SOCIAL TRANSFORMATION IN KASHMIR

SOCIAL TRANSFORMATION IN KASHMIR

A Study of Emerging Social Characters

B.A. Dabla

GYAN

Social Transformation in Kashmir:
A Study of Emerging Social Characters

ISBN : 978-81-212-1142-0

Published in 2012 in India by
Gyan Publishing House
23, Main Ansari Road, Daryaganj,
New Delhi - 110002
Phones : 23282060, 23261060
Fax : (011) 23285914
E-mail: books@gyanbooks.com
website: gyanbooks.com

Laser Type Setting : Rajender Vashist, Delhi
Printed at : Chawla Offset Printers, Delhi

Contents

Foreword

This is a delightful moment in my co-academic engagement to preface an excellent artefact by Professor B.A. Dabla. The other day when Dr. Dabla offered me a small space in his most creative and by now one of the most standard works –Social World of 30 Kashmiries – a sociological presentation was like making me feel big and blessed. Thank you Dr. Dabla.

The present treatise is a powerful social narrative with a commanding subjective approach.

A casual fiddling through the pages may lead you to an introspective error in which the treatment may look merely a biographic sketching or an artistic expression of mosaic reflections.

A social world of 30 Kashmiries in an objective placement of thirty characters in social context with special references to the variable like in and out of family environment, education and career, religious life, experience of conflict etc. My concept of objective placement may rightly irritate some readers because a context – specific narration merits only a non objective or qualitatively subjective dispensation. I am basing my argument on an integrative approach through a scheme of clearly stated parameters or the reference criteria.

Again it may seem very difficult to assign the book title to a wide expanse of case work. But the strength of the thematic connectivity of the cases is really we need to present a well planned and fine – tuned book as the present case.

Dr. Dabla has more than 15 published works to his credit, but I believe, he will be more clearly known and remembered because of the present work. It is exactly like the eminent cultural anthropologist - Margaret Mead - who is celebrated for her initial work "Coming of Age in Somua" only because of the way she narrated her observations with reference to a social context. Rest of her works are just knowledge-tied, scholarly written, research based and globally acclaimed master pieces in sociology, social work and anthropology.

Another importance feature of the present book is the concept of "folk-religion" Out of 13 variables, I am taking "folk-religion" as a strong component of Kashmiri personality. Major or minor ethnographic studies on Kashmir can hardly ignore the importance of folk religion while assessing the cultural roots of the basic Kashmiri individuality. In this regard a valid historical argument can be advocated to favour a balanced, peaceful and satisfied Kashmiri against any form of extremism.

To conclude a stray and discrete put-togetherness of the thirty cases may appear a clinical or diagnostic analysis but their standing on the predetermined socio-cultural products hints towards their integrative inclusiveness. I am sure that the present work of Dr. Dabla shall receive an overwhelming response and the readers, social workers, educationists, sociologist would enjoy the account and feel enriched.

April 7, 2011

Prof. A.G. Madhosh
Former Dean and Head
Faculty of Education
Kashmir University

Preface

When I joined JNU in 1976 for post-graduation in Sociology, I was surprised and shocked on the nature and level of ignorance about elementary knowledge related to Kashmir and Kashmiris among the common people there. Even literate and educated persons showed this type of ignorance. Not many people living there knew that J&K state had a separate constitution and flag. Notions that Kashmiris don't take bath for weeks and months and they keep arms with them always were commonly believed. Nobody bothered to enquire about these false notions and knows the reality. These baseless notions were transformed from generation to generation and this contributed to distortion of the realities about Kashmir and antipathy towards the Kashmiris. Thus these people remained apathetic towards their problems which they faced after the temporary accession of Kashmir to the Union of India. That was the condition of JNU society which was generally considered as an 'elitist place' in India and 'an ideological island in Indian society'. On the basis of this situation, one may imagine about the distorted images and spoiled reputation of Kashmir and the Kashmiris among the general masses in India.

This book stands as an academic attempt in that context which portrays a correct, real, actual, truthful and positive picture or image of the Kashmiri personality, Kashmiri society and its identity. In the background of falsehood and distortion, this effort aims at to present Kashmiris in their original and natural form, the attitudes they develop, and the behaviour they perform. It stands for a serious academic effort to portray Kashmiris as individuals and as members of their society; as they are and feel; as they think and understand; as they behave and operate; as they act and react; as they wish, aspire, practise and uphold distinctive ideas, ideals, views, opinions and perspectives about life and society.

Thus this book primarily and essentially explains the concept of 'social world' as believed and practised by a huge majority of Kashmiri masses and presents sociological perspective and assessment of their :

- Social ideas, views, opinions, ideals and ideology;
- Expectations, desires, preferences, priorities and desirables;

- Social institutions, organisations, agencies, associations and other situations;
- Social collectivities from family to religion, from ethnic group to global society and from religion to humanity;
- Social processes of transformation, particularly the processes of change, development and modernisation; and
- Social developments from birth to death at conceptual and practical level.

This book is directed towards academic as well as non-academic audience. It doesn't stand for abstract theoretical study. Since there prevails more illiteracy about Kashmir among non-academic sections of society, their levels and approach have been considered in the presentation and analysis of this book. In this context, this study was not followed by hard disciplinary limitations, rather liberal approach and unconventional methods and techniques were adopted for realistic understanding.

In brief, this stands for a sociological understanding of social characters representing social world of 30 Kashmiris who portray their selves and social images, ideal identity types, social system and social order, and political realities. In essence, it conveys a comprehensive picture about hardware and software of social life in Kashmir. Its focus is on present situations, past developments and future scenarios.

Bashir Ahmad Dabla
Department of Sociology and Social Work
University of Kashmir, Srinagar, J&K

Abbreviations

AIR	All India Radio
AMU	Aligarh Muslim University
MAKA	Maulana Abul Kalam Azad
BBC	British Broadcasting Corporation
BJP	Bhartia Janata Party
BPL	Below Poverty Line
CAAGI	Comptroller and Auditor General of India
ECI	Election Commission of India
FF	Family friend
GK	General Knowledge
GOI	Government of India
GSO	Global Social Order
HOD	Head of the Department
HOI	Head of the Institution
IH	Indian Hindu
IIT	Indian Institute of Technology
IM	Indian Muslim
INC	Indian National Congress
IPS	Islamic Political System
IQ	Intelligence Quantity
IT	Information Technology
JK	Jammu and Kashmir
JLN	Jawahar Lal Nehru
KAS	Kashmir Administrative Service
KM	Kashmiri Muslim

KMC	Kashmiri Muslim Community
KP	Kashmiri Pandit
MAAM	Maulana Abul Aala Maudoodi
MC	Muslim Conference
MKG	Mohanchand Karamchand Gandhi, known as Mahatama Gandhi
MLA	Member of Legislative Assembly
MMMF	Mirwaiz Molvi Mohammad Farooq
MMSM	Maulana Mohammad Syeed Masoodi
MP	Member of Parliament
MS	Masters in Surgery
MST	Maulana Sauddin Taraballi
NC	National Conference
NGO	Non-governmental Organisation
PAK	Pakistan Administered Kashmir
PBUH	Peace Be Upon Him (the Prophet)
PG	Post-Graduation
PTSD	Post Traumatic Stress Disorder
RSD	Right to Self Determination
RSS	Rashtriya Savak Sangh
SC	Scheduled Caste
SCI	Supreme Court of India
SMA	Sheikh Mohammad Abdullah
SSAK	Sir Syed Ahmad Khan
TB	Tuberclosis
UN	United Nations
UNGA	United Nations General Assembly
UNSC	United Nations Security Council
US	United States
VAW	Violence Against Women
VHP	Vishua Hindu Parishad
VOA	Voice of America

Glossary

Aakherat	The day of judgement
Aasthan Parasti	Saint worshipping
Awliya-ullah	Friends of God
Ahle-Hadies	A new school of thought among literate Muslims.
Alam Dare Kashmir	The upholder of Kashmir
Aligarian	One who was educated at AMU and stayed there.
Allah	GOD
Amir-zadegi	The life of affluence
Ajuman Nusratul Islam	*The educational* movement started in Kashmir in1860s by the Mirwaiz family.
Asna-Ashari	A sub-sect in the Shia Muslim Community.
Azaadi	Freedom
Bakra	A political group under the leadership of Mirwaiz
Baradarana	Brotherly relations
Barabari	Equality
Barelwi	A school of thought among the Indian Muslims
Batil-parast	Supporter of untruth
Bekaar	Useless person
Bihari	One who belongs to Bihar
Biradari	An association or community of the same occupations.
Brahmin	The higher caste in the Hindu society.
Challo call	A strike-call given by political parties
Chute Gharik	People of rags and filth
Dargah Sharif	The most famous Hazratbal Shrine in Kashmir.
Dev ban	One who has qualified from Dev Band university, U.P.
Dharma and karma	religious commitment and practical action

Dhobi	the washerman
Dua	the prayers to God
Eed	the Islamic festival
Eeman	belief in God
Faltoo	additional and extra
Goor bai	Milk-seller's woman
Gujjar	Hilly people in J&K
Gunnah	sin
Guroo	milk-seller
Guru	the guide
Haidth	the tradition of the Prophet
Hajj	the fifth pillor of Islamic faith and performed in Mecca.
Hanji	An occupation group/ caste in the Kashmir valley
Hanafi	One who practices the Hanafi school of thought
Harrijans	the out-castes in Indian Hindu society
Hartal	strike
Ha zuo payes peto	Oh self, think about yourself.
Heerath	the religious festival of KPs
Hindustanuk bate chew khewan	you survive on Indian support
Hunbalis	one who practises Hanafi school of thought.
Ibadah	the worship
Insaaf	justice
Insaniyet	humanism
Insaan khuda ke hazoor me	Man before God
Jagirdar	the landowners in feudal system
Jehadi	one who is engaged in a religious war
Juma namaz	the prayers on Friday
Kashmiriyet	the ideology of Kashmiri people
Khans	the middle caste in the Muslim society
Khan Saman	the person who serves the rich tourists/ visitors
- *Kharidars*	Customers
- *Khatem-e Sharif*	A religious function
- *Khudi*	feeling proud
- *Lok Sabha*	the lower chamber of Parliament in India
- *Mahr*	The amount of money paid by the groom to the bride on the marriage time
- *Maharaja*	the feudal lord in JK in 1947
- *Mahara*	the title KPs used for others

- *Malikis* the followers of Maliki school of thought
- *Mansabdar* an official in the feudal system
- *Mirwaiz* an institution created for religious propagation
- *Mohalla* a locality
- *Mohalla Masjid* a locality mosque
- *Molvi* a religious expert and preacher
- *Mullah* a religious parasite
- *Mard-e-Momin* a man of noble intentions and acts
- *Muztazzafin* the sufferers like proletariat
- *Namaz* the prayers
- *Naamdar* the graceful person
- *Namde-Gabbe* handicraft items for furnishing
- *Naya Kashmir Program* the official document adopted by NC in 1938 for future guidance.
- *Neo-Sayyids* those Sayyids who have adopted this title recently
- *Neyd* the haircutters
- *Najar* the carpenter
- *Nikah* the Islamic marriage
- *Numberdar* the officials in feudal system
- *Pahadi* People who live in mountains
- *Pandit* the Hindu saint
- *Panun ghare* my own family
- *Paper machie* art on paper in Kashmir
- *Patte bed* traditionally rich
- *Peer* a folk distinguished religious person
- *Peer-Mureedi* an institution of guide and followers related to religion
- *Peer Saheb* the person who has religious authority on his followers
- *Purdah* segregation and keeping women away from men
- *Qaleen-bafi* making of the carpets
- *Qiyamat* the last day of judgement
- *Quran* the most authentic book of Allah sent through prophet
- *Ram Navmi* the Hindu religious festival celebrated by KPs
- *Ramadaan* the month of fast
- *Risalat* the prophethood
- *Rishi* the mystic
- *Rishiyet* the mysticism in Kashmir

- *Roza* the fast
- *Sadre Riyasat* President of the state
- *Sanat-wel-jamaat* the mainstream group among Muslims
- *Sayyid* one who claims descent from the prophet's family
- *Sayyidization* *a* process in which people adopt Sayyid family names
- *Sarhad* periphery of the city
- *Shafis* followers of Shafi school of thought
- *Shariah* the Islamic jurisprudence
- *Shawl-bafi* the making of shawls
- *Shera* the political followers of SMA
- *Sher-e-Kashmir* the Loin of Kashmir
- *Sher-e-Kashmir ke dewaney* Fanatic followers of SMA
- *Shawls* a Kashmiri handicraft item
- *Shaitan* the great evil
- *Shais* the minority sect in the Muslim society
- *Shikara* the small boat for water-riding
- *Shikarawala* the man who drives the shikara
- *Sheikh sahib* commonly used in Kashmir for SMA
- *Sharaft* gentleness
- *Soor vael* vegabonds and rude people
- *Sufi* an occupational group/caste in the valley
- *Sufiana* classical Kashmiri music
- *Sunnis* the majority sect of Muslims
- *Syed-zadgi* posing as proud Sayyids
- *Taliban* a political movement originated from Afghanistan
- *Tawheed* oneness of God in the universe
- *Tawheed-parast* following the doctrine of tawheed
- *Ulema* the learned men of religion of Islam
- *Urs* *the celebrating of a particular day*
- *Ummat* the Muslim collectivity
- *Ummati* the member of ummat
- *Varna* *a* category which divides the Hindu society in four castes
- *Wahdat* unity
- *Wazir-e-Azam* *P*rime Minister
- *Wazwan* a special menu of dishes prepared in Kashmir
- *Zakat* a proportion of money to be spent fo. poor and needy
- *Zaildar* an official in feudal system.

1

Introduction

1. CONCEPT OF SOCIAL WORLD

(i) In simple terms, the concept of 'social world' essentially referred to the entire social universe, individuals and groups develop through experience at different stages of life in the ideational-theoretical and empirical-practical fields. The duration of this world starts with the day one takes birth and continues till the day one dies. According to Oxford Dictionary of Sociology, the concept of 'social world' was applied to the "universe of discourse through which common symbols, organisations and activities emerge." It involved central areas which could not be physically involved. In this thematic background, social world may be referred in cases of surfing, nursing, polity and so on.

(ii) James H. Ballantine and Kaith A. Roberts, in their book entitled *Our Social World* (2010) developed the concept of social world to "do" public sociology. They dealt with understanding social world in five parts with related contents for each part which follows:

(a) Part I : Sociology-A Unique Way to view the World

– Examining the Social World: How do we know?

(b) Part II : Social Structure, Processes and Control

– Society and Culture: Hardware and Software of Our Social World

– Socialisation: Becoming Human and Humane Interactions, Groups and Organisations

Connections that work

Deviance and Social Control

(c) Part III : Inequality/Stratification : Rich and famous or Rags and Famine

– Race and Ethnic Group Stratification

– Beyond "We" and "They"

– Gender Stratification

(d) Part IV : Institutions-family : Partner taking, People making and Contract Breaking

– Education and Religion

– Politics and Economics: Penetrating power and privilege

(e) Part V : Social Dynamics, Population and Health : The Process of Change:

– Can it Make a Difference ?

(iii) However, it is generally felt that the concept of social world has a long vague history in the area of symbolic interactionism. (*Ibid.*) Subsequently, many meanings have been attached to it which snatch its clarity and specificity. In other words, it stands not as a well-developed concept in terms of themes, concerns, features and so on. On the basis of sociological treatment of the subject, the following prominent features have been identified:

(a) the concept of social world refers to the largest social universe and covers entirety of human life. With the growth of this concept, its ideas and ideals got broadened. At the theoretical level, social world develops representation in terms of socially desirable and undesirable conditions which are concerned with :

- all social expectations, desires, preferences and positives;
- all social ideas, views, opinions and ideologies;
- all social processes of change, development and modernisation;
- all social institutions, organisations, agencies, associations and situations;
- all social groups, classes, castes, communities and sects;
- all social collectivities from family to nation, from ethnic groups to global society and from religion to humanity;
- All social actions, interactions and other collective actions;
- All socially preferable situations in the past, present and future;
- All socially relevant developments from birth to death; and
- All socially relevant ideational and behavioural changes.

(b) It has been observed that social world in operation always emphasizes particular social desirables and un-desirables, making some behaviour necessary and others redundant at the theoretical level. It also refers to identification and elabouration and practise of certain human behaviour in human society. It develops the goals which need to be fulfilled. Thus it represents sum total of feelings, wishes, expectations and other such variables. In this way, the notions of social world of individuals and groups emerge as preferable and achievable, which every one wants to attain.

(c) Taking into consideration the concept of the social world, in operational sense, we may formulate its three specific and inter-related successive stages which are as mentioned below:

– Stage I Features:	– Social context
	– In – family Socialisation
	– Out-family Environment
	– Education and Career
	– Occupation, Mobility and Association
	– Marriage and Family
– Stage II Features:	– Social Likes and Dislikes
	– Concepts of 'I', 'Me' and 'We'
	– Ideas about Equality and Inequality
	– The Ideal Character/Leader
	– Global Social Order
	– The Religious Life
– Stage III Features:	– The Kashmir Problem
	– Future Society of Kashmir
	– Experience of Conflict Situation
	– Social Problems in Kashmir.

(d) In the first stage of formation of the social world, the basic process of socialisation starts and is followed by further secondary socialisation. In this fundamental process, individuals and groups undergo the process of adoption of basic human and social traits required in that social situation. This stage provides the formulation of personality at individual level and nature-extent of the membership in social collectivities inside and outside family. The social actors who are involved in this socialisation composed of children and youth of all age groups. This early training also leads to internalisation of values, norms and social principles in general. This socialisation starts from family and is further carried out in the school, religion and community. This out-family environment is dominated by close-distant relatives, neighbours and personal-family friends. This path of socialisation determines the nature of social interaction, change, development, control and order. This stage also provides education, career, occupation, mobility, association and marriage-family. The dynamics of these actions follow the pattern as mentioned below:

– Modern Education > adoption of particular career>

– particular occupation > experiencing mobility >

– developing new association.

Thus this stage determined structural and functional features of the social world. In the context of its contribution, this stage may be characterised as a stage where a lot of input processes effect the thematic and functional contours of social world. While this stage concretise material basis of the social world, it also facilitates the theoretical and moral legitimacy of that type of world.

(e) The second stage of the social world was mostly based on the ideational and practical realities of the first stage. In this way, individuals and groups act, perform and assert according to pre-determined attitudes, behaviour and ideology. So, they tried to emerge as representatives of pre-determined ideals by adopting social likes, rejecting social dislikes, developing particular ideas about psychological notions of 'I', 'me' and 'we', concretising ideas about the phenomena of equality and inequality, giving ideational shape to the concepts of ideal leader/character and global social order. It provided the rationale for charismatic authority and to ideal social and religious order. Finally, all these attitudinal and behavioural trends reflected in religious life which was wholly determined by social forces generated in the first stage. In a way, the psycho-social developments in the second stage may be characterised as 'software of social world' and the first stage as 'hardware of social world'. Thus in this mature stage, the social world stood as 'direct outcome of the previous stage'. While the first stage was a formative stage, the second stage was an action-oriented stage. Further, it has generally been observed that social world was determined mainly by religious, political and economic factors.

(f) The third stage of social world represented the most mature stage. In this stage, one becomes super-conscious and higher-assertive about his and other's social world. While consciousness about one's social world emerged, there was simultaneous awareness of plurality, variety and diversity of the social world. Among other implications, there arises particularity and specificity of social world. One becomes sure about it and explains its lifelong objectives. This, in turn, gives rise to a particular perception or perspective and to a focused aspects of personality and society. In the case of Kashmir, the social world of its members was oriented towards the following four major aaspects:

– the Kashmir problem,
– Future society in Kashmir,
– Experience of Conflict situation, and
– Social Problems in Kashmir.

2. SOCIAL WORLD AND SOCIAL CHARACTERS

(i) The above explanation of the concept of social world reveals in clear terms that it represents social reality and social actuality. While it covers general and particular experiences, it revolves around the network of lifelong activities. In addition to social level of desires and expectations, its focus is also on psychological aspects of social life and make them focused items. Thus all important events, incidents and accidents become in-separable part of social world. In this way, it gives a rational, realistic, contextual and objective account of life. This gets related to the individual and collective identity and trace its problems in terms of particular historical past. When one develops full notion of social world, one becomes its proponent and ideologue and wants others to adopt it and follow in life.

(ii) The important point here is that the concept of social world is directly related to social characters in society. This relationship has two main features. First, concept of social world on the part of individuals and groups is generally created and developed in the light of life experiences, activities and expectations. The socialisation process inside and outside family concretize and rationalize its thematic and ideological contents. Second, in the later-mature part of life, the individuals and groups respond actively to these social actions and environment by developing the propositions of social world, concretising the specific contents and finally following all these social desirables in their life sincerely and with commitment.

(iii) In both the evolutionary stages, the concept of social world develops in a particular social-psychological context and is normally upheld by social characters through their actions and interactions in all fields of life. It follows that social world gets practically implemented or become operational through common actions of social characters which develop this relationship over a long period of life. In this context there emerged a necessary relationship between the social world and social characters wherein the former was followed by the latter as the ideal and preferable role in all fields of life. These social characters vary in their nature, role, status and other features. But, the dominant reality reveals that social characters share structural and functional characteristics which contributes to stability and continuity of social system with theoretical and empirical foundations. These 30 varying social characters in the Kashmiri society have been identified and explained with their functional utility and representative features as follows:

S. No.	*Social Character*	*Functional Importance*	*Representative Characteristics*
1.	The Folk, Kashmiri –Urban	– provided basic institutional structure and its effective control over social dynamics	– folk culture in its totality – retained religious practices in Kashmir – social integration, stability and cohesion – political identity at folk level – reflected composite culture of Kashmir
2	Academician and Administrator	– institutional and organisational control	– highly educated and intellectual class – ideal religious role and behaviour – experienced change and development – radical shift in edu., eco., asso. and mobi. – social-cultural-demo. transformation
3.	Academician: The Kashmiri Pandit	– professional and intellectual activity – the minority status	– level of intellect and innovation – model/ideal role in chang/developmnt – rational approach to religious ideology – plurality of region and culture – miserable lot due to mass migration
4.	Scientist and Academician	– professional authority – intellectual ethos – control	– highly educated and professional class – modernisation of attitudes and behaviour – rural – agrarian transformation – rational and scientific approach to life – overall and multi-dimensional develop

contd...

contd...

S. No.	*Social Character*	*Functional Importance*	*Representative Characteristics*
5.	Folk Kashmiri Woman – urban	– custodian of lower occupational structure and culture; – occupational basis of social	– life-sketch of service occupational groups – upholder of tradition and culture – less response to chang and development high degree of social and occupational mobility – women's new role in politics
6	Urban-educated Woman – housewife	– structural-functional element – providing institutional of work	– emerging middle class among KMs – emerging Muslim women in K. society – continuous edu., eco., soc., cul. Mobility – undergoing change and development – moderate moder. Response to religion
7.	Kashmiri Bureaucrat	– effective control of bureaucracy and its organisation	– highly educated and intellectual class – humble economic background – planning serious and tough strategy for life – between modernity and conservatism – educated and academic environment
8.	Urban-educated Working woman	– existing social position of women – institutional structure of role	– elite response to modernising process – changing women of elite-upper-family – legitimacy to new role of women – moderate response to religion – De-*sayyidisation* of certain families

contd...

contd...

S. No.	*Social Character*	*Functional Importance*	*Representative Characteristics*
9.	Small Businessman	– strong pre-requisites of organisation of occupational	– work ethics and moral ethic in business – standard occupa. attitude and behaviour – religion and business activities – rational response to religious beliefs – emerging middle class in urban context
10.	Table-boy and Businessman	– change in tradi. occupational activities – continuity and change in the	– unique features of social mobility – maintenance of folk character – belonging to extremely poor b.ground – honesty, commitment and hard work – occupational deviance and developments
11.	Lower Class Government Employee	– maintenance of entire system – through functional contribution	– lower class-caste occupational groups – reality of change and development – rational but traditional ideas and ideals – pattern of discrimination and exploitation – state response to problems of poverty
12.	The Kashmiri Youth: Rural-Urban	– structu. basis of rural-urban society and dynamics of change – functional aspects of world of youth.	– rural-urban migration in post-47 era – youth in rural-urban changing context – rational response to modernisation – rural-urban antagonism and its feature – positive response to religious trends

contd...

contd...

S. No.	*Social Character*	*Functional Importance*	*Representative Characteristics*
13.	The Kashmiri Scientist	-prof. authority for organizal. Status. -academic authority in different fields of life.	-educated and intellectual family context -academic elite as a class in itself -affluent and prosperous lifestyle -constant feeling of place of origin -highest degree of change and mobility.
14.	Political Ideologue	-social basis of politics -attainment of political power and authority -social impact of pol. Processes	-social mobility through politics -democratic background of politics -rural background of political system -new political ideas and ideology -political response to pol. Development
15.	Educationist and Social notable	-social legitimacy to systemic changes -rearrangement of structural Aspects	- feudal system face modern challenge -education and literacy increasing -ideology of reformation and revolution -an emancipated response to religion -modernised-westernised lifestyle.
16.	Kashmiri *Sayyid* Youth-Rural	-structural forms of rural social -change pattern in rural youth	-trends of change among Kashmir youth -attitude and behaviour of rural *Sayyd* youth -religious response to modernisation -rural conservative lifestyle -Sayyid and non-Sayyid rural hierarchy

contd...

contd...

S. No.	*Social Character*	*Functional Importance*	*Representative Characteristics*
17.	The Kashmiri Youth- and social developments	-radical response to political -political aspiration of people in Kashmir -political uncertainty in the System	-village dependency and isolation -youth's revolt against the Indian state -anti-India pol. attitude and behaviour -multi-farious background of K. problem
18.	Elder Kashmiri Intellectual	-changed conditions in quality of social life	-upcoming educated-intellectual class - intellectual ethos in/out of family -support to modernising forces -antipathy towards dogmatism and fatalis -modern worldview and future vision.
19.	Professional Doctor-Lower caste	-structural differences in the social system -mobility through self efforts	-professionals from lower caste -mobility among lower castes/classes -change from caste to class hierarchy -lower caste response to modernisation -incorporating revisions inrelig behaviour
20.	Doctor – Middle Class	-class structure and changes in it -dominance of political power and authority	-middle class b.ground of professionals -intellectual environment in midle class -overall mobility and change -different type of change in family -impressionistic role of doctor in society

contd...

contd...

S. No.	*Social Character*	*Functional Importance*	*Representative Characteristics*
21.	Fisherwoman	-structural requirements of Social system -functional pre-requisites of	-lower occup. Groups at lower level -primitive-tribal origin of occup. Groups -change, development, modernisation -primitive features of religious life -nature-reality of progress and develop.
22.	Shikarawala	-structural requisites of social System -functional aspects of occpat. System	-occupational plurality of K. society -lowest occupa. Groups in jierarchy -occupational changes and its adoptability -nature of mobility in occupa, groups -backwardness of life conditions.
23.	Religious Ideologue- *Sayyid* – Rural	-ideological aspect of existing system -exploitative nature of the System	-*Sayyids* at the top of social hierarchy -Erosion of *Peer-Mureedi institution* -no necessary rel. bet. status and change -implication of rural urban development -conservative relig. Response to moder.
24.	Professional Musician	-prof. contribution to the Functioning of integrative System	-secular and non-violent social ethos -emerging upper-middle class -composite culture and tolerance -positive response to change and moderni -out-migration-pattern and impact

contd...

contd...

S. No.	Social Character	Functional Importance	Representative Characteristics
25.	Professional Journalist	-prof. Character of the Functional dynamics of Social system	-growth of professions in Kashmir -represent. Charac. of media profess. -rational rural response to change and dev -rural dependenc and urban-independenc -reformed response to religion
26.	Milk-seller's Woman	lower occupational structure	-functions of lower occupational groups -lower class economic background -folk features in changing conditions -folk response to change and development
27.	The Kashmiri Youth - Lower Caste-Class	-composition of functional entities in social system -politicisation of masses -social functions of political authority	-political following of political leader -composition of class-caste youth -distinctive role of lower Caste Class youth
28.	The Kashmiri Engineer	-prof. contribution to social Structure -ideal values and norms in ideal	-social legitimacy of political leadership -social revolt against caste practices -mobility among lower occupations -positive educational response -adoption of realistic approach to religion -social ethics and cultural sense -serious opposition to corruption

contd...

contd...

S. No.	*Social Character*	*Functional Importance*	*Representative Characteristics*
29.	The Political Activist	-political socialisation and its Implications	-development of political culture -political domination and exploitation -political response to change and develop. -liberal religious attitude and behaviour -female education despite opposition
30.	The Young Advocate	-population proportions in Society and structural Stability	-religious response to pol. development -emerging middle class formation -generational shift in pol. Attitudes -professional ethics, morality and values -religious necessity in usual life.

(iv) The above identification and explanation of social characters in terms of their functional utility and their representative characteristics reveal three particular dimensions of 'social world' which are :

- Totality of the Social World
- Similarities of the Social World
- Dissimilarities of the Social World

First, totality of the social world of Kashmiris revealed clearly in all 30 social characters. It reflects in their actions, interactions, situations and developments. This totality apply to all individuals and groups and reveal crucial aspects of social statics and social dynamics. Thus, in essence, 30 Kashmiri social characters reveal :

- 30 comprehensive, composite and representative features;
- 30 holistic, common, deeply-felt and psycho-social images;
- 30 multi-dimensional socio-psychic looking self glasses;
- 30 sociological profiles of past and present life experiences;
- 30 sociological frameworks for future social vision;
- 30 sociological representations and ideal types of social system and social order;
- 30 sociological worldviews and future visions.

Second, similarities between social world of 30 social characters represent the natural and cumulative result of the experience of common life and its culture. In the context of above-mentioned social characters, the following features of their similarities may be noticed:

- Life experience in totality and at macro and mass level;
- In-family and out-family socialisation process and practices and resultant attitudes and behaviour on the part of individuals and groups;
- Direct and indirect impact of various social developments on the formulation, growth and evolution of the personality and its social ethos;
- Specific role of modern education and its direct contribution to the attainment of lifelong career, occupation, association and occupational-social mobility; and
- Most dominant and decisive roles of marriage members of different sections of society and the resultant family unit household and its multi-farious environments.

Third, on the other hand, the above-mentioned social characters reveal dissimilarities between prominent sociological features represented by these characters. The dissimilar features may be identified as follows:

- Social likes-dislikes, social desirables-undesirables, social choices, social images, social views, social opinions, social ideas and social impressions;
- Ideology, perception, perspectives, doctrines, principles, theology and so on;
- Ideal social characters, political leaders as per the nature and impact of their authority and power;
- Different class-formations such as class, caste, group, community, sect and so on;
- Diversity and plurality of culture, religion, values, traditions, customs, rituals, folkways and so on.

3. SOCIAL WORLD AND SOCIAL CHARACTERS IN KASHMIR

(i) All theoretical propositions related to 13 sociological variables of social world and 30 social characters of social world apply to the Kashmiri society qualitatively as well as quantitatively. This applications also reveals three prominent features of representative characteristics of 30 Kashmiri characters which are totality, similarity and dissimilarity. Thus the sociological presentation of 30 Kashmiris through their 13 sociological variables provide major social glimpses of their social world at ideational and practise levels. While it conveys their attitudinal and behavioural similarities in the context of social dynamics, it also reflects dissimilarities in their worldviews and future visions.

(ii) More important, it conveys the totality dimension of social world. In other words, all three features represent the totality of Kashmiri society and Kashmiri personality in the past, present and future. While as the focus of this study was on the sociological presentation of 30 social characters within broader sociological framework, i.e. application of sociological theories, concepts, principles, methods and techniques in the explanation and assessment of this society's statics and dynamics. It stands a scientific attempt in terms of sociological presentation of Kashmiri social characters which portray their whole social life at the individual and collective levels. In this way, this presentations conveys self and social images of Kashmiris supported by their views and perceptions as a distinct identity, distinct personality and distinct society with special attitudinal and behavioural traits.

4. OBJECTIVES OF THE STUDY

In the preceding thematic-theoretical background, this study was carried out with following objectives in consideration:

(a) Sociological description of main characteristic features of the concept of 'social world' held by individuals and groups of Kashmiris and interpreted in terms of 13 particular sociological features;

(b) Identification and explanation of 30 representative social characters of Kashmiri society which convey past, present and future developments in Kashmir and their presentations within sociological perspective;

(c) Discussing prominent aspects/dimensions of the concept of 'social world' (in terms of roles of 30 social characters) in its totality which compose similarities and dissimilarities in sociological framework;

(d) To make comprehensive, scientific and sociological presentation of crucial features of 'social world' held by 30 Kashmiri characters in terms of 13 specific sociological features;

(e) To make a sociological assessment of social world of Kashmiris with special reference to its society, social structure, social organisation, social system, social processes, social association, occupation, mobility, change and development, educational and family changes, social ideals, social desirables, social vision of present and future Kashmiri society, ideas of equality and inequality, ideal social character/leader, and major social problems and issues in contemporary times.

5. SOCIOLOGY OF KASHMIR

(i) Sociology of Kashmir deals with the statics and dynamics or structure and function of the Kashmiri society within the sociological theoretical-methodological framework. It makes a multi-disciplinary understanding and multi-dimensional study of all social developments in sociological perspective and related methodology. It gives sociological treatment to all social processes, institutions, organisation, associations, classes, castes, communities, groups, and other social collectivities. Finally, it provides a sociological assessment of all social phenomena, especially contemporary problems and issues facing the community.

(ii) The fact stands with evidence that not much significant academic work has been carried out in this important field. Some studies and researches have been carried out by local scholars, but, that amount of work and its quality-standard doesn't enable us to broader sociological understanding of the Kashmiri society and its different fields of life. A national workshop on the topic of "Relevance of Sociology in Kashmir" was organised by Department of Sociology at University of Kashmir in 1989 in this regard. The workshop made some recommendations for pursuing sociological research on the Kashmir society and identified some priority areas of research. But, this research could not be pursued seriously and systematically partly because of absence of commitment on the part of academic community on the whole and partly because of conflict situation just after the workshop. The present situation of sociological research in Kashmir may be characterised as 'unsatisfactory' and 'unexplored'.

(iii) In the preceding context, there seems an urgent need to initiate and to sponsor empirical sociological studies of the Kashmiri society and comprehensive sociological assessment of its various problems and issues.. The formulation and application of main sociological theories, concepts and methods will help positively in the sociological understanding of Kashmiri society. In this formal effort, the focus needs specially on various aspects/ processes of social transformation such as change, development and modernisation. Moreover, at this stage of the growth of this sub-discipline, the emphasis must be on the aspects of description of social phenomenon rather than on conceptual or theoretical aspects. At the same time, there seems a need to identify, select and apply pan-Indian concepts in the Kashmir context and explain the existing social reality here.

(iv) It stands clear from the title of this book that it deals with core aspects and themes of Kashmir Sociology, i.e. the Social World of Kashmiris. This academic study provides a sociological look on the totality of their social world as represented by 30 social characters.

(v) This study essentially stands as an initial effort and elementary attempt to explain social world of Kashmiris in the sociological perspective. Its focus is clearly on the sociological understanding of crucial aspects of Kashmiri society and personality in contemporary times. It is sincerely hoped that many such other academic efforts will follow this humble initiative.

[illegible] the concept [illegible] to primary social institutions in an [illegible] way which organises [illegible] those and [illegible] to other institutions. It also characterises [illegible] these social collectivities which [illegible] the concept was referred to the following [illegible]

- [illegible] family unit — [illegible]
- Mass [illegible] — [illegible] and [illegible]
- All professionals and technocrats — All engineers, doctors and associated experts
- Members of political parties/organisations — Members of a religious group
- Members of castes and sub-castes — Members of an ethnic community
- Members of an occupational group — Members of a particular sect

K-25 felt that there existed some negative features of the concept of "we". Thus, it was used for:

- Opponents of the political parties/organisations
- Proponents of religious organisations
- Ideologues of civil and democratic rights
- Opponents of the ruling party
- Opponents of democratic and secular system

[illegible]. IDEAS OF EQUALITY AND INEQUALITY

(i) K-25 believed in the hard reality of existence of inequality at all levels and in all fields of life world over. This was characteristic feature of pre-modern societies and it has survived in all forms of societies. Thus the system of inequality based on class, caste, power and gender have hurt the entire society. Taking into consideration its past record, it has always been disorganising and disordering and it could not be [illegible]

(ii) While K-25 supported absolute equality, he suggested that it [illegible] be made a reality through the establishment of its system. [illegible] all individuals and other social collectivities must be ensured and its ideological foundation and value-oriented principles must be evolved properly. The system must provide social justice to every social entity in all fields [illegible] egalitarianism and social equilibrium must emerge as guiding principles [illegible] cultural [illegible] ensure equal participation of diverse and different [illegible] the community must reflect all its forms and dimensions.

2

Methodology

1. SOCIAL WORLD AND SOCIAL CHARACTER

The main features of 'social world' and 'social characters' and their inter-relationship has been explained in the last chapter. While 'social world' conveys prominent features of social world of 30 Kashmiris through the contribution of the role of social characters, they reveal major aspects of social world through identifying functional features. In this interaction, both concepts represent ideational and practical aspects of that world of yesterday, today and tomorrow. Though these concepts also portray varying social images, social identities and social personalities, they portray, on the whole, the unique and distinguishing image, identity and personality at macro level. The aggregation and totality of social world consumes and accommodates both of its similarities and particularities.

2. THE BIOGRAPHICAL APPROACH

(i) In order to study the social world of Kashmiris through their social characters, a unique method of sociological analysis was adopted which was totally unconventional, qualitatively and quantitatively. It specifically referred to the application-presentation of biographical details in the explanation of their social world. In fact, the latter was the cumulative result and end product of the former. Thus biographical data provided basis for explanation/ analysis of life situation and particularly growth of social world. In this context, the personal life emerged as "embodiment of social life" and conveyed its self and social images. It was observed that the biographical approach and methods were commonly used in a variety of social science disciplines, especially psychology and sociology. This approach necessarily implied the list of characteristic traits with which social actors perform their ideal roles.

(ii) Sociologists and psychologists have undertaken several studies in cross-cultural context and explained social characters in terms of their features related to their social world. These features are as mentioned below:

- These studies identified the social universe adopted by individuals and groups and problems at theoretical and empirical level;
- The Roles of personal experiences and impressions seemed crucial and unavoidable;
- Propositions were based mainly on social contact, observation, experience, and impressions;
- Particular opinions and images emerged out of the observations of lifelong interaction;
- These led to life account which stood rational and reliable to the individuals. So, the life account stood as one's account in my language. It experienced personal experience only;
- It realised the source of biography through analysis, presenting the stories, and making statements valid and ethical; and
- It provided the necessary biographical data through intervening, training, analysing and writing up other details. (See Barbara Messill and Linden West, *Using Biographical Methods in Social Research, 2009,* University of Warwick, Sage Publications).

3. BIOGRAPHICAL APPROACH APPLIED

(i) The biographical approach and methods were applied extensively by Messill and West (see *Ibid.*) They characterised these methods as interdisciplinary with prominent features of sociological-psychological orientation, personal experiences and biographical data. According to them, several examples were available across social science disciplines in this regard.

(ii) While discussing biographical methods, the following thematic contents were identified:

- Biographical Methods :
  - Contemporary uses of biographical research
  - Identifying theoretical issues
- Illustrating Good Practices
  - Case studies
  - Interviewing and recording experience
- Making sense of biography
  - Analysis
  - Representing the stories
- Validity and ethical status of biographical research. (see *Ibid.*)

(iii) On the other hand, Kathleen M. White in her study entitled *Studying Families* (2009, New Delhi, Sage Publications) carried out such type of research on the basis of self reports of the family system functioning. In order to assess the individual's perception of his family environment, 90 particular and varying items of family environment scale, which was considered reliable and valid, were adopted in three different forms as follows:

(a) **Form R :** Real form which assessed individual's perception of their family Environment;

(b) **Form E :** Expectation form in which individual's expectations about family setting were assessed; and

(c) **Form I :** Ideal form which was directed to assess the conceptions of ideal family environment.

Thirty more items were added to bring up and assess the children's perceptions of their family social climate. This method of assessing perception of family social environment based on individual's experience and impression falls within the broader behavioural approach.

4.13 FEATURES OF SOCIAL CHARACTERS

The social world of 30 Kashmiri characters was approached through identification and analysis of 13 specific sociological variables. These core sociological features covering the entire life have become :

- Main instruments of observation;
- Recorded sheets of their past, present and future life;
- Objective statements about ideology, perspective and perception;
- Community political worldview; and
- Entirety of social vision engulfing individual and collective fields of life.

The nature, functional utility and methodological relevance and other necessary details of these 13 social characters were as mentioned below:

1. SOCIAL CONTEXT

(i) This variable is meant for tracing social background of particular social character in order to know about environment at early life and to be aware about personality traits. That enables to make sociological explanation of multifarious developments in recent past of the individual. These developments are related to the nature, growth, dimensions and change in a particular family, group, class, caste, community, association, neighbourhood and so on. Thus interplay of various factors, interactions between various social collectivities, mutual effects of culture and religion intensify the cumulative effect on family. It occurs through the operation of all social processes, institutions, organisations, agencies and so on. All these developments give rise to particular and general personality traits which characterize the social character.

2. IN-FAMILY SOCIALISATION

(i) It is a fact that the first stage of socialisation starts within one's family. It starts with the process of 'internalisation' of values, traditions, norms, principles, views, and ideals. It lays the basis for the formulation of prominent features of personality. It also creates conditions for ideas, opinions, view, ideology; attitudes and behaviour patterns; generational identity features, aspects of worldview and future vision; and major as well as minor aspects of social world. These conditions are shaped through parents' patriarchal authority, elders' and relatives' social and moral authorities; agencies of social control, consensus and harmony; and reduction of the levels of dissent, deviation, revolt and conflict.

(ii) All these processes and factors related to domestic environment of family which directly leads to socialisation of individual separately and in groups. This has direct bearing on formulation of early personalities in terms of its primary, hereditary and intrinsic features.

3. OUT-FAMILY ENVIRONMENT

(i) The second major effort on personality formation and its social characteristics comes from immediate social environment composed of members of neighbourhood, relatives, personal and family friends, teachers, colleagues and other acquaintances. The constant, repetitive, decisive and significant interactions between individual and members of these out family groups lead to the nature, quality, degree, direction and dimensions of this environmental impact. While in-family impact is more oriented towards ideational nature, the out-family impact is directed more towards behavioural nature, rather both. The out-family impact creates a social position of individual personality around which revolve all his roles, status and other social activities. Thus it is established sociologically that immediate social environment represented by certain groups have deterministic impact on individual. This impact may be in consonance or dissonance to moral and social ethos of society. While the former impact leads to stability and continuity, the latter creates instability and discontinuity.

4. EDUCATION AND CAREER

(i) Another important socialising agency after in- and out-family environment is represented by the institution of school which operates through school and creates conditions for career-making. While this stage of socialisation is considered necessary in changing/modernising societies, it was not considered so necessary in traditional societies. In fact, individuals and groups of individuals follow formal education and training and respective career in different fields of life. In that situation, individuals develop restive career roles, responsibilities and obligations. It was observed that formal career in present-day society is not possible without formal education and training.

(ii) Moreover, the adoption of formal education and career necessarily meant the dropping of hereditary and traditional occupations. All these features related to attainment of education and adoption of career shape the major aspects of features of social character which has ideational and behavioural conception and actions of social world.

5. OCCUPATION, MOBILITY AND ASSOCIATION

(i) Occupation generally refers to a particular set of activity in which an individual or groups are engaged throughout life. Its associated actions are vocational and so need skills and capabilities. This becomes source of livelihood in every type of society. In changing societies, occupational change takes place according to which (a) new occupation is adopted with the continuity of old occupation; and (b) adoption of new occupation with dropping of old occupation. While old occupation refers to agriculture, new occupation prominently includes government service. These features of occupation prevail in all societies.

(ii) The occupational change is generally followed by the process of mobility, upwards and not downwards in terms of social status and economic position. In this context, the grand general principle of mobility is from lower-esteemed occupation and lower economic positioned to high social esteemed occupation and high economic positioned. In principle, upward social mobility due to occupational change stands characteristic feature of modern society. In addition to social and economic impact, the mobility has educational, psychological, demographic, cultural, political and other implications for individuals and groups involved. Like other societies, the Indian society too has undergone deeply the process of mobility.

(iii) With adoption of new occupations and mobility patterns, the natural product comes in the shape of new social association which stands qualitatively different from old and relational association. In actuality, this process starts with attainment of education and adoption of career, and later on strengthened by experiencing occupational change and upward mobility. It represents new association in the material world. It gives birth to new contacts and relations in educational institutions, service offices-organisations, in-family/out-family environment, areas of activity-interest and broader society. This creates a new identity and broader purpose of life for individuals and groups.

(iv) All these features contribute towards formation and evolution of social character and scial world.

6. MARRIAGE AND FAMILY

(i) Marriage of an individual is needed and so it is considered obligatory. Normally, every individuals goes for this practice. In many cases, it seems just unavoidable. It qualifies a person for mature and major position in society. It leads to confirmation of responsible role. It provides institutional bases for family, group and community. Thus marriage emerges as one crucial institution which one adopts to register membership in mature society. More importantly, one undergoes extremely different experiences after marriage that influence the entire behaviour and gives rise to specific generational traits and personality type. It also determines social environment and its lifestyle.

(ii) The family represents basic and primary social institution which shapes the personality pattern by providing environment of socialisation at the initial stage of life. In comparison to other social institutions, it determines, dominates and makes effective the process of socialisation. Family effects in two stages, pre-marital and post-marital stage. While the first stage of socialisation is traditional, conventional and parental socialisation, the second stage of socialisation incorporates new attitudes and behaviour. Thus it leads to new world-view and future vision.

7. SOCIAL LIKES AND SOCIAL DISLIKES

(i) It has been observed that social world reflects through social likes and dislikes. It is because these likes-dislikes are based on images of others through interaction in and experience of the society. In order to follow lifelong lessons, one develops certain social preferences, priorities, preferred, and socially desired. They make conscious choice of social items like the selection in market. They opt some and drop others, desire some and reject others, and like some and dislike others.

(ii) Every individual and group, after reaching in the mature stage, makes these choices and preferences most sincerely and openly. Thus they make 'likes' like some individuals, groups, institutions, traits, features, attitudes, ideas, behaviour and processes. They follow the ideals of social world.

8. CONCEPTS OF 'I', 'ME' AND 'WE'

(i) These socio-psychic concepts are direct manifestation of individual's social world through different social characters. In actuality, the images and notions of social world reveal through these concepts of 'I', 'me' and 'we'. 'I' reveal individual personality and concrete impressions about social experiences. Thus one always talks or remains conscious about 'I' in the past. The second past of 'I' is related to the present, which is vehemently emphasised and stress upon his contribution to social order. 'I' also deals with the future too. Here the individual visualize his role in coming days.

(ii) 'Me' is similarly related to the psychological consciousness and used in the sense of 'my'. It reflects higher level of consciousness and is related to the immediate social context which is not the case with 'I'. 'Me' at the individual level has time dimensions too, i.e. past (my past personality and society), present (my present personality and society) and future (my future personality and society). It plays similar or dissimilar role in society at different times. In specific terms, it leads to static and dynamic aspects of individual and society.

(iii) The concept of 'we' refers to consciousness at high level, the domination of social environment and outcome of interaction and socialisation processes. Formulation of 'we' keeps in consideration past and present developments and future situations also. In this way, this consciousness reflects in actual that 'we' specifically points social collectivities in totality. With maturity, it deepens, broadens, strengthens and increases.

9. IDEAS OF EQUALITY AND INEQUALITY

(i) Every conscious member of society encounters others with whom one interacts and responds to their ideas and actions in terms of equality or inequality. This stands for a common conduct. In fact, in all human societies, there exist one or other type of inequality. No society so far portrayed absolute equality in all fields of life.

(ii) As every member of society face the situation of inequality, directly or indirectly, he develops ideas about equality, its nature, features, dimensions, relevance, impact and need. These ideas, views and opinions develop after observation, analysis, examination and criticism and become core ideas and ideals of their social world. These ideas are then categorised as 'desirable' and 'undesirable' from societal pint of view. The ideals of equality need to be achieved perfectly and all forms of inequality need to be negated and debased.

10. THE IDEAL CHARACTER/LEADER

(i) The ideal leader/character represents a social character which upholds ideological traits and ideological behaviour in the broader framework of social world by majority of societal members. This character leads to a dominant role which gets social and political legitimacy. The popularity of this role belongs to a particular person who has charismatic and others features. This establishes the relationship pattern between the leader and masses characterised with leader-masses inequality. While the ideal leader/character represents all interests and aspirations in his practical ideology, the masses follow seriously and sincerely with traditional, rational and legal authority. This gives the status of an ideal leader/character.

(ii) The entire social dynamics from initiation to perfection occurs in the background of social world which guides the leader and his followers. In other words, the ideal leader/character represents the ideals of masses which form their social world.

11. THE RELIGIOUS LIFE

(i) The entire religious life revolves around the beliefs and practices. Every religion determines functional aspects of social world. In actuality, religious life has deeper relations with the functional aspects of social world.

(ii) On the one hand, social world demands certain attitudes and behaviour in the cultural background of society. On the other hand, religion too demands certain beliefs and practices for ideational and practical guidance in life. Thus both contribute to social solidarity, coherence, consensus, harmony and integration. But, while social world may incorporate certain changes at different times, the religious life remains stable and static in maintaining beliefs, practices and principles.

(iii) On the whole, social world is perfectly reflected in religious life in terms of beliefs and practices which effects the entire life. The ideal character of social world is the direct creation of religious life.

12. GLOBAL SOCIAL ORDER

(i) Human society is characterised by different, but not necessarily conflicting conceptions of social world determined by religion, culture, ideology and so on. The humanity at large has a variety of social world for variety of factors.

(ii) But, at the global level, there exists the concept of 'Global Social Order' which refers to global type of social order established among different nationalities of the world. The example of this type of social order can be compared with UNO and UNESCO. It must necessarily reflect these features related to nationalities, ethnicities, cultures, religions, races and so on. In functional terms, this character must reveal in structure organisation, objectives and functioning.

13. SOCIAL WORLD OF PARTICULAR SOCIETIES

(i) As explained earlier, social world exists in different forms in different societies. It is generally believed that all societies in the world upheld no uniform but different and plural social worlds determined by their culture, civilisation, religion, ideology, social structure and so on. Similarly, the social world of Kashmiris have universal and particularistic features. In this context, we have focused on the Kashmir-specific social world. We have taken four major sociological features for explaining the social world of Kashmiris which are :

- The Kashmir problem;
- Future society of Kashmir;
- Experience of conflict situation; and
- Social Problems in Kashmir.

5. SOURCES AND METHODS OF STUDY

(i) The preceding account of main sociological features of social characters in aggregation, which contributed to the totalistic picture of their social world, were upheld by 30 representative Kashmiris. It also points towards sources of sociological information about concerned themes and topics, and methods-techniques used in this study. The explanation follows:

(a) *Observation:* This sociological observation is composed of two types: lifelong observation which is a sort of direct observation covering the whole life time of the individuals; and time-field bound observation which was carried out for specific time and in a specific field of the individuals.

(b) *Case Studies:* This sociological method referred to 30 specific social characters which were representative characters with particular as well as general cases. These two types represented the totality of social world of Kashmiris and its sociological features were aggregation, synthetic, reflective, contextual, and comprehension.

(c) *Recording of Life Experience:* This referred to the oral methodological technique in which life experiences and impressions were recorded which conveyed all important and trend-setting life events among individuals and groups. The recoding took place in two ways. In the first case, the recording was through remembering all major life events, achievements and changes. It may be named as mental remembrance type. In the second case, the experiences and impressions were remembered and confirmed through mental remembrance exercise and discussion with the character. This may be named as mental confirmation type. In this way, these exercises led to making sense of biographical details and data.

(d) *Life as most authentic and reliable source:* In case of requirement of knowing all important sociological details about social life in general and social world and social character in particular, life itself with all its major details emerges as most authentic and reliable primary source of information. While the authenticity and reliability of this comprehensive information was provided by the individuals themselves, the realistic assessment was also performed by individuals concerned. This does not represent subjective account of individual life, but essentially show the rational, objective and systematic account of his/her life. The various details explained, quoted and examined in this study played that methodological role.

(ii) This study through above-mentioned methods-techniques was enabled to make sociological explanations, assessment and interpretation of the phenomenon of social world on the one hand and social character on the other. Thus these two concepts played crucial role in this sociological study.

6. SAMPLE OF THE STUDY

(i) In general, the universe of this study was the broader Kashmiri society located within the valley of Kashmir. But, in actuality, the special focus of this study was limited to 30 contemporary Kashmiri characters whose representative character was at its highest level. These characters gave representation to all groups, classes, communities, castes, sects and other social collectivities prevailing in the contemporary Kashmiri society. This was done consciously in order to get totalistic picture about social world and social characters in modern era, especially in post-1947 era. Thus 30 social characters, their functional utility and representative features were noted and explained in social characters of Kashmiri society in chapter 1.

(ii) A point of methodological importance related to sample of social characters was 'Why 30, Kashmiris only?' Though this may be termed as subjective and arbitrary, it may equally be characterised as objective, comprehensive and representative. The number of social characters was limited to number 30 mainly because this number fulfilled the theoretical and methodological needs of this study. Moreover, this number of respondents enabled to give proper sociological treatment to the topic.

7. SOCIOLOGICAL AND SCIENTIFIC ANALYSIS

(i) As mentioned earlier, this study was carried out in sociological and scientific analytical framework. While the sociological character revealed in application of and analysis through sociological concepts, theories, themes, methods and techniques. In this context, we utilised the sociological concepts of 'social world' and 'social character' and methodological techniques of observation, case study, recording life experiencing and actual life realities.

(ii) This study was also carried out within a scientific framework by applying and following the sociological methodological principles as follows:

(a) First, the principle of objectivity was followed in all ideas, views, perceptions, perspectives, ideologies, worldviews, future visions and so on. Though the personalised accounts of personal lives and social experiences in their own phraseology were recorded and examined objectively, their contents were assessed and interpreted in most objective way through relevant methods and techniques. The personal perceptions and perspectives of 30 representative social characters were objectively measured and analysed.

(b) Second, the principle of totality involved the recognition and utilisation of the background facts related to plurality, diversity, similarity, dissimilarity and so on. It follows that no aspect of life was explained in isolation but in relation or association to whole social phenomena about social world.

(c) Third, the principle of rationality provided necessary and dynamic role in all statements of the study. All propositions about social world and social character were developed as per standard logic and related rules which have been mentioned in several chapters. No illogical or irrational argument was considered for inclusion in the thematic framework of the study. Thus logic and rationality revealed from beginning to the end of the study.

(d) Fourth, the principle of originality was upheld in the study of views, opinions, *perceptions*, preferences and sincerity of social characters in their notions, concepts and perspectives to the maximum extent. In this way, the concerned reality was exposed in its actuality and originality.

(e) Fifth, the principle of reliability was maintained after fulfilling sociological, methodological and scientific supports in all stages. This established the highest degree of reliability of all sources and aspects of information regarding social world and social character.

(F) Sixth, the principle of ethics was followed seriously. It was followed in social and academic fields. The former, i.e., ethics in the social field, was followed by maintaining the originality and specificity of various ideas, views, opinions and concepts of social characters. The latter, i.e., ethics in academic field was pursued by giving methodological treatment to the original ideas, views and concepts.

(g) Seventh, from the above explanation about this study in terms of certain central themes, this study was carried out in the sociological and scientific framework. All relevant propositions were explained/ analyzed and all related social developments were assessed and interpreted. This enabled to arrive at and formulate some basic features of the social world of 30 Kashmiris.

[illegible] [illegible] [illegible] [illegible] [illegible] [illegible] [illegible] by SMA [illegible] in any political developments, [illegible] [illegible] [illegible] [illegible]. In this way, SMA [illegible] women's power for his politics. K-26 [illegible] devoted to him without understanding his political ideals. She was a [illegible] follower of SMA.

(iv) Thus SMA and his leadership got the credit of giving legitimacy to the political [illegible] [illegible] [illegible] Kashmir. In fact, this new role stood unparalleled and unprecedented [illegible] [illegible] the Indian sub continent. In fact Kashmir was the first place where equal political rights of men and women were approved through their inclusion in [illegible] *[illegible] Program*. He also started efforts for their [illegible] education and employment.

(v) K-26 [illegible] that a leader like SMA never dies and can never be forgotten. [illegible] her devotion to his leadership remains still alive.

10. THE RELIGIOUS LIFE

(i) K-26 was a highly religious person but in a folk way. She had no knowledge about basics of Islam and no awareness about fundamental practices of this religion. Since she and her family were illiterate, they never formed the audience of religious preachers. They continued with the oral or folk tradition of religion. In fact, this community was kept away from ideal religious [illegible]. Its members, especially women, never got or gave time to listen to [illegible] religious preachers. They seemed neither interested nor involved motivated to develop proper understanding of Islam in their life. Illiteracy and ignorance further [illegible] their religious understanding.

(ii) In the preceding context, religion in K-26 family revolved around the performance of certain rituals, customs, practices and celebrations and so on. The major religious activities were identified as going to shrines regularly, following *peer-muridi*, celebration of particular occasions and days, [illegible] festivals and *urs*. In this type of religious environment, the role of the *mullah* and *molvi* emerged important but [illegible].

(iii) However, in previous decades some education has been [illegible] to the children of this community which led to some degree of understanding of [illegible] religion. Moreover, [illegible] [illegible] religious preaching [illegible] [illegible] Islamic [illegible] activities and [illegible] [illegible] organised by various religious organisations [illegible] different [illegible] contributed to some degree of understanding of real and [illegible] [illegible]. At the same time, this led to some [illegible] [illegible] and [illegible] [illegible] of basic Islamic ideas and ideals. [illegible] [illegible] [illegible] [illegible] [illegible] [illegible] [illegible] [illegible]

3

Social World of 30 Kashmiris

K-1 THE FOLK KASHMIRI – URBAN

1. SOCIAL CONTEXT

The service occupational groups were mobilised politically during the freedom movement in Kashmir in early 1930s. All these groups participated fully in political activities and got politicised fully. This situation provided the necessary background for overall developments in Kashmir in post-1947 period. However, the fact stands with clear evidence that, in that period, they responded late towards education and other changes in comparison to *Sayyid* and other groups which had adopted these changes earlier. Though educational, economic, political and other reforms in J&K were introduced in 1952-53, these groups generally responded late to basic changes due to lesser awareness.

K-1 belonged to one of the families of these service occupational groups which had specialisation in washing clothes and called *Dhobis*. In actuality, the families of *Dhobis* formed a community in the process of change and mobility which led to its total occupational mobility. Like in such other communities, the next generation/s dropped hereditary occupation and opted for new occupation of government service and small business. The traditional occupational activities were taken over by skilled and unskilled migrant Bihari labour in Kashmir.

It seems highly purposeful to present a brief sociological introduction of *Dhobi* community in the Kashmir valley. The total number of members of this community was not known. No survey or census has been carried out in this regard. However, different estimates conveyed their total number around several lakhs who live in different *Mohallas* in urban and rural areas in the valley. But, their heavy density and concentration prevailed in urban (old city) than rural (village) areas.

The occupation of this community revolved around washing all kinds of clothes. But, recent introduction of dry cleaning methods has reduced this activity. In the recent past, earlier manual-oriented washing was replaced by machine-based washing which has considerably reduced the labour-input in the process of washing clothes. However, the common methods used by washermen of Kashmir were traditional, primitive and obsolete.

Earlier their level of literacy was zero. But, later on, it improved significantly. As a result, 1/3rd of community members, especially young males, females and children, attained education significantly. Two points need, an explanation at this stage. First, this community responded to education late, i.e. from 1950s and 1960s, and more in urban than in rural areas. When the community members got free education in government schools in their localities, they didn't join in large numbers. Subsequently, those who got education tried for government jobs which they usually got. At that time, they dropped altogether old occupation and adopted new occupation fully. Then these occupational activities were taken over by migrant Biharis. In that situation, education and employment created a class of clerks and other government employees.

Culturally and religiously, this community was conventional and traditional. There was no radical change in the cultural life. In fact, its members were half modern and half traditional. At the same time, community members were generally conservative religiously and hardly any deviation had taken place. Religious beliefs and practices were still intact. They also observed strongly folk religious practices.

Politically, this community was still active with one or other political party. Its members were politically fully committed and were active in political participation. They were clear about political objectives and their proponents and opponents. But, they experienced lesser degree of political modernisation as they usually got involved in rigging, political corruption and non-democratic practices.

In terms of change and development, this community experienced lowest impact of these processes. While there was no major improvement in all fields of human development, no serious change could be observed in any field. Again, many families continued with the occupation in primitive conditions, there seemed no change in the social arena. There was not a single indicator which had been achieved fully by members of this community.

K-1 belonged to one such family of this community living in the central city. Basically, it was a traditional joint family unit but had responded to process of change through education which enabled its members to achieve highest degree of mobility.

2. IN-FAMILY SOCIALISATION

K-1 was socialised in a family which was half-changed and half-unchanged. It had not changed in cultural, religious and political fields. Culture because it retained old occupational life style. Religious because it maintained all traditional religious values and practices, folk religious practices. Political because it remained committed to its political leader and followed him seriously. At the same time, the family experienced change in educational and occupational fields. Educational because all its male members got education and one member got highest degree in the concerned field. While all children were enrolled in schools, only the elder females remained illiterate. Occupational because mobility enabled them to fully drop the old occupation and to adopt fully new occupation.

For some time, two occupations, old and new, existed in the family side by side. But, finally, old was dropped and fresh one was adopted. The entire changing pattern followed these developments seriously. Following this, a stage came when changed aspects dominated unchanged aspects. This happened in the context of adoption of new occupational role which led to significant degree of increase in social mobility.

K-1 got entangled in this environment where push and pull factors worked for every individual. He got education and parents paid for it. But, before he could go for higher education, he dropped and joined parents in their occupation. After some time, he found himself in undesirable occupation and dropped it. He got a government job which changed his entire role. Thus K-1 found himself in between two extremes and neither one was complete. In this situation, he developed a role characterised by half-old and half-new. This kind of situation dominated this family throughout.

3. OUT-FAMILY ENVIRONMENT

(i) Relatives: K-1 family was centre of attraction and interaction for all near relatives. This family was located at the central place in the city. So, all relatives visited this family repeatedly and regularly. In addition to providing entertainment and recreation, these meetings gave new ideas, views and so on, for new situation related to social roles and social action. Youth of these families developed same interest in a number of fields, especially related to career-making and programme orientation. They also helped each other. In this way, K-1 got deep influence of this environment dominated by relatives.

(ii) Neighbours: K-1 had faced deep impact of neighbours who belonged to same occupational community. Their social contact was close and deep and had emotional support too. They shared all life experiences and belonged to same educational, cultural and social background. They developed same social tastes, hobbies, actions and performances. This had total reciprocal impact on all of them.

There was another dimension of this neighbours' role, vis-à-vis the formation of the personality of K-1. It was belonging of K-1 and all his neighbours to the same local political group which had its own political ideology and political leader. This group had played and was playing a particular political role in Kashmir. This type of political socialisation effected the entire life of K-1 who, in response, developed relevant attitudes and behaviour pattern.

(iii) Family friends: The family-friends (ff) of K-1 included occupational colleagues, children's friends, clients and customers. While occupational community, professional and ff were of same social, economic and educational status, the clients-customers were of higher and much higher economic, educational, cultural and social status. The latter's economic standard reflected in getting their clothes washed by K-1 family. It had not rejected the impact of first category, though of lesser intensity. But, he and his family members were affected by the second category who included social notables, religious leaders and preachers, professionals, bureaucrats, officers, political leaders, doctors, engineers, advocates and white collars. All of them had positive impact on K-1 through interaction which was one-sided only. Those high status people (*oonche log)* used to emphasize on K-1, his parents and family members to pursue education. They also helped the family members for getting government jobs.

4. EDUCATION AND CAREER

(i) Education: K-1's primary to middle level education, like other children in the family, took place in a Muslim missionary school located in the heart of city. It was started by the Mirwaiz family in response to establishment of Christian missionary schools in Kashmir in late 19th century. It produced first generation/s of educated Kashmiri Muslims in modern times. It seems important to note here that this school was Islamic oriented and had some independent Islamic subjects, nearly half of the teachers there were the Kashmiri Pandits.

K-1 discontinued his education after 8th class due to personal reasons, for he disliked further education. He joined parents' occupational activities which he performed well. After some years of work, he changed his mind and wanted to qualify matric exam. for getting a government job. After very hard work, he got both.

(ii) Career: After a lot of efforts of K-1 and VIP customer (*kharidaar)*, the former got class IV job in a government office. He joined the job and was satisfied about it. K-1's opinion about this job was that there was no manual labour involved, while the occupational job was totally labour-based. Moreover, while there are holidays and fixed working hours in the present job, no such facility was available in the earlier occupation. In addition, he got a good salary. He continued with this government job and was later on promoted and got a clerical position, which was his long-time dream.

5. OCCUPATION, MOBILITY AND ASSOCIATION

(i) Occupation: There were occupational ups and downs in K-1's life. In childhood stage, he was a student as well as helper to parents in occupational activities. Then he joined the occupation on full time basis. But, some time later, he managed to get a permanent job in government office. At that stage, he dropped completely the traditional occupation and adopted fully new occupation. Subsequently, his parents too dropped the traditional occupation mainly due to their age factor. Thus there was K-1 family which experienced radical occupational change and this was followed in their life style too.

(ii) Mobility: Taking into consideration social esteem and economic value and different levels of input of manual labour in two different occupations, this change of occupations was significant and a radical step in the process of upward mobility for K-1 and his family. It was a positive achievement for him as an individual and as a member of family. In practical terms, it represented higher degree of change and mobility in terms of enhancement of status in life, income and social prestige among relatives and neighbours who were still engaged in traditional occupations.

(iii) Association: The occupational change and consequent mobility had not changed the association-pattern radically in the case of K-1. Since his family had the character of 'half changed and half unchanged' situation, the association with old acquaintances continued and, at the same time, the association was also established with new acquaintances. The old acquaintances included near and distant relatives, neighbours, political workers, ff and clients and customers. On the other hand, new acquaintances included official colleagues, class-batch mates, children's friends and new ff. These two patterns of association were different qualitatively as well as quantitatively. Both patterns had influenced the life of K-1 and, functionally, he had to maintain relations with both categories. Thus his situation of half-changed and half-unchanged got confirmed.

6. MARRIAGE AND FAMILY

(i) Marriage: K-1 was married after he got the permanent government job. The girl was his close relative. This type of marriage is common in the *Dhobi* community. Both partners belonged to same educational, economic, cultural and social status. It was an endogamous, monogamous and patri-local marriage. The girl was illiterate but intelligent, clever, alert and domestic-oriented. She took the control of joint family just after she arrived in K-1 family and managed to satisfy every member.

(ii) Family: K-1 and his wife lived in his joint family with parents and his married and unmarried brothers. After some time, she convinced her husband to establish nuclear family household. After he agreed, they constructed a new house in the outskirts of the city in a resettled colony. Now K-1 lives in his new house with his wife and married children.

7. SOCIAL LIKES AND SOCIAL DISLIKES

After going through life experiences, especially folk religious practices, K-1 have developed categorical choices as social likes and dislikes, some of which are mentioned below:

Social Likes	*Social Dislikes*
- a folk religious practice	- arrogance of rich people
- a *pir* and a *sufi*	- *corrupt* and incompetent officer
- Alamdar-e-Kashmir's poetry	- a non-trustworthy colleague
- religious-*thinking*	- violation of values and norms
- Kashmiri folk music and singing	- association with irreligious persons
- simple life with folk traits	- corruption and nepotism
- the poor family life	- a family having large number of members
- regular visits to relatives and neighbours	- the marriage with dowry
- regular celebration of festivals	- irreligious attitudes and ideology
- friends of *Awliya-ullah*	- a person with double standard
- a nuclear family household	- a hard and strict teacher
- close and reciprocal kinship ties	- a dishonest business man
- marriage between two equals	- a trustless neighbour
- taking care of poor relatives	- a non-committed relative
-traditional and conventional lifestyle of modern life	- not helping others in time of need
- controlled and disciplined children	- youth involved in abusing parental authority
- a highly qualified personality	- mental problems of children
- a credible and honest officer	- not to work hard

8. CONCEPTS OF "I", "ME" AND "WE"

(i) Since K-1 was lowly educated, culturally not exposed but politically active at lower level, his 'I' and 'Me' were not strong. The intelligent and intellectual superiority of his wife added further to his self-subordination. So, 'I' and 'me' were of submissive nature. In this context, 'I' and 'me' were used jointly for my past, my past history, my past work and achievement, my past struggle, my past association with VIP customers, my past of performance as a political worker, and my past political ideology and political party.

(ii) The concept of 'me' was further used which reveals it in my lowly educated childhood, my highly-educated relatives, my newly constructed house in middle class colony, my newly-adopted lifestyle, my new promoted job, and my religious-political association.

(iii) The concept of 'we' was developed by K-1 in special connotation in political and religious context. Since he belonged to a particular political party and a religious sect, the idea of 'we' was always alive. He often used it as 'we' as political party, our political leader, our religious sect and its identity, our customary behaviour, our traditions and values, and our own people.

9. IDEAS OF EQUALITY AND INEQUALITY

(i) K-1 followed the ideas of equality and inequality in rational and irrational ways. He favoured absolute equality in the folk *Sufi* and *rishi* traditions of Islam in Kashmir, wherein nobody is ousted and everybody is considered equal despite different social, economic, educational, cultural, political and other backgrounds. According to K-1, this concept of equality is also related to *pir-muridi* system. He believed that the *Pir* established a social order that treated every individual equally, the *murids* too considered themselves as equal to each other, at least in his presence. However, K-1 could not see the aspects of hierarchy and unequal relationship in this type of system.

(ii) K-1 believed that inequality of all types could be eliminated fully and effectively not in the materialistic framework, but in the spiritual framework. So, he suggested the adoption of *sofi-rishi* system which guaranteed equality in the absolute sense.

10. THE IDEAL LEADER

(i) The ideal leader of K-1 was *Mirwaiz Molwi Mohammad Farooq* (MMMF) who belonged to third generation of his family which was dedicated to the religious preaching in Kashmir. In the 19th century, this family extended its activities to the political domain. That was mainly because of political developments which hurt the Muslim interests at that time. The family also

(a) wanted to start influencing the emerging leadership in Kashmir; and

(b) wanted to establish its own political party, ideology and authority.

The family did it and *Mirwaiz* institution was politicised. Afterwards, this institution was known as religious as well as political in nature. The third *Mirwaiz, i.e. MMMF,* was installed on this institution in public and with full support of the state in 1962 after Holy Relic Movement (Tehriqi Moe Muqadas) and played religious and political roles simultaneously.

K-1 suggested five major reasons for following the supreme leadership of MMMF:

(a) he represented responsible religious and political position-authority which no other religious leader could hold;

(b) he was a folk religious preacher as well as leader. He used to teach and preach the Islamic religion in pure Kashmiri folk tradition. He used the *quran, hadiath,* and *Sheikhul Alam's* quotes to memorize by his followers;

(c) he was an accepted leader of a strong political group in Kashmir. He fought for independence of Kashmir, democratic system, and basic rights of the people. He represented people's political aspirations for which he never compromised.

(d) He represented the people's perception of the Kashmir problem which he wanted to resolve by granting the right of self-determination granted to them by the United Nations.

(e) His commitment to religious and political ideology was questioned. He fought for Kashmir and Kashmiris throughout his life and finally gave his life for the cause of Kashmir.

11. THE RELIGIOUS LIFE

(i) K-1 was sound follower of Islam. He believed in all fundamentals of Islam. Since he was educated, he had studied Islam from ordinary books. He was the regular reader of *Quran* and *naat* every morning.

K-1 was a equally a sound follower in primary religious practices. While he prayed five times a day regularly, he also performed other religious duties and obligations. He also performed all religious oriented day-to-day activities. He also remained committed to the concepts of good and bad deeds. He always opted for the former and avoided the latter.

(ii) K-1 was a strong believe in theory and practise of folk religion. He followed it like doctrinal religion. He gave equal importance to both aspects of religion, basic-central and associational-additional. He paid regular visits to all shrines in the valley. He celebrated certain particular days and dates in a week, month and year. Performance of customs and ceremonies was a usual affair at his house. He was not at all ready to listen against folk religious practices, as he was so confident about these. If somebody appreciated these practices, he used to feel delighted. It somebody didn't agree with him, he used to be annoyed with him. It is this kind of environment which has upheld the tradition of shrine-worship (*aasthan parasti).*

(iii) K-1 was not interested at all in reformative and radical trends of Islam in Kashmir. He considered these trends as deviation from traditional Islam. He also objected to these trends for their political objectives which, according to him, were their real purpose.

12. EXPERIENCE OF CONFLICT SITUATION

(i) K-1 felt that during last two decades conflict situation, it was workers, labourers and artisans who suffered more than other groups. They suffered at the hands of security forces, including the local police force. He maintained that workers and labourers could not work on all days declared as days of *hartal,* strike, declared/undeclared curfew, civil curfew, shutdowns, *challo* calls and protests-demonstrations. While they could not work and earn on current strike days, they usually could not get work in the winter season. So, they suffered for the whole year. According to K-1, some families of workers-labourers had to sell their domestic items to get money for the purchase of meals. Some of these families hardly get two-meals regularly. When they could not spend money for meals, how could they spend for education, health and other necessary fields. In fact, these classes faced severe economic crisis and it seemed difficult to come out of it. Some of them were seen begging also.

(ii) These classes and groups often became the victim of the fury and brutality of security forces. These were often made the target of security forces' violence while coming back or going to the working sites. K-1 had observed that while their men and youth were killed, tortured, disappeared, injured and disabled, their women and youngsters were raped, molested and dishonoured by the security forces repeatedly. This has happened in Kashmir despite the fact that both groups (Kashmiri workers and Indian security forces) belonged to the same class.

(iii) K-1 felt that artisans in Kashmir suffered more than other classes. These artisan workers, especially in the fields of *shawl-bafi, qaleen-bafi* and other handicraft experts were exploited to the maximum extent. While all of them were provided lesser than normal wages, they could not demand more wages due to no demand in the market in the absence of tourists in Kashmir. In comparison to these suffering classes, the middlemen and wholesalers of Kashmiri handicrafts got benefited much more in the national and international markets.

Thus the preceding explanation suggest clearly that workers, labourers and artisans, who all are daily earners, suffered more than other classes and groups during the last two decades' conflict.

13. SOCIAL PROBLEMS

(i) *Arrogance of Wealth:* K-1 had experienced many situations which revealed that some, if not all, rich individuals and families usually showed the arrogance of their wealth. This was directed towards lower economic classes and groups. It was mainly because of their accumulated wealth, collected mostly through immoral and illegal means, meant showing arrogance and abusing others. In fact, it was their wealth which spoke during the sessions of interaction with other classes.

K-1 felt that there were short-term and long-term social implications of this type of behaviour. Some of these implications were identified as follows:

(a) it divides (justifying and legitimising) the human society into opposite social categories of rich and poor, possessor and possessed, exploiter and exploited, masters and slaves, dominant and powerful and powerless;

(b) it created an unequal and unjust system based on the concepts of class, caste, power, gender and so on;

(c) it created antagonism and perpetual conflict between classes, groups an communities;

(d) it negated the concepts of culture, civilisation, values, ideals, norms and principles;

(e) it led to the processes of exploitation, domination, subjugation, and dehumanisation in human society.

Taking into consideration, disastrous social consequences of arrogance of wealth, this practise must stop immediately.

(ii) *Religious-Sectarian Intolerance:* Muslims in Kashmir constitute two major sects, i.e. Shias and Sunnis. Both sects have several sub-sects. While Shias were divided into Asna-ashri and, Sunnis were divided into *Hanafis, Shafis, Humbalis and Malikis. These* sub-groups are divided further into groups like *Ahle-Hadisth and Sanatu-wal-jamaat, Barelvi* and *Dev bandi* and Tawheed Parsth and *Aasthan Parsth.* All these groups and sub-groups belong to one religion, i.e. Islam whose fundamentals they believe in and practice. However, they got divided on different schools of thought, interpretation of religious concepts, and perceptions of Islamic reality and history. This difference of opinion was not on basics and fundamentals but on explanations-interpretations in different situational context. Ignoring their similarities, some Muslims focus on dissimilarities of opinions which often leads to antagonism and violence between various Muslim groups and communities.

In Kashmir, the major and minor sects have generally remained and lived in peace for centuries. These theoretical differences have not led to severe antagonism and violence, which violates the very essence of Islam. But, according to K-1, sometimes these differences are highlighted by vested interests in such a way that sectarian violence takes place and there occur human and material loss. He felt that this irreligious phenomenon represents exploitation of religion for petty and particularistic goals.

K-1 also felt that this behaviour also reflected in the practise of intolerance on differences on the part of some members of all sects. This intolerance was portrayed in presenting concepts and ideas and accepting or rejecting opinions and views. He was of the opinion that Islam never encouraged such pattern of attitudes and behaviour. These undesirable practices in the entire Muslim society must be stopped immediately.

K-2 ACADEMICIAN AND ADMINISTRATOR

1. FAMILY SOCIALISATION

K-2 took birth at a time when Kashmir was undergoing the greatest political upheaval in post-1947 period after the arrest of Sheikh Mohammad Abdullah (SMA), in 1953 on the part of government of India. But, the family background of K-2 was apolitical. In fact, he belonged to a humble *shawl-baf* family which had very meager income. Despite his humble background, all of his family members were sober, polite, intelligent, rational and gentle. His mother, though illiterate, was a lady of high standard in terms of her intelligence, performance and characteristic traits. From mother's side, K-2's relatives were comparatively prosperous and they provided emotional support to him and his family. The poor conditions of K-2's family did not stop him from going to a government school in his nearby locality for pursuing primary and secondary education. Since K-2 was intelligent and innovative, he qualified all exams. with distinction.

Since K-2 family environment was serious and religious, he developed his role accordingly. Even in his youthful days, his ideas, ideals, attitudes and behaviour were all religious-oriented. The main traits of his character at that time revealed seriousness, rationality, morality and calculated actions. While he followed respective patterns of interaction, he also developed respective association. At that time, he was an ideal religious person at home and outside. In this situation, K-2 lived a poor but dignified life.

2. OUT-FAMILY ENVIRONMENT

(i) The out-family environment of K-2 composed of *mohalla*-college-university environment and persons involved were relatives, neighbours, colleagues and personal-family friends (ff). K-2 started extending his social relations from *Mohalla Masjid* where he performed religious, social and other activities. Since he used to pray five times a day regularly, his activities expanded day by day and came in contact with people of different socio-economic and educational-cultural background. In the college and university, he continued the process of exposing himself to new social formations and social realities. While he concentrated on academic, literary and reformative activities during this college days, he worked with reformative-radical groups of a religious movement in the university. But, he was completely apolitical in character. Though he studied in a central university outside J&K, he was not exposed to national and mainstream political parties, organisations and groups.

(ii) K-2's neighbourhood was a mixed colony of different social, economic, cultural and educational families. Since the local mosque was a central place in the *Mohalla* community, his regular and repeated attendance enabled him to interact with all types of individuals, especially of intellectual type.

Individuals of such background had tremendous impact on his ideas and views at that stage of life. Some of them became ideal personalities and their families as ideal families for him. But, at the same time, he made a conscious distinction between desirable and undesirable neigbours. In this way, he accepted the influence of higher economic and educated families than lower economic and educated families. At this stage, he also got into permanent contact with an ideologue of a religious movement who made a radical change in his ideas and practices.

(iii) K-2's relatives were not many in terms of number, especially from father's side. While relatives from mother's side were engaged in small business, they had adopted prosperous lifestyle, the relatives from father's side presented a different social situation. When his family was passing through poverty, not many relatives visited his family. However, when the situation changed after he got a permanent gazetted job, relative started visiting his family often. In that situation, he was not influenced by poor relatives but the reverse impact took place. One of his near relative was an active member of a reformative religious movement and he encouraged him to participate in religious type of activities. Thus K-2's religiosity increased tremendously.

(iv) The colleagues of K-2 were his school-college-university batch-class mates and colleagues in different places where he worked. The personal and ff of K-2 were more or less of the same categories. A particular point worth mentioning is that K-2 was always selective in his friends and friendly colleagues. The criteria for selection was religious orientation and behaviour. Those who were seriously and sincerely religious became his friends and those who had irreligious orientation could not maintain friendship with him. So, it follows that all those who were his good colleagues and ff were completely religious in orientation and behaviour. They had significant degree of impact on K-2.s personality. He and all these people had reciprocal impact on themselves and their families.

3. EDUCATION AND CAREER

The entire primary and secondary education of K-2 was carried out in nearby locality government school where other children of surrounding localities were studying. Since he was intelligent and innovative, he passed all class exams. with distinction. Subsequently, he joined a city college for graduation. There he made distinction in literary activities. After that he joined a central university outside J&K for post-graduation in business-related subject. There he got exposed to national-level political, religious, ideological and social realities, especially related to the Indian Muslims.

Since he was a meritorious candidate, he got a gazetted job in a local college. It was considered a prestigious and status job in his entire clan in which most of the people were either illiterate or semi-literate. This was the happiest news and it was celebrated for months together. Thus K-2 started formal career with job which gave an improved economic condition to his family. After some time, he shifted to the local university where he was selected as a faculty member. He held several academic and administrative positions and finally reached to the position of one of the highest administrators in his institution. Though he always opposed this type of career, but finally opted for it. It seems that he wanted to avoid and negate the expected opposition by this ideational position.

4. OCCUPATIONAL ACTIVITIES

(i) K-2 was basically an academic professional. Within a brief period, he developed all necessary behavioural traits. The positive and negative features of his professional career follow. The positive features included straight and upright in approach, formal but hospitable, honest, sincere and considerate; helpful and appreciative; following all laws, rules, precedents and statutes of the institution,; more positive in response; not antagonistic to anybody; convincing power; rational arguments; and no compromise on principles. The negative aspects reflected in extremely formal and bureaucratic in approach, always not considerate, and wasting time in following formalities and procedures.

(ii) All his personal qualities got used in the system he works in. He represented a 'small instrument' in this machine-type structure and had to follow seriously all norms, rules, regulations, procedures, etc. without any question. He upheld and legitimised this corrupt system. Despite his honest leadership, corruption and nepotism continued. Despite his antagonism to the bureaucratic culture, he served like a humble servant of the system. In this situation, change in the system stands out of question and every action on his part strengthens the bureaucratic system. It was in the context of this bureaucratic culture that his image changed to an officer who was weak, ineffective, non-responsive, unrealistic and incompetent.

(iii) But, despite all religiosity, K-2 adopted modern technology in every department, office and section of the academic institution. All modern gadgets, instruments, tools and techniques, IT facilities were provided to all faculty members. He wanted to give the institution a modern look qualitatively as well as quantitatively. It gives us the understanding that religiosity does not necessarily lead to scientific and knowledge backwardness.

5. MOBILITY AND ASSOCIATION

(i) Taking into consideration, the parental occupation of K-2, the nature and degree of occupational mobility seemed considerable and that also only after one generation. From every aspect, this represented significant and irreversible occupational mobility. Consequently, this situation also led to overall social mobility which reflected in complete social transformation from old lifestyle to new lifestyle at home and outside. This also coincided with the adoption of 'syed' caste with his proper name.

(ii) The association pattern of K-2 followed closely his career pattern. Earlier his association was limited to his relatives, neighbours and close friends. This association was completely intimate with relatives and religious-oriented neighbours and close friends. While the association with relative was through reciprocal visits and interaction, the association with neighbours and close friends revolved around social, religious and cultural activities and functions. In the latter case, he spent most of his spare time. So, his image as a gentle, polite, helpful and religious person got popular. However, in the latter stage of his life, he expanded association to office and professional colleagues who belonged to the same economic, social and cultural status. They included academicians, professionals, officials, technocrats, religious preachers and leaders, and mass media experts. They also included different religious and ideological persons. But, his core associates were religious-oriented persons in whose company he felt at home. In this circle too, he became a popular character. In many cases, he was referred as role model for others. At the very late stage of life, his association developed the VIP character and he maintained that consciously.

6. MARRIAGE AND FAMILY

K-2 was married after he stabilised his economic conditions at home. He was married to a girl of syed family. At that time, the caste factor came in and he had to adopt the 'syed' title with his name. Thus apparently it was an endogamous marriage. But, in the contextual situation, it may also be considered as exogamous, hypogamous and parti-local marriage. The girl's family was quite ahead in education, culture and economic status. So, the marriage proved a step upward in the process of life-long social mobility.

Before marriage, K-2 was living with his parents in a nuclear family household. His wife joined that family. After some time of the marriage, he constructed a new house in a resettled middle class colony in the periphery of the city. K-2 lived in the new house with his unmarried children. Now, his children have settled abroad and one has also married there. His wife also seems committed to a particular ideology and she is devoted to missionary cause.

7. SOCIAL LIKES AND DISLIKES

After going through the principled, disciplined and serious life experiences, K-2 has developed some particular social likes and dislikes which Include the following:

Social Likes	*Social Dislikes*
- clean, decent and dignified personality	- music, dance, drama and art
- religious congregation of *namaz*	- cultural programmes
- religious awareness and knowledge	- radio, television and cinema
- home sickness	- wasting time without any purpose
- intelligent and intellectual friendship	- irreligious attitudes and behaviour
- prosperous life conditions	- extreme poverty conditions
- helping others financially	- watching girls and women unnecessarily
- loving parents, relatives and neighbours	- fashion and new cultural trends
- reading religious literature	- illiteracy and ignorance
- official titles, honour and prizes	- dishonesty, corruption and immorality
- hard working sincerely	- self praising and joking of others
- zero starter	- a feudal lord
- well mannered and open person	- sexual promiscuity among youth
- an intellectual and committed teacher	- social deviance
- ideal Islamic society and polity	- social apathy and carelessness
- stable moral relationship	- increasing criminal trends
- social ethics	- social pathology
- social revolution in practice	- violation of traditional values and norms
- family organisation and family control	- juvenile delinquency
- social change and development	- dehumanisation of police force

8. CONCEPTS OF "I", "ME" AND "WE"

Since K-2 was completely Islamic oriented, he developed the concepts of 'I', 'me' and 'we' in that particular background. In other words, the Islamic ideas, ideals and principles determined his conceptions. So, Islamic contextual background was necessary. 'I' was explained by K-2 in pure ideal and doctrinal terms. 'I' as pious Muslim, as god-fearing person, *Ummati* of Prophet Mohammad (PBUH), and sincere follower of Islamic religion. The ideal characters of 'I' in Islamic sense were four caliphs, Sidiq, Ummar, Usmman and Ali.

Similarly, 'me' was related to the Islamic ethos and Islamic history. So, 'me' was generally used in the sense of my Muslim community, my Islamic culture, my religious ideology, my religions traditions and principles, my religious perception. At the same time, the 'me' concept negated whatever was un-Islamic.

The concept of 'we' was used in the local, regional and global context. It portrayed similar as well as dissimilar identities, cultures and societies. It was also used in the situational context too. So, 'we' referred to we, the

Muslims of Kashmir, we, the Muslims in Asia and Africa, and we, the Muslims in the whole world. It mostly referred to their similarity in religious beliefs and practices. It didn't ignore the Muslim's ethnic and cultural diversity. In totality, 'we' was commonly used for the Muslim world.

In the background of explanation and use of social concepts of 'I', 'me', and 'we', all concepts of social collectivities such as class, caste, community, sect and tribe were negated completely. So, the former set of concepts were ideologically based for universal application.

9. THE IDEAL LEADER / CHARACTER

The ideal character of K-2 was Maulana Abul Aala Mawdodi (MAAM), one of the important Muslim thinkers in the Indian sub-continent in the 20th century. He stood parallel and equivalent to Sir Syed Ahmad Khan, Mohammmad Ali Jawhar and Maulana Abul Kakam Azad. He was not only a thinker, but a religious scholar, ideologue and political leader. He was the founder of *Jammat-e-Islami* in united India in 1940. After partition, while he migrated to Pakistan and his movement got divided in parties in India, Pakistan and Kashmir. Though these three parties have ideological similarity, they have serious political differences.

MAAM's writings represent master pieces in world Islamic literature in Urdu language. His religious scholarship was of the highest standard and unparalleled in his field. His famous books include *Tafheem-l-Quran, Pardah, JehaDi-fi-Sabilillah, and Khilfat-u-Malukiat.*

MAAM'S thought represented the Muslim response to their problems in 19th and 20th century, i.e. during colonial period. He made ideological, political and religious critique of the western powers and their civilisation. He challenged their 'superiority' and emphasised Muslims to withstand the Western challenge with Islamic revolutionary ideology. So, he emerged as one of the relevant, impressive and influential thinkers in the Indian sub-continental countries.

Though he and his movement stood for establishment of ideal Islamic society and Islamic state, he could establish none in Pakistan after 1947. While he was arrested there several times, his movement could not get more than 4% votes in national elections. Finally, he died in the lap of same advanced technology which had become the target of his criticism.

10. IDEALS OF EQUALITY AND INEQUALITY

(i) K-2 was a strong follower of Islam and so rejected all forms of inequality. He argued that Islam establishes an egalitarian system, equitable relationship, and debased all types of social inequality. The only difference it makes is between those who believe in oneness of Allah and final prophet-hood of Mohammad (PBUH) and perform Islamic practices and those belief in all these basics. But, this Islamic egalitarianism was de-shaped by the prevailing practices of caste and class among Muslims in Kashmir and elsewhere. Apparently, they claim to be equal but are not so in reality.

(ii) K-2 didn't believe in class composition of society in the Marxian sense. He felt that this framework puts the economic interests of different classes in opposition to each other. So, it leads to perpetual conflict and antagonism in society in place of harmony and integration. But, he had to accept certain existential realities of this perspective.

(iii) Regarding caste, K-2 felt that while it awards sacred and supreme position to certain castes, it has thrown out certain castes even within the societal framework, i.e. outcastes. Moreover, giving upper or lower social status just on the basis of heredity, descent and occupation, does not seem human criteria. The idea that one who was born in a particular caste has to die in that caste without any possibility of change is certainly cruel.

(iv) K-2 felt that women's role has to be seen in terms of equality but in different roles for men and women. He is in favour of different status and roles for different sexes. This according to him, stands normal, natural and beneficial. So, he opposed mixed education and favoured segregation of sexes. But, the system, in which he works, this was not allowed. Even in his personal life, he could not avoid this kind of interaction.

11. IDEAL SOCIAL ORDER

(i) K-2 upheld the Islamic perspective of ideal social order which reflected certain particular ideas, ideals and principles. The basic Islamic ideas and ideals of this social order were *Tawheed*, which revealed unity of God, nature and religion, relationship between these three units, and supremacy of God; *Risalat,* which revealed in finality of the prophet-hood of Mohammad (PBUH) who was sent to the whole humanity; and *Qiyamat, which revealed in* final assessment of good and bad deeds and rewards/punishment for these actions.

(ii) The ideal Islamic social order is based on some principles, some of prominent ones are as follows: (a) Principle of Equality: It emphasised that no caste or class division or stratification must be considered in the human society. All individuals in that society, irrespective of the belonging to different social, cultural, economic, educational and political groups, must be treated equal. The distinction and honour will be for those whose individual and social record will be best. The concept of *Ummat* has all these features. Since absolute equality doesn't seem a possibility in some cases, those deprived of equality must be compensated. He opposes both capitalism and socialism and wants a system which will ensure every individual his/her due share without hurting the collective interest. (b) Principle of Democracy: It emphasised the representative and participatory character of the social order which K-2 preferred. There will neither be political elites nor ruling classes. All citizens will have equal political and civil and legal rights within the system. That order will be integrative, cohesive, and will not encourage alienation. (c) Principle of cultural plurality: Since Islam spread outside Arabia an d covered the whole world, different cultures and societies were involved in it. All these cultural entities responded to Islamic religion in their own cultural context. So, the plurality of these cultures has to be safeguarded.

(iii) The Islamic ideals to be achieved, according to K-2, included establishment of global community, interaction and inter-relationship between various cultural and social entities, positive integration and solidarity, avoidance of cleavage, conflict and confrontation, ideological consensus and similarity in attitudes and behaviour patterns.

12. THE RELIGIOUS LIFE

(i) K-2 was a firm believer of Islamic belief system as well as pattern of necessary religious practices. He learned Islam directly from *Quran, Hadith* and standard Islamic literature, original and permanent sources. He was puritan and original in following Islam in totality and sincerely. He followed religious duties in daily life and any problem or confusion arose, he used to consult these original sources. He was in constant touch with Islamic literature for developing and accumulating standard knowledge about Islam and its application in modern life.

(ii) K-2 had the opinion that there was hardly any relevance of folk religious practices to pure Islam. He viewed the former against the essence of the latter. Since he was the sincere follower of doctrinaire religion, he disassociated with these practices and considered them as irreligious. He characterised these practices as corruption and distortion of Islam.

(iii) K-2 maintained the religious ethos in his home and outside but with reformed, emancipated and modernised version. In this way, he accommodated both features in his social environment which suited the composite cultural practices in Kashmir. In totality, he emerged most tolerant, humane, considerate and liberal towards other religions and cultures, especially of Kashmiri Pandits (KPs). Some of his best friends were non-Muslims. Thus he maintained the plural character of social and religious ethos.

(iv) K-2 was never impressed with the radical trend of Islam in Kashmir and kept himself away from it always. He considered its objectives misplaced, strategy wrong and actions counter-productive. In comparison to this, he opted for reformative trend of Islam which emphasised complete change in society before the radical change of the state.

13. POLITICAL IDEOLOGY AND KASHMIR PROBLEM

(i) In actuality, K-2 was apolitical person and depoliticised personality. So, he always kept away from active politics. While he never participated in any political meeting, protest or demonstration, he never cast his vote in elections. It seemed that processes of political socialisation and modernisation were not relevant to him. He felt that there was no political role for him. So, he felt himself engaged in establishing an ideal society which will give birth to an ideal political system, which symbolised in the system established by the prophet (PBUH) and four caliphs.

(ii) The Kashmir problem and its resolution was not central to K-2's thought and actions. Since he was professional and distinguished person, he developed special views about Kashmir problem. According to his perspective, this problem must be related to broader change and reform in this Kashmiri society. An Islamic, emancipated and reformed society can liberate the Kashmiri society and give it proper, ideal and necessary political system. An unprepared society cannot replace the corrupt and degraded political system. So, the attempt should be to carry forward the mission of establishment of Islamic society at the first stage.

At the same time, K-2 was not clear about the future of Kashmir. The choice of independence stands adoptable in case there is appropriate society available which is not the case in practice. The Indian option cannot be accepted because it stands un-Islamic. Moreover, the emerging revivalist forces in India will never allow KMs to live in peace. The Pakistani choice stands acceptable partly because of the national and sub-national questions there. The questions of particularity of Kashmir stand in contradiction with the ideology of Pakistani state.

In the present context, K-2 fully supports the *Azaadi* uprising for political reasons like its mass support, opposition towards the oppressive policies of Government of India, and reflect people's political aspirations.

14. EXPERIENCE OF CONFLICT SITUATION

Though he was not directly involved, K-2 was affected by the conflict situation like an average Kashmiri living in Kashmir. In fact, every individual and group was engulfed in the impact of this disturbed situation. K-2 felt this serious impact on the work culture in the offices. During those days, everybody felt tense, depressed, insecure, uncertain and disturbed. No professionalism was possible in this abnormal situation in the offices. No technical programme could be carried out. No innovative work, no scientific research and no serious academic assignment could be materialised. Even the regularity and punctuality in attending offices could not be ensured. There was total social apathy and hardly anybody was interested in following rules, norms, regulations, statutes and so on. It seemed that work ethic had gone and everybody was interested in his/her personal security. Moral and ethical standards were violated very easily and frequently. While lethargy and pathology dominated every working place, corruption, nepotism and other related practices were in vogue. This was a kind of situation which can be characterised as chaos or crisis which hurt the society as well as state.

15. SOCIAL PROBLEMS IN KASHMIR

(i) Orphans and Widows: Among various social problems faced by the present-day Kashmiri society, K-2 identified two major social problems. The first problem was the emergence of a huge number of orphans and widows mainly because of the armed conflict in Kashmir from 1989. He quoted an estimate according to which there were 32,000 widows and 98,000 orphans in Kashmir in 2008. There prevails no organised and systematic and continuous help and any credible livelihood resource for these suffering groups. So, there seemed an urgent need for continuous maintenance and lifelong rehabilitation.

There exist a lot of original, sincere and committed organisations working for their welfare. But, there are equally a lot of fake, insincere and self-committed organisations which work on the name of these unfortunate groups and grab the entire amount in their pockets. There are dozens of orphanages run by local organisations, in which thousands of orphans have taken the shelter. They represent even not 5% of the total number of orphans in Kashmir. The state government too provides some kind of monetary help to some hundreds of orphans and widows. Some of these suffering groups are taken care of by relatives, neighbours and family friends.

But, all these efforts represent a smaller effort while as there is the need of wider and larger support, which can be provided by the governmental and non-governmental organisations and agencies. K-2 was associated with the welfare of the activities related to these suffering groups. This work has to be carried out on short-term and long-term basis.

(ii) Corruption and Nepotism: Among the implications of conflict was the rise of corruption and nepotism in government offices. K-2 felt that these practices were so widespread that it was really difficult to get work done without corruption. He had personal experience in this regard. Even handing over the file from table-A to table-B, there is a demand for bribe. People have no option to this type of system. He agreed that he supervised the corrupt system.

With this practice, the practise of nepotism got also regularised. The family members, friends and other relatives of employees get their genuine and fake works done. Even modern technology is used to encourage this undesirable practice.

K-2 felt that the important point is that this practise of corruption has got mass social approval and nobody feels shy in corrupt dealings. He suggested that there is the urgent need of organised and unorganised efforts to stop it by NGOs and government agencies. The state and civil society have to work united.

K-3 ACADEMICIAN – KASHMIRI PANDIT

1. SOCIAL CONTEXT

(i) K-3 was born in mid-1930s in a situation which determined whole politics of Kashmir in modern times. In fact, the freedom movement at that time gave rise to a group of Kashmiri nationalists who worked for radical transformation of the Kashmiri society, especially after 1947. It was essentially in the context of this transformation which ensured maximum degree of change and development of majority Muslims and put a challenge to the traditional KP domination. K-3 was conscious of this situation of change.

(ii) K-3 was born in a modest and humble family. Economically, his family could not be characterised as prosperous. The head of the household was a teacher and his wife; though semi-literate, was housewife. This family was religiously conservative and his mother represented tradition and culture and was responsible for socialisation and transformation of this heredity to next generation.

(iii) K-3 was born in a rural background in a famous town in Kashmir. So, his personality reflected rural traits which continued through out his life. The 'rural solidarity', in opposition to the 'urban solidarity', was used by him as one of his 'operational strategy' in the urban social theatre of society. This enabled him to attract some friends but, at the same time, made some foes also. But, in the over-all balance sheet of social life, he got benefited by this strategy.

(iv) K-3 was brought up in a family which composed partly of a larger Muslim *mohalla* community. The relations between different families were cordial and intense relationship was intact. In fact, KM and KP families were tied in a reciprocal relationship which had deep effect on K-3. Most of his friends, neighbours, classmates and others in the locality had all effected his behaviour in the childhood and younger stage.

(v) K-3 was born in KP family which had no high caste status. His family caste was considered lower than other castes, especially high castes in urban areas like *Kaul, Dhar and Bhan.* But, he didn't felt disillusioned because of his family company with the surrounding Muslim families.

(vi) K-3 lived in a family which was a joint household unit but disintegrated soon. It happened in normal social dynamics of change and mobility. When A-3's brother got employed in armed forces, he shifted from home and established his nuclear family unit in Jammu. When K-3 himself got employed, he too shifted to city after establishing nuclear family unit. Then his parents also followed the migration. Though his parents, especially mother, faced certain social and cultural problems, they stayed in the city family unit for K-3, his wife and their little children. She took care of little kids and socialised them in KP religious traditions.

2. KASHMIRI PANDIT COMMUNITY

(i) K-3 belonged to the KP community which is known for its intelligence, excellence, higher education, statesmanship, scientific temper and academic progress. It will be highly useful to present a brief sociological profile of this community. It will also introduce K-3 and other KPs in this book in proper perspective.

(ii) Demographically, KPs constitute a minority religious community in JK state. They feel different from other religious communities in the Indian sub-continent. They had more similarity with KMs than with other Hindus in India. They were composed of 2.7% of the total population in the state in 1991 and their proportion must have reduced in 2001 and 2010 because of migration in 1989-90. They lived in urban as well as rural areas but not in hilly areas.

(iii) Educationally, KPs stood as highest literacy community. In fact, it represented one of the few distinctive communities in India which have maintained 100% literacy standard. They got education in all professional, technical, higher, most modern in scientific and super speciality fields.

(iv) Economically, KP community provided upper and lower officials to the state for centuries for carrying out its official activities. It was because of education that it provided official services from top to bottom, to all rulers in Kashmir, alien or local without any consideration of religion, language, race and ethnicity. In modern times, they provided the entire bureaucracy in the state. In a way, 'government service' emerged as a status symbol. It was considered so necessary that it became a necessary factor for getting a desirable partner in marriage. However, after 1947, some KPs deviated from the traditional occupation and started business.

(v) Culturally, KPs may be considered as cosmopolitan. They have usually adopted other cultural traits and, at the same time, maintained their own cultural traditions. They have strong sense of their past and they are proud of that. Sometimes, those sentiments reflected in their arrogance vis-à-vis other cultures. They still like to call themselves as *mahara* – an equivalent to *maharaja.* They expect every KM to call himself by this title. Usually, they were practising endogamy but it has changed now significantly. Similarly, the joint family is fast replaced by nuclear family units but its joint relationship had not changed radically.

(vi) Politically, KPs stood as a passive political community. They have always remained dependent on others for political leadership. Despite undergoing a serious tragedy, they failed to throw up representative leadership.

(vii) The KP community had repeated experience of migration. Their first migration took place in medieval times during the alien rule in Kashmir. They migrated from Kashmir and settled in different areas of undivided Indian sub-continent. Jawaharlal Nehru belonged to one such family which had settled in Allahabad after migration. Then KPs started migrating from Kashmir after 1947 mainly due to shrinking share in state government jobs. In that situation, while highly educated KMs started getting jobs in large numbers and the state government encouraged this trend, the highly professional KPs were compelled to go to different cities of India to get appropriate jobs. This pattern of migration has occurred in different states of India, especially in Tamil Nadu. Finally, the mass migration of KPs from Kashmir started in 1989-90 when militant movement for *Azadi was* launched. They got threatened in that situation and the government of that time encouraged this sentiment. As a result, about 80 to 90% KPs migrated to Jammu and Delhi, Chandigarh as well as other cities of India. Most of them left their moveable and immovable property in the valley, which was looted by hoodlums and forces. In this way, this community was uprooted and torn apart. It got lost in the wider ethnic plurality of India. In reality, it lives a diaspora life. It seemed that the community's total return is totally difficult if not impossible.

3. OUT-FAMILY ENVIRONMENT

(i) K-3's out-family environment composed of his neighbours, relatives and colleagues. His life-long neighbours were his colleagues, KMs, KPs and Indian Muslims (IMs) and Indians Hindus (IHs). Since IMs and IHs were culturally, religiously and socially liberal and maintained migrants' culture, he visited them often. His immediate neighbour was an IM professor who was in Kashmir for several decades. K-3 showed extreme degree of cultural liberty at home and enjoyed life with them. He liked aloofness and never joined the social mainstream except with some particular neighbours, with whom he shard social and academic activities. He was also impressed by some *Aligarian* colleagues and maintained social contact with them. Among the local-origin neighbours, he had relations, a few among them all Muslims.

(ii) K-3 had none of his relatives living in Kashmir. All of them have migrated to Jammu and other cities in the country at different times for education and employment. His nearest relative, elder brother, lived in Jammu and never visited him, K-3 used to visit his house in Jammu.

(iii) In the institution K-3 worked, he preferred some colleagues who were not of his own community. He preferred the colleagues who were IHs, IMs and KMs. He was not at ease with his community colleagues except some, one among whom was very liberal and entertaining. K-3 shared many of his traits like attending social parties, social gathering, modern lifestyle and entertaining programmes. Except these traits, he stood for opposite personality traits. In fact, K-3 was jealous of his career, social, cultural and personal engagements.

4. EDUCATION AND CAREER

(i) K-3 got his primary education in the government locality school in the town. He had to shift to proper town for secondary and higher education. *After graduation* in social sciences, he shifted to Chandigarh for pursuing higher education leading to the doctorate degree in his subject. Despite getting highest degree education in a cosmopolitan environment, it seemed that he had its lesser effect. Thus his rural Kashmiri traits continued throughout his life.

(ii) K-3 started the career with a teaching job in a rural school, then in a college and later on in the university. After several promotions, he became senior professor and head of his department. But, he didn't want to continue for personal reasons and so resigned after a brief period. He retired as senior professor with dignity and respect. His contribution was that he produced several generations of educationists and scholars in the field. He was in touch with eminent experts and scholars in the field. He often visited centres of excellence in his discipline. He prepared and published several papers.

5. OCCUPATION AND MOBILITY

(i) K-3 was an academician, though he was not carrying out all academic activities. His occupational activities were limited to teaching and research, in which he was regular, strict and open. His father was also a teacher but K-3 had higher degree of education, exposed to outside influence, married to a non-Kashmiri girl, reached to highest administration position in his department, and experienced highest degree of social mobility. He also improved his standard of life and spent most of his savings on acquisition of property in Panjab which he later on gave to his children. During his last days of academic career, he used to conduct a class, some research and read daily newspapers and listen to radio in the evening. This reflected an ideal behaviour-pattern of the KP teacher in the valley during normal times.

(ii) Taking into consideration the humble occupational background of K-3, he made tremendous upward mobility. He reached to the highest position in his concerned department and he became an eminent expert in his field of research. Moreover, he produced a number of high quality scholars. That gave him academic credibility and satisfaction. In addition, he developed elevated status due to educational qualification, marriage with non-Kashmiri bureaucrat woman of high economic standard and partly of westernised life style. This gave him highest degree of satisfaction about his mobility in life. In fact, he could not have dreamed more than that.

6. ASSOCIATION PATTERN

(i) K-3 had not determined any particular social objectives of his association in life. In actuality, his association depended exclusively on the situational needs. When he was outside Kashmir, he got exposed to urban people of other cultures. In that situation, he responded by convincing himself to marry a girl who belonged to different cultural and linguistic group. But, later on, when he came back to Kashmir, he changed his orientation towards social association, including marriage. The major social associates of K-3 were his colleagues in his profession. He made conscious interaction with some specific and not all colleagues due to his psychological orientation. He was always against academic bureaucrats and used to criticise them off and on.

(ii) At the same time, K-3 was fond of children and neighbours. While he loved all children by giving them sweets and chocolate, he used to exchange pleasantries with selected neighbbours. He had developed a lot of association for a Muslim neighbour whose boy he used to take to his home.

(iii) K-3 had also special attachment to lower class workers and lower occupation women. This reflected in his behaviour with sweepers, scanvengers who used to come to his flat for cleaning toilets and bath rooms. After their work, he used to serve them with tea and food items in addition to due wages. This behaviour also revealed in his dealing with fisherwomen who used to come to his flat for selling fish.

(iv) The above paragraphss assessed K-3's social attitude and behaviour which represented three main features. First, his social attitudes included liberty, frankness and openness, no communal approach, no communal discrimination, scientific and practical orientation, appreciation of innovative things, and no caste or class biasness. Second, his social orientation was relevant, pragmatic, realistic and so on. Third, his approach was directed to help others, fulfilling domestic needs and keeping everybody concerned happy.

7. CULTURAL LIFE

(i) Some aspects of the cultural life of K-3 may be explained as follows. Though the KP culture was an existing reality, it was non-existent for K-3 partly because he had left the KP social background long back and partly because he was now a part of KM social background. His approach was practical and reconciliatory. He could not be differentiated from KMs culturally. He dressed like Muslims, ate like Muslims, and behaved like Muslims. He visited Hindu temples occasionally, neither he installed any statue of God or Goddess in his home. He also didn't celebrate religious festivals with devotion. On the other hand, he participated in the Muslim festivals and other occasions. It may be observed that functionally he felt at ease with folk Muslim culture in Kashmir and had much knowledge about Islam than many Muslims.

(ii) His cultural identity can be related to the composite culture of Kashmir which K-3 was proud of. He usually commented that "what these outside Indians know about our culture". In actuality, he identified completely with the majority community. He thought and behaved like majority members and established a permanent contact with them. Here a question of basic importance arose, i.e. whether this attitude and behaviour on the part of K-3 was a life-long objective or strategy.

(iii) This Muslim-dominated Kashmiri ethos was upheld by K-3 and it reflected in dress, food, interior decoration, entertainment pattern, personal hobbies, guest-host relations, relations with others and so on. This life-style of K-3 was similar in Srinagar and Chandigarh where he had two residential flats. Thus the life experience of mixed Islamic, Hindu and other religions and cultures had given rise to a composite cultural framework in which he lived. In this framework, K-3's KP identity was not torn apart. But, he remained conscious about this identity for particularistic ends.

8. MARRIAGE AND FAMILY

(i) As has been explained earlier, K-3 proved unconventional in the case of marriage. Though he was conservative in marriage matters, he forgot his conservatism when he came in contact with a girl of his liking in the university who was a non-Kashmiri Panjabi. Going against his tastes, lifestyle and normative behaviour, he fell in love and was married with an alien girl. Thus his marriage was exogamous, uni-local and of hypergamous type. This marriage provided a plus psychological point for K-3.

(ii) After marriage, they lived together for some time in nuclear family household, some time in Srinagar and some time in Chandigarh. He enjoyed her family and she was entertained by his family, but for brief periods. Since they had good government jobs in different cities and different states, they could not live together for long time. Thus the family units established by them got disintegrated. In this situation, the wife used to go to Kashmir in summer for some time and the husband used to go to Chandigarh in winter for some time. In this way, they continued their marital relations. He bought several flats in Panjab for keeping permanent contact with his wife. There also he never forgot his roots and used to enjoy the company of folk KM labourers there. They used to do all his jobs, while he fulfilled their petty needs.

(iii) The flat in Panjab was a house but not a home. There was no social-cultural environment, no socialisation of children, no family relations and no family solidarity. All members lived separately which effected their attitudes and behaviour. The only person who could socialize children in Kashmiri culture was K-3's mother, but she passed away when their children were in early age groups. This family got dismembered after the daughter was married to a top Orriya journalist and son with a Delhi girl. In actuality, this represented common phenomenon of their joint families among KPs. Accordingly, when KPs get higher education and higher jobs, they usually marry high status non-Kashmiri girls and usually live outside Kashmir. In this process, the lost their identity and roots.

(iv) At the last stage of his life, K-3, like many other KPs, live alone in private accommodation in Srinagar and in Chandigarh.

9. SOCIAL LIKES AND DISLIKES

After going through different life events and experiences, K-3 developed the following likes and dislikes:

Social Likes	*Social Dislikes*
-System of social equality	-system of social stratification
-education as ideal in itself	-education as a commodity and means of profiteering
-artisans and labourers	-religious orthodoxy
-lower castes, communities and groups	-continuous use of vegetarian foods
-higher professional and technical education	-most modern dresses
-self-made personality	-communalism and sectarianism
-preference to girls against boys	-any kind of discrimination
-good non-vegetarian foods	-some non-local colleagues
-Muslim liberal ethos in Kashmir	-communal political leader
-folk religious practices	-top academic bureaucrats
-least dress consciousness	-child-domestic labour
-gender equality	-gender violence
-occupational practise in related fields	-drug addiction among youth
-reading daily newspapers	-juvenile delinquency
-knowledge about social issues	-poverty and poverty culture
-endogamous type of marriage	-illiteracy and ignorance
-civil marriage without dowry	-reservation of any type
-folk culture and music	-corrupt academic practices
-company of children	-child abuse by parents
-cultural roots of person	-no cultural attachment

10. CONCEPTS OF "I", "ME" AND "WE"

(i) K-3's concepts of 'I', 'Me' and 'We' were shaped mainly by contemporary cultural developments in Kashmir. His 'I' stood for bi-dimensional personality. While one dimension was related to traditional Pandit culture and ethos, other dimension was associated with Muslim tradition and culture. So, 'I' stood for both aspects of the social reality in Kashmir. These aspects were in constant interaction, inter-communication and mutual adjustment.

(ii) In this context, 'me' stood for synthesising process of religions and cultures in Kashmir. So, everything involved in this process belongs to 'me' and my actual religion and culture. That was empirical reality 'me' stood for.

(iii) 'We' was the cumulative result of all these developments in the shape of a living community which had distinct historical past and contemporary relevance in terms of its ethnicity and so on. It stood for holistic character of all that Kashmir represented, conveyed and aspired.

11. IDEALS OF EQUALITY AND INEQUALITY

(i) K-3 upheld the view that absolute equality between human beings was possible and it must be established necessarily. He opposed all in-equal systems which perpetuate the practise of injustice. He opposed class differences of any kind which will put some classes to injustice and misery. So, he showed clear opposition to feudal and capitalist systems. But, he was not clear about the alternate system of equality and justice.

(ii) K-3 was a strong opponent of religious differentiation and discrimination. He interpreted it as the most inhuman practice. He argued that all religions stood for a way of life which will not recognize any sort of inequality, injustice and division. If the same institution was used against to our own or other people, it leads to its dehumanisation. He felt that religion in practise has taken up a dominant negative role at micro and macro level. In this situation, he preferred to be an irreligious person.

(iii) K-3 abhorred caste stratification and considered it absolute system of inequality, domination and exploitation. He criticised proponents and upholders of caste which was endemic among KPs. Since he felt belonging to lower or middle caste, he showed antagonism towards upper castes, which, according to him, were perpetrators of injustice and exploitation. On the other hand, he used to listen about Islamic egalitarianism but, at the same time, he used to observe some caste practices among Muslims.

(iv) K-3 was not a believer of gender differentiation and discrimination but wanted equal role and status for women. In order to establish basic and larger gender equality, radical change was needed in a broader society. The processes of secularisation, modernisation, industrialisation, urbanisation, educational advancement and women empowerment will help significantly in this regard. This was one of the aspects of social life among KPs about which K-3 was satisfied, i.e. KP women enjoyed more or less equal status.

12. RELIGIOUS LIFE

(i) K-3 was basically an irreligious person in attitude and behaviour. He hardly took care of his religion and religious community. He hardly visited religious gatherings, congregations, festivals and temples. He had no association with religious organisations and parties. In his discussions, he always revealed irreligious orientations.

(ii) He considered the religious factor/variable as backward. He considered every extreme religious person as undesirable and so avoided them. However, some times, he participated in religious activities for social pressure, especially *tul mulla* festival once a year. He had not kept any portrait or statue of God and Goddesses in his residential flat.

(iii) However, K-3 was fond of folk religious practices and functions, especially related to language, music, Sufism, *Rishism*, and religious songs. He never believed or worked for establishment of religion-based associations, but was always active for composite cultural-religious activities. This religious tradition, according to K-3, was essence of Kashmiri culture. So, he sometimes visited Muslim shrines and showed his obedience.

(iv) K-3 was allergic to reformative as well as to radical trends in Islam in Kashmir. It was because of his feeling that these movements will ultimately destroy the composite culture in Kashmir. So, these trends were dangerous for Kashmiri culture, Kashmiri identity must be avoided and rejected. But, in public, he used to appreciate persons associated with these movements and sometimes became their good hosts.

(v) K-3 had special interest in *Sufi* Islam. So, he enjoyed *Sufi* music and the company of Muslim mystics. One of such mystic was his permanent guest. He used to visit regularly K-3's office and residence and get material and monetary help. K-3 always participated in all folk religious celebrations of Muslims and he had no inhibition about it.

13. IDEAL SOCIAL ORDER

K-3 never thought in theoretical-abstract terms about social order at the global level. However, he presented some ideas which reflected certain positive features of the global social order. These features included equality among all human beings based on humanity, sentiment, liberty in thought and action, cultural plurality, safeguards to all minorities, cultural synthesis, limited role of religion in social and cultural affairs, secular ideology and secular practise in state affairs, and upholding distinctive features of Kashmiri society and culture.

14. POLITICAL IDEOLOGY AND LOCAL POLITICS

(i) K-3 was a non-political person. He neither supported any political party nor voted in any election. He had no practical political ideology to follow. Despite being minority conscious, he hardly thought in political terms to serve his community. But, due to militancy in Kashmir, he was compelled to develop certain political ideas. In general, he supported broader objective of secular Kashmir in future. He wanted special protection of religious minorities. Sometimes, he supported the withdrawal of occupying Indian forces from Kashmir and criticised their abuses of human rights.

(ii) In private meetings, he used to criticize India as well as Pakistan for creating and then not resolving the Kashmir problem. According to his views, it can be resolved by granting 'right to self determination' to people in JK. When India refused to solve this problem peacefully, the Kashmiri youth was compelled to rise in revolt against the Indian state. It was in this context that militancy started in Kashmir in 1989.

(iii) But, at the same time, K-3 had also critical views about militancy and militants. He maintained that militancy was not in the sincere, mature and credible leadership and it stood mis-directed. In some cases, even hoodlums (*munje gre)* and petty people (*soor val and chinevel)* became its local leaders and representatives. They had neither any ideology nor any commitment and political cause. According to him, they used the movement for their petty selfish or family interests. He also believed that there were some sincere, mature, committed and credible leaders and activists in this movement, because of whose commitment the militancy survived and continued.

15. EXPERIENCE OF CONFLICT SITUATION

(i) Many militants and activists used to visit K-3's flat. In fact, they had developed trust in him mainly because of their feeling that security force will not doubt him because he was a Hindu. He also proved a good host to them always. But, despite being a Hindu, he was treated well by security forces. He was harassed, tortured, humiliated and offended like other Kashmiris. He was often furious about it, especially in relation to women, children and elders. The forces' alien background (like Bundelkhand) and no proper training made them just unbearable. Their superiors just ignored their vulgar and inhuman behaviour despite complaints from the local people.

(ii) One particular experience of conflict situation of K-3 was related to how innocent civilians got involved in the armed clashes. Cross-firing between militants and security force was a common feature of daily life in busy streets in Kashmir during 1990s. During those days, K-3 had gone to the market for purchase of bread when cross-firing took place there. After the firing, the militants and all civilians started running to protected areas, so did K-3. While running to his flat, the militant too was running behind K-3. He came near to K-3 and shielded his rifle in his blanket and ran away after saying "I will collect it in the evening".K-3 had no alternative except to take rifle to his flat and kept it at a safe place. In the evening, the militant came and took it back.

16. FUTURE KASHMIR SOCIETY

(i) K-3 was a proud Kashmiri and he maintained this position even in India. He had developed some particular ideas and ideals about future Kashmiri society which include the following features. Politically, he wanted a state based on the principle of liberty, freedom and independence. He favoured an independent Kashmir in future which will have friendly relations with India and Pakistan and will safeguard all ethnic identities in Kashmir. He wanted establishment of this state through political and peaceful means.

(ii) Educationally, he wanted a Kashmiri society in which every member is literate, qualified in higher, technical, professional and most modern educational fields. All educated youths must be provided suitable jobs in public and private sectors. Education must not be made a material commodity in the market, rather it must be made free to all citizens, especially to socially disadvantageous groups. The private sector must play a limited but specific and focused role in order to fulfill societal needs.

(iii) Culturally, while the state must maintain all legal formalities of secular ideology, the society must practise values and norms related to secular ethos. The composite character of religion and culture must reflect in all fields and at all levels. This cultural heredity must necessarily be shifted to the next generation.

(iv) Socially, Kashmiris as a distinct community must emerge with multifarious features of traditional family ties. He wanted safeguards against change in existing marriage practices, especially endogamy. K-3 gave a conservative view that all values and norms must be consciously followed, even in changing situation.

17. SOCIAL PROBLEMS IN KASHMIR

(i) *Social Apathy towards suffering masses:* According to K-3, a socially important problem was general apathetic attitude towards the suffering of lower classes and groups in the Kashmiri society. This problem not only led to social deterioration in their life conditions, but involved the whole social fabric. This also led to continued social antagonism and conflict between varying classes in the broader society. K-3 felt that this situation stood highly undesirable and so must be changed completely and effectively. That was necessary for establishing equitable and just social order.

(ii) *Corrupt Practices:* K-3 was astonished when he came across minor details about nature, enormity and level of corrupt practices in the entire Kashmiri society. His estimates and observation revealed that all fields of life, especially political, legal, administrative, economic, cultural, educational, professional, police and bureaucrats were heavily corrupted. While the government agencies and organisations encouraged it consciously, the civil society too gave it a helping hand. Thus our society became fully corrupt from top to bottom and 'Transpirancy International' had to rank it as 'second most corrupt state in India' recently. K-3 felt that our society was totally drowned in corruption and wanted a stronger and broader social initiative to root it out.

K-4 SCIENTIST AND ACADEMICIAN

1. SOCIAL CONTEXT

(i) K-4 was born in mid-1950s in a rural family in a small town when radical changes started in the agrarian society in Kashmir after centuries gap. Consequently, the traditional pattern of life started undergoing serious and basic changes mainly because of introduction and implementation of famous land reforms and other revolutionary measures enshrined in the *Naya Kashmir Programme in 1938.* Now, the villagers in Kashmir, got some land of their own after centuries and consequently got sustenance of life in terms of production of rice. As was expected and imagined by the rural masses, the land reforms and other measures didn't prove revolutionary. These reforms didn't benefit people equally but unequally. While some got more than their needs, others got less than their needs. Again, some emerged as orchardists after getting more land, while others remained small or landless peasants. In this way, the net effect was that a significant number of rural peasantry was not in a position to produce sufficiently for their yearly needs.

(ii) K-4 belonged to one such family which had neither sufficient land nor sufficient production. It had to work for other occupation for livelihood needs. In this context, this family was bi-dimensional in occupation, i.e. agriculture and service occupation. Later on, the family developed other two occupations, i.e. government service and business.

2. IN-FAMILY SOCIALISATION

(i) In the post-1950's changing agrarian situation because of implementation of land reforms, K-4 family could be categorised neither in middle class nor in lower class but in between the two. Since land distribution had benefited the family partly, this family was not fully agricultural. In addition to owning limited land, other factor responsible for this character was K-4's mother's urban origin and family engagement in occupational activity. So, this family represented qualitatively a different type from other rural families. It was particularly different because of its response to modern education. At that time, even KMs in urban areas were not getting education at large, there was least possibility for inhabitants in rural areas. But, this family proved as an exception.

(ii) Consequently, all children in the family were educated, even highly educated and for both sexes. In this situation, the family developed bi-dimensional feature socially and culturally. It was traditional in terms of cultural, social and religious ethos (represented by parents) and modern educationally and professionally (represented by children). Both these aspects determined the direction of change of the family in future. Despite living in the village-small town, all urban features and facilities were available in this family house.

(iii) Thus this family which was poor earlier now emerged as a prosperous unit partly due to changed agrarian situation and partly due to educational and occupational mobility. The family emerged as a distinct unit now. K-4 was socialised in this type of family. His attitudes, behaviour, personality and entire career were developed in this environment.

3. OUT-FAMILY ENVIRONMENT

(i) The environment which effected K-4's personality intensively were his rural-urban community, neighbours, relatives and family and personal friends. The rural community was generally illiterate or semi-literate and composed of agriculturists. There were also rich peasants and orchardists who had close interaction with K-4 who gave him regard and respect and, in exchange, he helped them all times. On the other hand, the urban community (from mother's side) was comparatively more educated, exposed, mobile, changed and developed. K-4 had intense interaction with this community too and got benefited by urban benefits and its centrality. In this way, both urban and rural environments contributed to the development of his personality.

(ii) His neighbours in the village were living in close-knit society and were mostly illiterate. They mostly belonged to lower classes and were culturally unexposed. They had particularistic interaction with K-4 and had different impacts on each other. They generally held him in high social esteem and considered him a social notable. Even educated and well-off families were impressed with K-4's life achievements and established permanent contact with him. He always helped them, especially in educational matters. Even in the younger age, he proved all helpful, considerate and open-minded.

(iii) K-4's relatives were many and belonged to rural and urban areas. Nearly all of them belonged to same educational, economic, cultural and political status. They were mostly engaged in different occupational activities. K-4 had developed close relation with all and visited them often. So, he had accommodated all complex features in his personality. While he was liked by all relatives, he too showered affection on all of them. So, they had a reciprocal impact.

(iv) K-4's personal and family friends were his personal and his brothers' friends who used to visit his office and home. In fact, he attracted a large number of friends with extremely different belongings and his office used to be crowded all times. These friends were generally highly educated, serious-minded, intellectual-oriented, rural-urban, from all classes, communities and groups, and undergone change and mobility. He certainly got influenced in attitudes and behaviour.

(v) K-4's personal friends belonged to many nationalities; cultural-linguistic groups; occupations-professions; classes, communities, sects and groups; all regions and age groups; and all economic classes. Majority of these friends were engaged in scientific, academic and development research and strong profile in this regard. Ideologically, most of them like K-4 were committed and dedicated and had clear religious orientation in life in the positive sense. They were eminent scholars in their fields of specialisation. A significant number of them composed of different Kashmiri individuals but who all supported the sacred cause of Kashmir and Kashmiris. In regard to these personal friends, K-4 had the experience of reciprocal impact, especially in the ideational fields.

4. EDUCATION AND CAREER

(i) K-4's early education was carried out in the government school in his small town. For college level education, he had to shift to the city where he pursued graduation. This shift contributed to his broadened vision, expanded horizon and exposure to new world of social-cultural-economic realities. As was expected, K-4 made excellent performance in all classes and exams. Subsequently, he shifted to a central university for post-graduation in sciences. Though he excelled there and scored high, but he was not impressed by its academic mileau and standards. It was mainly, because, all including academic, activities revolved around the 'minority conscience'. Following the higher academic objectives, he got into contact with a centre of excellence in scientific research in India (IIT) where he joined for doctoral research. Here he got exposed too world class academic standards and practices. Moreover, the faculty was of global resources, socially open and represented the elite in its subject/specialisation. K-4 was impressed with this environment and developed highest degree of academic excellence here.

(ii) The first appointment of K-4 was in a central university where from he had done post graduation. Though it was practically very difficult for a KM to enter as faculty in that university, he managed to get in because of his highest merit. So, his appointment pleased some but displeased many others. K-4, after some years of work, proved a distinct academician in terms of his academic credibility, academic performance, national-international academic contact, scientific research, rational-academic bent of mind and commitment to academics. He got recognised at the national and global levels, especially in Western Europe. Despite antagonistic approach towards his progress, nobody could stop his promotion in the university. Then he shifted to his motherland and joined as head of his department. It was a home return after a long gap and he wanted to utilize all his faculties and experiences to make his department a centre of academic excellence. So, he started working for that objective seriously. But, after some time, he felt that there existed certain serious structural and functional limitations inherent in our system that hurts the academic progress and development. He also felt that deeper and larger social initiatives were needed to negate these limitations completely.

5. OCCUPATIONAL ACTIVITIES AND MOBILITY PATTERNS

(i) The traditional occupation of K-4 family was related to agriculture and service occupation, and adopted government service and business later on. While K-4 and his brothers-sisters were working in new occupations, his parents were related to old occupations. In this context, this occupational shift represented absolute upward social mobility which not many families in the villages in Kashmir had experienced in modern times. In a way, this may be considered as 'unprecedented' pattern of mobility. This had a direct impact on the family life, especially its new lifestyle which reflected in all urban facilities in the house, expenditure-consumption pattern, entertainment-engagement pattern, new status and role and so on.

(ii) K-4 was in real terms an academician, intellectual, scientist and researcher. All sorts of academic activities like teaching and research were his favourite. He never missed them. He used to work for academics for more than 15 hours. He was an eminent expert and specialist in his areas of specialisation and known for his expertise in India and abroad. He often used to visit Western Europe, especially Germany and Italy for academic discourses. He used to get invitation for different academic assignments from the whole world. In brief, his academic excellence was seriously noticed, discussed and analysed the world over. Since he was an intellectual-oriented person, he used to involve his friends and colleagues in serious discussions on political, religious, economic, social, cultural, national, international, science, psychological and all other topics related to human life and society. He put forth new and original ideas on all these topics. In reality, his intelligence and intellect represent a gift of God which not many human have.

6. CULTURAL LIFE

(i) K-4 had a rich cultural life whose main features were plurality, tolerant approach, work ethic, linguistic multiplicity, objective analysis and scientific orientation. Since he upheld the ethos of plurality of regions, religions and cultures, it enriched his life. He wanted all cultures to bloom and develop freely. This may provide the basis of a global social order, he opined. He also represented a liberal tradition of religion in theory and practice. He was not for regression, backwardness and fatalism but for regenerative, progressive and innovative role of religion. He felt that religion and culture must be used to develop human communes at local, regional, national and global levels. It should be the source of peace and development and not conflict and underdevelopment.

(ii) His work culture was based on ethics and morality. He sincerely followed the objectives of his profession. He believed in the sacred value of *halal* income, so he worked sincerely and seriously. In this environment of work culture, he advocated the ideals of scientific temper, universal orientation and application, rational arguments and propositions, human perspective and utilisation for humanity and not against humanity. Thus in his ideal academic cultural life, K-4 developed the features of objectivity, secular outlook, humanity as the supreme cause, future vision, positive ideas and ideals, global orientation and application, dealing with issues and problems with humanitarian point of view.

7. THE ASSOCIATION PATTERN

(i) K-4's association was of open type. There was hardly any consideration of region, religion, culture, language, ethnicity, language, education, demography, sex, community, caste and class. Even age was not considered as the factor. Males and females were his close associates. He had close friends belonging to Ks, KPs, IMs, Hs. His friends belonged to all cultures from Kannadas to Biharis and from Panjabis to Tamils. He had the association with friends at national as well as international level, belonging to U.S., England, Europe, Middle East, South East Asia. The important feature of the association of K-4 was that he fulfilled all social obligations of this relationship.

(ii) The association of K-4 was characterised by the similarity in ideas, ideals and ideology. The friends in association were all liberal, pro change, non status quo, anti-establishment, pro-poor and anti-colonialism. So, they were progressive, futuristic, humanitarian and enlightened. They hardly supported sectarian, communal and pro-establishment views in society in general and in politics in particular. They always favoured the objectives, methods, techniques, concepts and theories of change and development in India and the developing world. They all opposed the colonial-imperialist western powers, their political, economic and cultural domination. They opposed kingship in Saudi Arabia, repression of Palestinians in Izreal, and suppression of Kashmir in India.

8. MARRIAGE AND FAMILY

(i) K-4 was married in the occupational group of the same class. The girl belonged to upper economic and educational background. She was highly educated and culturally exposed. Both of them arrived in the marriage market late. They married when K-4 was working in the central university. Since she was highly educated and self earning, she proved an ideal partner in the marriage. This marriage proved a step forward in the social life of K-4. It was an exogamous, monogamous and neo-local type of marriage to which he was always committed in theory and practice.

(ii) At the time of marriage, K-4 was living in his nuclear family unit outside Kashmir. However, she joined his joint family household in the town and shared its social life for some time. Afterwards, she shifted to out-Kashmir nuclear family unit of her husband. There she was interacted and got exposed to India academia. After coming back to Kashmir, they established a separate nuclear family unit in the official residence. But, at the same time, they maintained cordial relations with the parents' joint family in the town. Some time back, they constructed a new house in an elite colony outside the city and shifted there recently and live there at present.

9. SOCIAL LIKES AND DISLIKES

After going through long and serious experiences in life, K-4 had developed the categorical choices as social likes and dislikes some of which are mentioned below:

Social Likes	*Social Dislikes*
-decent social behaviour	-an arrogant and uncivilised officer
-serious and strict application of laws and rules	-a corrupt politician
-commitment to monogamous type marr.	-corruption and nepotism
-close kinship ties	-crime and drug addiction among youth
-scientific analysis of social problems	-violence against women
-self confident personality	-academic backwardness
-honest, humble and open bureaucrat	-a person who avoids hard work
-moderate religious attitude and behaviour	-the political dictator
-sincere, competent and regular teacher	-inequal and unjust social system
-liberty, freedom and democracy	-the caste hierarchy among Hindus.
-intelligent and hard working girls	-communal-sectarian ideology
-people of low caste origin	-inequality and discrimination
-egalitarian social order	-gender discrimination
-social initiatives for literacy	-child labour and domestic labour
-collective ideals of Islam	-extremely irreligious behaviour
-cultural and religious pluralism	-forces of suppression and oppression
-development of poor countries	-western global domination
-moderate life style	-ultra modern social life
-a person who had started from zero	-social apathy and social pathology

10. CONCEPTS OF "I", "ME" AND "WE"

(i) K-4 had strong sense of all three concepts. Since he had passed through harsh, hard and tough experiences in life in the past, he was always conscious about these psychological identities. 'I' reminded him immediately his past and his courageous struggle. He was also reminded of his positive and negative experiences and his positive response with positive values and ideology. 'I' also reminds him to see the present situation and present a self which stands objective and humane. That reflects in his response to known and unknown individuals and groups. His domestic behaviour has also been shaped by his 'I'.

(ii) The concept of 'me' also conveys my past and my present. It coincides with past and present experiences positive and negative, religious and irreligious, and nationally and globally. So, he often talks of my education, my achievements, my foreign trips, my academic contribution, my home, my family, my friends, my ideas and ideals, my character and my association. 'Me', according to him, refers to academic profession and its history in the global context. This stands as one of the most confident aspects of K-4's life.

(iii) The concept of 'we' was an umbrella concept. For K-4, it stood for academic fraternity with all its characteristics, features, distinction and hard realities. It also stood for community of Muslims called *ummah* which established equal status and membership irrespective of social, racial, cultural, economic and other differences. It elevates one from static lower position to a dynamic membership of global implications. Finally, 'we' for K-4 was his community of locals, i.e. Kashmiris who maintain a distinct history, culture, language, ethinicity and so on. Though they have been suppressed, dominated and ruled by aliens, they aspire political independence, for which they have given unparalleled sacrifices. K-4 does not stand for ethno-centric ideology but he believes in mutual respect for mutual survival. His conceptions of 'we' have no contradiction because social collectivities have their respective spheres of influence.

11. IDEAS AND IDEALS OF EQUALITY AND INEQUALITY

(i) K-4 had clear ideas about social differentiation and social inequality. Broadly speaking, he supported any type of system which will ensure social equality and, at the same time, proscribe social inequality. Regarding class differentiation in society, K-4 felt that it was inhuman and makes differences on the basis of economic standing. It dehumanizes the concept of equality and it creates antagonism and conflict in society. Moreover, it has failed to create an egalitarian social order.

(ii) On the other hand, caste stratification also dehumanizes the concept of equality because it grants upper or lower status on the basis of hereditary status and occupation. Moreover, it keeps *Harrijans* outside the framework of caste. It stopped their liberation and emancipation. It also stood illogical and undesirable. It allows upper castes to exploit the rest of castes. In comparison, he presented the Islamic conception of equality which stood logical, scientific, human and beneficial. But, he accepts the reality that, despite Islamic prohibition, some Muslims practise Caste in Kashmir and have also been involved in the process of *sayyidisation.*

(iii) K-4 opposed gender discrimination in clear terms. He felt that since women have been exploited, mal-treated, abused and molested throughout history, they must be ensured equality and justice now. Religion, culture and ideology must never come in this process. But, at the same time, he accepted the existing reality related to gender injustice and violence against women. He wanted legal and social measures and initiatives in this regard. He opined that women's initiative in this connection will prove more purposeful and productive.

12. THE IDEAL CHARACTER

(i) One of the ideal characters of K-4 was world famous Noble laureate, Professor Abdul Salam of Indian sub-continent and later shifted to Italy where he works in an international research centre in Triest and where he worked for noble prize work.

(ii) K-4 felt impressed with Professor Salam for his academic commitment, excellence in scientific research, world-class quality research, continuous, dedicated and hard work, scientist of the first order, his religious devotion and scientific temper. He was also a humble follower of Islam. More important, he has maintained these qualities despite his downfall in health seriously.

(iii) K-4 has visited the research centre in Triest and had seen Professor Salam working in his lab. This was real treat for him. He felt extremely influenced after seeing his commitment to educational advancement, scientific temper, science education and religious consciousness and identity of Muslims in the Indian sub-continent. Professor Salam worked for this cause even in his later stage of life.

13. THE GLOBAL SOCIAL ORDER

(i) According to K-4, the contemporary global social order was directly related to the equitable distribution of power at global level. It was because no global social order can survive without the support of global political powers in the present-day context. In other words, he felt, this referred to the polity of social order in which there must be no manipulation, no exploitation and no domination. This also means equality between developed and developing countries. In this context, multi-national companies must work for economic benefits to developing countries, especially their labour force. This may be considered in humanistic perspective. This must not be treated as charity in lieu of colonial economic past. The political economy of this order must serve and safeguard the interests of these suffering people.

(ii) As per the ideals of K-4, the global social order must represent an egalitarian social set-up, otherwise it will prove purposeless. This order must specifically reflect no division, no stratification, no differentiation and no inequality on any basis. All these systems of differentiation, stratification and exploitation must be debased and demolished.

14. POLITICAL IDEOLOGY AND LOCAL POLITICS

(i) K-4 was politically passive and he never participated in active politics. It was because he believed that professionals like academicians must restrict their activities to their own fields only and politics must be left to professional politicians. But, at the same time, must take serious and continuous assessment of the role of politicians and must develop a realistic and objective critique in the light of national and international political objectives. This role stood primarily ideational and not involve participatory role of professionals in politics.

(ii) K-4 stood as a man of political vision and had innovative political ideas related to local politics, especially Kashmir problem and its resolution. According to his views, the origin of Kashmir problem could be traced to the partition of 1947 in the Indian sub-continent. This tragedy led to other tragedy of Kashmir. Subsequently, while the Kashmiris got trapped, India and Pakistan got entangled in complex problem. These countries developed extreme form of antagonism and conflict and made this problem more complicated. While Pakistan demanded right to self determination to the people in JK, India took all steps necessary for total Indianisation of JK into its broader whole. In this political environment, the primary stakeholder, Kashmiris, struggled for their freedom but were suppressed always. They continued their political struggle against India and the uprising in 2010 was last in its series.

(iii) The resolution of the Kashmir problem can be resolved only when the political aspirations of all people in JK are taken into consideration in totality and involve its units and elements. There must be realisation on the part of India and Pakistan that the primary party in this dispute, Kashmiris, have suffered too much for four generations. Now, this problem must be resolved to the satisfaction of all parties, all partners, and necessary regions, religions and identities. It must also involve regional as well as global powers. India and Pakistan must take this initiative at the earliest possible opportunity and resole it taking into consideration their bilateral and Kashmiris' interests.

15. EXPERIENCE OF CONFLICT SITUATION

Like all other Kashmiris, K-4 was equally effected by the two-decade old conflict situation in Kashmir. He observed its crucial implications related to the erosion of 'work ethics' and 'work culture' in work places and in civil society. He felt that the conflict situation directly led to increase in social apathy and lethargy. During and after high-militancy, there were a lot of *hartals,* strikes, curfews, civil curfews, cross firings, bomb blasts, crack downs, search operations, daily killings and shoot-outs, and other disturbances. This situation led to complete collapse of social life and reduced the working hours/days in offices, work places and even in markets. Nobody could work daily and for the whole day. This had serious and disastrous impact on the work ethic and work culture in urban and rural areas. This was like 'total social collapse'. While there was not any performance of work in office or home, even the feeling about this loss was non-existent. In actuality, there was wastage of days, weeks and months, but there was neither any serious feeling nor any negative reaction about it, as if social conscience had died down. This environment created a common habit of workless-ness and wasting time and a bent of mind not to work but get wages regularly. Thus a whole nation collapsed and became a victim of wages without work. This was like a disease which hurt the working health of society. The diseased society could never think high and cannot transmit a culture of work to the next generation.

This situation created social apathy and social lethargy. While social apathy affected general social attitudes and behaviour in all fields of life which encouraged static rather than dynamic implications. People lived with four walls of home and that was their social world. They were not concerned about what happened outside. They felt no motivation for social wellbeing, social problems, social relations, institutions, processes and roles. They even didn't care about important matters such as health, education, sanitation, environment, diet, and cleanliness. Their living standards got degenerated to the lowest possible level and nobody was bothered to take care. In these conditions, people didn't live but survived only.

16. FUTURE KASHMIR SOCIETY

K-4 had clear ideas about the future society in Kashmir. He maintained clarity, specificity and preciseness of ideals in this regard. Politically, that society must have democratic and liberal system and equal political rights must be provided to religious and ethnic minorities. Socially, an egalitarian social order must be established which will negate completely inequal basis of caste, class, power and so on. Economically, a just and equitable system must be established which will benefit maximum and hurt minimum number of people. It must ensure minimum economic standard for every family unit. Legally, a formal constitution and the structure based on it must be framed and implemented sincerely. Educationally, the system must make it possible to reach education to all, especially illiterate, sections of society. Professional, technical, IT and super-speciality fields must be priority fields of education. Internationally, that state must prove a source of peace and not of conflict.

17. SOCIAL PROBLEMS IN KASHMIR

(i) *Educational Backwardness:* K-4 held the view that the first and basic impact of militancy in Kashmir was felt seriously in the increase of educational backwardness among KMs. It had affected negatively short-term and long-term objectives of processes of change, development and modernisation in the state. Though the KMs had started coming out of educational backwardness due to increase in literacy, they have started going back to that stage again. This dangerous trend has already started its effect. So, it must be controlled and directed towards educational advancement.

K-4 also held the opinion that militant-political organisations-parties must ensure modern education to new generations of Kashmiris. It will certainly play a positive and productive role for future generations in Kashmir.

K-4 also put forward the view that KMs learn from KPs in this regard. Despite mass migration and its problems, education of children remained their first priority. In this way, they were able to solve many of their problems.

(ii) *Anti-Kashmiri Sentiment:* Another crucial social aspect of the impact of militancy, according to K-4, was rise of anti-Kashmiri sentiment outside Kashmir in different cities and towns of India. This problem, generally unnoticed, was identified by K-4 as he used to visit different places in India for professional activities. It was faced mainly by Kashmiri businessmen, students and tourists. He felt that this hate campaign was the cumulative result of the activities of communal political parties and organisations, like BJP and RSS, and of presentation of distorted and communal version of the Kashmir problem by national-regional print and electronic media.

This anti-Kashmiri sentiment and environment has affected adversely Kashmir and Kashmiris. In these political conditions, when any Kashmiri young man reaches to any city of India, he is dubbed as anti-national, terrorist, *jehadi* and member of different religious-oriented parties. They are being arrested and lodged in prison without producing them before courts. Hundreds of such Kashmiri youths are suffering in different jails in India. On the other hand, the fact stand with sufficient evidence that these youths were never involved in militancy nor in any act of terror.

K-5 FOLK KASHMIRI WOMAN–URBAN

1. SOCIAL CONTEXT

K-5 was born in a poor working class family which was a component unit of occupational community. This family had lowest economic standard and low social status. It represented an important unit in the local occupational community in a particular urban locality, which had the high degree of social solidarity. In actuality, it was mixed locality of KMs and KPs, in which KPs, *sayyids, khans*, other occupational communities and castes formed the main composition. K-5 family had developed close and intimate relationship with KP and *sayyid* families, which were educationally advanced, economically well off and culturally exposed. The interaction with these families had long-term impact on K-5 family. As a result, K-5's brother got higher education and also was employed in a government office. This led to the occupational mobility and improved economic conditions in the family. However, this proved a short-term change. It was because, after getting education and employment, her brother migrated to Pakistan and settled there. In that situation, the family had to turn to old days of poverty. Though all members were working in the occupational field, the family income was low and it survived at that level.

2. FAMILY BACKGROUND-SOCIALISATION

(i) K-5 was married in a family of same social and economic status. So, it was not difficult for her to get socialised in new family-clan traditions, conventions and overall behaviour. She did that successfully and became proponent of new family, *panun ghare,* rather than that of her parental family which she could never forget but maintained relations with that till she passed away. This represents the traditional type of relationship which Kashmiri women maintain with their parental family throughout their life. K-5's new family was poor, uneducated and lived in folk style in an Urban area. Since she was intelligent, innovative, social and cautious observer, she introduced all new ideas in her family despite traditional restrictions and limitations. Despite vagaries of that family life, she established the family and gave a direction to family members.

(ii) K-5 lived a rough, tough and most difficult life. She faced extreme form of poverty and its imposed culture. Her family was so poor that used to spend the amount of money in the evening which they earned in the day. It was the environment in which if you had lunch but were not sure about dinner. So, she and her family members had to work daily in order to get regular meals. So, she worked very hard in order to survive. Her hard work could have hardly any parallel. She used to work from morning till late evening and remained busy in her activities throughout the day. In this way,

K-5 faced poverty boldly and bravely in 'proletarian' tradition and gave a decent life to her children and other family members.

(iii) Despite these poor conditions of life, she lived a life of dignified woman and maintained her position vis-à-vis relatives, neighbours and family friends. She learned about new role of children from the *sayyid* family. Keeping in view her intimate relationship with KP at her parental family, she was oriented to follow the educated path for her children. Her children performed all occupational and domestic jobs. At the same time, she sent all her children to school. In this process, an illiterate woman produced educated children. All of them had higher education in different fields. One of her sons got the highest degree in his particular field of study in a prestigious institution in the country. Thus she may be considered as important lady in the cause of educational advancement, for which she deserves numberless prizes and appreciations. In fact, her contribution to educational advancement among lower sections of society can never be forgotten. In a way, she gave the family a new identity, new status-role and new future.

3. OUT-FAMILY ENVIRONMENT

(i) K-5 lived in a congested urban locality inhabited by various petty occupational communities, but the *mohalla* solidarity was also prominent and effective in social life. So, she lived in a locality in which maximum people were poor. But, at the same time, some business and *sayyid* families were also living in that colony. K-5 was able to develop close relations with *sayyid*-business and lower occupational families. The neighbouring *sayyid* family proved lifelong supporter to K-5 family in all respects. The former was traditionally rich, *patte bed,* educationally advanced and culturally exposed and helped neighbours in all situations and at all times. This family provided all emotional and material help to K-5 in educating all her children. In return, the K-5 family used to provide occupational and other services to that family.

(ii) The second intimately-related neighbouring family of K-5 was a poor occupational family with large number of children. The senior lady of that family was K-5's close confidant and used to share life experiences and life secrets with her. She was so poor that she could not afford even a cup of lipton tea. But, she did not learn any social lesson from K-5. She had large number of children and all were illiterate. They had to adopt petty occupations in life like wood-carving, *shawl-bafi*, auto driving, foot-path vendor and so on.

(iii) K-5 had many near and distant relatives who belonged to service occupational group. One of the close relatives of this family lived in the periphery of city and was engaged in the same occupation. The level of poverty in that community was that there was a lone trouser for all males of the community who used to wear it one after the other especially when they had to visit in-laws family. Among all relatives of K-5 family, this relative family only was able to produce first graduate in the entire clan partly because of his intelligence and hard work and partly because of the encouragement of KPs. Later on, he got a job in a central government office in Kashmir. He became the 'ideal for progress' in the entire group of families.

4. OCCUPATIONAL ACTIVITIES

(i) In actual life, K-5 was always practical, positive, responsive and realistic. While she provided practical solutions to all problems of life, this response was very positive in terms of its response and implications. She always thought of high standards at ideational level, but never proved to be an idealist. She approached every problem in its realistic and rational perspective. She was conservative to a certain level, but innovation used to dawn upon her at last. She proved to be highest degree responsive, especially to human concern. She always responded humanely to the requests of people for help. No beggar could go without anything from her home. She often shared her food with them.

(ii) She had a particular attitude to the concept of work ethic. That was positive, rational, practical, realistic and humanistic as well as objective oriented. She believed that work stood for worship for life. She had extreme notion of work ethic and made it a reality through continuous work during entire day from morning till evening. She worked for family, occupation, association and so on, but never felt tired and bored. She worked on every front and satisfied all involved. She was an ideal type of work-ethic and wanted others, particularly her children, to be of the same character.

(iii) K-5's total activities inside as well as outside her family clearly reflect in her regular daily activities from morning till evening. The details are as follows:

Morning	Day	Evening
-morning prayers	-day prayers	-evening prayers
-domestic jobs	-domestic jobs	-domestic jobs
-preparing children for school	-receiving guests	-occupational activities
-serving morning tea and bread	-occupational activities	-receiving guests
-taking bread and milk from market	-serving lunch to f. mem.	-preparing and serving dinner
-cleaning utensils, crockery, etc.	-buying vegatables	-visiting relatives and neighbours
-occupational activities	-buying daily-need items	-cleaning crockery and utensils
-all other works	-treating children	-all other works
	-serving afternoon tea	
	-visiting neighbours, relatives	
	-all other works	

5. ASSOCIATION PATTERN

(i) K-5'S association were determined by the occupational ties with the community, relation with neighbourers and family friends. This type of association was strong and reciprocal visits was considered a usual affair.

(ii) In addition to this type of traditional association-pattern, K-5 family had developed political type of association with a political-cum-religious group under the leadership of *Mirwaiz*, who had pitched himself against the popular leader, SMA. This particular group developed its own identity and played a significant role in the politics of contemporary Kashmir. In this well organised religious-political group, the role of women was equally important. K-5 was a strong follower of *Mirwaiz*, she participated in all his religious and political activities. In this way, she developed association with other women of the same group, in addition to getting politically socialised in particular political culture. This religious and political association proved helpful and purposeful for K-5 and her family. Though her children didn't continue this association, K-5 maintained this association till last stage of her life.

6. CULTURAL LIFE

(i) K-5 lived in cultural environment characterised by Kashmir's folk culture having two dimensions: cultural and religious. The Kashmiri folk culture referred to common usage of Kashmiri language, folkways, folklore, ceremonies, practices, values and norms. That folk environment had its specific social context and social reference, including concepts of 'we' and 'they'; 'our' and 'their', insider and outsider and local and alien. These features determined entire social and political ethos in the valley.

(ii) On the other hand, the religious dimension in folk tradition which referred to a particular religious order called *rishi* order whose ideational focus was on the other world after death than on the present world before death and philosophy of purity of self (*ha zuo payes peto)*. Death was the border line between two worlds and humans must care about the final stage of life after death.

(iii) The other important social feature F *rishi* order was composite culture determined by religious activities and beliefs of a number of communities. This religious orientation and resultant activities revolve around similarities of various religions. This set of ideas had pre-Islamic Hindu religious orientation. The main ideologues of this syncratic Kashmiri folk tradition were *alamdar-e-Kashmir,* Sheikh Noor-ud-din Noorani and Lala Ded (also known as Lala Aarifa). The disciples and followers of this tradition gave it social legitimacy and made it a part of Kashmir's social ethos.

(iv) Though K-5 was illiterate and was not aware about origin and history of distinctive religious-cultural tradition, she was performing the religious role within its framework. She and her family members visited shrines, peers, and rishis regularly, celebrated specific days of 3rd, 6th, 11th, 13th and so on. They used to prepare special tea, drinks and meals for distribution among people at shrines. Though all these activities were not obligatory in Islam, but considered these as 'must' and on inseparable part of folk religious practices.

7. MOBILITY PATTERN

(i) As is clear now, K-5 belonged to a service occupational group which had lower economic standard of life. Her children lived in that abject poverty in which even two meals a day was not sure. In that situation, the social status of her family was not high. In those harsh economic conditions, she worked in her occupation and managed to send her children to school. After decades' efforts, her children were able to get government jobs, even of higher status. Thus that educated environment created by an illiterate lady got transformed into a prosperous family in the economic sense.

(ii) Taking into consideration the occupational, economic and educational conditions of K-5 family earlier, it has undergone tremendous degree of overall mobility during past few decades. In reality, this type of mobility represented a general type of occupational and social mobility in the Kashmiri society where thousands of families in urban and rural areas have achieved this new position and status after getting education and government employment during previous few decades. Like other families, K-5 family has certainly experienced this radical transformation. This revealed a historic and revolutionary social change in Kashmir after 1947.

8. MARRIAGE AND FAMILY

(i) K-5's marriage took place at an early age which was a customary practise in the family. In the selection of her marriage partner, she had no say. She was married in a family of same economic, occupational and educational status. Since she was intelligent, innovative and catious observer, she introduced some changes in the family in this regard. This was a marriage of equals, so proved highly stable till last. This marriage may be categorised as parents arranged, endogamous and patri-local marriage. It was considered productive and successful.

(ii) K-5 joined the joint family household of her husband after marriage and lived in that family for a longer time. This was a large family unit composing of the members of her husband, his parents, his unmarried and married sisters and brothers. She served the family sincerely and with humility. However, after marriage of husband's sisters and brothers and death of father-in-law, this family got divided into several nuclear family units. She too established her separate nuclear family unit in poor conditions. But, due to her strong will power, continuous hard work and struggle, she was able to make it a prosperous family unit.

(iii) After her children were married, they lived together in joint family for some time under the supreme authority of the couple. However, after some time when all children were established in economic fields, this family got divided into several nuclear units. While some children bought land and constructed new houses in resettled colonies outside city, others preferred to live in ancestral house. So, K-5 established all nuclear family units in her life time. Finally, she passed away in one of the nuclear family units before her husband which she had prayed for. After one year, her husband joined her in that world. Thus the unclear families of their children were left to manange themselves.

9. SOCIAL LIKES AND DISLIKES

After going through toughest and hardest experience of crude life, K-5 had developed clearly social likes and dislikes and she used to express these openly at appropriate times. Some of these were identified as mentioned below:

Social Likes	*Social Dislikes*
-emancipation of socially downtrodden	-social hierarchy of caste and class
- higher education and higher government jobs for socially lower classes.	-child and domestic labour
	-social antagonism and political conflict
-equality and justice for all	-a mean and fradulent administrator
-no discrimination in any field	-living without earing in the family
-maintenance of work culture, work ethic	-close-minded and secretive-natured person
-a sayyid family with egalitarian orientation	-following alien culture and lifestyle
-no caste barriers in social relations	-stopping others from making progress in life
-lower group social solidarity	-unemployed educated young man
-family conventions, traditions and practices	-wasting life without any purpose and achievement.
-social cooperation and social consensus	-avoiding hard work at home and in office
-marriage among equal partners	-poverty and poverty culture
-fulfilling needs of all family members	-gender discrimination and gender violence
-equal education for boys and girls	-inequality and injustice of any type
-submission to the will of husband	-role of fake mullas in religious garb
-folk religious beliefs and practices	-corruption and nepotism in offices
-cultural reforms for all	-moral degeneration among professionals
-religious orientation and behaviour	-sexual permissiveness
-positive response to social work	-a corrupt politician
-good and same-status neighbours	-dowry and other new cumstoms in marriage
-controlled and properly socialised children	

10. IDEALS OF EQUALITY AND INEQUALITY

(i) Since K-5 had lived in folk egalitarian set-up, she upheld the related ideals of equality. At the outset, it may be specifically mentioned here that she opposed any system or order of inequality irrespective of its difference. According to her, there could be no justification for inequality and its existing systems or orders because it hurts the essence of humanity. So, it must be deconstructed and destroyed. She always emphasised the graceful and forceful struggle against inequalities at individual and collective levels. She had done it in her life and wanted others to follow it.

(ii) K-5 was apathetic and allergic to caste inequality in particular. She termed it as a 'disgrace for humanity'. She always felt against the so called upper castes, particularly *sayyids* and was completely hesitant to accept their superiority.

(iii) K-5 was more concerned about gender inequality even in her joint family which was endemic in the Kashmiri society. Even in changing situation, the related practices were in vogue This, according to her, was crude reflection of male domination, exploitation, harassment, abusing and domestic and criminal violence. She opposed these practise vehemently and saved some women from this brutal practice. But, in the long run, she developed such a social environment in which maximum degree of gender equality was ensured. But, at times, she succumbed to the practices of gender discrimination in her own family when she had to support her male children in opposition to her daughters-in-law.

(iv) The overall response of K-5 can be traced from her experiences of folk equality in Kashmir. This arrangement of individuals as equals among themselves within the traditional framework of culture was worth mentioning. In this framework, women and men played equal roles in their respective fields. This reflected in male-females roles in occupational communities in urban and rural areas. There was hardly any scope for sexual segregation and practise of *purdah*. The folk equality revealed a type of social situation in which there existed lower level of consciousness about private property, sharing with others, sharing mutual social experiences, emphasize highest degree of social cohesion and solidarity and lesser degree of social antagonism and conflict within this working community. Thus folk equality stood for an ideal for K-5, which she made a 'living reality' in her family.

11. IDEAL SOCIAL ORDER

K-5 was not literate and was not exposed to non-Kashmiri societies and cultures. So, she could hardly imagine about global dimensions of social order. But, her ideas and views about ideal social order could be gauged from her morning prayers (*dua)* which she used to make every day in the morning after formal prayers and before starting her day work. The gist of this prayer, with its liberal translation in English, is given below:

Dua in original Kashmiri language	*Liberal translation in English language*
-*Ya Allah, sare thawuk warie*	-Oh God, keep all human beings well.
-*sarevie baliev te bemari ev nishe rachtak*	-*save all Hindus and Muslims (and all others)* from sare *Hinde te musalman all* disasters and diseases.
-haq *te hamsaye thau tak varie*	-keep all relatives well.
-*me deke poshenevzem*	-*keep my husband* alive till my last breath.
-*sehte badan te rehte jaan*	-grant good health and wealth to me
-*kudrev bemarev nishe rachzi hindis te musalmanus*	-keep away all Hindus and Muslims (and others) from chronic diseases
-*kule aalemeken bacchan seth menen baccan*	-grant good health and wealth and life security to all children. Including my children.
To shet-u-samati	
-*manen bacchankaamyabi te kamrani kuli*	-grant success and prosperity to all children, including my children.
Aalamen ken bacchan saan	
-*pannane taleem-e manz kar tek kamyaab*	-give all of them success in their education
-*panen yaere te barkat*	-grant all of them favours/pleasure prosperity.
-*kule aalamus manz amun te amaan sane*	-establish peace and tranquility in the whole
Kashiri seeth	*world,* especially in our Kashmir
-*sen kasheer rach ten balaiv nishe*	-save our Kashmir from every disaster
......*Fasade nishe*	-......disturbances/destruction
......*tazaade nishe*	-......conflict and war
......*toofane te waba nishe*	-......epidemic and air waves
......*zalime sende zulume nishe*	-......Cruelty of the cruel ruler
......*Gasebe sene gasube nishe*	-......occupation of the illegal occupant.

12. THE IDEAL LEADER

(i) K-5's ideal leader was the *Mirwaiz* of Kashmir, the hereditary religious head of a group of Sunni Muslims in the valley. This institution was established in Kashmir centuries back in order to preach religion in folk tradition. At early stage, it was restricted to the religious preaching but, later on, it got politicised and played a political role, especially in freedom movement during 1930s. It was under the influence of this institution that an organised movement for modern education among KMs started in 1865 on the name of *Anjuman Nusratul Islam.* It played the basic role in the educational advancement of KM community in modern times.

(ii) K-5's ideal leader, Molvi Mohammad Farooq (MMF) was the third generation *Mirwaiz* from his family. This religious cum political character established the authority and gave his group prominent political identity. He was reformative in orientation and worked in several fields. While continued vigorously folk religious preaching (in which the speaker and audience recited religious quotes loudly and repeatedly, so that the latter remember these), he carried out social works in his areas of influence. He was also seriously engaged in educational advancement of his community. Finally, he was actively involved in politics, mainly against the popular political leader of SMA and government of India. But, he could not get popularity in the state. He was killed during high days of militancy by unknown militants. During his life time, he always took care of his followers and visited them often. K-5 was also felt pleased, when he visited her home.

13. RELIGIOUS LIFE

(i) The religious life of K-5 revolved around folk religious beliefs and practices, which operated at two levels. First, at the ideational level, and, second, at the practise level. While the ideal beliefs referred to belief in oneness of God, final prophet-hood of Mohammad (PBUH) and day of judge-ment, the folk religious beliefs referred superstitions. In the case of practice, while the former pointed towards *namaz* and *roza*, the latter reflected in shrine attendance and customs. It seemed that two social phenomena were not separate and parallel entities but, as K-5 believed, were related and accommodative entities. The two entities, according to her, must be seen in association and not in dissociation. In a way, these two entities were interacting in a way which engaged these in a close and intense relationship.

(ii) K-5 had developed such a type of religious behaviour inside and outside her family. She had absolute belief in *tawheed, risalat and qiyamat* and pursued vigorously daily prayers, fast, honesty, sincerity, help, co-operation, simplicity and other social virtues. At the same time, while she believed in superstitions, miracles and other irrational ideas, she attended shrines regularly and prayed there necessarily. She made these visits daily, on special days in a month, and special days in a year. She regularly celebrated birthdays and other occasions of the Prophet, caliphs and *awliullah.* On all these occasions, special meals, drinks and tea were prepared and distributed among people.

(iii) K-5's family environment was dominated by this type of folk religiosity. She had not visited any temple or any other religious place, but had regards and respect for those sacred places. She felt it as 'duty' of KMs to provide safety and security to KPs. She had special consideration for KPs as they had contributed to her family's emancipation and development. She used to say her children "you would not have done some bad act, if you had been a Pandit". Thus KPs represented a reference group and ideal type for her. In this way, K-5 established, maintained and safeguarded the composite cultural practices of tolerance, plurality and patience.

(iv) In the folk religious environment, which she had developed at home for decades, she was neither satisfied nor impressed by the arrival of radical or militant Islam, especially with its alien contents. She followed strictly the traditional interpretation of religion given by *Mirwaiz,* which emphasised on the ideals of peace, coexistence, tolerance, harmony, and solidarity. Moreover, she opposed the militancy trend because of two reasons. First, she liked peaceful and non-violent lifestyle as per traditional Kashmiri cultural traits developed by *rishi* order. She could not compromise on this aspect of life. Second, she was allergic to gun, gun-culture and gun-exploiters. In this way, she kept distance from militant Islam but her children followed different views. Some of them supported this trend of religion due to political reasons but none of them joined militancy.

14. POLITICAL CHARACTER

(i) Basically, K-5 was not a politically conscious person in terms of thinking about and practising political ideas and ideals. May be they were not expected to do it. But, their political situation compelled and dragged them to adopt particular political views and their relevant behaviour under the influence of *Mirwaiz* and his politics. It was intensified by the competitive varying political grouping and leadership's particularistic approach. In this game, while the leader and his close associates emerged as political elite, others became the masses and ruled. Thus the religious leadership was able to give this group a political identity and was subsequently related to certain political interests.

(ii) In that situation, K-5 was not interested in politics but was involved through religious persuation. This resulted in her occasional participation in religious cum political meetings, rallies and demonstrations. Since anti-India sentiment remained dominant in the post-1947 era in Kashmir, K-5's political leader utilised this sentiment to continue his hold over his group, which always provided him the political support.

(iii) The Kashmir problem, according to K-5, was a simple problem. As per the folk version, which was conveyed to them by their leader, India had occupied Kashmir illegally and by force. So, it was complete injustice with Kashmiris. The occupation by Indian troops must end by withdrawing them. The leaders representing India in Kashmir will not solve it because they were corrupt and insincere. K-5 felt that the KP can be resolved by its accession to Pakistan but stands ignorant about its pros and cons.

15. EXPERIENCE OF CONFLICT SITUATION

(i) As most of the Kashmiris felt, K-5 had horrible experience of conflict situation mainly due to inhuman and humiliating behaviour of security forces. She used to mention about offensive-atrocious language of these forces during security checks and crack-downs of localities in urban and rural areas. She upheld the view that Kashmiri women became the main target of these uncivilised forces which left no opportunity to tease, molest and rape them. She remembered the days when she advised her locality women to prepare for death than to bear the brutalities of these forces and to face wrath of forces collectively and not to allow them to capture and torture women on individual basis. She also asked pretty girls in the locality to blacken their faces, so that security forces don't get attracted to them. She had heard about several cases of rape, never gave their details so that girls' marital interests may not be hurt.

16. FUTURE SOCIETY IN KASHMIR

Though K-5 was illiterate and not exposed to other cultures and societies, she could not draw an exact portrayal of Kashmiri society in future. However, she had developed some distinctive ideas in mind about that society which include the following:

- equal social status and economic opportunities for all women;
- equality of all human beings before law and God;
- no system of differentiation and discrimination must be allowed to exist;
- mass level social solidarity with workers and artisans;
- upholding the cause of Kashmiri language and culture;
- strongly supporting the ideology of Kashmiriat;
- tolerance of all religions and religious communities;
- no harassment and violence against women inside and outside their homes;
- maintaining folk character of religion in Kashmir;
- all practices and processes related to change, development and modernisation must be revived;
- all folk aspects of Kashmiri society must be safeguarded.

17. SOCIAL PROBLEMS IN KASHMIR

(i) *Exploitation of Workers:* K-5's general feeling was that nearly all workers were exploited, even harassed, by their masters, middlemen and entrepreneurs. Most of them worked in different handicraft sectors such as *qaleen bafi, shawl bafi, paper machie,* wood work, *named-gabbe* making and other fields. She had no estimates and other details about lesser wages they got in lieu of their hard labour. But, her interaction with all of them gave her the exact idea of level of exploitation. She upheld the view that they were getting their due wages, so injustice stood a common practise with them. These wages could not fulfill even basic needs of these families.

According to K-5, this was a clear case of injustice with workers. While they themselves and their children were working day and night on handicraft items, they could not even establish and maintain minimum standard of life. They could not think of a decent lifestyle and savings for hard timings. Though they produce most beautiful *shawls, paper* machie decoration pieces and carpets, their life doesn't stand beautiful but all ugly. K-5 felt that entire benefit in this field of business was grabbed by middlemen and wholesalers and that that also at the cost of workers.

(ii) *Extravagance on various occasions:* One of the specific social problems in Kashmir, according to K-5, was extravagance on various ceremonial occasions, especially on the preparation of eating delicacies called *wazwan* (a cosine of about 20 dishes all based on meat and prepared by professional cooks called *wazas*). She characterised this preparation as 'arrogance of wealth 'as it aims at showing the host's economic standing than providing a quality food items of non-vegetarian type.

This type of extravagance thus referred to the behaviour of some big business, rich and elite families, which spend lavishly on different ceremonies, occasions, and other celebrations in order to convey their image as the top affluent families. In a way, this has become a 'status symbol' for these and other classes and groups. These families have initiated it and maintained consciously and seriously in order to continue superior status, irrespective of the consideration of its impact on middle and lower class-groups.

K-6 URBAN-EDUCATED WOMAN–HOUSEWIFE

1. SOCIAL CONTEXT

(i) K-6 was born in early 1960s represented a phase of continuity and change. It follows that, in the post-1947 period, while some members in an average family lived a traditional life, other members were undergoing processes of change in their entire life. In actuality, what happened before 1947 was that Kashmiri nationalists, who were secular and progressive in their orientation under the leadership of SMA, got committed to the ideals of *Naya Kashmir Program.* This document stood for land to the tiller, abolition of centuries old usury system and forced labour, free education to all, gender equality and voting rights of women. After 1947, when this leadership came to power in J&K, it started implementing these ideals. Exactly after 4-5 years, the famous land reforms were initiated.

(ii) Since majority of population in Kashmir composed of Muslims and they represented the only suffering lot during the alien-feudal rule, they got benefited because of these reforms. Sine KPs and other groups were already educationally advanced, employment ensured and associated with state apparatus, these sections were not benefited with debasement of old system. In this way, the KMs started undergoing irreversible change. In rural as well as urban areas, economic and educational reforms started revolutionising the entire society. While age-old agrarian structure gave way to new agrarian social order in rural Kashmir, more or less same situation started emerging in urban Kashmir. K-6 family too was undergoing these processes of change and development. This family was half educated and engaged in traditional occupation, while it maintained continuity of tradition in social and cultural fields. But, at the same time, education, employment and exposure led to adoption of new occupations, so it had initiated formally elements of change in social cultural life.

2. IN-FAMILY SOCIALISATION

(i) This family was passing through a process of transformation which finally led to radical changes in its structure and functions. This transformation may be explained in terms of placing the family in two extremes of tradition and modernity and direction of change was towards progress. The social and cultural phases of family was dominated by tradition but ongoing processes were heading towards the objectives of modernity.

(ii) K-6 was component part of this family. Like other members of family, she was getting socialised in that particular environment, some of whose features were as follows. Educationally, most members of family were literate. This family was headed by a literate female, who after going through education and professional training, was engaged in nursing profession in a local hospital. She had direct command of the family and controlled it effectively.

She emerged as the ideal character in the entire clan. She represented the first KM women's generation which responded positively to modern education. She was effectively able to direct the family towards the goals of modernity. The family had an educated daughter-in-law, which had affected its collective psyche and its daughters were sent to education on priority basis. K-6 was also encouraged to get highest available education.

(iii) In the field of occupational-economic activities, the eldest member of this family was engaged in some petty occupation. The present members of family had adopted different occupations which had given them middle-level income, which ensured economic security, minimum life standard and related status and position. In this situation, K-6 got exposed to multiplicity of occupations.

(iv) In the social and psychological fields, the family members experienced all-round mobility. They were specifically exposed to KP and non-Kashmiri communities. The intense interaction with alien culture and society gave the family a secular and liberal character. Thus K-6's social horizon widened and worldview broadened.

(v) In its lifestyle, the family adopted new cultural and social patterns from that of the traditional one. Education, employment, exposure, mobility provided it a strong base to join the status of emerging middle class in Kashmir. In that changing situation, extreme conflict between tradition and modernity was not prominent, but modernity was systematically replacing tradition in all fields of life. Thus deviation from traditional practices became easy and desirable. At the same time, extreme violation of religious values and norms were punished. In this way, K-6 enjoyed benefits of change and got socialised in that type of ethos.

3. OUT-FAMILY ENVIRONMENT

(i) The K-6 family with the neighbouring community was restricted. It had intimate relationship with a few neighbours. That community was highly stratified. While a few families were called *pate baed*, other families belonged to middle class of that time. The majority of families were engaged in occupations and were poor. In fact, their conditions had started changing as a result of governmental measures. That community was highly politicised and participated actively in political activities. They were staunch supporters of SMA (called *shers)* in his fight against the *Mirwiaz* family.

(ii) One of the intimate neighbours of K-6 family was an elderly person of the common name of *Sulle Mir*. He was well respected and social notable and was engaged in a petty occupation which gave him meager income. He had taken care of K-6 family after its senior members passed away. He was a usual visitor to the family and even participated even in decision-making process. He also played the role of advisor and protector of the family. Like his neighbours, he too was strong follower of SMA and his charismatic leadership. He was ready to do anything in life, even to sacrifice himself, on the orders of his supreme leader. He had absolute faith in his leadership, who, according to him, liberated Kashmiris from centuries-old slavery and alien rule. This was the generation which made SMA as *Sher-e-Kashmir* and gave him absolute political support irrespective of his changing political decisions. For this generation, while SMA was a legendary leader during his lifetime, he attained the status of 'super hero' after his death.

(iii) K-6 had close interaction with all relatives which affected his life intensively. The relatives of family used to visit her family often and exchange gifts and reciprocate invitation. One of their relatives was a man of high intellect and of literary taste. He was a strong disciplinarian and a follower of religious as well as modern ideas. He was highly community-conscious and social work initiator. He always emphasised upon his children and relatives' children to study seriously, opt for science and professional fields of education, achieve higher grades and loyalty to the parents. He was a well read person and stressed upon youngsters to read good and quality books on science, technology, religion, politics, fiction, literature, fine arts, history and Kashmir.

(iv) K-6 family had developed friendly relations even with outsiders who became family friends. It played the role of socializer,and, at the same time, got socialised with natives. One of the family friends of K-6 family was an elderly Christian lady associated with Srinagar branch of Indian Red Cross Society. She developed friendly relations with eldest female head of this family and stayed with them for about a decade. She shared all life experiences with members of this family. In addition to feelings of plurality of religion, culture and language in the home environment, her stay at home had generated a secular outlook and orientation. Every religion and culture was dealt with regard and respect at ideational and practical levels. K-6 had accepted and adopted this influence to the maximum extent. Thus the lady's stay had certain implications which included family's response to other religions, cultures and languages, women's emancipation and empowerment, encouragement and achievement of modern education among girls, and performance of social work activities by children.

(v) This was not one way socialisation. The alien lady had adjusted in the local cultural ethos. She had adopted local dress, attained working knowledge of local language, enjoyed local cultural practices and customs. In this way, she approved cultural differences but encouraged cultural interaction and adoption. K-6 had developed many cultural traits from this environment. It was essentially in this social-cultural background which shaped lifelong attitudes and behaviour of K-6. In her practical life, she adopted some of these cultural traits which she transformed to her next generation.

4. EDUCATION AND CAREER

(i) In the changing family environment in K-6 family, all children were sent to schools. K-6 too started primary education in the near-by government school in the locality. That was the only educational institution available for girl's education. She completed her secondary education in that school where most of female teachers were KPs. Following this education, K-6 got into a college, located at far-off place, which was a minority institution established by KPs for the benefit of entire locality. In this institution, while majority of students was of Muslim girls, teachers and staff was KPs. The institution had established reputation in imparting quality, professional, skill-based and technical education. K-6 had free interaction with KP girls and developed friendship with some of them. From here, K-6 joined the university where she was exposed to many influences, some of which she adopted in her life.

(ii) Since K-6 was married while she was pursuing education, she could not follow a regular career. Even after completing education, she could not follow a regular career because of going outside JK with her husband. After some time, they came back and tried to get a job which she could not get partly because of passive attitude and partly because husband's inability to approach the higher ups in this regard. However, she got a supervisory job in a private educational institution. While her performance was appreciated by all concerned, she performed supervisory role of Principal with responsibility, dignity and upright manner. But, she left this job after 5 years. She gave two arguments for this. First, she felt that educated women must be committed primarily to their families than to their offices. After taking up jobs, they were torn apart between two extreme roles, domestic and official. Second, she felt that domestic work must be valued in equal terms.

5. OCCUPATIONAL ACTIVITIES

(i) The adoption of the role of housewife was a careful and conscious decision. She argued with others on this issue and accepted all its implications. Thus she was a perfect 'housewife' performing all types of household jobs related to family members and all their matters. In social terms, she became :

- good mother for children,
- good wife for her husband
- good host for all guests
- good helper for all patients,
- good daughter for parents
- good sister for all brothers and sisters,
- good manager for domestic affairs,

- good cook for family members, relatives and guests,
- good budget-maker for domestic and non-domestic affairs, and
- good social friend to all friendly people.

(ii) The house-wife career for K-6 was a lifelong career. She performed all related roles honestly, sincerely and demanded no price for that. She used to say "Allah will pay back in the hereafter." She was found extremely busy with home affairs day in and day out and from early morning till late night. The ordinary activities of domestic life reveals in the following list:

Morning:	-prayers	-cleaning
	-cooking	-preparing children for school
	-washing clothes	-listening radio
	-preparing and serving tea and meals	-listening songs
Day Time:	-gardening – lawn	-gardening- kitchen vegetables
	-house keeping and cleaning	-washing clothes
	-shopping for household items	-shopping for family members
	-shopping for family friends and relatives	-home management and care taking
	-serving guests	-visiting relatives, neighbours and others
	-guiding children in school work	-waiting and receiving children
Evening:	-cooking and serving dinner	-preparing and serving afternoon tea
	-watching television	-listening radio
	-discussion with husband on family and other matters.	

6. CULTURAL ENVIRONMENT

(i) The cultural life of K-6 family, from which she got inspiration throughout life, was characterised by cultural, religious and linguistic plurality. K-6 family environment can be explained in terms of existence of different cultures of local and non-local origin. It follows that Kashmiri culture existed side by side of non-Kashmiri cultures. The concerned attitudes and behaviour reflected specifically in practice at the time of celebration of different festivals of different communities such as *Eed*, *Heerat,* Christmas and *Diwali.*

(ii) The religious plurality existed in K-6 family not only in theory but in practise too. The ideas and ideals related to great religions were all respected. The family used to celebrate different festivals, fairs, customs and occasions, which were local and non-local in origin.

(iii) The linguistic plurality K-6 family revealed in the usage of different languages such as English, Urdu, Hindi, Kashmiri and Panjabi. In addition to enriching the local language, it contributed to their intellectual improvement.

(iv) All these factors of culture in K-6 family reflected changing dimension of cultural milieu of the family. But, traditional local cultural practices were in operation in family. While relations with and role of Christian lady represented the changing dimension of culture. By following both these dimensions, K-6 family was not following conflicting practices but complementary practices. It meant that different cultural practices were followed sincerely at different times, situations, and contexts. The occasions and celebrations were not conflict but consensual. All these facts got a place in the social life of K-6 and her family. Broadly, it can be related to the situation of the cultural continuity and change, discussed earlier in this chapter. This situation also explains earlier introduction of television and family-watching of movies in K-6 family. While the former referred to introduction of television in KM society at a stage when not many families in Kashmir had introduced it in their homes, the latter referred to a practise according to which all family members, males and females, watched Hindi films together, giving it social acceptability.

7. MARRIAGE AND FAMILY

(i) K-6 was married when she was studying in the university and was of marriageable age. She was married to a Kashmiri academician who was working in a central university. So, after the marriage, she had to go outside JK and live there for few years. K-6's marital family was a humble family and was in the process of emerging middle class mainly due to occupational mobility. In fact, this mobility pattern was common in Kashmir, according to which, when members of an occupational group attained education and got government jobs, they usually left their traditional occupations which were taken over by rural labour or migrant labour. K-6 belonged to a family which was ahead of husband's family in educational, economic and cultural fields. So, this marriage was in a way a step forward for husband. In fact, K-6's marriage symbolised continuity and change. This marriage was exogamous and patri-local type.

(ii) During her post-marital stay outside JK, K-6 had intensive interaction with all communities and groups of Indian society, especially those of IMs. This, on the one hand, exposed her to social life of Indian society in general and IMs in particular, and, on the other hand, doubled her experience of multi-cultural life. Taking into consideration of all positives and negatives of social life, she preferred the Kashmiri society, as according to her, it had ideal social life features. But, at the same time, she felt at home in changing life conditions. In all these homes, she made no compromise on basic values, norms, roles, status, traditions, customs and so on. Ethics, morality and religiosity were preferred principles for her family life. In that situation, K-6 learnt how to adjust in changing situations and how to develop social cooperative network.

(iii) After the marriage, K-6 joined joint family unit of her husband. After a brief period, she established an independent nuclear family unit outside Kashmir. She enjoyed the sole authority in that family. After coming back to Kashmir, she continued with her nuclear family unit in her husband's official accommodation. After some years, the husband of K-6 constructed a new house in a new colony on the periphery of city. Subsequently, she and family shifted to that house where they live at present.

8. SOCIAL LIKES AND DISLIKES

In the context of her socialisation and life experiences, K-6 had developed particular social likes and dislikes, some of which are mentioned below:

Social Likes	*Social Dislikes*
-helpful to neighbours, poor and needy	-dual role and dual personality
-lawn and kitchen gardening	-helping others with material consideration
-always responsive in attitudes and behaviour	-boosting of class-caste status background
-equal regards for all religions and communities	-communal views and communal ideology
-constant interaction with neighbours and relatives	-inequality of all types and forms
-no hidden social agenda and social deals	-religious fanaticism and fatalism
-modern scientific, technological education	-gender inequality and gender violence
-ideal guest-host relationship	-no regard for values and norms
-social consensus and responsibilities	-no consideration of role and status
-upholding moral ethics and social order	-corruption, nepotism and bribe
-fulfillment of health needs	-poverty and its life conditions
-change and progress for all social groups	-extremely westernised way of life
-multi-cultural social ethos	-conflict situation and its impact
-a clean, well-dressed and un-dogmatic person	-social pathology and social apathy
-a prosperous and qualified person	-abnormal socialisation
-controlled and disciplined children	-using religion for personal interests
-sharing social life with others	-a marriage of un-equals
-a competent and hard-working teacher	-sub-standard teaching in schools
-ideal follower of one's own religion	-any stratification system in society
-modernity with rational limits	-following practices of decaying culture.

9. CCONCEPTS OF "I", "ME", AND "WE"

(i) K-6 was very clear about concepts which she had developed in her personal life and in interaction with other groups, communities and classes. The views were clear and contextual as follows: K-6's concept of "I" essentially represented her personality traits developed through her hard-soft and complex-simple and multi-cultural and uni-cultural life. These traits included dynamic personality, respecting others irrespective of their status and position, positive humanistic views, no humiliation and denigration of others and their cultures, respecting others' views and ideas, multi-dimensional social-cultural traits, secular-scientific-progressive orientation, no religious fatalism, open, frank and social relations with all, pursuing human objectives in life, always hard-serious-quality work, and keeping family and community always happy by one's practices.

(ii) The concept of "me" for K-6 was primarily contextual. It was a social self she developed in life during in-family and out-family experiences. It directly and indirectly referred to her upbringing and consequent habitual behaviour of children, her life-long contribution to home and family, human and modern life style, internal-external decoration of home and house, parents and elders' contribution to the culture of family units and so on. In brief, 'me' for K-6 meant a good mother, good wife, good neighbour, good relative, good host, good sister, good daughter, good home manager, good home keeper and proud religious and cultural character.

(iii) The concept of "we" as held by K-6 may be characterised as multi-layer, whose apparent identities were overlapping each other. This was highly contextual and had more political contents. She felt a proud member of KMC, KM Urban Community, KM Sunni Sect and so on. She also felt more anti-Indian and less anti-Pakistan in political perspective. She consciously upheld and asserted, especially after visiting different parts of India, the historical identity of Kashmir and Kashmiris. She upheld the Kashmir cause despite opposition from inside and outside communities. She always felt aligned with the worker's lot and had progressive worldview. She also felt an active supporter of the housewives. Last but not the least, she was a staunch supporter of modern, professional and technological education for all intelligent children, boys and girls, of modern Kashmir.

10. IDEAS OF EQUALITY AND INEQUALITY

(i) In general, K-6 stood for absolute equality between members of society irrespective of their status, position, and power. Taking into consideration the complexities involved in this objective, she revised the position and argued for maximum possible equality in which no particular individual or group suffers. In fact, K-6 had a distinctive perspective regarding equality which she developed from her life experiences. She approached the problem by a question, whether inequality exists in human society? She answered the question in positive. She argued that since inequality exists in most societies, it stood as a social reality and a fact of life.

(ii) She felt that inequality can be properly treated by developing a mechanism to reduce it, to control it and to debase it. This may be done by processes of change, development and mobility in relation to class as well as caste. The class inequality, according to her, could be reduced, controlled and finally debased through educational, occupational and mobility. This will provide the institutional support to new social order where maximum degree of equality will be evolved through competition among all.

(iii) K-6 also argued that caste inequality can also be reduced, controlled and debased through the processes mentioned above. She characterised caste as inherent and legitimised social order, which gives superior status to a particular caste of *sayyids,* though it was completely negated by Islam. The *sayyid* caste was considered like the *Brahmin* caste. Both groups were self-serving at the cost of other social groups. K-6 argued that monopolistic position and exploitative role can be demolished by attaining education, employment and mobility. In the democratic and competitive framework, this will ensure the gradual debasement of Caste order. In this regard, the doctrine of Islam, whose main sources are *Quran and Haidth,* can be of tremendous help.

(iv) K-6 felt that gender inequality reflected mainly in gender violence which included the practise of wife beating. She had observed this phenomenon existing in many Kashmiri families. She was in total opposition of this practise theoretically and practically. After dealing with this problem, she upheld the view that it continued partly due to women's submission and partly due to inactive role. *In this context,* she made debasement of gender violence as one of her life objectives.

11. THE IDEAL CHARACTER

(i) The ideal character of K-6 was her father who lived a humble life but gave all life benefits to his family. Though he had limited income, he fulfilled all needs of the family in a systematic way. In actuality, he preferred family needs to personal needs. He had a multi-faceted personality. He performed all his works himself which included domestic jobs, market shopping and day-to-day purchases. He also did these jobs for his near relatives. Since he was a hard earner, he had the habit of hard spending. He never felt dependent but always kept the spirit of independence, initiative and innovation open.

(ii) K-6's father was faithful and a devoted follower of his religion. Though he had not much first-hand knowledge about religion, he represented an absolute believer of Islam. His religious beliefs and views were not against any other religion or its practising community but for personal purification and social perfection. His religious practices never antagonised anybody but led to cordial relations with followers of other religions/sects. In fact, he practised the ideas which were emphasised by Sheikh-ul-Alam and Lala Arifa in Kashmir.

(iii) K-6's father had ideal social personality. It specifically reflected in his commitment to maintenance of close social ties with near and distant relatives, neighbours and family friends. He had made distinction in visiting regularly his relatives and kept himself aware about their family conditions. He also interacted with neighbours daily and kept himself well aware about situation in his neighbourhood. His personal friends belonged to different religious communities, sects, castes, groups, occupation and demography and so on. This had enriched his life with a variety of experiences.

(iv) His personality may be characterised as an ideal human being with ideal human traits. He respected everybody irrespective of position, status and whereabouts. He hardly antagonised anybody during his life time. He could never speak a lie and never deceived anybody.

12. RELIGIOUS LIFE

(i) K-6 was a strong and firm believer, whose beliefs were related to the fundamentals of Islam and derived from *Quran* and *Sunnah.* She was a devoted Muslim doing everything material and non-material nature by considering it as 'worship'. She offered prayers regularly and observed fast. She also practised all other Islamic duties and responsibilities in day-to-day life. At the same time, she was a keen follower of folk religious practices. Though she was not a saint-worshipper, she visited shrines regularly. She felt that some of the activities performed at shrines had non-Islamic character. Moreover, these shrines have given rise to group of *mullas* who have used these places for their monetary gains. In the business on shrines, they even violate basic principles of *tawheed.* In totality K-6 followed a mixed brand of religion in which some ideal and some folk features of Islamic religion were integrated which suited the Kashmiri psyche.

(ii) K-6 felt no attraction for radical or militant orientation of religion in Kashmir. Some times, she was allergic to these religious orientations and at other time apathetic. In practice, she kept herself and her family away from this religious persuasion. She characterised these religious perceptions as deviation from ideal Islam, intolerant form of religion, contribution to disruption and downward economic mobility, gave rise to conflict situation, gender biasness and other problems.

(iii) K-6 was a strong upholder and oral supporter of composite culture and concerned religious ethos. In reality, she had inherited this culture from parental family and attempted to transform this culture to next generation in her family. Even in long period of conflict, she maintained personal contact and family relations with KPs and KSs.

13. GLOBAL SOCIAL ORDER

(i) K-6 stood in favour of global social order which will eliminate gender inequality and establish equality in institutional form. She felt that women in that social order must play multiplicity of roles and these must be accepted formally. So, formal legislative sanction and consequent laws and rules must be formulated. First of all, she has a role in her family as a sole agent of procreator and socialize. A new generation in her hands stood safe. Educationally, she may prove much-needed tutor for developing in-family and out-family roles and multi-faceted personality. She will enable elder generation to younger generation the cultural tradition. Politically, she may participate in formulating and implementing relevant legislation for laws for gender equality. She may also serve this cause by joining elite political class at the global level.

(ii) She asserted that women can participate in economic activities in all sectors with equal responsibility and equal wages. While in some sectors, she was necessarily needed, in other sectors, she may be considered undesirable. Religiously, she will play positive and humanistic role at global level. She may prove a good religious preacher, ideologue, teacher and reformer and will safeguard at all levels and in all spheres. She may play meaningful and effective role for gender cause in inter-religious interaction and dialogue. In the field of health, she may prove a best doctor for all in humanity. In the overall process of change and development, her role will be crucial at the national and international levels. But, this gender role has some limitations which must be recognised by all, felt K-6.

14. POLITICAL IDEOLOGY

K-6 never felt in terms of political ideology mainly because she was politically apathetic and held no political role. She felt no need and practical utility and relevance for that. She never participated in political discussions, a common social feature in Kashmir. She considered it the duty of some particular individuals and groups to become political ideologues and political roles must be assigned to them. In other words, she argued that political ideology and political role must be limited to the people composing the political class which sponsor, monopolize and exploits political events. They develop career in this field and make it a life-long practice. However, K-6 became conscious and active political supporter when it came to the question of India-Pakistan cricket match. On that occasion, she used to take pro-Pakistan position. Moreover, in normal discussions with relatives and friends, she took position in favour of Kashmir and against India and Pakistan. Thus K-6 behaviour reflected the usual KM attitude in this regard.

15. EXPERIENCE OF CONFLICT SITUATION

K-6 felt deeply concerned by short-term and long-term implications of conflict situation in Kashmir in all fields of life. Here we will mention her views about this impact on women's day-to-day life. She felt that perpetual conflict disturbed entire life of women and their families. They could neither maintain normal standards of decent life for themselves and their children nor could they establish and improve existing quality of family life. The family was transformed into a cage and no normal interaction with outsiders could take place. No regular health care for children, especially immunisation of infants in regularity could be carried out in urban and rural areas. The problems related to pregnancy and delivery became acute and dangerous. This led to increases in the rates of mortality deaths. No proper socialisation of children could take place and so children faced acute psychological problems related to stress, anxiety, depression, tension, and PTSD mainly due to bomb blasts, cross firing, crack downs, and security checks. N those conditions, no short-term or long-term home-management or planning was possible. That was the situation of mere survival in the surrounding environment of social insecurity for women.

16. FUTURE KASHMIR SOCIETY

(i) K-6 had developed a framework of policy in abstract terms for future Kashmir society whose prominent features are mentioned below:

- Politically, it must be independent from all countries and subservient to none, especially the U.S. and Western Europe.
- Economically, it must develop self-sufficient and self-reliant economy by utilising all its economic resources like water, forests, and climatic conditions. There should be full growth of indigenous economic sectors like power, tourism, horticulture, handicrafts and forests.
- Educationally, it must follow liberal-progressive vision in order to follow the objectives of modernisation, secularisation, professional and technological development in the state.
- Socially, that society must belong to all and none must feel deprived and isolated. The citizenship must supersede all other considerations. The distinctive identity, *kashmiriat,* must be upheld and safeguarded by constitutional and political measures.
- Culturally, that society must be plural, composite, interactive and realistic in institutional and organisational form.
- That society must have its own flag, constitution, territory and so on.

17. SOCIAL PROBLEMS IN KASHMIR

(i) *Marital Problems:* After achieving significant degree of material change in the Kashmiri society, certain serious social problems related to marriage emerged. Common among them were late marriage, post marital discard and mal-adjustment, domestic violence and dowry. In this background,

K-6 felt that Kashmiri girls of marriageable age faced tremendous problems. They faced these problems even after marriage. The continuous conflict in Kashmir had also negative implications for marital affairs before and after marriage. K-6 identified these problems as very late age of marriage, about late 20s /early 30s for girls; shortage of eligible grooms in the marriage market; specific problems of higher education of girls and lesser education of boys; post-marital problems of less adjustment and lesser number of children or no child at all; heavy amount of dowry paid to boy's family by girl's family before and after marriage, domestic violence against newly married women and other problems. This situation has affected personal as well as social aspects of marriage, making it disastrous for both partners, children and the society at large.

(ii) *Social Deviance:* K-6 felt that most parents in Kashmir valley faced the problem of social deviance on the part of their children. They often challenge the patriarchal authority of the family head, usually their father. They also refuse to follow the authority of their relatives, family friends, neighbours and teachers. They have gone out of the institutional control and were consciously involved in violation of traditional values and norms, especially religious based. This pattern of social deviance gave rise to a parallel situation of value free and norm less society, in which youngsters felt free to carry out illegal, immoral, undesirable and dangerous social activities. If the social order has to be maintained, these serious acts of violation need to be controlled, stopped and negated through institutional means.

K-7 KASHMIRI BUREAUCRAT

1. SOCIAL CONTEXT

(i) K-7 was born in early 1950s of the last century when mass-level mobility was experienced in the Kashmiri society. As the fact stands, Kashmir throughout medieval period was dominated, suppressed and subjected by alien rulers irrespective of their religious affiliations. During that period, Kashmir was ruled without caring about its inhabitants. In addition to imposing worst kind of life conditions, they were never opted or appointed in the state apparatus for different positions, high or low. In reality, non-local people, both Hindus and Muslims, and local KPs were co-opted for running affairs of the state. Since KMs were not educated and not equipped with skills to deal with statecraft, they were left out of the state.

(ii) In modern times, a deep concern and anguish was expressed by some intellectual Kashmiris "living outside Kashmir" about these conditions which were highlighted by the then only political party, MC, in its resolution in late 1920s which was presented to the Galancy Commission. SMA exploited these sentiments and established his leadership under the MC political platform. This party was later on transformed into NC due to progressive ideology impact and to accommodate KPs in it. The NC adopted a progressive program in 1938 called *Naya Kashmir Program* for future guidance. After 1947, when the Kashmiri nationalists assumed power in JK, they started implementing radical economic, social, educational and other reforms. The success rate of these reforms was much higher in the national context. When implications of these reforms started effecting society within a decade's time, a small number of KMs got modern education, government service and felt overall mobility. The state government consciously encouraged this new trend which took place probably for the first time in modern history of Kashmir. K-7 belonged to that generation which took birth in urban Kashmir at that time.

2. FAMILY BACKGROUND AND SOCIALISATION

(i) K-7 belonged to a family which may be characterised as a real BPL family. In actuality, it was the status of poorest of the poor. It had lowest possible living standard at that time. The family was engaged in a petty occupation that didn't gave them minimum required income. It was partly because poverty created 'poverty-culture' and partly because some members of the family were not fully functional. So, it could not manage the occupation which led to its intensification of poverty. But, this family environment did not effect two family members and both proved exceptions. Their behaviour can be explained in psychological and other factors. Taking into consideration family conditions, K-7's brother was taken by a relative for education, whose family had come under the influence of *Mirwaiz* and his educational program.

After shifting from parental house, the brother got higher professional education and subsequently higher government position. There were only some local Muslims on such positions in the state.

(ii) How K-7 got out of the impact of his parental family, still stands a mystery which could hardly be explained in material terms. The basic question arises why K-7 didn't join the traditional occupation despite having extreme poverty at home? Apparently, in the sociological framework, this may be explained in terms of repulsion of psychological traits and, at the same time, more acceptance of the impact of external social environment. It was a kind of negative reaction to in-family compulsions and positive response to out-family environment. Other observers explain it in terms of role of 'unknown force'. In other words, it was 'God's will' and so it happened. An eminent sociologist of Iran characterised this phenomenon as the "role of accident" in the history of individuals and groups. So, by accident and pre-determined destiny, the individual follows god-ordained career.

3. INTERACTION WITH OUT-FAMILY ENVIRONMENT

(i) K-7's response represented a rational choice and intelligent reaction to the out-family environment which was dominated by the presence of *Sayyid* colony, *Mugge* tailor's gossip shop, milk-seller's shop, intellectual and literary centre in his neighbourhood. In this type of social situation, K-7 was influenced more by institutions and organisations than by individuals. Thus he had three different institutions and some individuals who had life-long impression on him.

(ii) The first institution was a reading room which was established in K-7 locality by a reformist religious movement. He was a usual visitor to its library and read good books on religion, politics, history, philosophy and Urdu poetry. So, even in his early age, he stood well read in literary, political, academic and religious fields. He had developed intellectual orientation and started writing articles in local newspapers. In this way, he was taken away from usual social activities.

(iii) The next source of inspiration for K-7 within and outside family was his elder brother who was a top official during 1960s and who stood for highest degree of religiosity. He was always helpful to others who were intelligent and hard working boys. Moreover, he was dedicated to the cause of modern education among KMs, especially those who belonged to lower social and economic classes. He was also devoted to K-7's higher education in highest institution of the country and ensured highest degree in the field. K-7 was also emotionally devoted to his brother and got inspiration for his life achievements.

(iv) In the case of K-7, near and distant relatives were not effective at all due to their extreme backwardness. But, *Mugga's* tailor shop became an agent of politicisation, especially in determining his political attitudes. This was a meeting place for many people of the locality who were interested in politics of local, national and international level. Mugga's political analysis was highly realistic and contextual. Many of his political predictions proved correct. Many locals, particularly political activists, educated, intellectuals and others used to discuss Kashmir politics for hours together there, till they were called back by their families. K-7 too used to be involved in political discussion and discussed current political developments. This activity had lifelong impact on political ideas and attitudes of K-7.

4. EDUCATION AND CAREER

(i) K-7, like other boys in his locality, got his primary and secondary education in his locality government school. He qualified all stages of this education without any failure. Subsequently, he joined a city college where he got introduced to eminent academicians, poets, writers, experts and professionals and got influenced by them. There he also got exposed to new social roles, social associations, social organisations-societies and social world. This was also due to his personal relations with others. At that stage, boys wanted to be associated with him and he reciprocated them.

(ii) K-7 post-graduation education was carried out in a central university where he studied national and international politics. The actual realities of politics dawned upon him at that stage. He was always critical of the Indian polity primarily for its diacotamy in theoretical and practical terms. He also got intense interaction with the IMs but did not appreciate their 'minority politics' which was usually exploited by certain religious and feudal-oriented individuals and groups.

(iii) Then K-7 shifted to another central university for doctoral research. This was not only a new academic institution but much higher and modern than the earlier one. For him, this shift proved as journey from old fashioned institution to a place which was highly innovative, inspiring and creative in ideas, attitudes, behaviour, lifestyle and ideology. In actuality, it was an opening in a new world with new vision and new worldview. There he was attracted and then appeared in IAS exam. And was successful in first attempt. Subsequently, he joined the elite bureaucracy of India through the gates of Lal Bahadur Shastri Academy of Public Administration where they were taught all about 'bureaucratic culture'..

(iv) Before joining IRS, one of the premier services in India, field post, he was baptised at Masoori in bureaucratic formalities, traditions, conventions and other practices. Socially, it meant that he was elevated to the status of superior person from rest of masses. This orientation on the part of Indian bureaucrats was not different from the practices of colonial administration. K-7 started his career as an officer in a central government office. After accumulating service and experience, he was promoted to the highest position in his department in his region. During his career, he was posted in different states and different cities in the country. Thus he became pan-Indian bureaucrat because of getting countrywide experience. During his career, he visited abroad too and had firsthand experience of economic, political social system of countries in Europe and America.

5. ASSOCIATION AND MOBILITY

(i) In the context of the above, the association pattern of K-7 followed his professional career and intellectual development. While the former led to his association with bureaucrats, administrators, officers, colleagues, professionals, politicians, social notables and so on, the latter exposed him to literary, academic, media and intellectual personalities. As in his younger age, he was greatly impressed by a literary figure like Professor Akbar Haiydri and eminent journalist cum politician like Shamim Ahmad Shamim, this association with other such personalities expanded and deepened. He felt deeply interested in such kind of activities and such company. In reality, he became 'an intellectual bureaucrat'.

(ii) In the preceding context, the adoption of service career from a petty traditional occupation represented grand-level change. It may be characterised as the century's jump from one extreme occupation of lower social status to other extreme occupation of highest social status. This also reflected a radical type of social mobility not observed often in our society. In fact, it matures after generations and after centuries. Thus highest degree of upward mobility was experienced by K-7 and his family, of which he was sufficiently conscious.

6. MARRIAGE AND FAMILY

(i) K-7's marriage reflected a social crisis in marriage market of Kashmir. When lower classes/castes got higher education and employment, they underwent overall mobility and change in their social status. In practice, it affected endogamous and exogamous practices of marriage in Kashmir at that time. It so happened that lower class/caste but highly educated and employed boys could not get suitable girls within their endogamous circle. So, they were compelled to come out of the limited circle and search for a suitable match on competitive terms. In practice, they faced several difficulties and complexities. In totality, the above situation in marriage market had the following patterns of marriage:

(a) Boys of upper caste/class > girls of upper/lower caste/class;

(b) Girls of upper caste/class > boys of upper/lower caste/class;

(c) Boys of lower caste/class > girls of lower/upper caste/class; and

(d) Girls of lower caste/class > boys of upper/lower class/caste.

In the preceding framework, K-7's marriage fit in 'C' pattern. After a lot of investigation, a suitable match with education and business background was found, with whom K-7 married. On the day of marriage, the entire city gentry and business elite was present on the occasion of *nikaah.*

(ii) K-7 was married at a time when he was living in a nuclear family unit established outside the state in place of working. After marriage, he established neo-local household temporarily in Kashmir and another family unit at the place of work outside JK. Subsequently, his nuclear family household (in which he, his wife and unmarried children lived) became a moving unit as it shifted from one city to another city with his transfer. After some time, K-7 constructed his own house in a posh colony near the city and used to live there during vacations. Thus he had two residences, one permanent in Kashmir valley and other temporary in different cities of India where he and his family lived. After marrying of his child, this family has two members, i.e. he and his wife who live a peaceful life.

7. SOCIAL LIKES AND DISLIKES

In the context of lifelong experience at different places in the country, K-7 developed particular likes and dislikes, some of which are mentioned below:

Social Likes	*Social Dislikes*
-well-informed person on international affairs	-poverty, poverty conditions and poverty culture.
-helping others without any consideration	-wasting time in useless activities.
-participation in political debates and discussion	-*Syed-zadegi and amir-zadefi*
-*writing for* newspapers and magazines	-caste as the operational social unit
-reading daily newspapers regularly	-spoiled children due to economic affluence.
-loving and caring for parents in older age.	-*Sayyids* who claim higher social status.
-Informal and decent bureaucrat with human approach	-persons who always dominate, manipulate, exploit Traits and harass others.
-visiting all friends irrespective of their status	-a person having no knowledge of religion and politics.
-always an excellent host	-corruption and nepotism.
-Kashmir experts and Kashmir lovers	-a person with selfish orientation
-liberal religious-mindedness and sober behaviour	-corrupt politicians and dishonest businessman
-equal regard for each religion and region	-incompetent and inefficient teacher
-historical sense in national/international affairs	-anti-gender ideas, values and norms.
-treating domestic servants with dignity	-the practise of shrine worshipping
-a nuclear family unit	-social deviance and crime
-self arranged marriage	-unemployment
-secular attitude and behaviour in public	-political suppression and oppression
-cultural emancipation in society	-denial of basic human and civil rights
-gender equality and justice	-exploitation of workers and artisans
-free education to all poor students	-free competition in education and employment.

8. CONCEPTS OF "I", "ME" AND "WE"

(i) K-7 had a strong sense of 'I' and consciously maintained the status of this concept. It represented a positive personal worldview and vision of achievement. It was also related to work ethics in the whole of life and a response of hard-regular performance. Emotionally, he felt that the concept revealed his past and present and predict about the future. K-7 felt that 'I' represented his personal charisma in later part of his life, status and image of bureaucrat and his authority and power over a number of people. Finally, while this concept emphasised following strictly values and norms in personal and social life, it provided eternal strength to value-based attitude and behaviour.

(ii) The concept of 'me' reflected his social world around him which he inherited or created. Though both were separate and different, they had a dialectical relationship. While the former negated some behavioural traits, the latter stressed for adoption of new behavioural traits. Broadly, it represented the institutional aspects of 'my' Kashmir, 'my' society, 'my' home and 'my' family. It also pointed towards my social choices, social preferences and priorities, my education-socialisation, my job-occupation, my engagements-achievements, my contribution and my attitude and behaviour. Finally, it revealed the reality of my generation and the following generation.

(iii) The concept of 'we' upheld by K-7 was most clear, revealing and contextual and was preferable in his life. He always talked about 'we' the Kashmiris, the KMs, the Indians, the Pakistanis, the workers, the artisans, the occupational group, the lower-middle class, the bureaucrats-officials, the friends-colleagues and neighbours-relatives.

9. IDEAS OF EQUALITY AND INEQUALITY

(i) Taking into consideration his social background, K-7 always upheld ideas and ideals of equality and emphasised debasement of inequality in all forms and at all levels. The concept of inequality for him stood unjustified and unbearable in theory or practice. In reality, it was a concept which must be annihilated and erased from the memory of human beings world over. For him, it could never be justified on any criteria, especially class, caste and power.

(ii) K-7 understood well all major formulations and their practical implications of major variables of social stratification, i.e. class and caste. He had gone through Marxian, post-Marxian and non-Marxian notions of class and their variability and applicability. As per the thinking of K-7, the concepts of class and caste led to the establishment of systems of inequality and injustice. But, various classes also get divided which in all situation lead to domination, exploitation, antagonism and conflict. Though he felt high degree of class consciousness and sense of affiliation to the *proletariat,* he never felt convinced about the "class war" in the human society and establishment of socialist or communist society. This, according to him, failed even in the Mecca of socialist society, i.e. erstwhile USSR and other backward agricultural and forward industrial society in China and Europe respectively. But, K-7 always remembered the contribution made by Karl Marx in understanding social dialectics and raising the consciousness among workers against exploitation in the capitalist society.

(iii) K-7 explained caste in terms of a system of stratification which stood most unequal and unjust and was against the notion of humanity in nature, contents, practices and implications. It created varna groups of upper, lower and middle status and threw others outside its framework. This status was hereditary and irreversible in this world. Thus it had dehumanised the entire system. K-7 argued that a human being cannot be called of upper or lower status just because he was born in a certain family. According to him, it was the action and performance of an individual which made him of upper or lower status. In a social situation, an individual or a group must carry out social efforts in an environment of equal opportunity and competition. Those who perform well and contribute positively must go up in the hierarchy and those who contribute negatively must go down in the hierarchy. He was much concerned about the treatment SCs get in the society. By calling them *Harijjans,* they were made socially disabled permanently. They bear the real rot of caste system in Indian society for centuries.

(iv) K-7 had observed that practices of gender discrimination were common among all classes, especially the lower class, in the Kashmiri society. He was of the opinion that this situation was the result of poverty and 'poverty culture' and has recently given rise to gender violence. These practices negated the gender justice and women were left uncared. In this situation, according to K-7, the need emerged was that there must be formulation of social legislation, implementation of these laws-rules through agencies of crime-control and judiciary, and finally the initiatives on the part of civil society must take its care.

9. THE IDEAL CHARACTER

(i) Mawlana Mohammad Sayyid Masoodi (MMSM) was one of the ideal characters of K-7. He belonged to Gujjar community inhabited in hilly areas of the state and lived in Kangan area. He was an eminent religious scholar, social notable and political leader. He had got religious as well as modern education. He was a man of future vision and historical sense. His intellectual and political orientation drew him to the freedom movement in Kashmir. After 1947, he continued to play certain role in Kashmir politics. He remained a faithful colleague of SMA before and after 1947 and always maintained his distinctive positions on various issues inside and outside party, the NC. He was killed by unknown militants in the early stage of militancy.

(ii) Due to his intellectual-political approach to the Kashmir politics, MMSM was given distinctive position in the constituent assembly of JK in 1948-49. He also played an important role in the constituent assembly which approved the draft of the Constitution of India. He was respected for his simple lifestyle and realistic political ideas in all political circles, even outside the state. So, he played an important role in all political developments till 1960s. He was a prolific speaker and impressed even large gathering of people by his oratory. He used to deliver long speeches in public gatherings but the entire audience listened to him silently and seriously. Later on, people used to quote him in political discussions and other gatherings.

(iii) K-7 was highly impressed with contents, composition, themes, ideas and delivery of MMSM's speeches. He became his fan for some time during his younger days. He found his approach to politics as scientific, realistic and pragmatic. He visited his residence several times and had discussion with him. He was highly impressed with his simple and primitive lifestyle. He observed that despite his excellence in scholarship and political thinking, he lived an isolated, uncorrupted and simple life, which has no parallel with present day political ideologues. Thus MMSM played a crucial role in maturity of political ideas and political assessment of K-7.

10. GLOBAL SOCIAL ORDER

K-7 put forward the point that there must be no political consideration in the establishment, maintenance and continuity of global social order. At the same time, there must be no differentiation and no discrimination in the origin and ethnicity of the people involved in this order. Moreover, there must be constitutional, organisational and formal safeguards and measures for this consensus based social order. After these political precautions, K-7 believed that the great job of establishment of global social order must be done in association with and organisational support from global religions, regional cultures and local ethnicities. The functioning of this order must be carried out on the principles of plurality, equality, justice, democracy, liberty, secularism, tolerance and balanced representation. Finally, this global order must be protected by all states through ideological commitment, constitutional measures, multi-cultural efforts, and social institutional arrangement.

11. RELIGIOUS LIFE

(i) K-7 upheld the type of religious life which was partly religious and partly secular. These two aspects of his life were not conflict in relationship but complementary and reciprocal. While his personal life stood for ideal religious beliefs and practices, his personal life also revealed secular aspects. In his personal life, he was deeply religious by upholding all positive qualities of religious personality. But, at the same time, he stood irreligious in professional life which meant that he had no consideration of religious affiliation in official matters. People of different religions visited his office and he treated them with equal attention and consideration.

(ii) K-7 believed that religion stood for way of life which provided guidance for all fields. It stood for two component parts, theoretical and practical. Theoretically, Islam stood as an ideal and supreme religion with belief in its fundamentals revolving around *tawheed, risalat and aakherat,* which determine the belief system, attitudes and behaviour pattern of the believer. K-7 often prayed, observed fast regularly, paid *zakat* and performed all activities related to the noble religious-human cause. He rigorously followed all desirable-preferable social practices, equal treatment to all, honesty, sincerity, work ethics, commitment to profession, regularity, punctuality, discipline, quality and excellence. He didn't practise any harassment, exploitation and manipulation of clients. He never involved himself in bribe, corruption, nepotism and red-tapism and followed laws and rules strictly with no exception or deviation.

(iii) Islam stood as an ideal religion for K-7 and he understood it from literary tradition, i.e. from authentic sources such as *Quran,* Haidth and other credible Islamic literature. This method of understanding religion stood parallel to traditional folk method under which *molvis, mullas* and *ulema* and other preachers used to preach people verbally in the cultural framework. K-7 was a well read person in religion and had proper understanding of basic ideas, concepts, views and so on. He was better equipped with religious knowledge than many religious scholars. He corrected them at times.

(iv) K-7 was a strong believer in doctrinaire Islam which meant that he was not following folk religious practices. Accordingly, he never visited shrines and never celebrated any particular day in a week or a month or a year. But, at the same time, he held all mystics in high esteem whose shrines lie inside and outside Kashmir and who did tremendous job in the cause of Kashmir. Inside Kashmir, the shrines of these great people are used by *mullas* as places for monetary purpose.

(V) K-7 represented the composite culture of Kashmir at ideational and empirical levels. At the ideational level, he was a firm believer in religious plurality and interaction between culture and religion in Kashmir. This kind of environment gave rise to a culture which has been shared and upheld through out history. Thus he considered KPs 'a component part' and 'in organic relationship'. In this context, he felt that Kashmiris of his generation can hardly fall apart.

(vi) In practice, he developed composite cultural traits at personal, family and societal level. In addition to several personal friends, K-7 had many KP family friends who used to visit his house on usual occasions. Finally, he had a large number of friends and colleagues from the KP community who had constant interaction with him and shared his life experiences. In fact, K-7 had special attraction for KP intellectuals who used to discuss various issues and problems for hours together. In this way, he felt that Kashmir fraternity never ends.

12. POLITICAL IDEOLOGY AND POLITICAL ROLE

(i) Since K-7 had studied politics and was an expert on political affairs, he used to be critical in his discussion related to political ideology. In fact, he proved to be a political analyst than a political ideologue. He was specifically critical about political ideology of political leaders, parties and politics of minorities and presented these themes in critical perspective. Among political leaders, SMA was one of his targets. He used to criticize great political leader for his political ideology. According to him, SMA didn't follow a consistent political ideology regarding Kashmir. He maintained different political positions in 1931, 1947-48, 1953, 1975 and 1982 which benefited neither the Centre nor the state. It only contributed to political instability and political uncertainty and alienation of masses in the state. While he was highly critical of all political parties in the state, ruling as well as opposition parties, for their role vis-à-vis Kashmir problem. Another focused area of his political criticism was the 'minority politics' in India which he felt was exploited for electoral political gains.

(ii) Formally, K-7 played no major or minor political role. He was a political analyst and deliberated but not participated in political developments. He also didn't work for political modernisation in and out of his family. In earlier years of his life, he used to listen to the political speeches of eminent leaders in public rallies but this practise was abandoned later on. Now, he used to read newspapers in detail regularly for getting these details. He also used to listen news bulletins from Radio Kashmir, All India Radio, BBC and VOA. He also used to watch regularly the news from Doordashan, PTV, Zee News, NDTV, CNN and BBC. In this way, he used to get real and factual information on political developments at regional, national and international level.

13. EXPERIENCE OF CONFLICT SITUATION

K-7 kept himself well informed about all developments in Kashmir through regular-intense study of newspapers and magazines and through interaction with the local people. He had read in regional and national newspapers a lot of stories about brutal torture of youth in prisons and interrogation centers because of which many of them died. K-7 got confirmation about these inhuman incidents from the local people. He had also read about these grave incidents in the writings of Basharat Peer, Shahid Agha, Seema Qazi and B. A. Dabla which caused pain and anguish in him.

14. THE KASHMIR PROBLEM

K-7 provided a distinct perspective regarding nature and resolution of long-pending Kashmir problem. He maintained that this problem has three distinct dimensions which are as follows: Politically, it was primarily a political problem. While its origin was purely political, its resolution too lie in political action. Other non-political aspects, such as, economic, social, cultural, religious, demographic and psychological, were also necessary aspects of the problem, but politics remained dominant. These aspects stood peripheral in comparison to the political factor. According to K-7, the resolution of Kashmir problem can be seen at three different levels. First, at the regional level, a political consensus has to be evolved between different political entities represented by political parties. Second, at the national level, India and Pakistan have to develop political consensus within their own countries and between these two countries, keeping in view their respective national interests. Third, at the international level, political consensus has to be developed among the U.S., the lone super power, and Western allies on the one hand and Russia, China and South Asian neighbouring states on the other.

Historically, K-7 maintained that since the Kashmir problem was left unresolved, it developed its own history which was necessary to study for its totalistic understanding. He put forward the proposition that Kashmir problem has become extremely complex due to historical complexities started from 1947. In the post-1947 period, both India and Pakistan followed their respective policies and politics of their own countries in order to follow their national interests. In 1948, India took this issue to the UNSC and was internationalised. On the home front, Kashmiris could not develop uniform political ideas and a consensus-based perspective for final resolution of Kashmir problem. On the other hand, both countries followed a similar policy of integration within their parts of Kashmir. Though people on both sides resisted this process, it made the problem more complex.

15. FUTURE SOCIETY IN KASHMIR

K-7 thought that future society in Kashmir must represent a broader political unit, representing all sub-entities and sub-identities in an umbrella fashion for peace and development and not for conflict and underdevelopment. It also represent multi-cultural, multi-religious, multi-lingual, multi-ethnic ethos. It must seem another Switzerland and next Vianna in the Indian sub-continent.

However, the important question for K-7 was : How to establish this ideal society in the world of conflict.? He held that this distinctive political entity in Kashmir can be established through processes of political modernisation at —

(a) regional level, involving all principal actors in the region;

(b) national level, involving two major regional states in the Indian sub-continent; and

(c) international level, involving the U.S. and other global and regional powers.

All this will contribute to a durable and humanist construction of future state and society in Kashmir.

16. SOCIAL PROBLEMS IN KASHMIR

(i) *Poverty and Conflict:* K-7 felt that poverty stood as the most crucial problem of present day Kashmir. In fact, this global problem reveals in least economic-social development, sub-human standard of life, and minimum basic facilities of life such as food, mental-physical health facilities and education. In most of the cases, it also led to the processes of degeneration and dehumanisation. K-7 felt that in Kashmir, this type of situation has been intensified mainly by perpetual conflict for last two decades. Consequently, the quality of life has gone down to the minimum standard. So, he also felt that this alarming situation needed to be controlled and arrested immediately through formal policy-planning and implementation of relevant programs through official agencies and organisations. At the same time, NGO sector must be involved in this grand effort. Special focus must be on exploitation of conventional resources and traditional sources of local economy. K-7 further held that with these processes of change and development, the political resolution seems a must.

(ii) *Unemployment in Kashmir:* K-7 considered unemployment as the crucial and chronic problem in Kashmir. As per official sources, there were 5.5 lakh unemployed educated youth in the state in 2009. However, he was primarily concerned with unemployment among lower occupational groups which could neither compete with upper classes and forward groups nor had direct or indirect access to higher authorities or positions of power. Though children of these backward groups in general even with higher qualifications, have no jobs for them in the public or private sector. At the same time, they were not in a position to pay bribe for getting jobs. In this way, corruption and nepotism have denied them government jobs; frustration among them was the logical result.

K-8 URBAN EDUCATED WORKIING WOMAN

1. SOCIAL CONTEXT

(i) At the turn of 19th century and arrival of 20th century, Kashmir was ruled by alien feudal rulers, while the society was generally illiterate. But, there were some families which proved an exception to this situation. As has happened in other societies, these economically affluent and politically influential families had attained modern education and were serving the state at various positions. These families in Kashmir may be identified as KP, business and *Sayyid* families. The last category was the first generation of KMs which played a crucial role in grand transformation from tradition to modernity, especially in the field of education, in the Kashmiri society. In some cases, not only men but women too were educated in these families. These women proved 'change initiators' and 'change carriers' and affected attitudes and behaviour in the KM community. While at attitudinal level, they created scope and relevance for change betterment of all and, at the behavioural level, they realised gains of change and development and provided 'ideal cases' in this regard. They also introduced the culture of education and employment at that time.

(ii) The preceding situation led to some basic changes in the Kashmiri society mainly because of women's involvement. Though they didn't develop completely 'dual role' and 'role conflict' for themselves, but they emerged as 'role model' for rest of women in society. In that situation, especially during 20th century, women developed a new role in society, i.e. modernising role. Though they also got education and employment, they were not fast in adopting corresponding change in role and status partly because of traditional factors of *purdah* and segregation in their families and partly because there was no motivating agent or agency available. Though these women got emancipated, their social role was restricted. Later on, it was mainly because of processes of political socialisation in the 20th century that Kashmiri women at large participated in socio-political life.

(iii) K-8 was born in that context of political, economic and social developments in the modern history of Kashmir. Her generation got all that was modern and was needed in new society. While their ideas, attitudes, and worldview changed considerably, they developed a parallel behaviour pattern to that of their ancestors two generations back. In terms of role and status, they experienced radical transformation which covered all in-family and out-family situations. An important point which needs to be noted here is that social transformation at that time was experienced in elite and upper families only, which were educationally forward, economically prosperous and culturally exposed. This type of change cannot be generalised and applied to all KM women who were totally illiterate, extremely poor, culturally not exposed, politically suppressed and socially dominated. K-8 was socialised in the elite family which had experienced revolutionary change on the one hand and was aspiring to adopt new modern way of life on the other.

2. IN-FAMILY SOCIALISATION

(i) K-8 was socialised in elite families of Kashmir in middle decades of 20th century. While her paternal side belonged to upper economic and social status family, maternal side belonged to upper economic and *Sayyid* status background. Thus she was the product of such elite social environment. The convergence, interaction and finally matrimonial relationship between these sides led to the establishment of new elite family unit whose prominent features were educational advancement, adoption of professional career, economic affluence, political influence, psychological stability, cultural exposure and so on. The non-traditional situation in the family gave its members new ideas about their role in broader society. It was essentially in that context that K-8 followed newly-developed behaviour pattern which was characterised with attaining higher modern education followed by adoption of professional career and changed pattern of social life.

(ii) This process of change in elite family of K-8 got initiated in a particular background related to the role of religion. As the fact stands, Islam never discouraged adoption of change and progress through education. In the case of this family, Islam played a significant role in the emancipation of women. While it restored the human dignity of women, it also established an egalitarian gender relations with institutional, organisational and legal support. It also determined rules, codes, conventions, values and norms accordingly. In actuality, Islam in Kashmir had a folk character with two prominent features. First, it referred to ideal Islamic beliefs and practices which emphasised equal and just social status to women. Second, it referred to negation of the pre-Islamic notions and practices which were unequal and discriminatory. While the former tradition helped women to emerge as an 'emancipated lot', the latter helped in the continuity of traditional differentiation and discrimination. In this situational background, Islam as a reformative religion played a very positive role in the process of emancipation of all in two ways. It maintained the local cultural standards and didn't allow their debasement, and allowed selective adoption of modern standard practices in social life.

(iii) K-8 was brought up in the preceding social dynamics and developed two life-long traits. First, she maintained faithfully traditional values and norms. Second, at the same time, she adopted selective traits of modern life. While in the former case, beliefs-practices of religion and concerned attitude-behaviour were upheld consciously, in the latter case, a career-oriented life which was unconventional, un-dogmatic and unprecedented was established.

In actuality, K-8 represented assimilative and synthetic aspects of social-cultural life. For her, these traits were not in contradiction but co-relative. However, like other members of elite family, she too had developed these characteristic traits which could be distinguished from common traits. The elite traits reflected in her attitudes, behaviour, ideas, views, ideals, ideology, values, norms and judgments.

(iv) K-8's life represented another particular feature which was uncommon in elite families. Since she had extensive social interaction with members of non-elite families, she had developed cordial and open ties with the latter. This mass-oriented life pattern had led to her revolutionary worldview, progressive ideas and radical, political, economic, social, educational and other views, especially related to social equality, change and progress. Though K-8 had not de-classed herself, her association with other classes were cordial, open, direct and end-oriented. Thus she was popular and sociable person in her social circle. In this lifestyle, she represented some ideal personality features such as regularity, punctuality, frankness, truthfulness, cordiality, sincerity, ready to help others, making more friendship and less enemies, and due regards to elders.

3. OUT-FAMILY ENVIRONMENT

(i) The impact of out-family environment was limited at the earlier stage because K-8 family had shifted to a new house in the outskirts of the city. The children of the family were not allowed to interact freely with the children of surrounding colonies there. The residents of those colonies provided several services to the family. However, K-8 had certain definite impact from near-distant relatives and pitri-matri kins. They and their children used to pay regular visits to K-8 family. They usually met or gathered in K-8 house on different occasions. This environment affected K-8 in terms of developing particular hobbies, entertainment patterns, social images of different individuals and groups and elite families general lifestyle. In this social situation, K-8 was also made class-elite conscious. Then came the impact of family friends which was felt specifically in areas concerned with professional career, its market chances and problems. She developed many attitudes, behaviour, engagements and interaction due to this particular impact. In actuality, it was observed that pattern of association was slowly determined by this impact of family friends.

4. EDUCATION AND CAREER

(i) The primary and secondary education of K-8 was carried out in one of the missionary convent schools in the city. This was first of a series of schools which the catholic missionary started in the valley in mid-19th century to impart modern education to locals. The concerned school provided modern education in all fields in English medium. The missionary managed the school fully and taught according to Christian ethics and practices. Though it faced little resistance at that time, it did not stop the mission of education. Thus this school, after a lot of efforts and problems, produced first generation of educated Muslim men and women in the 19th century. As this missionary school provided modern version of education and it had deep effect on its students like that of K-8. Most of these convent-educated belonged to elite families and upper-middle classes and made distinguished careers after they left the school.

(ii) After this schooling, K-8 joined a local college for under-graduate course. Subsequently, she got in the university in the field of mass media where she spent two years. The university social ethos proved absolutely new and different for elite girls like K-8. She had not observed this culture among the relatives and family friends. However, the impact of university culture stabilised and strengthened her modern personality traits. So, she was quite ahead of others in this field. The university's contribution was that she got established rightly in the field and got a suitable place in it.

(iii) E-8 started her career as a journalist in a state English daily newspaper. She was a social journalist dealing with issues of women's problems, social problems and impact of science and technology. In her presentation, she appeared more as a social activist than as a social journalist. Her write-ups were full of arguments in strong and stylish language. After some time, she got a job in academics which she considered all time blessing for her. So, she decided to develop a professional career in the field of mass media.

5. OCCUPATION AND MOBILITY

(i) In her profession, she stood as a committed teacher, serious researcher and sincere academician. As a teacher, she was most successful and impressive. In addition to the advance preparation, she used to take classes regularly and punctually. She stood as a reputed, successful and popular teacher. As a researcher, she was involved in all types of research, theoretical, empirical, academic and sponsored. She produced some good reports about social change and mass media in Kashmir. She always remained busy with serious research work. As a sincere academician, she carried out all types of related activities such as research, teaching, publications, discussions, lectures and so on. She used to come to office early in the morning and left late in the afternoon. During the day, she performed following academic activities:

Morning;-Classes	Day:	-class	Afternoon: -research
-practical/assignments	-practical	-publications	-reading

She also participated in regional, national and international conferences and seminars and presented her papers. Her presentation was always impressive, logical and professional. In this way, she developed academic credentials. But, due to this outstanding academic performance, she has attracted criticism from academic faculty and academic bureaucracy.

(ii) Taking into consideration of occupational activities of three old generations of K-8, she and her family experienced certain degree of occupational mobility. While the earlier generations were engaged in large business and bureaucratic jobs, the new generations adopted occupations of government servants, professionals and technocrats. Two points need emphasis here. First, this process of mobility involved men as well as women, which was not the case with earlier mobility. Second, the present pattern of mobility was different from that of the earlier pattern. While the former was economic, social and cultural, the latter was economic only. Again, the latter was more family oriented, while the former was individual oriented.

6. MARRIAGE AND FAMILY

(i) K-8 was married to a businessman in her family clan. Both partners were educated and highly qualified. In reality, this marriage represented an emerging phenomenon of late marriage and changing marriage practices in Kashmir. Thereafter conflict started influencing the society after 1989. In that marriage market situation, girls of higher qualification, advanced age and from elite-upper families had to opt for boys of lower qualification, advanced age and from upper-middle classes. It was mainly because of shortage of eligible males in the marriage market of Kashmir from early 1990s. This shortage was caused mainly because many males of marriageable age group were killed, injured, disabled, disappeared, left Kashmir for education abroad, and joined their family business outside state. The shortage of grooms had immediate effect on the existing practices of marriage related to endogamy, exogamy, hypergamy and hypogamy. In practical terms, it meant that girls of upper classes and *Sayyid* castes were compelled to go for marriage with boys of middle-upper classes and non-*Sayyid* castes. Moreover, both partners were advanced in age. K-8's marriage was performed in this social context. Her marriage was endogamous, monogamous and patri-local type and proved a step forward in the life of both partners.

(ii) At the time of marriage, K-8 joined the nuclear family household of her husband which became a joint family because brother of K-8's husband was also married at the same time and he too joined this family. For some time, this family household survived. But, before the death of her father-in-law, K-8's husband's brother opted out of this joint unit and shifted to his newly constructed house in a posh colony. Thus K-8 was left with her children and husband and lived a comfortable nuclear family life. Her husband preferred to live in the ancestral house than to construct a new one.

7. SOCIAL LIKES AND DISLIKES

In the background of socialisation in in-family situation and experience of out-family encounters, K-8 developed social likes and dislikes during her mature age, some of which are mentioned below:

Social Likes	*Social Dislikes*
-persons who started their career from zero	-arrogance and uncivilised behaviour
-a committed, hard-working academician	-criticising others without reason
-competition in all fields and for all members	-*chamchagiri* of officials and seniors
-self-confidence, and self-initiative	-discrimination with poor and lower classes
-social-economic mobility for all members	-social pathology and social apathy
-focus on performance and achievement	-perpetual tension and conflict situation
-highest positive performance by children	-deviant and delinquent young generation
-ideas, ideals and values of social equality	-bureaucrats with their rigidity and formalities
-defending ideals of consensus and harmony	-politicians with their visionless personalities
-gender equality with gender responsibility	-wasting time without any meaning full purpose
-socially conscious young generation	-negative, lazy and compromising attitudes
-committed, competent and trained teacher	-violation of religion-based values and norms
-always helpful to social workers	-crime against women
-a serious and sincere researcher	-obscene television programs and advertisements
-no consciousness of caste in social affairs	- parents having no control over children
-government offices without corruption	-social inequality of all types
-work culture and work ethic in office	-erosion of ethics and morality in broader society
-invitations and celebrations	-priority to bureaucracy over academics
-professionalism in life	-corruption in academic field
-primary necessary education for all	-poverty and underdevelopment

8. CONCEPTS OF "I", "ME" AND "WE"

K-8 had strong sense of all three concepts of 'I', 'me' and 'we'. Since she was self-achieving, she had developed strong notions of these psychological feelings. Her consistent work and continuous social exposure was maintained by these notions. 'I', according to her, stood for self-independent, self-reliant and self-confident. I also meant a hard, long and serious struggle for life. This 'I' gave the human being the character and direction. She upheld that 'I' belonged to the :

- past : portraying the ideal life of forefathers;
- present : reflecting the life struggle of contemporary generation of parents and children; and
- future : showing the human path to the young coming generation.

All these aspects were bright, positive and progressive in the context of Kashmir. Thus 'I' pointed towards psychological support and social legitimacy for the human network in future.

(ii) K-8 has also got high sense of 'me' which she equated with 'my'. So, 'me' conveyed belonging of the social self. According to her, 'me' specifically referred to :

- the person developed physically and mentally in a family, community and society;
- a citizen of a country – its history, culture, social set-up, and level of economic development;
- an inhabitant of a continent – its history, culture, plurality, ethnicity, economic and social condition;
- the member of human society – its social and economic conditions related to egalitarianism;
- the member of a class without domination, discrimination and exploitation;
- the member of a professional community in which she remained active, answerable and responsible.

(iii) Finally, K-8 had also strong notion of 'we' which was related to social collectivity and specifically referred to Kashmiris in general as—

- the citizens of an independent country,
- sufferers of self-established system,
- ideologically and politically non-consistent people,
- trapped in the inferno of violence, crime, drugs and moral anarchy, and
- as a group which has lost its identity, past and direction towards future.

9. IDEAS OF EQUALITY AND INEQUALITY

(i) K-8 had developed clear characteristics of class which stood for unjust system of stratification imposed forcefully by interested classes. She felt hardly any justification for a stratified system on moral, religious, cultural, educational, economic and social grounds. The three-tier class system, upper, middle and lower, hurt the two lower classes and benefited only the upper class. The two-tier stratification of capitalist and worker classes also exploited the masses by top few and chosen few. So, both systems must be dislodged and an egalitarian system must be adopted for whole of humanity which can be helped by religious ideas and ideals.

(ii) K-8 considered caste as most unjust system in human civilisation. She raised the fundamental question as to how and why a human society can be divided into unequal castes just on the basis of their birth in a particular family or group? She got no legitimacy for the existence of this system. So, she felt that the ideal caste system needed total debasement and disorganisation. Even among Muslims, the *Sayyid* group phenomenon represented anti-thesis of the concept of equality propounded by Islam, wherein no one is superior because of relation and lineage. So, dominant status of *Sayyids* and *Mullas* in the Muslim society stands redundant.

(iii) K-8 felt that gender equality as the supreme social ideal and must be strengthened. There seems no alternative to this system, so it must be established. But, at the same time, K-8 put forth some critical views about this theme, especially related to violence against women (VAW) in Kashmir. While it represented an inter-sex affair, it also showed intra-sex character too. While the former type of violence was crucial by men against women, but the latter type of violence was carried out by women against women. While the former must be opposed, the latter too must be identified and opposed equally. K-8 also mentioned about an important aspect of gender equality campaign. It was related to gender arrogance which some women use for personal interests. In a way, they misuse the ideology of gender equality. She felt that the trend must be discouraged.

10. GLOBAL SOCIAL ORDER

K-8 understood the importance for establishment of global social order based on humanistic ideas and ideals and through democratic-peaceful methodology. It had to represent all sub-regions, regions and continents in the world. This order was based, among other ideological and political features, on two universal principles of social equality and gender equality. Without these principles, this order will prove useless for the whole humanity. While social equality referred to a situation in which there will be equal relationship between various groups and classes in the whole world, gender equality ensured the gender relations characterised by equality of genders in their role and status (and required support of ideology, religion and so on) among the nations of the world. This bi-dimensional social order will serve humanity in a purposeful way.

11. THE IDEAL CHARACTER

(i) The ideal character of K-8 was her mother who had developed unparalleled personal and social traits in her impressive and popular personality. She developed reputation of a good wife, good mother, good socializer, good trainer and good teacher in her home and outside. Culturally, she represented two generations, one, which was hardly exposed to modern influences in the 19th century and, second, which was completely exposed to new impact, got modern education and adopted working career outside her family.

(ii) She proved a good wife because she got well adjusted with her husband and his joint family despite belonging to a different background and developed successful and productive post-marital life. She proved a good mother because she had eternal love and affection for her children whom she brought up, socialised, trained and taught traditional and modern values, religious and secular practices, and scientific-innovative attitudes and behaviour. She proved a good trainer because she trained properly and carefully all her children in academic, social, cultural, psychological, political, economic and other affairs. She proved a good teacher because she impressed all with her academic performance, taught children everything needed in life, and satisfied everybody who came in her contact.

(iii) More important, though she worked inside and outside her home, she had no a 'dual role' or 'role conflict'. She adjusted and reformed her life in such a way that she served to the highest degree of satisfaction official as well as domestic duties. She provided an ideal example for K-8.

12. RELIGIOUS LIFE

(i) The social-cultural environment established by K-8 family was characterised by religious as well as secular features. She believed in all fundamentals of Islam and abide by all its rules, codes and guidelines. She prayed daily, observed fast and performed all daily-activities like a humble believer. But, at the same time, she hardly considered religion in worldly, especially professional matters.

(ii) K-8 was also a strong believer in folk religious practices and its theory. Following these practices with dedication, she, along with children, visited shrines regularly (weekly or monthly) and offered prayers there. According to mystic tradition in Kashmir, she used to celebrate particular days in a week, month or year, prepared special items on those occasions and distributed among the needy. While she organised *Khateme Sharif* regularly, she followed the tradition of *Peer-Mureedi.* Though she stood very clear about real *tawheedi* ideas of Islam, she upheld all folk customs, rituals, and practices. For K-8, these two forms of religious life were not contradictory but complementary. The folk religious practices represented the localised adopted version of doctrinal universal Islam.

(iii) K-8 never felt attracted to the trends of reformative and radical Islam in Kashmir. It was mainly due to strong impact of family background. It can also be explained in terms of following religion in traditional framework. Thus she was away from these new religious trends in Islam.

(iv) As per the family practise of K-8, every religion was given equal regards, which among other things, suited its cultural and material interests in the long run. The religion of KPs had special regards because it was a native religion and different from mainstream Hindu religion. This treatment of KPs was in vogue even in conflict situation. Moreover, she felt that KPs and their culture represented "the component part of Kashmiri society" and "part of the body culture of Kashmir". Following these ideas, K-8 had developed intimate relations with some KPs and other religious communities, usually interacted with them, even outside Kashmir, and discussed all matters with them. She found their company interesting, refreshing, and open. She visited them on festival occasions also. They reciprocated and visited her home. Children of both sides used to interact freely and knew each other.

13. KASHMIR PROBLEM

(i) K-8 was not interested in politics and usually avoided it. Since Kashmir issue could not be avoided always, she developed certain ideas related to its importance and final resolution. She pointed out that dominant role of Kashmir problem in determining Kashmiri psyche, Kashmiri identity and Kashmiri daily life in contemporary times. So, she identified and upheld some political ideals in relation to the resolution of this problem. Ideally speaking, she found ideal solution of this problem in an independent state with its component parts in different regions. This state can be established with political support of all neighbouring countries, India and Pakistan, and with the help of economic resources generated from hydro-electric power, forest wealth, tourism, handicrafts, horticulture and other productive sectors.

(ii) According to the perception of K-8, all Kashmiris at large suffered during last 61 years because of its non-resolution. Now, it needs resolution on priority basis. Among other benefits, that will ensure security concerns of India and Pakistan and political stability in South Asia.

14. EXPERIENCE OF CONFLICT SITUATION

(i) Like other people in Kashmir, K-8 had some crude experience of conflict situation in Kashmir. It was related to utilisation of militant movement or the gun for personal, family or group interests by some petty elements within the movement. This resulted in alienation and isolation of sensitive elements of the movement during and after mid-1990s.

(ii) K-8 observed that at the time of the *Azaadi* movement, some petty elements used the gun for selfish and groups interests and demanded and accumulated large sums of money from all sorts of people in Kashmir. The government sponsored-patronised militants minted large amount of money in this way. These acts of loot-like situation on the part of fake militants for some years discredited the movement for some time and reduced its quality support among the masses.

15. FUTURE KASHMIR SOCIETY

K-8 had developed some particular ideas and ideals which she would like to be associated with future society in Kashmir. Some of these were as follows:

- pursuing the process of modernisation with retention of the rational part of the tradition;
- maintaining plurality of cultures and religions, their toleration and equal treatment in social life;
- Modern education, especially in professional and technical fields, for all members of society in an open and competitive system;
- upholding formally and practically the supreme principle of social equality and social justice;
- to pursue the processes of change, progress and development and providing equal economic benefits to all classes, groups and communities;
- to uphold the ideology of independence, liberty and equality; and
- to prepare for real humanistic social order in future.

16. SOCIAL PROBLEMS IN KASHMIR

(i) *Children doomed by affluence:* K-8 was highly conscious of the fact that many, if not all, children belonging to elite, business, upper and middle class families faced chronic problems created solely by their affluence and lifestyle. In fact, this problem referred to a situation in which, after getting all basic necessities of life in abundance, children of these families were provided all luxuries of present IT, particularly television, computer, internet, mobile and new vehicles and so on. They got engaged in these items and got entertained regularly. K-8 felt that these kids wasted their whole spare time with these instruments like sports items. And Surprisingly, parents never objected to this affluent entertainment.

K-8 felt that patterns of affluent entertainment by affluent children never represent productive and beneficial to them. In reality, it hurts their material and non-material interests. This type of entertainment never stood as productive use of time but sheer wastage of time. She argued that those children don't get awareness about the nature of struggle which their parents had carried out in their life. The IT engagement kept them ignorant about actual and hard realities of life. They never visualise about problems which they may face in future.

So, this IT engagement activity on the part of children stood not beneficial but highly undesirable. Ignoring some positive benefits of IT for all generations, she advised for its partial stoppage on the part of children of affluent families.

(ii) *Social Impact of Mass Media:* The second important social problem raised by K-8 was that of the impact of mass media, especially television and cinema, on children. Taking into consideration, totality of this situation, she concluded that this problem was the "root problem". She clearly identified some of its social implications which included the following:

- attitude and behaviour of life got vulgarised;
- human, religious and cultural values got delegitimised;
- traditional values and norms were not considered in actual life situations;
- dehumanisation of sacred and marital relationship;
- creation and extension of the environment of sex;
- deviant and delinquent trends in social life;
- crime and drug addiction among children and youth of all areas;
- no positive life ideology and positive worldview; and
- increasing trends of violence against women.

K-8 upheld that all such and other grave problems were experienced in society. So, there arises the need to control this situation, otherwise more social disasters will follow. In this connection, all mass media agencies, particularly television and cinema, must be used for productive-positive objectives, gain of children and youth, and betterment of whole society.

K-9 SMALL BUSINESSMAN

1. SOCIAL CONTEXT

(i) K-9 was born in a social context which reminded one horrible times in Kashmir in the past, i.e., 19th century. In that situation, poverty was so deep, intense and cruel that even two-time meals in a day or all clothes on the body was possible with a lot of difficulty. Educational, social and cultural progresses near to impossible. Several European visitors to Kashmir at that time have recorded those sub-human conditions in their books. In that situation, two important social developments were noticeable. First, the formation of occupational communities was emerging with specialised economic activities related to daily life-needs in Kashmir. Second, since Kashmir stood as the most scenic beautiful spot in the world, increasing number of European, especially British, tourists used to visit Kashmir during colonial era. They felt impressed with special beauty of Kashmir and they used to come here repeatedly, which increased the number of English tourists who stayed here for considerable time. The arrival and stay of those tourists in Kashmir directly gave rise to a group of servants, servers, suppliers, *khan saman and others* for fulfilling their daily needs and supply essential daily need items and facilities.

(ii) In the context of increasing occupational activities of this group, its economic conditions improved relatively and they were able to get two-time meals on their own income. This was followed by extension of their occupational activities and further improvement in their economic status. This was also followed by educational initiatives, social progress and cultural exposure in this group which belonged to the lower class in the past. It was this socio-economic context in which K-9 was brought up, educated and finally started an occupational career.

2. IN-FAMILY SOCIALISATION

(i) The ongoing changes mentioned above were further expanded by macro-level political changes in JK after 1947 in the field of economic development, social mobility and educational advancement. In that environment, K-9 family started minor business activities which gradually expanded and gave this family minimum economic strength. The concomitant effect was felt in the field of education when K-9, his brothers and sisters were educated which enabled the former to start their business in traditional and non-traditional occupations and the latter were able to get good marriage partners from business and other families. This situation provided necessary inspiration for higher education to their next generation boys and girls.

(ii) It seems interesting to note that expanding economic activities related to supply of various items and facilities to English tourists led to 'psychic mobility' and social status of K-9 family. Moreover, some of its members, who were more exposed and interactive with tourists, adopted their version of English language. In fact, this language change represented a phenomenon according to which local serving people came in close contact of English tourists and adopted many words and sentences, not the whole language, in their day-to-day life.

(iii) K-9 was socialised in this type of changing economic, social and cultural family context and adopted occupational skills efficiently. He opted for his traditional occupation after getting education. Subsequently, he proved a successful businessman because of his personal qualities of hard work, innovation, openness, frankness, discipline, regularity, punctuality and concentration.

3. OUT-FAMILY ENVIRONMENT

(i) The impact of out-family environment in K-9's life was dominant. This environment composed of neighbours, relatives, family friends and business colleagues. The K-9's family neighbours were other occupational communities like that of his own, which were in separate *mohallas*. One such community was *Mullas* of the big shrine in the locality. The occupational role of that community was protection of shrine and shrine culture. Though there existed no such role in original Islam, this had developed according to folk tradition. This role stood folk-oriented and exploitative and had pre-Islamic origin. Other occupational groups had developed an antipathy towards this particular group and opposite of it was also correct. But, at the same time, occupational groups used to approach this group for 'folk healing' and other ritual performances. In return to these services, this group was paid in cash and kind. Thus a 'functional dependency' among occupational groups had emerged in society.

(ii) The second influential group helped in socialisation of K-9 was of near and distant relatives who mostly belonged to the same occupation. In actuality, they affected his basic attitude and behaviour that oriented him towards the occupation. The continuous interaction and regular visits to each others houses increased occupational solidarity and general material benefits to all kin members.

(iii) K-9s ff composed of individuals and families of same and other occupations. They were usual visitors to each other's families and exchanged gifts on religious, cultural and social occasions. They always provided mutual help and cooperation and functioned like guilds. They became high conscious about their identity and also entered into matrimonial relations.

(iv) Another group which influenced socialisation of K-9 was of "market guys" who used to work there like him. They used to work in company for the whole day and shared joys, sorrows, secrets, experiences and so on. K-9 developed cordial, open, helpful, understanding and realistic relations with them, while they usually reciprocated. The regular interaction and consequent stable relationship provided a social situation which benefited everybody's interest. In a way, he helped others and was helped by others. Through his personality traits, business ethics, honest and open dealings increased his social intimacy among the *biradari.* His treatment to clients gave him a distinctive image, reputation and credibility. Clients trusted him and he trusted clients. In this process, both sides got benefited.

4. EDUCATION AND CAREER

(i) K-9's primary, middle and secondary educations carried out in a government school in his locality. In fact, under the benefit of free education in the state, all children of his family were educated. Since K-9 was not interested in further education, he opted for career in his traditional occupation. This was a conscious and rational choice for his life-long career. So, he always behaved reasonably and responsibly. He handled the entire business single-handedly but efficiently. It was also because of his professional and scientific approach that he developed in life.

(ii) In his occupational career, he stood as a perfect businessman and best retailer. He always kept all original and necessary items available, maintained fixed prices with specific brands-standards, kept no option for bargaining, and never wasted client's time while shopping. He stood excellent in business ethics and business courtesy. It was because of these reasons that he had attracted a long list of clients who included the following:

- Scientists	- Teachers	- Academicians
- Bureaucrats	- Locals and outsiders	- Youth, especially girls
- Doctors and engineers	- government officials	- religious leaders and preachers
- Elite family members	- business classes	- upper class families.

5. OCCUPATIONAL ACTIVITIES AND MOBILITY

K-9 was considered most successful businessman in his locality. All socially important and relevant persons were used to shopping from his shop and most of them felt satisfied. Thus he was popular, credible and authoritative shopkeeper in his entire market. It was mainly because of his occupational traits which he developed in business life, some of which were as follows:

- Making available all national and international standard-branded items, especially in the fields of toiletries, perfumes, dry foods, drinks, luxuries, dresses, fancy items and so on.
- Since he was television advertisement conscious, all those items which were shown on television were made available in his shop in the first opportunity.

- Since his distinctive clientale included elite families women from surrounding colonies – he used to keep all – most recent and new fashion and most-modern luxury items – in the shop, and which were usually used in Paris, London, New York and Delhi.
- He used to get orders for those international items and got in the shop in shortest possible time.
- Due to these occupational features, K-9 was considered in the area as the ideal retailer. So, anybody who heard about him wanted to visit his shop and make purchases there.

(ii) K-9 had undergone radical type of mobility in occupational and social fields. Taking into consideration occupational-economic conditions of this family at the dawn of 20th century, it has experienced unprecedented process of mobility which, in actuality, has given its members new lifestyle. K-9 in person too had experienced multi-farious mobility.

6. ASSOCIATION PATTERN

(i) In the broader context of in-family and out-family socialisation and subsequent experience, K-9 developed an association pattern which revolved around the activities of occupational community, clients and general public. In the first case, he developed permanent and reciprocal ties with its members which lasted for long. Since it contributed more positive features to his family life, he deliberately continued this relationship.

(ii) In the case of clients, K-9 felt seriously that his life style and business were dependent on 'sweet approach' of clients towards him. So, he gave sincere regards to them and fulfilled all their needs, priorities, choices, brands, variety and so on. He accepted exchange of things and return of spoiled things. He took full care of spouses and children of his clients and developed personal relations with them.

(iii) In the case of general public, K-9 proved a formal business-like person, end oriented person, no personal consideration in person, no interference in others' lives, kept away from socially undesirable persons, and never liked social chaos, animosity and conflict.

7. MARRIAGE AND FAMILY

K-9 was married to a distant cousin who was living within the boundary of his occupational community. In the sociological typology, this marriage was within local endogamous circle but with a little difference. K-9 in-laws family had attained higher economic and social status due to large business of Kashmiri handicrafts outside JK. In actuality, this proved a forward step in the broader process of overall mobility. After the marriage, K-9 and his family joined the joint family with his parents, married and unmarried brothers. But, when the number of its members increased, this family got divided into several nuclear family units. With that, K-9 and other brothers shifted to new colonies after constructing new houses there. He too established new nuclear family household composed of the couple and their little children. Though occasional differences emerged, he maintained decent relationship with his brothers. The new family unit represented a middle class home and a modern family where all modern luxury items and facilities from toiletries to perfumes and from modern dresses to all fashion items were available.

8. SOCIAL LIKES AND DISLIKES

After going through in-family and out-family socialisation and developing vast experience in the occupation, he made selection of social likes and dislikes some of which are mentioned below:

Social Likes	*Social Dislikes*
- Affluent business families	- narrow-minded religious orientation
- Rich lifestyle in general	- corrupt and selfish political leaders
- Maintaining social consensus and harmony	- corrupt and inefficient bureaucrat
- Showing social concern always	- communal and extremist political party
- Discussing social issues with others	- one who cheats and plays fraud
- Rational analysis of social problems	- begging in its forms
- No scope for social duplicate behaviour	- bargaining in business transitions
- Happy children of decent families	- wasting one's own and other's time
- Practices of business ethics and courtesy	- undesirable social dependence
- Sincere and honest social life pattern	- extreme fashion adoptions by young
- No bargaining in life and business	- anti-religious attitude and behaviour
- Self-confidence and self assessment	- anti-people stand on various issues
- Necessary basic education for all	- usual disturbances and strikes
- Never forget old parents and other elders	- one who is unclean and unhealthy
- Religious and modern life in balance	- constant conflict and its negative implications
- Tolerance and respect for other religions	- unnecessary gossip about others
- No politics in human life relations	- joint-family household and its ideal relationship
- Religious rituals to be performed	- corruption and nepotism
- Disciplined and controlled children	- drug addiction of youngsters
- Nuclear family household	- negative impact of mass media.

9. CONCEPTS OF "I", "ME" AND "WE"

(i) K-9 had a strong sense of 'I' in the context of vast and varied life experienceS. He was reminded of all experiences in his 50 years of busy life. On the one hand, he got memories of those horrible days when even daily meals was not a possibility. On the other hand, he was witness to the present youngest generation who have all necessities – basics and luxuries of life available in abundance. This, according to K-9, happened within two generations time. All this was achieved through individual 'I' and collective 'I' and their consistent struggle for improvement in life conditions. He developed 'I' in this broader context that contributed to more change for betterment.

(ii) K-9 had also strong notion of 'me' which he usually equated with 'my'. He considered this concept as main contributing factor in individual and collective life. In fact, 'me' existed for him more at the social level and in all fields and represented his past, present and future. It involved the society at macro and micro levels. K-9 felt that, without the psychological support of 'me', there was lesser possibility of change and mobility in life. So, he kept the sense of 'me' high in letter and spirit.

(iii) K-9 had a broader view of the concept of 'we'. It covered micro social units like family and macro social units like nation. Preferably he adopted this notion in a limited framework of Kashmiris. So, he had various types, images and faces of those people some of whom include the following:

- We, the distinctive people in a distinct region
- We, the rich and upper class
- We, the occupation holders
- We, the scientists, academicians and researchers
- We, the teachers
- We, the workers and artisans
- We, the religious followers
- We, the professionals and technicians
- We, the ideologues and idealists and
- We, the observers

10. IDEAS OF EQUALITY AND INEQUALITY

(i) K-9 had clear conception of class according to local standards. He equated class to his occupational community and showed his solidarity to this social collectivity. He wanted relations between various classes of competitive nature and not of conflict nature. This peaceful competition will ensue change and mobility of all deserving. In brief, K-9 life experience revealed an unequal class reality, but he felt the consideration of change and mobility of equal importance.

(ii) K-9 was highly conscious about his caste affiliation. But, at the same time, he used to threw his caste origin into background and was more concerned about exploitative role of upper caste *Sayyids* and their passive opposition to general Muslims advancement. He also stood a blind follower of folk practices and followed customs, rituals and so on. But, he opposed their status and role assigned to them. He opposed upper caste domination in education, employment, business and other fields in the present situation.

(iii) Regarding gender, K-9 was a firm believer in gender equality because it fits in his human perceptions. In his personal life, he was considerate to women always. He also felt that equality between males and females stood also in accordance with Islamic principles of equality. He made an observation that women in his occupational group enjoyed safe and equal status than women in other groups and classes.

11. IDEAL SOCIAL PRINCIPLES

K-9 maintained that he didn't believe in ideal leader or character as none of them lives nowadays. In contrast to this, he believed in some ideal social principles which stands for assessing the ideal leader or character. These principles were as follows:

- There should be traditional, dignified and simple marriage among al groups and communities.
- No foreign or westernised culture must be adopted completely.
- Religious guidelines must be followed strictly in social and business life.
- No practise or corruption, nepotism, bribe and moral turpitude in home and outside.
- Self- confidence, self-dependence and self-assertion in social life.
- Taking due care of all family members, especially elder family members.
- High, technical, profession and most-modern education for all groups, classes and so on.
- Equal position to women in every field of life.
- Necessary public help to the disabled and injured. and
- English language must be taught at every stage of education.

12. RELIGIOUS LIFE

(i) K-9 was a staunch believer in Islamic fundamentals and wanted other Muslims to believe in same way. The beliefs include *imaan,, namaz, roza, zakat and hajj*. Following this ideational framework, he followed all necessary practices. His attempt was to follow all Islamic guidelines in social life. He equated these guidelines with humanistic social principles and provided for him *solid* social actions.

(ii) At the same time, K-9 was a strong believer of folk religious practices. He thought that there was a dynamic relationship between universal Islam and local folk religious practices. For him, there was no divergence and no contradiction between the two. While he used to pray *jumma namaz* in only a particular shrine, he visited regularly this and other shrine in Kashmir. He believed in magic and superstitions. So, he used to give preferential treatment to some in comparison with other customers. He used to celebrate some particular days in a week/month/year at home.

(iii) In this type of religious environment, there was hardly any scope for reformative or radical trends of Islam. He was consciously or unconsciously away from their influences which he considered as irrelevant.

13. POLITICAL IDEOLOGY AND KASHMIR PROBLEM

(i) K-9 was politically conscious person. He followed every political development in the world. But, he stood non-participatory in the political process. Though he was politically apathetic, he stood politically more aware about political developments at local, regional, national, continental and global levels. Despite heavy schedule in the shop, he had acquired good knowledge about national-international affairs, which was much better than many teachers, scholars and students. This also reflected in his knowledge about the facts of global politics. Some of these objective facts which he mentioned to friends included the following statements:

- Erstwhile Soviet Union could not face the U.S. due to its inferior military status, weak economic position, ideological crisis and political illegitimacy;
- The lone super power, U.S., has established global position through its military might in all regions;
- China and India were fast emerging economies in the world which will certainly hurt the global American interests;
- Europe will always follow America in world politics because of former's inherent limitations;
- China will soon dominate the Indian and other world markets due to its fastest growth in its economy;
- U.S. intervention in Iraq and Afghanistan have proved counter-productive to the super power vis a vis its global interests.

(ii) K-9 had very critical views about resolution of Kashmir problem to the political satisfaction of masses. His criticism was all major political leaders and parties, which all betrayed people repeatedly. Neither these leaders nor their parties were sincere in their politics. He was critical of NC as well as INC which played the politics that made the problem of Kashmir unresolvable. He was critical of other political parties and organisation for not fulfilling the people's aspirations. This also applied to major and minor separatist political leaders who, despite having a sole political cause, could not unite on one platform. Thus they could not utilize the opportunity created during 2010 *azadi* movement in all parts of Kashmir.

(iii) K-9 wanted final resolution of Kashmir problem through granting freedom which will benefit not only people of Kashmir but people of whole Indian sub-continent.

14. EXPERIENCE OF CONFLICT SITUATION

K-9 always showed serious concern about the impact of usual strikes and other disturbances on his occupational community's business shops. As per his calculations, 20% working days were closed days, so were lost in the total working days due to strikes, curfews, civil curfews, and other related disturbances. Again while existing business could not be stabilised and expanded in that situation, no new business initiatives could be taken during this period. Moreover, many short-durable items got spoiled and wasted, while profit proportion got down completely. Thus his business community suffered financially more than any other communities.

15. FUTURE KASHMIR SOCIETY

(i) During his career as a small businessman, K-9 had developed appreciation for world-class standard society in Kashmir, in which every citizen will be affluent and there will be no trace of old poverty. However, he was not sure about the time when this dream will be materialised. He was sure that this society will not emerge in his life time. He was not clear about its clear dimensions. But, two points were clear in K-9's mind. First, the future Kashmiiri society must adopt global standards in every field, especially economic and educational. That must also reflect in whole of life, particularly lifestyle and consumer-pattern. The English were the ideal in his life in this regard. The modernity of that future society must not be of material nature only, but non-material too. He meant that international standards must reflect in education, economy, science-technology, overall progress and development, social-cultural life, and conflict-free, exploitation-free and discrimination-free social order.

(ii) Second, at the same time, K-9 wanted future society of Kashmir to be characterised with religious and cultural plurality. He wanted to make it sure that 'humanity' will be supreme guiding principle in that society. Overall, the dominant features of that society must be multiplicity of religion, culture, ethnicity, nationality and regions. That is possible only after Kashmir emerges as an independent entity.

16. SOCIAL PROBLEMS IN KASHMIR

(i) *Fashions among youth:* K-9 was highly critical of the local youth which has adopted latest fashions in extreme form. He felt that they have lost or deformed their original form in this process. By these abnormal actions, while they have repudiated their cultural identity and heredity and adopted alien and foreign cultural identity and heredity. They had hardly any reason or rationality in those acts. It reflected complete imitation and taking things without their context and utility. Moreover, extreme adoption of fashion acts have physical, psychological, social, cultural, economic, religious and other implications which proved disastrous for the society. So, these fashion acts must be avoided necessarily. However, fashions within decent and cultural limits have no negative implications.

(ii) *Disorganised Social Life:* K-9 upheld the view that social life in Kashmir was disorganised, particularly during last 20 years of conflict situation which has turned it in to an anarchic place'. In fact, social disorder reflected in the Kashmiri society in the entire social situation of crisis. So, it was observed that no social institution, organisation and process was unaffected by this disorganisation. While it appeared within families in violation of parents' authority and no proper-desired socialisation of children, it also revealed in new emerging trends of deviation and delinquency and no regards for elders-teachers-seniors outside families. This large scale disorganisational effect glaringly reflected in all social, political, economic, cultural, psychological and other fields of life. K-9 felt that this situation will negate the essence and ethics of social order, so must be controlled and negated.

K-10 TABLEBOY AND BUSINESSMAN

1. SOCIAL CONTEXT

(i) After 1947, there were continuous political instability and uncertainty in JK due to unique circumstances of accession of the state to the union of India. But, all state governments were able to carry out some reforms such as land to the tiller, abolition of usury system, and free education for all. Subsequently, planned efforts under policy direction, welfare programmes and particular schemes for overall change and development were carried out. This certainly helped in the improvement in conditions of life among lower classes and occupational groups in Kashmir. The people in general were benefited by state sponsored reforms and other measures. Those who utilised these reforms and measures quickly improved their life conditions considerably. They were also in a position to accumulate some wealth and moveable-immoveable property, particularly land, gold, property and so on. All this led to the environment change and mobility among certain groups in certain areas.

(ii) During the same period, the population of Srinagar city started increasing. Some families and groups expanded beyond normal limits. So, the shift of these people to periphery, called *sarhad* areas, took serious turn. They bought lands and constructed new houses there and established new fashionable but unplanned colonies there. These developments made special focus on the peripheries and started new economic, educational and social activities there. In addition to giving rise to groups like *Drals,* who deal with buying, selling, transfer and other dealings with land, an environment of non-conventional economic activities and possibility of fast mobility in erstwhile villages on peripheries of the city. As a result of this mobility, inhabitants of these former *sarhad* areas developed new identity. K-10 was born and brought up in this kind of social environment.

2. IN-FAMILY SITUATION AND SOCIALIZATTION

K-10 belonged to an ordinary family in a village, now an urban area, on the periphery of city. Like other families in the village, his family too had no land and was not involved in agriculture. The nearness to the city had given it the character of *Sarhad. K-10 family was backward* in educational, economic, social and other fields. The non-agricultural economic activities within and outside community made subsistence level possible. He had a large family with several brothers and sisters. Among all of them, he stood most sober, gentle, social, kind, considerate and intelligent.

(ii) In the situation of free education in the state, K-10 family took benefit and got free education with parental encouragement. The other major contributing factor was establishment of the university in neighbourhood of his locality. While it encouraged education among all locality members, it also opened new economic and other opportunities for residents of surrounding areas. Thus many youth from K-10's locality got engaged at lower positions in the university. This also gave boost to some economic activities in the area.

(iii) K-10 was highly benefited in that situation. He responded to that situation in a different way. He got lower level education like his brothers and got a petty job. But, he never remained static and played an active role at every stage. Consequently, he experienced continuous upward mobility unlike his brothers.

3. OUT-FAMILY ENVIRONMENT

(i) K-10's out-family environment was composed of his relatives, FFs, neighbours. His relatives and FFs belonged to same occupation and had very less or no impact on K-10. In fact, he impressed them and affected them. However, neighbours and neighbourhood proved dominant in his upward career. Though he lived in his community, he didn't like career of petty occupational activities. He wanted new, improved and better version of occupation. At the same time, he loved his locality people and showed solidarity with them always.

(ii) When K-10 started a petty career outside his locality, he came into contact with a family which proved as the main instrument of mobility. That family encouraged him to follow a new career and provided him monetary and non-monetary support. He maintained that without constant support of that family, he could never achieve such mobility. Thus this support helped him in making future career.

(iii) Another very significant factor at that stage was establishment of university in the neighbourhood which had long-term implications for inhabitants in surrounding areas. That new environment had decisive impact on K-10's life. It gave him a new world for future progress and life long career. It provided him broader vision of life and ideas of struggle for achieving it. Finally, it gave attitude and behaviour to be adopted for life objectives

(iv) Thus K-10 followed the path of life whose inspiration was from above-mentioned environment. In this process, he reached to such a position which not many people achieve, even after hard work.

4. EDUCATION AND CAREER

(i) The entire in-family and out-family environment of K-10 was characterised with complete illiteracy and ignorance. The dominant majority of the community was engaged in many petty occupations and children were not sent to school for education. It was in changing conditions that K-10 and his brothers got interested in getting in government school with parental consent and encouraggment. But, the level of education didn't cross over middle or matric stage. In practice, K-10 was lowly educated who could not attend the school regularly.

(ii) It seems clear that K-10 followed seriously the options of career in his life. After primary education, he started working in a cafeteria as a Tea-Boy who used to serve tea to customers and all other petty jobs there. He did it seriously, efficiently and without any guilty conscience. During his interaction with different people and assessing their roles, he got the idea of changing his occupational role. So, he did that and adopted different roles one after the other and reached to a position where not many people reach easily. In this long process, he adopted the positions and respective roles of cafeteria owner-manager, retailer-shopkeeper, bookseller, electronic items dealer-supplier and finally an investor in education and corporate sector.

5. OCCUPATIONAL ACTIVITIES

K-10 adopted different occupational roles, some of lower social status and some of upper social status. In every occupational career, he proved an honest, sincere, committed and hard worker and never ignored occupational interests and responsibilities. In this way, he as well as his superiors got benefited financially. The distinctive feature of his occupational career was his continuous positive and dynamic role at every stage. He maintained strictly standard work culture and work ethic in his office and impressed all others to follow same values and norms. Moreover, he was extremely polite and gentle in his business and personal dealings with all who interacted with him.

6. MOBILITY UNLIMITED

(i) K-10's occupational mobility was highest possible according to local worldly standards. He stood at the top among the friends and relatives. It was complete mobility, not only in occupation and economy but also in social, cultural and psychological fields. This gave him a new role which was unconventional, influential and had high reputation and mass popularity. In reality, his occupational change represents a phenomenon of 'mobility unlimited'. This role started from Tea Boy and concluded as Big Businessman which stood unprecedented and unparalleled.

(ii) In his entire occupational career, K-10 never thought about the lower positions. In this context, an important question arises why he didn't adopt same occupation which his brothers adopted and how he achieved highest degree of mobility? This may be explained partly by socio-psychological reasoning. But, the proper explanation came from the factors of 'divine role', 'God's intervention', and 'pre-determined destiny'. The famous sociologist of Iran, Dr. Ali Shariati characterised this phenomenon in terms of "accidents" and "exceptions" of history which were solely determined by the will of *Allah.* Thus K-10's mobility was achieved with the blessings and pleasure of God, as he believed. The nature and pattern of mobility performed by K-10 revealed in the following chart:

Nature of Mobility and Occupational Activities of K-10

S.No.	*Occupational role*	*Time schedule*	*Nature of activities*	*Mobility*	*Clients*
	Hotel Tea Boy	9.00 - 6.00	-serving tea	Up	-students andteachers
			-cleaning utensils		-employees
			-serving proprietors		-all others
	Retailor/ Shopkeeper	8.00 – 10.00	-selling all items -students, scholar	Up	-locality people -common people
	Supplier	9.00 – 6.00	-supplying items	Up	-HODs/HOIs
	Electronic Individuals	to offices. Org. -professors	-Administrators		
	Book-supplier and Publisher	8.00 – 8.00	-supply books to all deptts, teachers, students, etc.	Up	-Univ. teachers, students and officials
	Investor in	whole time	edu.l management	Up	-academicians, govt.
	Edu. Sector	and administration	officials and educators		

(iii) In the preceding background, K-10 developed relational association outside his family. Since he was deeply involved in the occupational duties, it gave rise to intense association with his clients. Thus he was associated with students, scholars, teachers, employees, professors, HODs, HOIs, governmental and non-governmental officials, administrators and so on. This was a new association for him and his family. In this environment, he felt satisfied and happy. He hardly felt upset or frustrated in his career.

7. MARRIAGE AND FAMILY

K-10 was married during his mid-career in his own kin group in an endogamous type. His wife belonged to same socio-economic background. He had relatively a simple marriage. Till that time, he was living in his parental joint family household, wherein his parents, married and unmarried brothers and their families were living. After the marriage, he added one more person to the already crowded house. Since they had purchased fresh land in the vicinity, he and his brothers constructed new houses separately. Subsequently, all of them shifted to their respective houses. In this way, the great joint family got divided into several nuclear family units. That represents the ideal pattern of transformation of joint into nuclear family in Kashmir. In this way, K-10 established his independent family unit with his wife and children with a different identity and distinct responsibility.

8. SOCIAL LIKES AND DISLIKES

After passing through different stages of life, K-10 was in a position to develop particular social likes and dislikes some of which are mentioned below:

Social Likes	*Social Dislikes*
- Purity and sacredness in thought	-social negligence and social exclusiveness
- A committed and hard working employ	-not maintaining social awareness
- Educated and civilised youth	-not caring about family and its dependent members
- Value based ideal life-pattern	-poverty in any form in society
- No injustice with any community	-inequality and discrimination in any form
- Self-sufficient and prosperous life	-trend of violence against women
- Decent family life	-dishonest and narrow-minded personality traits
- High regards to women and girls	-marriage with customary dowry and fun fare
- Taking care of one's family and comm.	-spoiled, undisciplined and uncivilised children

contd...

contd...

Social Likes	Social Dislikes
- Safeguarding occ. group interests	-deviant and delinquent youth
- Helping others in difficult times	-drug addiction among boys and girls
- Feeling other's pain and anguish	- unethical attitude and thinking bad about others
- Understanding others problems	-disrespect or dishonour others in any way
- Following values and norms	-thinking not about higher stages in life
- No antagonism with others	-no cordial relations with friends and relatives
- Feeling component part of family	-not respecting elders, teachers and women
- An efficient and honest officer	-arrogance of wealth
- Being gentle and polite with all	-uncivilised police official
- Thinking of higher positions and roles	-highly modernised lifestyle
- Processes of change and development	-disorganised and discredited family

9. CONCEPTS OF "I", "ME" AND "WE"

(i) K-10 had simplistic, humble and folk notion of I, Me and We. Though he had no professional and technical details, he could think on his own level. His raw ideas about these three identities were as follows. His notion of 'I' was in reality submissive, polite, gentle and far from arrogance or ego. 'I' for him stood for sustained and hard work in proper direction and with dedication. There must be no compromise or alternative to this ideal. 'I' stood for commitment and forward looking which help in achieving lifelong objective. 'I' also stood for accumulated sum of experience which guides for future expectations. Finally, 'I' for him was his 'individual one' and for the like-minded who compose one.

(ii) K-10 upheld the notion of 'me' in a way which he equated with community orientation, various roles which coincided in his life over a long period. Thus it was related to lifelong association which he developed consciously. Earlier, this association was limited but in the present situation, it was not limited. In the last, it will be unlimited in future. In material terms, the notion of 'me' could be related to social collectivities of community, group, friends, government officials, clients, suppliers and administrators.

(iii) K-10 had also same kind of notion about the concept of 'we'. In precise terms, it stood for :

- We, the economic class sufferers
- We, the members of occupational community
- We, the poorest of the poor
- We, the proponents and supporters of the poor

- We, the hard working, dedicated and honest workers
- We, the lowest status group
- We, the exploited and dominated lot
- We, the suffering lot in all fields. And
- We, the poor Kashmiris

10. IDEAS OF EQUALITY AND INEQUALITY

(i) At the ideational level, K-10 could not make difference between various concepts of social stratification. For him, inequality was inequality as the composite reality. It represented an unequal situation which reflected the consciousness on the part of poor people. He always talked about absolute equality between different human groups and opposed inequality in any form, in any pattern, in any factor and in any degree. This was mainly because of his religious and humanitarian orientation.

(ii) K-10 explained his views about inequality by saying that all humans were equal before God and no difference can be made on the basis of caste, class, culture, religion, region, race, language and so on. For him, religiosity in life meant equality of all men and women before God which reflected in daily prayers.

(iii) He viewed the ideal of equality by arguing that when God created human beings with equal status, why should we create inequality? If we do that, it will be against religion, nature and justice. He upheld the idea that priority and preference to human beings must be granted on the basis of their worldly acts. At the same time, those whose material acts suit family, community and society must be appreciated and rewarded.

11. RELIGIOUS LIFE

(i) K-10 stood as a strong believer in Islamic fundamentals. He also stood loyal to the folk religious practices for which family members and friends gave him regards. He visited regularly all shrines and believed in practices of magic, miracles and superstitions. He used to organise ceremonial functions on particular days in a week/month/year and prepared and distributed specially prepared foods and drinks among neighbours or at shrines.

(ii) K-10 showed no response towards the emerging trends of reformative and radical Islam, for which he showed no interest. But, he had close friendship with some KPs and he used to visit their families, especially on occasions. He held them in high regards and considered them highly intelligent and capable people. Though he was not aware about the concept of "composite culture" of Kashmir, but, in practice, he participated in many such related acts.

12. THE KASHMIR PROBLEM

The perception of the Kashmir problem upheld by K-10 may be characterised as simplistic and folk-oriented. The prominent ideas of this perception were as follows:

- Kashmir as an independent state, having its territory and independence
- Kashmir with the greatest economic benefits
- Kashmir with equal status to men and women
- Kashmir as a disputed territory and problem to be resolved
- Kashmir having people who have been denied basic human rights by India
- Kashmir will provide safety and security to all in sub-continent
- Kashmir and its people suffered because of wrong policy of Indian government
- Kashmir problem should be solved once for all

13. EXPERIENCE OF CONFLICT SITUATION

Since K-10's shop was a common place where selected few of the locality visited regularly for gossip, the police officers and other officials too used to come in the shop to participate in ongoing gossip over a cup of tea. As per this gossip, K-10 heard, the police and security forces were often involved in all offensive and inhuman acts during detention, arrests and interrogation at different police stations and interrogation centers. This has brutalised and dehumanised the entire police environment. It was revealed to those who were present there that, few days back, a person of grandfather's status was arrested on the charge of a petty theft. He was made fully naked infront of his son as the punishment. All of them felt sorrow and shameful.

14. FUTURE KASHMIR SOCIETY

K-10 had no specific but general ideas about future society of Kashmir, which essentially reflected common people's wishes and aspirations. Those ideas included the following:

- A society with no inequality, discrimination and exploitation
- A society with no corruption, unemployment and moral degeneration
- A society with freedom, liberty and democracy
- A society with respect to basic human rights, economic affluence and ethical standards

15. SOCIAL PROBLEMS IN KASHMIR

(i) *Elders' Problems:* K-10 was more concerned about the care and treatment which elders got on the part of youngsters inside as well as outside their homes. In some cases, it was just inhuman where children left their parents alone without any safety, security and care. Some of them were left here and children settled outside state and country. Others were living separately in the same city. All this, according to K-10, stood against basic principles of humanity and religion. These elders faced acute problems such as loneliness, dependence, health deterioration, safety-security, economic hardships and overall survival. K-10 felt seriously about the pathetic situation of elders in Kashmir. So, he felt an urgent need to arrest this social trend.

(ii) *Wastage of Wazwan:* K-10 felt that Kashmiri *wazwan* stood as most delicious menu served at the time of marriage and other occasions. It is based on 25-30 distinctive dishes, all based on meat. It is prepared delicately by professional cooks with their hard labour for the whole day. The problem arises when, after serving the dishes to the guests, they don't consume it fully. As a result, the left-over amount of *wazwan* gets waste and was usually thrown in some river or some lane. Thus *wazwam* gets completely wasted partly due to host's as well as guest's mistakes. K-10 strongly felt that this extravagance of *wazwan stood against* everybody, so must be stopped as early as possible.

K-11 LOWER CLASS GOVERNMENT EMPLOYEE

1. SOCIAL CONTEXT

(i) As was expected by the government and leaders of political parties of that time, famous land reforms and other radical measures in JK in 1952-53 didn't benefit all groups equally, especially the lower classes in rural areas. It was observed that while politically active and connected families got benefited, politically non-active and unconnected families were not benefited. In actuality, it was not equal distribution of land among landless or land according to family needs. Thus inequality on the basis of land ownership was not dismantled or disappeared. Some studies in this field have confirmed these propositions.

(ii) It clearly revealed in several studies that while some groups got more land and other groups got less than their needs. Other groups didn't get at all. In that changing agrarian situation, the lower classes and groups and occupational communities were altogether left out. These groups either got very less or no land at all. Practically, it was left to the ruling party functionaries who determined and distributed land in association with government representatives. They often benefited their related families and groups. In that situation, there emerged an 'orchardists elite' in some areas in the long run. It follows that many families and groups, which got more lands than their needs, converted their agricultural land into orchards and this gave them huge economic benefit in the following decades.

(iii) In that situation, free distribution of land among villagers had no desired or radical impact on the position of lower classes and groups. Their condition remained same as in pre-1953 days or worked in traditional occupations or worked as landless or shared workers in new peasants' lands. Some of them were compelled to migrate to Srinagar city and settled there. They worked there in their own occupations and some of them got petty government jobs. This helped him in improving their economic condition and lived comparatively a better life in the city.

(iv) In that situation, K-11 got attracted to migration and one day he left for the city with his relative and settled there.

2. IN-FAMILY SOCIALISATION

(i) K-11 was born in a rural family in a far-off village that represented poorest of the poor in that area. The economic standard of that family, and of occupational community at large, was near to zero, which meant that two meals per day was possible with difficulty. This type of poverty existed in the valley till 1947. Since poverty breeds poverty culture, this entire community of K-11 was engulfed in that culture.

(ii) Socially, this occupational community was considered 'undesirable'. While it stood at the lowest level of class/caste stratification in the village, the class/caste of it was related to their factors and activities in life. In social concerns, this community was discriminated, exploited, and depressed.

(iii)) Educationally, this community was totally illiterate. Children used to waste whole day in their homes or outside in meaningless and unproductive activities. This put them in undesirable socialisation that increased their deviation and backwardness. Neither its community members felt conscious about attainment of education nor others attempted to do this job. So, they remained illiterate, generation after generation.

(iv) Culturally, this community was considered degraded and looked down upon. The role and status of this community members were neglected and they were treated in-equally. No normal action took place between this community and rest of society. In this situation, they felt psychologically depressed and socially downtrodden.

(v) The community occupations were sweeping, shoe-repairs, folk singing and other such occupations which were considered in the broader society as 'unclean' and 'petty'. When they could not get regular job, they worked as labourers in their own and surrounding villages.

(vi) The community members usually lived in unhygienic conditions that affected their health and gave rise to chronic and dangerous diseases. Various high death rates were also observed among them.

(vii) Though Islam provided them equal role and status, that was not a practical reality in the village. Though members of this community could not be denied the entry into mosque to perform prayers, they were isolated and segregated socially-culturally in clear violation of Islamic orders. But, the situation of this community was altogether different which may be characterised as 'normal as others'. The members of this community in city were neither segregated nor discriminated. Their social, economic and cultural life was not bad relatively. Some of them lived in "special localities" established for them only in some areas and maintained their separate identity.

(vii) But, the situation of this community in urban areas was completely different with the SCs or *Harrijans* in India. It was because this had no scheduled legal status. They don't face life situation which SCs face in India. In actuality, they live in Kashmir like other lower class/caste groups They interact freely with other groups without any hesitation or limitation. With economic improvement, many of them have achieved social and cultural mobility in urban areas. Many of them have government jobs and that has enabled them to elevate their status. More important, the liberal and emancipator force of Islam has legalised and legitimised their equal status and role in society.

3. OUT-FAMILY ENVIRONMENT

(i) The out-family environment of K-11 was not different from in-family environment. Practically, it was the same environment in which relations with outside world were limited to families of same occupational community. This mutual interaction was intense and deep. Since they were socially segregated, their internal solidarity was prominent.

(ii) In that situation, the members of this community followed a pattern of association which may be characterised as 'segregated type of association'. Thus they followed a limited social world through life. However, the community members in urban areas were not so restrictive but had full, free and regular interaction with all classes and groups. In reality, they created a space for themselves through roles in towns and city.

4. EDUCATION AND CAREER

(i) K-11's family and community were completely illiterate, so was he. Earlier he could not go to school because there was neither any motivation nor any financial support for this objective. But, later on, his personal inclination and intelligence directed him to the school for formal education which he pursued till the matric stage despite tremendous financial problems. Only he knew the enormity of problems which he faced during the course of his formal education.

(ii) The distinctive traits of K-11 were seriousness, reasonableness, higher IQ and fast understanding, which contributed to his formal education in illiterate community. As was done by many of his community-family members, he migrated to the city after education, got a lower class government job and settled there. In the city, he was able to perform certain petty jobs of domestic nature which gave him further financial standing.

5. OCCUPATION AND MOBILITY

(i) In the city, K-11 came in contact with a top government officer who developed sympathy for him and engaged him in his office. The city story of K-11 started from that day. He served the officer in office and at home in a pure traditional manner. He performed all jobs seriously, silently and without any question. That led to his appreciation by all. At that time, his behaviour revealed dedication, submissiveness, politeness, order-following, commitment, work-fulfillment and sincerity. After some time, he became a permanent employee which enhanced his salary and thus strengthened his economic status further for the whole life. He used to do extra-work in morning, evening and on holidays, which increased his income further. Subsequently, he established a family unit in the city, first in rented accommodation and then in official accommodation. The nature of activities K-11 performed included the following:

Official Works

- All class iv works in the office
- Regular cleaning and dusting of furniture
- Serving tea to all employees in the office
- Serving guests on all occasions in the office
- Taking care of personal needs of officers and employees
- Photo-copying
- Distribution of the post inside and outside the office
- All clerical works
- Security jobs related to the office
- Opening and closing of the office
- Cleaning toilets, urinals, bath rooms and other places
- Bank transactions.

Other activities

- Work as a labourer in different fields
- Skilled and daily-wage worker
- Electric mechanic
- Motor mechanic
- Horticultural works in orchards
- Agricultural farming
- Vegetable growing construction works
- Garden development.

(ii) How K-11 got formal education from primary to Matric standard stood as a mystery, which can be explained by role of social-psychological factors. The role of divine factor cannot be ruled out. Despite these explanations, the objective fact stood that K-11 was able to get education in totally illiterate community. This education was the minimum level required for getting a government job. Thus his educational qualification enabled him to get a job which stabilised his personal and family life. The continuity of extra work strengthened further his economic condition. In this way, the mobility pattern which he followed can be explained in terms mentioned below:

Education > Employment > Higher Status > mobility

This type of mobility was uncommon in his village community. It was unmatched, unconventional, unprecedented, and of the highest degree. It could not be achieved by many in his community.

6. MARRIAGE AND FAMILY

(i) After getting a job in the city, K-11 married a girl from his village occupational community and both established a nuclear family unit. The wife gave him emotional and material support in the processes of psychic mobility, social progress in addition to improvement in economic conditions. She was exposed to urban environment and proved a helping hand to K-11.

(ii) In the post-marital life, both of them were able to change their backward status into a normal lifestyle. This crudely reflected in their food habits, sending children to school, and wearing decent clothes. Though K-11 was highly conscious, they could not provide high or quality education to his children, he sent them for the primary education. In fact, this pattern of sending children to school for early education was common as it qualified them for getting a government job and subsequently get a suitable match in marriage.

(iii) The improvement in economic and educational conditions affected K-11's family unit in the city. It represented extremely different kind of family from that of village family. After some time, K-11 got his new house constructed in the village with the help of bank loan. This was a descent house in the whole community. He shifted his family to the village and lived a single life in the city and visited village family unit weekly.

7. SOCIAL LIKES AND DISLIKES

After going through tough conditions of life, K-11 developed hard choices of social likes and dislikes which include the following:

Social Likes	*Social Dislikes*
- A person of high education and good job	-usual political and educational disturbances
- Absolute social and economic equality	-corruption and nepotism
- Children to be maintained at early age	-belonging to lower class and caste
- Youth must get suitable jobs in time	-bossism and issuing orders every time
- Family with limited number of members	-arrogant, corrupt and rude official
- Planned and limited expenditure in family	-exploitation of labour and women
- Conflict free and peaceful society	-no formal education for children
- Following of values and norms seriously	-dependence on others in social matters
- No violation of moral codes	-interference in other's private life
- No extreme freedom to youth in society	-a corrupt police officer
- Self-confidence and self- initiation in life	-children not under parents/teachers control
- Constant interest in social work	-conscious abuse of family-school authority
- Maintenance of work ethic and work culture	-stopping women from working outside home
- Serious criticism of communal politics	-inhuman attitude and behaviour in life
- Satisfactory work at home and outside	-always dominating and humiliating others
- Always ready for facing difficulties	-incompetent and untrained teacher
- Always treating others well	-losing patience with lower-status people
- Showing hospitality to all guests	-not taking care of elders at home
- Socially polite, humble and submissive	-harassment of juniors in office
- Decent standard of life for everybody	-poverty and poverty culture

8. CONCEPTS OF "I", "ME" AND "WE"

(i) It was observed that K-11's ideas of 'I', 'me' and 'we' were determined by his psychological traits. He had developed some elementary views in this regard. He felt that 'I' generally represented all that which came under areas from submissiveness to surrender. In actuality, it conveyed the pattern of life in which there seemed no scope for sensitivity, innovation and creation in following orders. For him, 'I' stood for a person who was always kept down by the dominating, suppressive and exploitative forces for maintaining their economic and social superiority. In brief, 'I' represented a person who was always *ghulam.*

(ii) For K-11, 'me' represented a life of antagonism between ruler and ruled and between inferior and superior. This concept explained human life in terms of whole human beings composed of haves and have nots. 'Me' also remembered the idea of my family, my community and my conditions. It also reminded the process of change which changes this situation completely.

(iii) In comparison to two preceding concepts, K-11 had some clarity on the concept of 'we'. It referred to his family and group which have suffered at the hands of other groups through out history and have never protested against the unjust treatment. He believed that nobody from his group will rise in revolt. This pessimistic view of 'we' stood as common culture in his community. Though religion gave them equal position, they followed neither religious nor secular ideology to establish an honourable community.

9. IDEAS OF EQUALITY AND INEQUALITY

K-11 was not clear about formal concepts of equality and inequality. He had some elementary notions. But, he stood as a firm believer of the existing fact that inequality in some form conveyed the reality. Whether this inequality will be dismantled and replaced, he was not sure. According to him, this inequality existed in its folk form in the village. Some main types of inequality were as mentioned below:

- Inequality between various classes and groups
- Inequality between various castes and sub-castes
- Inequality between men and women members of society
- Inequality between regions and religions
- Inequality between various races and cultures and
- Inequality between nations of the world.

10. RELIGIOUS LIFE

(i) K-11 stood as a practical religious person than in theoretical-ideological terms. He had not studied basic religious sources of Islam, neither he was trained by folk religious preachers. So, he lacked basic knowledge of religious fundamentals, but that didn't stop him from following religious practices. In fact, this can be generalised about the whole village community, especially among their women, in which there was no formal and necessary arrangement of religious teaching.

(ii) K-11's practical religiosity reflected in his views at large. He didn't give importance to doctrinal ideas, principles, legal codes, ideological views and so on. He felt committed to folk practices of religion. So, he regularly visited shrines and prayed there. Earlier, he was not praying regularly but later on he prayed regularly, especially *jumma* prayers. It was mainly because of pressure of making good social image.

(iii) He didn't involve himself in other folk practices for financial expenditure. But, he believed in magic, superstitions and so on. His family celebrated all Islamic festivals and other usual festivals. In actuality, his religious life stood full of rituals and ceremonies which he celebrated with special preparations.

11. EXPERIENCE OF CONFLICT SITUATION

(i) K-11 was very conscious about serious economic implications of two-decade long conflict situation in the Kashmir valley. It was because he was not able to go out and work to earn more for his family on all days of strikes and civil-curfews and undeclared official curfews. In that situation, many of his colleagues either fled back to village or migrated to outside JK to work as labourers.

(ii) K-11 used to convey his experiences about economic impact of strikes and curfews on particular class of daily labourers from rural and urban areas in Kashmir. This period proved an 'economic disaster' for all of them. Living in those disturbed conditions, they could not earn for their families meals. As per his information, while some of them had to borrow loans, some of them had to approach NGOs for help. Others were compelled to sell their domestic items. Moreover, when they could not earn in summer season, they could not save any amount for harsh winter days ahead.

12. FUTURE KASHMIR SOCIETY

K-11 had developed some raw and folk notions about future society in Kashmir. These were solely determined by his early life experiences in the village which he has not forgotten. These notions seem rough ideas but revealed greater social realities related to the village life in Kashmir. He always presented ideas about future village society in negative ways which included the following:

- A village society with no poverty which he had experienced there
- A village society with no segregated and discriminated social life
- A village community with no social apathy towards problems of the village.
- A village with no political confrontration and conflict.
- A village society with no caste and sub-caste system.
- A village society where nobody remains illiterate and ignorant.
- A village society where nobody remains unemployed.
- A village where nobody waste time.
- A village where no molestation could take place.
- A village where everybody remains busy in purposeful activity.
- A village where every urban facility was available.
- A village where there will be no crime and drug addiction.

13. SOCIAL PROBLEMS IN KASHMIR

(i) *Poverty in villages: As* per K-11's perception, the first basic problem in Kashmiri villages was poverty which still stood in large scale and is deep rooted. He explained that poverty in terms of extreme conditions in which villagers were not able to get even basic needs fulfilled.

Another point he revealed was that poverty in all possibilities gave birth to poverty culture that had dangerous implications in two fields. First, poverty led to deterioration in health standards which had undesirable impact on population growth. That ultimately led to high death rates among poor and ignorant villagers. Second, it made individual and group life extremely backward in all fields. Thus poverty culture emerged as dominant trait of village which still continues.

K-11 pointed towards an important aspect of poverty-alleviation programes and schemes sponsored by the government. He felt that these efforts will not succeed in eradicating poverty mainly because of prevalent corruption. Most of the amount was grabbed by government officials, engineers, employees and others. He felt that this situation had turned pathetic.

(ii) *Illiteracy and Ignorance in villages:* K-11 considered illiteracy and ignorance as grave problems in Kashmiri villages, especially among lower classes and castes. In many cases, poverty gave rise to these problems. He had personally experienced these problems.

K-11 wanted eradication of these problems which hurt the processes of change and progress in the villages. But, in practice, the governmental efforts are with a lot of corruption by government officials and others involved. So, he wanted non-governrnental efforts in this field.

K-11 was specifically concerned with these problems in relation to lower classes and castes in villages. He emphasised special and repeated efforts must be carried out to attract, mobilize and involve these lower sections of village society for that success of concerned progrommes.

K-12 THE KASHMIRI YOUTH: RURAL AND URBAN

1. SOCIAL CONTEXT

(i) The renowned 'land to the tiller' reform had not benefited all groups equally in the villages in Kashmir. As a result, it increased inequality by owning disproportionate amount of land. K-12 family got sufficient amount of land which was more than their needs. So, this family, like other families, converted some agricultural land into orchards. With this ongoing development, these middle status families got attracted to modern education introduced in the state from 1952 and, subsequently, got government jobs under liberal policy of successive governments.

(ii) In this changing social dynamics, the middle status families in villages got benefited economically and educationally and later on socially and culturally. The concomitant effect was felt in the adoption of urban lifestyle which happened in the process of migration from villages to city. After migrating to the city, they settled here permanently and adopted urban traits like dresses, foods, engagements, culture, language, habits and so on. They sent their children to English medium schools inside or outside JK. They constructed houses and established new colonies in the city peripheries. Some of them married city girls and lived in their houses after matri-local marriage. Religiously, they were still conservative and never behaved irreligiously. Some of them were strong followers of religious practices. As a result, many among them were attracted to the reformist and radical trends/ movements of Islam. In practice, they attempted to adopt both, modernity and tradition, in a balanced way which for them were not conflictual but accommodative. They represented KMs' new generation after 1947 which was educated, economically well-off, culturally exposed, socially stable and were modern, innovative, positive and career-oriented. K-12 was the product of this generation of KMs.

2. IN-FAMILY SOCIALISATION

(i) K-12 family was originally rural based but shifted to city later on and lived there permanently. The patrilineal family in rural area had not the highest status. But, the grant of land in 1952 made it 'above average' family in the rural context. Since its members got modern education and employment, it gave the family new position, new social standing and new social image. While in the agrarian hierarchy, it was one of lowest families before land distribution, but experienced change, progress and upward mobility after that. It converted some land into apple orchards because of three reasons. First, all members of family got education and government jobs. Second, they were not interested in working on agricultural lands. Third, most of these members migrated or were in the process of migration to the city and settle there.

(ii) The family in the village had hardly any attraction for K-12, so its effect on him was minimum. The other factor for lesser effect of family unit was K-12's education in a boarding school outside Kashmir whose socialisation effect was more dominant. Moreover, the features of modern lifestyle, learnt by K-12 outside, had no match with other factors. But, at the same time, he maintained contact with that family unit mainly because of taking care of immoveable property and resolve matters related to share-cropping with labourers.

(iii) In direct comparison to this family unit, the city family of K-12 was socially more relevant because this unit stood educationally forward, economically prosperous, professionally career-oriented, culturally-lingual exposed and modern in lifestyle. It was radically different from the rural unit. So, this unit had naturally lesser effect on the life of K-12 who enjoyed urban facilities.

3. OUT-FAMILY ENVIROONMENT

(i) After family units in rural and urban areas, the next major sociological impact on K-12 came from out-family environment represented by near-distant relatives, neighbours, ffs and colleagues. K-12's relatives were in rural as well as urban areas and they were more impressed with the latter and had their impact. In fact, those relatives, who had migrated to the city and settled there, were in close contact and in regular interaction. They often provided help and cooperation to each other. In a way, they formed a 'solidarity group' for their mutual help in getting admission for children in prestigious schools, career building, getting employment, social recognition and so on. So, K-12 had every reason to get affected by this group. He developed intimacy with most of them, visited their houses and developed close relations.

(ii) The group of neighbours were families of rural origin and some of them were also his relatives. The neighbours families formed a 'fraternity' for reciprocal help among their members and in the process had reciprocal impact, on K-12, especially in his career-making. In fact, he was selective in accepting this impact. He accepted only that impact which was beneficial to his career, preferable in life and desirable in society.

(iii) FFs of K-12 belonged to rural and urban areas and they accepted the impact of the latter. Those who belonged to villages originally belonged to his family status and were educated, employed, migrated, exposed and well-off. They formed a close solidarity group for social, economic, educational, cultural and other purposes. This group played certain positive social functions in the city context related to needs in different fields at different times.

(iv) The other group of K-12 FFs was of original city dwellers who too had features of solidarity, cohesiveness, identity, interaction, reciprocal relationship and mutual help. At times, this group came in competition or conflict with villagers' group. However, both groups were interlocked in constant interaction which resulted, in some cases, inter-group marriages, i.e. marriage between boys and girls of both areas. In this broader social dynamics, educated-employed village boys married educated-employed girls of city and the reverse also took place. This happened in a situation of marriage market in Kashmir which had marriage feature of the availability of

(a) highly educated and employed eligible village grooms;

(b) lower educated and business engaged city grooms;

(c) highly educated and employed-unemployed city brides; and

(d) lower educated and unemployed village brides.

In this situation, the preferred marriage was between 'a' and 'c' and between 'b' and 'c'. In fact, that pattern of marriage was one of the common types of marriage in Kashmir after significant social changes at the end of 1947. It may be interesting to note here that K-12 parents were married on this pattern, though they belonged to one endogamous group of relatives.

(v) K-12 faced both groups of FFs and applied his practical knowledge and operational strategy and developed positive social place and image among both groups. This behaviour may be explained partly because of K-12's different training in school and partly because of liberal ideology and personality. Though he maintained relations with both groups, he accepted the influence of city group more seriously.

4. EDUCATION AND CAREER

(i) The entire primary and middle level education of K-12 was carried out in a boarding school outside Kashmir, established by the central government for wards of its employees. The school was fully modern and a reputed one in education and training. It trained its students for all fields of life, academic as well as non-academic. With all these positive qualities of life, K-12 came back to Kashmir and got admitted in a local college for graduation which he qualified in three years. Subsequently, he joined the university for post graduation in social sciences, whose completion led to pursuance of the highest degree of research, i.e. Ph.D. This he completed in a record time.

(ii) Since K-12 was dynamic initiator and worker, he started working in other fields such as journalism and small book business, in addition to academics. He used to spend 14-18 hours a day for activities in these fields. He got a teaching job in a university which he worked for a few years. His performance in this field proved satisfactory and impressive. At the same time, he became a successful businessman due to his practical intelligence, wider experience, mass social contact, hard work and scientific orientation.

(iii) The third field of his activity was life-long career in government job which started in a gazetted position. His competitive spirit, social contacts and hard work enabled him to reach at number 2 position in his departmental hierarchy in shortest possible time. This official career stood most crucial for him and he used this position to expand his social network and his popularity.

(iv) However, he abandoned the work in journalism solely because he had neither patience nor time for that job. In place of that work, he adopted the field which may be given the name of 'social marketing'. He considered the social situation like a 'social market' in which he was always involved in buying and selling 'social commodities'. In this context, 'social buying' referred to continuous help which he provided to others, for whose confidence he always tried and usually succeeded. So, in this way, he earned good will and positive image. The 'social selling' in this context meant the behaviour which he adopted during the course of helping others. In this way, he made purposeful and productive use of his distinctive faculties. In these 'social transactions', he used to get 'social commission' and 'social discount'. Thus social ties too benefited him in the material sense.

5. OCCUPATION, ASSOCIATION AND MOBILITY

(i) K-12 had very busy schedule of occupational and other activities, which reflected in the following set of activities:

-Morning	-Domestic works	-Child care	-House care
	-shopping	-office works	
	-visit to neighbours, relatives and others		
-Day time	-official works	-journalist work	-academic works
	-business works	-hospitality	-visits to relatives, friends and
	-home works	-receiving guests	
-Evening	-home works	-shopping from market	-extra curricular
	-child care	-domestic works	-health care
	-hospitality	-social work	-business work
	-visits to relatives, neighbours and friends		-receiving guests

(ii) As revealed, K-12 spent most of his time in government office and business. Rest of his time was devoted to social networking. He was always on move from one to other individuals. While government service occupation was started by his parents, business occupation was his own innovation. These occupations determined his association pattern. It was basically the occupational links which created 'association links' with various individuals and groups. Comparatively speaking, K-12 had largest social network of associations which included the following individuals:

-politicians	-government officers and bureaucrats	-administrators
-journalists	-researchers	-writers
-intelligentsia	-technocrats	-businessmen
-teachers	-shopkeepers	-doctors and engineers
-females	-scholars	-academicians
-lawyers	-students	-outsiders

His association links were so large that even his telephone and engagement diaries were always over booked. He received hundreds of calls daily. It seems interesting to note that despite detailed schedule of daily activities, he stabilised and maintained all his social contacts through visiting, telephone, writing and conveying verbally. He used all these contacts for professional, social and economic objectives related to him and his business.

(iii) Taking into consideration previous occupations, agriculture and service, K-12 adopted a new occupation of business and continued the old. This represented the basic occupational shift and mobility followed by other types of upward mobility. These gave a new status and function to him, his family and provided strong economic basis for next generations. Though this process was tough and full of problems, K-12's dedication, commitment, hard work, sincerity and scientific bent of mind made it possible in two decades time to emerge as a successful man. In this way, he and his family achieved upward mobility in absolute terms.

6. MARRIAGE AND FAMILY

(i) K-12 was married with a girl in the near kin-group. Though many relatives were not satisfied with this match, this endogamous and neo-local type of marriage was carried out. While K-12's family was educationally and economically ahead of his wife's family, the latter had a working job which helped in the economic stability of new family unit established by the couple. This marriage proved a step forward for the bride.

(ii) After the marriage, the wife of K-12 joined the joint family household in which lived his parents and unmarried sisters. She stayed there for some time and later on established her own independent nuclear family household in a rented accommodation. Both husband and wife with little children live in this small family unit. They have constructed a new house in the periphery of city and intended to shift there shortly.

7. SOCIAL LIKES AND DISLIKES

In the light of experiences in his hard life, he developed clear likes and dislikes in social life, some of which are mentioned below:

Social Likes	*Social Dislikes*
- An honest and confidential officer	-a stratified social order
- Achieving status through struggle	-caste and class character system ideology
- A person who started from zero	-discrimination against lower classes/castes
- Deep commitment to values and norms	-exploitation of workers, labourers and artisans
- No rituals, customs and other practices	-agrarian inequality
- Educational and cultural progress	-underdeveloped conditions of life
- All regards to elders and parents	-social apathy and social pathology
- Religious beliefs and practices in ideal form	-highly anti-social attitude and behaviour
- Gender equality with suitable roles	-no morality and no ethics in social behaviour
- Tough life experience and training	-denial of gender justice
- Full cultural exposure a must for all	-social exclusiveness and discrimination
- Highest degree of social networking	-crime and drug addiction among youth
- Close relations with influential persons	-dowry and customs in marriage
- To care more about objectives and goals	-obsolete social customs and traditions
- To help others in times of need	-complex social problems
- Upholding ones cultural identity	-an unintelligible person and his traits
- Positive social relations with neighbours	-not a well-informed person
- Keeping in touch with friends and relatives	-social deviance and crime among youth
- Adopting Kashmiri culture completely	-immoral and illegal practices
- Social change and development for all	-pre-marital and extra-marital sex

8. CONCEPTS OF "I", "ME" AND "WE"

(i) K-12 stood conscious of all three socio-psychological concepts. In fact, he was lesser conscious about 'I' in comparison to 'me'. For him, 'I' stood for struggle, activities, and experiences in the past. Again, 'I' passed through three stages of evolution. First, when social efforts of the individual started. Second, stability and continuity in these efforts. Third, realisation of fruits of difficulties. In this way, the concept of 'I' matured with life and its struggle. As per K-12, 'I' favored those who favour life. Thus it favors those who dream, expect and aspire for higher ideals of life. It stood must for conscious individuals, groups, communities and societies.

(ii) K-12 felt more seriously about 'me' which stood as a higher stage of 'I'. In this context, 'me' represented the present life, struggle, efforts, culture, social system and economic organisation. At another level, it referred to family, clan, community, association, organisation and other social institutions. K-12 felt that 'me' reflected a particular society, religion, nation, region, culture, language, ethnicity and so on.

(iii) K-12 upheld the view that 'we' represented the collective whole of society at different levels and in different fields. So, it was essentially to 'we' Kashmiriis, Indians, Pakistanis, nationalists, regionalists and internationalists and so on. It also pointed towards 'we' the workers, labourers, and artisans in the Kashmir valley. Finally, 'we' referred to particular and specified social and academic categories, such as sociologists, anthropologists, social scientists, economists and geographers. At last, it pointed towards the oppressed, dominated, humiliated, exploited, murdered, killed, tortured, injured and disabled.

9. IDEAS OF EQUALITY AND INEQUALITY

(i) K-12 was deeply aware about concepts of equality and inequality. He also knew about their origin: class in agricultural-industrial society, caste in pan-Indian society, and gender in global society. Since he had social science background, he knew chief characteristics of these concepts. He consciously opposed these concepts because of their impact of exploitation, discrimination and dehumanisation.

(ii) Caste discriminated individuals and groups on the basis of birth, hereditary status, occupation, *dharma and karma* and purity and pollution. On the other hand, class discrimination was carried out on the basis of economic position, social status and political power. Other contributory factors were cultural, educational and historical. Similarly, the concept of gender discrimination was based on existing notions of inequality suggested by tradition and religion.

(iii) In the same way, caste divided the society into upper, lower and out-castes which had their respective status. This naturally led to exploitation of lower and out-castes by upper castes. On the other hand, in the name of superior economic position, some groups exploited the inferior economic position which established the exploitative systems of feudalism and capitalism. Finally, gender exploitation took place on the basis of ideas of inferior status of women in comparison to men.

(iv) Dehumanisation in society took place in the case of caste when human beings were treated just on the basis of birth and occupation. Similarly, the concept of class treated human beings as mere material categories that automatically gave rise to non-human considerations. This situation led to its dehumanisation. Finally, gender was also considered as cultural or religious category. This characterisation of gender led to its dehumanisation.

10. GLOBAL SOCIAL ORDER

(i) K-12 opined that GSO represented a multi-national institutional order and organisational arrangement at the global level. The representative character of this order stood of primary importance. So, all nationalities, ethnicities and continents must be its composite parts. In order to prove purposeful and meaningful global order, it must have three specific features:

(II) First, the structure, composition and functions of GSO must not reflect any shade of discrimination against any human group or sub-group. Rather, it must demolish all basis of inequality established on different basis and factors. It must reflect real human global character. Second, GSO must not become a tool of exploitation of one or other group or force. Third, GSO must reflect humanitarian character in all its functioning. All these objectives must be followed systematically and with policy and planned framework.

11. THE IDEAL CHARACTER

(i) K-12 had no ideal leader, at least in Kashmir. However, he thought in terms of ideal characters, not one but many, in the Kashmiri society. The ideal character of K-12 was represented by a retired academician, who was still active in his field. His commitment and sincerity to academics stood unparalleled as he always remained busy in one or other activity of academics. In addition to producing many generations of students and scholars, he was published at national and international level. In this way, he developed excellent reputation in the field of specialisation. K-12 was impressed with this academic character because of particular considerations mentioned below:

- his scientific, innovative and realistic orientation in teaching and research;
- following seriously life-long academic career with sincerity and dedication by him;
- identifying and analysing main/major social concerns in his academic framework;
- carrying out systematically and consistently all serious academic efforts by maintaining standards of work ethic; and
- continuous supervision and guidance by him to generations of Kashmiri scholars and students even at the advanced stage of life.

12. RELIGIOUS LIFE

(i) K-12 family was influenced by the reformist trend of Islam in Kashmir. Later on, he too accepted this impact despite his irreligious impact of outside schooling. Thus his family understood Islam rationally through the doctrinal tradition. It meant the total understanding of Islam from its original and authentic sources, i.e. *Quran, Haidth and Shariah* and other relevant literature. Since K-12 and his family members studied these written sources, they developed basic knowledge about fundamentals, concepts, beliefs, practices, principles and so on. So, while his belief was sound and rational, his practices followed the pattern of beliefs.

(ii) In this way, K-12 followed scriptural Islam, i.e. he followed what was written in scriptures. He didn't follow those which were not mentioned in scriptures. But, he didn't offend or antagonize anybody in this regard. Despite irreligious schooling and broader social network, he attempted to follow a genuine Islamic religious life.

(iii) K-12 had no attraction for folk religious practices as he considered them as 'not necessary' and 'extra'. Consequently, he never visited shrines, never celebrated particular days, and never believed in magic, superstitions and *peer-mureedi.*

(iv) Though K-12 understood trends of reformative and radical Islam and came near to some of their ideologues, he was never convinced to join these movements. He always maintained a distance and difference with both. That also suited his social and professional life.

(v) His relations with Hindus, especially KPs, were as cordial as with Muslims. Most of his colleagues in office and business belonged to other religious categories, but maintained friendly relationship with all. In some cases, they loved and respected him more than Muslims. He was more near the KPs too inside and outside Kashmir and used to visit them often. They figured prominently in his social network. He specially took care of those KPs who opted to stay back in Kashmir during early 1990s at the time of their mass migration. He visited them often and fulfilled many of their needs.

13. THE KASHMIR PROBLEM

(i) K-12 observed that the Kashmir problem was the creation of partition of 1947 when Kashmiris were denied their right to self-determination to decide about their political future and same continued till date. The U.N. and Indian leaders promised for this right but forgot in course of time. Every Prime Minister of India revived that promise but never fulfilled.

(ii) K-12 also observed that Kashmiri people continued their struggle for this right of freedom, but have not been successful so far. Many times, they rose in peaceful uprisings like those in 1931, 1953, 1962 and 2010. They also made armed revolts in 1973 and 1990. But, both these types of struggle have not yielded any result.

(iii) The Kashmir problem, according to K-12, stood where it was in 1947. India needs to adopt a political, realistic and human approach towards this problem for its final resolution.

14. SOCIAL PROBLEMS IN KASHMIR

(i) *Women's Suitable Role in Society:* K-12 believed in gender equality absolutely. No law, custom and tradition must go against it. Similarly, violence against women should be opposed. In order to make the equality of women a social reality, social legislation as well as practical social efforts are required. At the same time, he felt in terms of the biological and social suitability of women's role in broader society. What he meant was that women's unlimited role outside family has led to many undesirable effects such as harassment, eve-teasing, torture, crime, molestation, etc.

In this situation, there seems a clear social desirability of selecting special areas of activity for women outside family. This will suit her biological make-up also. In order to make women's role more effective, productive and purposeful in Kashmir, K-12 felt the following fields as ideal working fields for women:

- Medicine and health care
- Nursing
- Teaching and research
- Scientific research
- Academics
- Broadcasting and telecasting
- Hospitality areas
- Mass media
- IT areas
- Managerial areas.

(ii) *Heavy amount of Dowry:* This problem emerged in the Kashmiri society recently when the girl's family demanded heavy amount of *Mahr* to be paid by the boy before solemnising marriage at *Nikaah.*_This amount had usually gone above the economic standard of the groom. If the bride's side remained adamant on this heavy amount, the groom felt compelled to opt for alternative in which he paid some amount of *mehr* and the rest was deferred for future payment, which was hardly paid later on.

K-12 felt seriously about this practise and found it socially and religiously undesirable. So, this practise must be discontinued as early as possible. The *mahr* must be demanded and paid on time according to the economic standard of the boy/groom.

K-13 THE KASHMIRI SCIENTIST

1. SOCIAL CONTEXT

(i) During medieval times when Kashmir was ruled by alien rulers, Kashmiris in general, both Muslims and Hindus, were compelled to migrate outside Kashmir mainly for political reasons. As a result of suppressive policies of alien regimes, a significant number of Kashmiri families experienced out-migration at that time. While KPs migrated and settled in north and central Indian cities and towns, the KMs settled in north Indian urban areas. They established residential colonies in several areas in united India. Pandit Jawaharlal Nehru and Dr. Mohammad Iqbal represented two distinctive Kashmiris of those migrant communities outside Kashmir. This process of migration continued till freedom movement in Kashmir started in 1931.

(ii) But, another type of migration started afterwards among KPs which was broader and deeper in effect. In the earlier decades of 20th century, many KPs started migrating from Kashmir for education and employment purposes and in anticipation to the political situation in JK. But, after 1947, a significant trend of out-migration among KPs was observed for education and employment purposes. This could also be explained in terms of downfall of *Maharaja* and emergence of Kashmiri nationalists under progressive political leadership. After some decades, especially after implementing successfully famous reforms, KPs had to face tough competition from newly-educated local Muslims under liberal policy of the government. In fact, a new situation emerged in which more local Muslims than local Pandits applied for limited number of government jobs and the former got more share than that of the latter.

(iii) In that economic and political environment, many KPs felt about their job security as their traditional share was threatened. So, they felt safe by sending their children to outside Kashmir for higher education and for getting jobs there. This explained the phenomenon of the presence of KPs in all cities of India. This trend of migration got boost in the second half of 20th century because of KMs' anti-Indian uprisings in 1931, 1953, and 1963. In anticipation of these political sentiments in Kashmir, many KPs migrated and established their colonies in Jammu, Chandigarh, Delhi and other north Indian cities.

(iv) In this socio-political environment, K-13 left Kashmir for higher studies and research in the scientific field in which he showed excellence. After completing his research courses, he got a job there and subsequently settled there with his family. In this way, the son of mother Kashmir got settled outside Kashmir for ever.

2. IN-FAMILY SOCIALISATION

(i) K-13's family belonged originally to a town in the valley. Due to education and employment, it migrated to the city permanently and settled there. But, some of the folk features of the cultural life of this family had not changed completely. This family environment, which had tremendous influence on the personality growth of K-13, had three features First, all male members of this family were officers of higher cadre and females used to take care of domestic affairs. The male KPs were serving in all government, non-government and semi-government sectors. They had developed partly official, aristocratic and bureaucratic culture in the family life. Second, certain traditions of knowledge and education were fully maintained with all social support from the family. Thus all male members of family developed huge material and spiritual knowledge and formal education in terms of highest education. Third, culturally, this family was known for religious tolerance, politeness, generosity, helpfulness and other such features. They proved extremely gentle and were considered *sharifu nafes* in multi-religious locality. They always benefited their neighbours and helped them in getting government jobs.

(ii) This attitude and behaviour reflected in the personality of K-13 who was considered as embodiment of *sharafat* among his neighbours. He represented supreme moral ideals of gentleness, solidarity, submissiveness, kindness and so on. At the same time, he proved intelligent, intellectual, scientific, creative and innovative. The cumulative impact of these family features has influenced K-13 totally and he developed 'humble personality' liked by everybody. He was popular inside and outside family and there was none who could oppose him.

3. OUT-FAMILY ENVIRONMENT

(i) This wider environment was composed of and connected with his relatives, neighbours, FFs and colleagues and others. While most of his relatives lived in urban areas after migrating from the town, some of them still lived in rural areas. All these relatives of K-13 belonged to same economic, social and cultural status. They were serving in government and non-government offices at higher positions. They had established close and reciprocal relations through usual visits and exchange of gifts. It was in this type of social atmosphere that all members including K-13 got affected attitudes and behaviour.

(ii) The neighbourhood of K-13 was of multi-religious character and Muslims, Hindus, Pandits, Sikhs and others lived together from historical times. K-13 family's relations with all of them were friendly, cordial and *baradarana*. They had shared the joys and sorrows of life and were sharing positives and negatives of life together. They celebrated festivals and other ceremonial occasions jointly. K-12 family always helped their neighbours in fulfilling their material and non-material needs. More important, this family, despite high education and higher economic standard, shared all cultural practices of Kashmir within and outside family, especially dresses, food-habits, lifestyle, ritual practices, attitudes, traditional behaviour, language and so on. In terms of social estimation, this family stood as one of the respected families in the locality.

(ii) K-13 family had a lot of FFs who were their former or present colleagues in their offices and they belonged to different religions, cultures, regions, languages and ethnicities. That interaction and intimacy with aliens gave his family the experience of multi-culturalism. Some of these features were also adopted by K-13.

(iiii) Others who visited K-13 family included VIPs, social notables, dignitaries, different professionals, and high-level government officials. They too had certain impact on the psyche and interaction pattern of K-13.

(iv) All this social environment outside family gave K-13 some characteristic traits related to his life, particularly future career. He adopted common scientific-creative orientation, national-global cultural values and social norms; preference for Kashmiri culture in lifestyle; making habit of reading books, doing research and other academic works; positive future image and scientific bent of mind; and finally, most humble attitude and behaviour which became his life treasure.

4. EDUCATION AND CAREER

(i) K-13 had his entire primary and secondary education in the locality government school. He proved an exceptional student throughout this period, he scored high in every stage. At his school age, he was less interested in extra-academic activities and used to do science-oriented things. In fact, he started developing scientific bent of mind from that stage.

(ii) K-13 joined local university and completed graduation and post-graduation in sciences there. Subsequently, his interest and family encouragement led him to apply for research in a prestigious institution of the country. Due to top merit at all stages and his impressive performance in interview, he was selected in that institution, which gave him everything in life, especially status of a noted scientist. After doing some necessary courses, he carried out some serious research which impressed everybody there. Even at this stage, his research was valued in the country and, later on, this was quoted in the country and abroad. This reputation as a noted scientist enabled him to get a permanent academic job in that famous institution. Thus he stayed there in official accommodation and got settled there permanently.

5. OCCUPATION

(i) As K-13 was academic-oriented from his younger stage of life, he succeeded in getting a suitable job, which not many people get easily. So, he adopted this academic job as lifelong occupation. Though it represented a different occupation and lifestyle, his family appreciated it. In fact, this profession suited his life as he had developed fully research bent of mind. Thus what he aspired for in life, he got that in abundance.

(ii) K-13 started formal academic career in a reputed institution of India. His academic activities included teaching, research, guidance, publications and academic administration. His research supervision proved so effective and excellent that he earned high reputation in the country. The earlier image of K-13 as a serious researcher increased tremendously. Now, his scientific research reflected national and global standards and it could be compared with any research piece in the world. This image and reputation was possible only because of his dedicated, continuous and quality research work that clearly revealed in his daily schedule of research work and other academic activities which are enlisted below:

Time duration	*Place*	*Academic activities-research*
-08.00-01.00	-Labortary -Department -Office -seminars-conferences	-Teaching -Research supervision-guidance -meetings
-01.00-02.00	-residence -rest and entertainment	-lunch
-02.00-04.00	-Lab. -Department -office -visits – courtesy and academic -seminars-conferences	-Teaching -Research supervision/guidance -meetings
-04.00-04.30	-canteen	-tea break and gossip
-04.30-07.30	-lab. -department	-research supervision/guidance -self-research
-07.30-08.30	-residence -dinner	-refreshment
-08.30-10.00	-lab.	-self research

(ii) After years of continued research, he got recognition as a reputed scientist in his areas of specialisation. At that stage, he was referred, quoted and consulted by researchers and scholars in the whole country. That gave him the elevated status of 'I' and 'Me' and in the process he emerged as a noted scientist. By continuous and rigorous efforts in the scientific field, he attained the reputation of serious scientific researcher at international level too. At that time, he also got into contact with individuals and groups of eminent scientists and started getting invitations from international agencies, organisations, institutions and other bodies for consultation, perceptions, and advice in different scientific matters. That also opened his doors for repeated participation in international conferences, seminars and workshops.

(iii) At that time, K-13 was at the height of his career. He used to visit all important and developed countries of the world and used to go to the U.S. every year on the invitation of different departments, institutes, agencies and organisations there. His institution was also liberal in granting him leave for this purpose. He remained busy in academic research activities even after retirement and continued scientific research in government and non-government institutions, organisations and agencies. In this way, he lived a full professional life.

6. ASSOCIATTION AND MOBILITY

(i) K-13's association pattern was determined mainly by his professional activities. So, in his life, he got exposed to and had deep experience of the academics throughout world. At national and international level, he developed intimate relations with government officials of highest order, academicians, bureaucrats-administrators, professionals, experts and so on. He also developed close association with academic individuals and groups in India and abroad. Finally, he developed permanent association with eminent individuals, families, groups and circles related to his profession.

(ii) In the above occupational and associational background, K-13 experienced highest degree of social mobility. Though he belonged to high social status and economically prosperous family, he reached to the highest possible heights. It was the longest jump in the career among his contemporaries and also fulfilled his lifelong ambition. In this way, he experienced absolute personal and social mobility.

7. MARRIAGE AND FAMILY

(i) K-13 was married in his own community with a girl of conscious choice of his own in an exogamous type of marriage, as most of KPs were marrying in those days. His in-laws' family, though well educated and well employed, belonged to lower economic and social position. The marriage was solemnized in a traditional manner as was the wish of his parents. Subsequently, he started family life in a nuclear family unit established in his official residence outside Kashmir. He didn't close his contact with parental family in Jammu and Srinagar and used to visit them during vacations. Since his wife provided a satisfactory company, he had peaceful and happy marital life. In fact, this family had harmonious relations after marriage. They had children who were brought up and socialised in traditional as well as modern cultures. At the fag end of his career, K-13 shifted to his grand house constructed recently. Later on, his children left for education to the U.S. and got settled there. Here in their grand house, husband and wife lived a lonely life.

8. SOCIAL LIKES AND DISLIKES

After his long experience in the academic profession, K-13 developed some particular social likes and dislikes, some of which are mentioned below:

Social Likes	*Social Dislikes*
- Extremely gentle personality	-a person with dual character
- Intelligence, excellence and innovation	-corruption, exploitation and discrimination
- Dedication to one's profession	-gender inequality and violence against women
- Full care of parents and elders	-not allowing democratic system to function
- Not disturbing others uselessly in work	-exploitation of the working class
- Living a peaceful and prosperous life	-in-equal social, economic and political system
- Not forgetting one's past	-oppression against lower castes and SCs
- No conflict, no domination and no tussle	-treating education as a material commodity
- No sexual harassment and exploitation	-reform-oriented political participation
- Academic credibility with honesty	-moral-ethical degeneration
- Serious teaching and research supervision	-having no scientific temper
- Following values and norms sincerely	-living like a dishonest man
- Religion purely a personal affair	-communal disharmony and disturbance
- Ideal modern education for all	-use of religion for personal ends
- Good child upbringing and socialisation	-corrupt academic practices
- Friends with trust and confidence	-extreme form of westernisation
- Liberal and progressive ideology in life	-revivalist politics in India
- A competent and trained teacher	-wasting whole day in useless activities
- Professional ethics and standards	-sub-standard scientific research
- Work culture maintenance	-illiterate and ignorant society

9. CONCEPTS OF "I", "ME" AND "WE"

(i) K-13 had no strong sense of 'I' but, later on, got its strong version. Two of its dimensions were revealing which were 'in-home I' and 'out-home I'. The main features of these features are as follows:

Features of In-home 'I'	*Features of out-family 'I'*
- *Gentleness*	*-bold and assertive*
- Submissiveness	-academic leadership
- Seriousness	-innovation and creation
- Responsiveness	-well defined expertise
- Positive and open-mindedness	-distinctive research findings
- Compromising attitude	-distinctive research supervision
- Just, fair and honest in approach	-innovative methods of teaching
- Religious beliefs	-competition but not conflict
- Emotional involvement	-logical-rational arguments

As per the calculation of K-13, his 'I' represented two extremes which got mixed in between life. At time 1, he adopted one set of 'I' qualities and at time 2, he adopted another type of 'I' qualities. These qualities balanced each other and provided a humanistic dimension to this professional work.

(ii) K-13 was always conscious about 'me'. It reminded him of his entire past, near and distant. Some times, he equated it to 'my'. In reality, the concept of 'me' was evolved slowly over whole period of life with his successful performance in life career at every stage and in all fields. It finally reached to its mature stage. In this thematic conference, 'me' referred to :

- My work	-my struggle	-my efforts
- My services	-my reputation	-my contacts
- My orientation	-my expertise	-my research work
- My disciplined life		

He felt that 'me' remained alive even upto later stage of life in comparison with 'I'.

(iii) K-13 had also strong notion of 'we' and was careful about it. This developed in evolutionary way and was strengthened by progress stage by stage. The first stage of 'we' was referred to as follows:

- We – the whole of family
- We – the whole of community
- We – the whole of society
- We – the whole of academic group
- We - the whole of middle class

The second evolutionary stage of the concept of 'we' was revealed in competition :

So, he used to think

- We, the academicians, professionals and experts
- We, the Kashmiris, Indians and internationalists
- We, the businessmen, bureaucrats and administrators

The third stage of 'we', according to K-13, was of different identities. It reflected ideally in a situation in which he held different identity cards for different groups of people, different times and different places. Every situation had its separate causes and consequences. But, 'we' represented all situations and at all levels.

10. IDEAS OF EQUALITY AND INEQUALITY

(i) K-13 had not specifically studied theoretical concepts of equality and inequality but had developed some particular ideas in this regard. First of all, he was a strong supporter of equality among all individuals and groups. Though he was conscious of the fact that absolute equality stood a distant dream, he talked in terms of equality according to needs and resources of each. Conditions for equal competition must be created in order to provide equal opportunity for change and mobility.

(ii) K-13 was basically against the basic system of caste founded on 4-layer *varnas*. Though it seemed an undesirable unit of stratification, it stood undesirable due to its functional relevance. Similarly, the unit of class proved unavoidable due to its crucial role in change and development. So, the caste and class inequality must be made effectless, if not dismantled. That seemed the practical solution of inequality in India.

11. GLOBAL SOCIAL ORDER

K-13 upheld the view that ideal GSO in future must be by states and societies of the whole world in the scientific framework. He characterised it as scientific future social order with distinctive features, some of which are mentioned below:

- Scientific orientation – complete science based policy, programs and their implementation.
- Scientific character - overall scientific attitude and behaviour in the evolution/emergence of future social order.
- Scientific character in representation - global representation for all sub-global groups, communities and societies and sub-global agencies and organisations.
- Scientific reality to multiplicity of
  - regions, sub-continents and continents' :
    - Religions and cultures,
    - Ethnicities and races,
    - Classes, communities and groups;
- Scientific features in organisational functioning to pursue long-term and short-term goals scientifically:
    - Scientific criticism in terms of - overall functioning of the global order, especially its implications on regional and continental identities.

12. RELIGIOUS LIFE

(i) Though all social traits of religious life, i.e. truthfulness, fraud-less and corruptionless life, high standards of morality, following values and norms seriously, no gender discrimination and gender violence, no disturbance to others, no social suppression, maintaining a public and desirable image, and so on, reflected in his attitudes and behaviour pattern, K-13 considered himself an irreligious person. It was partly because of his extreme commitment to scientific research and values, and partly because of the progressive non-religious environment in his academic institution. He upheld the view that religion was meant for human beings at their individual level. So, it must not be utilised for economic, political and social objectives, which has already the undesirable consequences in the past.

(ii) K-13 was a Hindu by belief, but it was a half belief. Since he had not got rational and scientific explanation of many basic beliefs and ideas of ideal Hindu religion, he could hardly believe in them. He had in mind the ideas like Hindu gods as mythical characters or caste justification. He was not against the institution of religion but against its exploitation by some sacred groups for their monetary interests.

(iii) In the preceding framework, though K-13 was not an ideal religious person, he followed all social-human traits in life for which he was known in his entire group and locality.

14. **FUTURE KASHMIR SOCIETY**

(i) K-13 was a scientist and an idealist as well. He wished to create an ideal society in a land which he left long back. His dream about future society in Kashmir revolved around following attitudes and behavioural traits:

- higher degree of literacy and education;
- higher degree of gender equality;
- higher degree of – humanistic orientation;
- tolerance of religions and cultures;
- composite cultural traditions;
- scientific orientation among students, particularly girl students;
- scientific temper in life;
- professional, technical and IT education;
- exposure to and understanding with other communities;
- jobs for all youngsters.

In reality, K-13 wanted the Kashmiri way of life in future with

- Social life oriented towards scientific principles in totality
- Social life oriented towards scientific temper and related ethics
- Adoption of scientific ideas and ideals for better life conditions
- Adoption of scientific methods resolving various problems.

14. SOCIAL PROBLEMS IN KASHMIR

(i) *Illiteracy:* In general, K-13 argued that literacy elevates an individual from sub-human to human status. At the same time, it emancipates society from extreme backwardness to extreme forwardness in all fields of life. In totality, it takes human society from darkness to light. He observed that illiteracy became the sole stumbling bloc in the processes of change and development.

He viewed the literacy situation in Kashmir with concern. As per his estimates, though a significant portion of population has attained literacy, but still a dominant portion of population, especially in rural areas, were still illiterate. There were multiple factors responsible for this situation. He was of the view that in case this huge illiteracy was not reduced considerably, no purposeful and scientific development could take place.

In order to eradicate illiteracy in Kashmir, local government needed a clear policy document, program framework and implementation strategy. Moreover, it needed dedication and commitment to achieve the desired goals within a timeframe. In this regard, the state government must seek the help of international agencies and organisations.

(ii) *Lack of Scientific Temper:* The scientific temper referred to the totality of attitudes and behaviour on the part of general society in accordance with scientific principles of man, nature, universe and whole human world. K-13 was of the opinion that scientific temper stood as basic feature of modern society and civilisation. So, it seemed a pre-requisite for long-term process of change and progress.

He was of the view that Kashmiris in general lacked the scientific temper which had effected their entire life adversely. The younger generation stood main victim of scientific apathy, while it stood necessary for radical change in it.

K-13 was of the opinion that the civil society has more responsibility than the state in creating awareness and adoption of science education by majority of students, especially girl students, at secondary and higher stages. It can also take it in domestic sphere where this objective can be made a reality through sustained training and socialisation. The out-family environment can also be oriented towards this objective. K-13 hoped that the Kashmiri society will certainly adopt many features of scientific temper at individual and collective levels in the 21st century.

K-14 THE POLITICAL IDEOLOGUE/POLITICIAN

1. SOCIAL-POLITICAL CONTEXT

(i) Political sociologists divided society in two major political groups of people on the criteria of possession of political power. This dichotamous characterisation of society identified the classes of rulers and ruled. The society was further divided particularly on the basis of factors such as population and its dynamics. In actuality, this led to political division of people on their urban, rural and hilly characteristics of inhabitance. In this context, we may explain this phenomenon in terms of role of centre and periphery which emerged in the background of in-equal type of development. While people in urban areas developed central character in political developments mainly due to their proximity to the corridors of power, people in rural areas could not perform in the same way as they stay away from official areas. The people in hilly areas generally remained isolated and hardly developed political contact of significance and importance. In other words, distance of areas and inhabitance of people affected nature of centrality from centre of power. Since people in urban areas were within a short range of centre of politics, they got fully participated and benefited. Since people in rural areas were not in such a position, they were participatory and more benefited. The people in hilly areas were not connected with the centre of politics in urban areas, they got least benefited.

(ii) This situation provided opportunity for all political parties to use one population group or the other or one population group against another for petty political interests, especially at the time of elections. These parties identified particular issues and problems of these groups and manipulated entire political process. Though there existed different levels of economic development in different areas, political leaders dominated the situation in such a way that they apparently pleaded for every group's support at the time of elections. The state of JK, particularly the Kashmir valley, experienced this kind of politics right from 1947. The central government continuously utilised different population groups or groups against each other for its political interest, i.e. forceful integration of the state with India. It led to a situation that gave rise to antagonistic relationship between urban and rural groups on the one hand and between rural, urban and hilly groups on the other.

(iii) In the preceding political environment, people in urban areas, especially the city, played a dominant role in all political developments right from 1931, when the first organised political movement of KMs started in Kashmir. They were at the forefront of all political uprisings in 1931, 1953, 1962, 1973, 1989 and 2010. Since they lived in city, they showed first political reaction to all political developments. Consequently, they suffered in material terms than any population group. Thus they played anti-establishment role throughout post-1947 period. The political parties pitched rural and hilly areas people against them, in which they were successful through the politics of rural versus urban versus hilly areas.

(iv) The rural population too played decisive political role due to their numerical strength, especially after 1953 land reforms which benefited them a lot. With this impact under the leadership of SMA and NC, they participated more in electoral politics in comparison to other population groups. At that time the SMA was alive, they always played pro-establishment role in politics and got benefited in education, employment and other fields. This situation was efficiently exploited by their political elite and it pitched them against urban and hilly people under the 'rural-urban-hilly politics'. However, after SMA's death, political role of rural people turned opposite mainly due to radical religious impact in Kashmir. This new development proved anti-establishment in character and it was also pitched against urban and hilly people by interested elite groups.

(v) But, the hilly people, commonly known as *Gujjars or Pahadis,* played a political role which suited to their existing life conditions which were miserable and pathetic. While basic life facilities like water, electricity, health care and literacy were not available, even 'two meals a day' was difficult for many people. As per economic standards, it was of 'under-developed character'. So, these people were always dependent on the state's help. This made them pro-establishment throughout post-1947 period. In that situation, political parties and their political elite too convinced them about 'discriminatory treatment'. In this way, they were pitched against urban and rural people. This situation was also exploited seriously by the central government and always patronised them and their political activities. It was in that background all their educated people preferred government service and local administration, while their intellectuals got safe positions in all regional and national political parties. This also explains their top positions in all parties.

(vi) In this political context, three different political roles were played by different population groups in Kashmir. These were :

- Always anti-establishment role by urban people.
- Some times anti-establishment and some times pro-establishment roles by rural people.
- Always pro-establishment role by hilly people.

In this political environment, while the first group suffered extremely, the latter two groups were benefited comparatively. K-14 belonged to that elite category of people in hilly areas who belonged to a humble background but emerged as one of the prominent political ideologue and politician.

2. IN-FAMILY SOCIALISATION

(i) K-14 family was folk and pre-modern joint family unit having many members of patri-lineal descent. This big family in a hilly village had some distinction because of economic, religious and cultural reasons. This family had a huge house and other ancestral property in the village. It had the reputation of having a member who lived the lifestyle of a *darwesh.* Then the family was exposed to other cultures due to his followers' attendance every day. In reality, he had not established *pir-muridi* but a folk institution of *darwesh.* In this institution, he adopted a particular type of religious-ritual type of behaviour after remaining aloof from this world and its material comforts. He lived only for ideals related to his religious life without any return. People from all places and all backgrounds used to visit him for getting his blessings. The material things and eatables which they used to take to his house, were kept in the common kitchen and were served to other guests there. Nothing was left unconsumed. This was the real essence of the institution of *darwesh.*

(ii) K-14 came from this family background and he had ingrained some traits of this folk environment. That is why he was referred by some as *darwesh sifat.* At this stage, he accepted other religious impacts, which emphasised the study of basic and written sources of Islam, *Quran* and *Hadith,* for its real understanding. This doctrine-oriented and scripture based approach to Islam represented a new trend different from traditional folk approach. This happened immediately after he was exposed to the external family exposure. Thus his personality was shaped with both old and new religious orientations and forces.

3. OUT-FAMILY ENVIRONMENT

(i) K-14 had considerable impact of out-family environment. Since he was a son of *darwesh,* he could have been the same. That would have been the easiest choice in his life. But, he consciously opted for difficult type of occupation and career. How it happened – can be explained partly by socio-psychological factors and partly by destiny predetermined by Almighty *Allah* in advance, as explained by Dr. Ali Shariati, famous sociologist of Iran.

(ii) Since his image outside family was of a man from a noble family, he got preferential treatment there. People liked him and showered affection on him. But, at the same time, he didn't accept everything which came in his life. He was choosy and selective. This trait continued in his life throughout and he proved choosy about individuals, groups, occupation, career, and everything in life. He was selective even in the field of politics, a rare trait in present-day politics.

(iii) However, after coming out of family influence, he accepted impact of some individuals, groups and institutions which, in the long run, shaped his mature personality and determined his political career. They included his relatives, teachers, neighbours, personal-family friends, party colleagues and political ideologues and institutions/situations of backwardness, exploitation and petty political culture. This practical experience of existing realities in Kashmir gave rise to his particular attitude and behaviour in politics.

(iv) His relatives belonged to lower socio-economic status, so, K-14 had learned about reality of poverty and poverty culture. He accepted no effect from them, but gave them regards, respect, visited them and helped them too. So, their effect on K-14 was minimum, rather his impact on them was maximum.

(v) K-14 was highly impressed by some teachers who were intelligent, intellectual, committed, sincere, regular and punctual. Throughout his life, he paid them high regards and accepted them as ideal human beings. He saved their interests always and never allowed them to suffer in life. While he accepted their impact completely during his formative years, he remained committed to these ideals even in his later life.

(vi) The neighbours of K-14 were people of his region, religion, culture, language and historical background. He was socialised among them in traditions, customs, conventions, folkways, rituals, values, norms, ceremonies and other folk practices. More important, his religious attitude and behaviour were determined by his actions and interactions in his neighbourhood.

(vii) The personal and ffs of K-14 changed from time to time. They included top elite family members, they also belonged to humble socio-economic background. While some of them were modernised and highly professional individuals, others were tradition-bound individuals. Their variety ranged from modernity to conservatism, rich and poor, rural and urban, young and old, men and women, highly and lowly educated and social notables. Most of them visited his official or personal residence. He felt inspired with their company and was exposed to their intellectual and cultural tendencies. He proved a helping hand to all of them before, during and after his official positions. However, he was selective in family friendships. He never encouraged consumer society people, richest elite families, extremely westernised males and females and so on.

(viii) Then came the influence of party colleagues in K-14 life at the mature stage, i.e., during and after the practical political life. He was constantly exposed to new political ideas and ideologies through interaction. He got introduced to actual world of politics, its dynamics, problems, powers, recruitment, limitations and its role as an instrument of change and progress. The new political experience gave him the political wisdom and perspective of complex political career which he adopted after a lot of assessment. At this stage, through wider interaction with political circles, he was also exposed to extreme forms of political dissent, conflict and so on. But, he was attracted to certain values in the processes of political socialisation, culture and modernisation. This was considered as most prominent aspect of his political personality.

(ix) Finally, K-14 was exposed to political ideologues and functionaries in the party and outside, which shaped his particular views about various problems and issues. His understanding about political problems stood unmatched. One could disagree with him but could not ignore his ideas. So, his political views were adopted in most of policy and program documents of his party. There was hardly any party document which could have been passed without his approval.

4. EDUCATION AND CAREER

(i) K-14's elementary religious training took place at his home. But, for modern elementary and primary education, he had to travel to nearby village. For secondary education too, he had to go to nearby town. In this way, he completed graduation in his own areas and then shifted to the city where he got enrolled for law course in local university. He was not much excited on this development mainly due to earlier urban exposure. During his college-university days, K-14 was a serious and sensitive student and had strong likes and dislikes. He had strong observation sense and eye. Among academic themes, he was interested more in Kashmir political developments and complex political topics like political socialisation-culture and participation. He continued studies even after becoming MLA from his area.

(ii) K-14 started his career as a party worker and political activist. He maintained several positions in the party hierarchy. In fact, he used to be popular in the party due to his organisational skills and capabilities. He attracted to his party many intelligent-intellectual youth. He was always interested in making party a cadre-based organisation after proper training in its ideology and programs. Subsequently, he contested for MLA from his area and got elected. This electoral success conveyed his personal popularity. As the legislator, he emerged as a serious, careful, alert and positive politician who was always interested in introducing new ideas in drafting and discussions on draft legislations. In actuality, he stood as the architect of many important legislations in the state assembly.

(iii) At this time, K-14 came in contact with SMA who was impressed by his ideas, attitude and behaviour. So, he took him in his party and his ministry where he performed miraculously. So, he gained Sheikh Saheb's confidence who used to entrust him some of his own work. In this way, his integrity and talent paid him at the younger age in life. Afterwards, he became important person in the government as well as in the party. After SMA's demise, he could not be ignored and was among a few old guards in the new cabinet. Because of his personal capabilities, he emerged as one of the influential ministers in the government and party. Hardly any decision was taken without his consent. Bureaucrats and administrators were fearful of him due to his critical approach, objective assessment and honest dealing. He was so assertive that his advice could hardly be ignored in the government. At that particular time, his government was toppled by the central government, but he remained committed to his leader and party. After many years, he was fielded for the election of MP (*Rajya Sabha)* which he contested and won.

5. OCCUPATION, ASSOCIATION AND MOBILITY

(i) K-14 opted for political career and this occupation was different from his ancestral occupation. He consciously adopted it after careful thinking and put his life to a 'risky career'. But, his intellectual and value based behaviour made him successful repeatedly and he reached to the highest level of political power in the state. Not many individuals in his generation made such a jump in political career. From a common man in a hilly village with no political background, he achieved highest degree of upward mobility possible in this material world.

(ii) As K-14 changed his occupation and positions, he adopted and changed the network of association. One status position led to another position and one type of association was followed by another type of association. Going through positional changes, he developed a wider association at all levels, in all fields and with all people. While he had associations with all classes, castes, communities, sects and groups, he was cordial with all rural-urban-hilly people, rich and poor, religious and irreligious, radicals and conservatives, young and old, men and women, and so on. He had also developed close association and mass contact with all those who were related to social, cultural, religious, economic, psychological, literary and other fields. But, in this type of association, he always remained selective in government, policy and his personal and social life. He had liking for certain categories of people who included 'zero starters', humble background individuals, open-minded people, moral charactered, religio-oriented, tolerant, multi-cultural, learned, academic and so on.

(iii) Thus K-14 had multi-faceted selected association. He often invited them and was invited by them too. At times, he felt comfortable among these categories of people than among political colleagues, leaders and activists. Some times, K-14 felt 'odd man out' in this political company. In reality, he wanted to follow certain values in life which was not possible in the prevailing political context in Kashmir.

(iv) K-14 experienced highest possible degree of mobility. How was this possible? It can be partly explained by socio-psychological factors. But, complete explanation can be carried out by theory of 'eternal destiny' which is determined in advance by Almighty *Allah*. In other words, this happened mainly because it stood "God willing". K-14 was a firm believer in that explanation and he never felt arrogant and always pleaded with humbleness and dignity. He respected every person, that is why he was respected by all.

(v) It seems important to note here that he used the highest mobility for overall benefit of his family, community and society. At the family level, he educated and employed all near-distant relatives from paternal, maternal and in-laws sides. As a result, they improved their educational and economic conditions. At the community level, he helped every individual and family which came in his contact. In addition to education and employment, he provided them every financial and non-financial help to emancipate in life. He made it certain that all his neighbours and acquaintances in his native area are fully benefited. At the societal level, he helped all those who came in his contact irrespective of their affiliation to politics, ideology and religion. He was all out for their help and saw it personally that their works were carried out. He also used to contact concerned officers himself in this regard.

7. PERSONALITY TYPE

(i) In the existing political environment, K-14 developed a personality which can be characterised as a distinctive type with particular attitudinal and behavioural features. This type of personality represented a sum of activities and experiences in life in general society and in politics in particular. The characteristic traits of his personality type were as follows:

- K-14 developed a simple and folk-type as well as modern lifestyle, which were utilised at different occasions and were not in conflict but in consonance.
- He never developed any feeling or idea of inequality, inferiority-superiority, and stratification. He never differentiated friends and acquaintances on the criteria of any inequality.
- During his entire career, he had the habit of all out help to deserving people, even at the cost of his personal risk.
- K-14 had developed some super-human qualities which included not having too many clothes, not possessing too much wealth, and not using many luxuries despite their availability in abundance. Despite being a leader of higher position, he always dressed moderately. His family budget used to be within the limits of his limited income. This seems unbelievable in these days.
- He had the higher degree of intellect and innovation power. He was most well read legislator, minister and party leader. He used to be well aware about all national and international political developments. So, he registered a marked impact in the legislative assembly proceedings, governments files and party documents. His views could never be ignored by party leadership. Even senior bureaucrats were conscious

about his level of intelligence and they used to do homework before presenting pleading their cases with him.

- K-14 was a man of ideas and ideals with radical humanist orientation. His political life in legislative assembly, government, party and home reflected his humanist perspective.
- He never played a dual role in politics and remained committed to his principles. No power could change his mind in this regard.
- He was highly literate in religious knowledge. He was well aware of all schools of religious thought, traditional and modern religious ideas and concepts, major trends and movements and basic-authentic sources of Islam. He had also developed comparative religious understanding.
- K-14 was a *darwesh sifat* man and wanted to reach to the expected standards of behaviour.
- He was unique in his hobbies. Unlike common politicians of present generation, he had following set of daily hobbies:
- book reading - meetings with political ideologues, intelligentsia;
- newspaper-magazine reading intellectuals, academicians, experts, notables, etc.
- Television-Radio news - BBC radio and television and VOA radio.
- K-14 was found always a busy person. He must not have wasted a minute in his life. It can be gauged from his daily schedule of official and political activities which follows:

- MAJOR POLITICAL ACTIVITIES

- Meetings with academicians, experts, bureaucrats and officials.

Meetings with national and international thinkers and scholars.

.... political ideologues, leaders and workers.

.... intelligentsia and intellectuals.

.... opposition political leaders and workers.

Participation in conferences, seminars and workshops and other gatherings.

- MAJOR OFFICIAL ACTIVITIES

- Meetings with top bureaucrats, administrators and high officials;

.... professionals, technocrats and experts.

.... personal and official staff.

Attending regular cabinet meetings.

.... Ministry and departmental meetings.

.... Cabinet committee and sub-committee meetings.

Other official and non-official meetings outside secretariat.

8. MARRIAGE AND FAMILY

(i) k-14 got married with a woman from a family of equal economic and social status in same hilly area. This was endogamous and patri-local type of marriage, in which the endogamous circle composed of patri-kin group members. This marriage provided a perfect match and helped in his psychic and social mobility.

(ii) K-14 remained a component part of huge joint family in the village even after marriage and his wife settled in his household. But, he had to establish a nuclear family unit in city because of his usual work there. This gave unusual features to nuclear and joint families. It followed that though structure of joint family could not be saved completely, joint family features like close relationship-association, usual visits and taking care of others could not be discontinued. His family in city used to get near and dear relatives and other guests from the village. In that situation, while continuous contact with village family could not be disrupted, relations with other families remained intact.

(iii) It was observed that the family culture of K-14 was characterised with tradition as well as modernity. It followed that the family in city adopted modern way of life in areas of education, training, mass media, cultural practices, role and status. But, at the same time, it maintained traditional values, norms, ideals and old way of life.

9. SOCIAL LIKES AND DISLIKES

After going through different political situations, K-14 developed particular choices for social likes and dislikes, which he always held and wanted others to adopt, some of which are as follows:

Social Likes	*Social Dislikes*
- Social equality and social justice	-a corrupt and dishonest person
- A sober religious personality	-a person preaching communal disharmony
- An honest, efficient and committed officer	-economic underdevelopment of any class
- Minimum economic benefits to all	-educational and technological backwardness
- Emergence of elite families	-political antagonism and armed conflict
- An ethical and moral social order	-politics of defection and deception
- Self integrity and self confidence	-the incompetent and uncultured teacher
- Necessary study of books and literature	-arrogance of wealth and heredity

contd...

contd...

Social Likes	*Social Dislikes*
- Regular reading of daily newspapers	-the feudal system and its features
- Public standing and moral character	-discrimination in any form and on any name
- A well informed person on global	-denial of political and civil rights
- An ideal teacher	-capitalist life style
- The charismatic leader	-extreme cultural modernisation
- Simple and timely marriage	-deviant attitudes and behaviour of youth
- Study of relevant books by politicians	-corruption and nepotism in any form
- Helping all needy and deserving people	-juvenile injustice
- Gender equality and gender justice	-equal agrarian structure in villages
- Ideas of conflict resolution	-inefficient and corrupt officer
- Political consensus and political culture	-political differences lead to political conflict
- Role of political party in democracy	-violence against women
- Political socialisation in values and norms	-principle of no salary without work
- Social ethics and work culture	- social evils and social pathology

10. CONCEPTS OF "I", "ME" AND "WE"

(i) K-14 had a strong sense of 'I' because he had constructed it. 'I', in his view, represented stages of evolution which improves and enlarges it as per social conditions of individual personality. These stages and their features are as follows:

I Stage	*II Stage*	*III Stage*
• Less mature	> Mature	> More mature
• Childhood	> Youth	> Elder
• Less political	> Normal political	> More political
• Local identity	> Social identity	> S-P-C identity
• Uni-dimensional	> Bi-dimensional	> Multi-dimensional

(ii) The concept of 'we' was also strong in the personality of K-14. It rises fully after the third stage of 'I' matures. Thus it matures through different stages whose details follow:

I stage

- It starts with consciousness of local status, identity, culture, family, and kinship.
- It remains limited to close interactions within closed social situations.

II stage

- It leads to further but limited social exposure related to enhanced status, improved version of identity, encountering other cultures.
- It broaden its social arena/limits through wider interactions and exposure.

III stage

- It emerges as a particular political concept and social-political ideal to be followed in life.
- It provides thematic clarity and theoretical justification of the concept.
- It gets exploited for self and social purposes.

Finally, it leads to the consciousness of particular region, religion and culture as a distinct political phenomenon. This may force an individual to enter into a zone of conflict which may be utilised by vested interests for political purposes.

(iii) K-14 felt that it stood as idealised form of 'me'. In volatile situation such as in Kashmir, it emphasised and focused on differences rather than on similarities. In this way, it created a strong consciousness about different cultural regions in a broader political unit. People argued in terms of 'we' the people in similarity and 'we' the people in dissimilarity. In that situation, while the state stressed for integration, cohesion and stability of the collective 'we', the civil societies opted for opposite directions for the individualistic 'we'. This led to the political crisis of identity at ideational and practical levels. Thus, according to K-14, the concept of 'we ' was explained in terms of 'the Kashmiris in whole of J&K', 'we' the *Dogras* in Jammu, and Ladakhis in Ladakh.

11. IDEAS OF EQUALITY AND INEQUALITY

(i) Since K-14 was a well read person, he was aware fully about actual realities related to equality and inequality in society. He had read a lot about these concepts and their social implications in Indian society. He specifically highlighted the following features of these concepts:

(a) Class: It referred to inequality between lords and serfs during feudal period and between capitalists and workers in capitalist society in Marxian framework. He upheld that it also indicated inequality between upper, middle and lower classes in American and European societies. He also felt that it included division between rulers and ruled and between political elites and masses in political sociologists' framework.

(b) Caste: It referred to inherent and absolute inequality between various castes among Hindus in India, some of which were considered upper castes and some lower castes. Still some were considered as 'out-castes' or SCs or *Harijjans*. All these in-equal classes were legitimised by *Dharma*.

(c) Gender: It meant social inequality between men and women in society, based on biological notion of physical dissimilarity in the human body framework.

(ii) Against all these concepts of inequality, K-14 introduced some local concepts for explaining his desirable pattern of equality. These included the concepts of *insaaf, barabri and insaniyet*. According to him, the principles based on these concepts will certainly contribute to determination and evolution of egalitarian framework by treating human beings primarily as human beings. The contribution of *tawheed*-oriented religion to the system of equality stood considerable. However, non-religious material factors play decisive role.

12. THE IDEAL LEADER

(i) The towering personality of Kashmir in its modern history, SMA, was the sole ideal leader of K-14 who was his fan and follower. K-14 had three specific reasons for this choice. First, he felt that SMA represented the top most political leader of Kashmir known throughout the world and comparable to any Indian sub-continental political leader. It was due to the struggle under his leadership against feudal rule and representation of political aspirations of people that he became a charismatic leader in Kashmir. During his lifetime, he could not be challenged either by his traditionalist rivals or his modern political opponents. Thus he and his party was able to dismantle the *dogra* rule in JK. K-14 sincerely felt that Kashmir had not produced any such leader before.

(ii) Second, K-14 considered SMA as the architect of *naya Kashmir program*. By introducing and implementing land reforms and other revolutionary measures such as abolition of usury system and forced labour and free education, congenial conditions were created for radical transformation in rural society and agrarian sector. These reforms and measures destroyed the structural and functional basis of centuries old poverty and feudal system and elevated the Kashmiri society to a dignified position. These efforts led to unparalleled, unmatched and organised struggle against unjust and unequal political system and social order.

(iii) K-14 felt (and many may disagree with him) that SMA was a man of political ideas and ideals. But, he could realize or implement these. He felt that SMA had idealistic approach, realistic orientation and pragmatic perspective in his lifelong politics. According to K-14, as an idealist, SMA upheld ideas and ideals of complete independence of Kashmir right from 1931, a political unit which will have all political features of a sovereign state. But, as a realist, he felt that post-1972 situation, in which Pakistan was divided into two separate countries, that goal could not be realised. So, he made a compromise which led to Indira-Sheikh accord of 1974. Finally, as a *pragmatist*, he entered into political and constitutional relationship with the union of India under article 370 which guaranteed 'special status' to JK.

(iv) But, at the same time, K-14 opined that SMA never forgot betrayal of the government of India repeatedly and its leaders, particularly Jawaharlal Nehru and Indira Gandhi. His autobiography, *Aateshe Chinar* is full of such stories.

13. RELIGIOUS LIFE

(i) K-14's personality represented primarily a religious type. But, religious dimension never meant expulsion of logic, rationality, scientific and material considerations. In fact, he explained religion in traditional as well as modern terms. He found no dichotomy between the two.

(ii) He believed strongly in all fundamentals of Islam and tried to make practical reality. Despite heavy public rush, he managed to pray during the day. It was observed that he followed most of the order of Islam for day-to-day life. He was considered most gentle, most humble and most hospitable person.

(iii) In his religious behaviour, K-14 followed reformative trend of Islam which he considered was 'pure' form of Islam without local distortion and adulteration. He was impressed by this trend because it retained originality and primary character of Islam; it emphasised on scriptural-doctrinal approach of understanding Islam; it was not associated with the state; and its practices and behaviour was simple and not related to any ritual. So, despite having village origin, K-14 performed no saint-worship, never visited shrines, and never celebrated any particular day in a week/month/year and was not involved in any other folk religious practice.

(iv) At the same time, K-14 stood against the trends of radical and militant Islam because they distort religious objectives and religious ethos. Moreover, it has defamed Islam Which is portrayed as a religion of violence, intolerance, conflict and terror. This characterisation of Islam can be interpreted as 'desacredisation' and has hurt the followers of Islam throughout the world. But, at the same time, he understood the context of its emergence which was directly related to the colonial and imperialist policy towards the Muslim world.

(v) K-14's relations with KPs were highly positive and friendly. In fact, this relationship was established through mutual confidence and affection. Since he paid highest regards to teachers, he treated the KP teachers in the same esteem. He considered them as potential factors in the literacy of KMs. Even his children were also going to KP teachers for private tuitions. He never allowed them to suffer in personal and official matters. They visited his house regularly and on festival days in particular.

14. GLOBAL SOCIAL ORDER

(i) The GSO, according to K-14, represented one humanistic social alternative at global level for entire humanity. Its causation must be oriented towards needs of humanism and its institutional-organisational and structural basis. Its implications must also be directed to the benefit of whole humanity in the long run. While the former must touch upon human sufferings and concerns, the latter must lead to their emancipation.

(ii) The GSO must represent and safeguard all social-political interests of all regions, sub-continents, continents, countries and nations. It must provide suitable representation to all nationalities and sub-nationalities. It must absolutely reflect the plurality in terms of religion, ethnicity, culture, language and so on. It must not allow certain world powers to dominate and manipulate in order to grab global benefits.

(iii) K-14 felt that GSO must demonstrate global, secular, liberal, egalitarian and non-discriminatory character. So, it must contribute to world peace and not conflict, to integration of the world and not disintegration, and tolerance and not intolerance in all fields of life. This order, if established properly, may lead to a new era of global association covering all human groups.

15. THE KASHMIR PROBLEM

(i) K-14 had all sorts of views about the Kashmir problem. In fact, he stood as the 'moving encyclopadia' on Kashmir affairs. He had full knowledge of many apparent and hidden aspects of all developments and events. He also played a certain role in many related political developments after 1947. Among all these views, K-14 had specific views about lasting resolution of six-decade-old problem.

(ii) He observed that the Kashmir problem was concerned primarily and necessarily with Kashmiri people and countries of India and Pakistan were secondary to it. So, Kashmiris of all opinions must be involved in final resolution. He opined that Kashmiris must be necessarily granted some form of freedom which must fulfill their political aspirations. The political and constitutional aspects may be discussed later on. That political framework of freedom must benefit both India and Pakistan in terms of positive benefits from the state of JK. Though these ideas seem simple and of easy option, this will prove highly meaningful. So, a dialogue among all major and minor partners of dispute must initiate. The dialogue process, though difficult, may lead to be initiated realistic, durable and purposeful solution of the problem.

(iii) K-14 maintained that the future state in Kashmir must benefit Kashmiris of all belongings and must serve the interests of all countries involved. An atmosphere must be created in which Kashmir's beauty, resources and potentialities will benefit all surrounding countries..

(iv) K-14 put forward two more related points. First, the future political unit in Kashmir must be safeguarded politically and constitutionally agreed upon by the joint Kashmiri leadership and India and Pakistan. Second, after raising basic question of who will represent the Kashmiri people, he felt that they have to decide about it in advance.

16. FUTURE KASHMIR SOCIETY

(i) K-14's humanitarian approach and perception reflected in his ideas about future society in Kashmir which is as follow:

- that society must essentially reflect the composite culture and society; all major and minor social collectivities must get sufficient and appropriate place in that society;
- all social, cultural, demographic, ethnic, linguistic and other identities must be fairly integrated and made component part of 'Kashmir collectivity';
- that society must upheld a constitutional system with dominant features of decentralisation of power, democratic functioning, representation to all irrespective of their religion, region and culture, liberalism, humanitarianism, safeguard of all political, civil and human rights, guarantee for educational and other social facilities to all, equality and justice for all, no discrimination at all, cultural and political freedom to minorities, and safety and security of all citizens;
- that society must maintain the ideals of nationality and sub-nationality in equal order;
- that society must provide equal representations to all religious, cultural, ethnic, racial and other relevant groups and communities; and
- that society must uphold the humanitarian principles of tolerance, plurality, similarity, consensus and avoid conflict, difference and dissent.

K-15 EDUCATIONIST AND SOCIAL NOTABLE

1. SOCIAL CONTEXT

(i) Like other societies, the Kashmiri society faced a stage of development called "feudalism" with its associated socio-economic features. However, this institutionalised system had a particular political feature, i.e. the rulers in this system were alien, which had specific implications in all fields of life. These alien rulers came to Kashmir and ruled till 1947. This system was generally associated with inequality and inhumanity. Kashmir represented an extreme example of that. Politically, people were completely dominated and suffered through force. Militarily, they were disarmed in order to stop them from rising in revolt. Economically, the masses suffered extremely. The poverty level was so low that even 'two meals in a day' was considered a luxury. They lived in sub-human living conditions. Peasants in villages and workers-artisans in urban areas were taxed so heavily that their life and work became meaningless to their life. Forced labour from locals was a common practise in which members of every family were involved. Religiously, the masses suffered and were humiliated and religious places were desecrated or closed. The local culture and language was never considered for promotion. The local traditions, customs, folkways, ceremonies and other cultural practices were never encouraged. Illiteracy was rampant among the people. Even religious education to children was hampered. In that situation, the masses were generally discriminated, humiliated, tortured and threatened.

(ii) The feudal set-up in Kashmir in pre-modren times was further stabilised by some local classes, groups and families. The alien rulers, in order to make the system functional and effective, recruited them in their administration on different positions with material benefits. They also empowered different notables as *Jagirdars, zaildar, numberdar, mansabdar* and so on for representing the regime, collecting taxes and imposing regime's orders. The properties and entire villages and areas were awarded to them for their services to the regime. All this was done irrespective of religious consideration. The sole purpose of these exercises was to get legitimacy of their rule in Kashmir, as was done in other parts of undivided India. In that situation, all religious communities were involved and these individuals and families served the feudal regime sincerely. Since KPs composed the only local literate community, they got many positions in all regimes, whether Muslim or Hindu or Sikh.

(iii) In that feudal situation, some local aristocratic families too served the feudal regimes, for which they were provided material benefits. However, the younger generation in these families had gone for modern education mostly outside the state, which changed its response qualitatively towards alien rulers. Though this generation didn't revolt against feudal regimes but showed sympathy with suffering Kashmiri masses. They expressed their concern about extreme backwardness, inhuman treatment and sub-human living conditions of locals. Though these individuals had not de-classed themselves, they had conveyed 'silent solidarity' with the suffering Kashmiris. When the opportunity came, they came out against these atrocities and injustices on the part of feudal rulers. In this process, some of them had to face downward economic mobility. All that happened in the context of political developments in Indian sub-continent in general and in JK in particular.

(iv) K-15 belonged to those individuals who may be characterised as 'conscience keepers' of that time. That educated and modernised generation responded differently from its families towards the feudal regime in Kashmir. Though they were not declassed but they suffered by not getting jobs, perks, benefits, services and properties. It seemed that they played this role consciously and were ready to face the consequences in their solidarity with the masses. K-15 stood as the 'shining star' among those individuals who played that historic role in Kashmir.

2. IN-FAMILY SOCIALISATION

(i) K-15 family was a prominent sect-based religious family which had achieved social distinction primarily because of religious esteem. That type of distinctive religious family existed in the India sub-continent only and it cannot be traced in Arabia. This family status was hereditary and performed all ritual practices in daily life. It was considered as sacred by people of the sect and stood highly respected. All members of the family were supposed to all laws of *Shariat* and maintain leadership of the community.

(ii) K-15 was early socialised in this kind of social environment and got elementary religious education and training at home. But, subsequently, he got into a missionary boarding school outside Kashmir, where he found different, especially liberal, social environment. So, he was exposed to that environment and early family influence started decreasing in his life. During that long period of exposure outside Kashmir, he developed modern attitudes, ideas, behaviour and lifestyle, which were devoid of religiosity and far from traditional values. In that situation, K-15 deviated from many family norms and practices. But, all this violation was tolerated in the family keeping in view his future career and material life conditions. At that stage, he started developing his identity in terms of self preference, positions, likes and dislike.

(iii) Later education of K-15 also took place outside Kashmir in the pan-Indian secular environment, especially after independence in 1947. This further reduced the family impact on him. On the other hand, his attraction to modern way of life got further inspiration. But, a peculiarity of K-15 was observed according to which he never felt detached from Kashmir, its people, its culture and its beauty. That was despite his entire education and socialisation outside Kashmir. In reality, Kashmir was always alive in his blood and soul.

3. OUT-FAMILY ENVIRONMENT

(i) K-15 had a complex, even conflicting, effect in the out-family environment. On the one hand, there were near-distant relatives who were either extreme conservatives or extreme modernists. While the latter were educated, young, influential, authoritative and rulers, the former were religious educated, elders and having religious-based influence. He encountered both trends of influence but preferred to opt for the former trend.

(ii) The second component of out-family environment was neighbours and followers. K-15 family lived in a congested sect-based locality in the city. The social, economic, educational, political and cultural status of these neighbours-followers was much lower than his family. It was observed that there was absolute one-sided effect of this family over others who considered this 'family elders' as hereditary leaders. This led to their lifelong submission to the authority and orders of the family. K-15 was a keen observer of these practices but usually ignored them in his social life.

(iii) The FFs of K-15 family may be categorised as (i) a group of elders, religious oriented, having long-term relationship and having same political ideology; and (ii) a group of youngsters, usually irreligious, having short-term role and having different political ideology. K-15's option was clear. He preferred the company of the latter who composed of bureaucrats, administrators, social and political notables, intellectuals and so on. The effect of those FFs was significant as well as longest and rise to an association of aristocratic families. Those FFs belonged to different cultures, religions, regions, languages and so on and they exposed K-15 to the plurality, diversity and multi-cultural dimensions of the Indian society. This kind of social impact started in K-15's life from school environment and matured with this interaction with FFs. In this way, the entire personality of K-15 was shaped inside and outside family environment.

4. EDUCATION, CAREER AND MOBILITY

(i) At the earlier stage, K-15 was given basic religious education and training at home. But, it was lost in his long life experiences. His modern education was continuous and systematic. The primary and middle level education was carried out at the missionary boarding school outside Kashmir. This educational environment had serious influence in his academic and non-academic life in future.

(ii) The higher education of K-15 was carried out at Aligarh Muslim University (AMU) and Jamia Milliya Islamia (JMI) during the hey days of Dr. Zakir Hussain, the first Muslim President in independent India. He got highly impressed with the secular ethos of IMs. He was encouraged to pursue higher studies by Dr. Hussain and his colleagues at AMU and JMI like Professor Mohammad Habib. He also got interested in Maulana Abul Kalam Azad (MAKA)'s, first Minister of Education in independent India, philosophy and methodology of education in Independent India, particularly related to the IMs.

(iii) Later on, he got the opportunity to visit Europe and the U.S. for further studies. There he got impressed with new educational technology and methodology. After coming back from the West, he wanted to implement those new ideas, concepts and method of education in a small society like Kashmir.

(iv) After completing higher education in India and abroad, he returned to Kashmir, as was not expected here. The political regime of that time appreciated his return to his native land and offered him several positions to introduce and implement new ideas in education in the state. But, when his radical views and innovations started showing positive results, he was stopped to work. He made no compromise on his ideals and principles he had developed. He was offered several higher positions in the field of education, from Chief Inspector of Schools to Commissioner of Education in the state. Bit, in undesirable situation created by bureaucrats, politicians and others, he opted out several times due to serious differences on education policy and academic matters.

(v) His constant, stable and dynamic career proved a grand success when he joined the local university. There he emerged as the most impressive academician. Teachers, scholars and students felt honoured after attending his classes. His academic arguments, logic and methodology was considered matchless. No other teacher could make a parallel image.

(vi) In addition to these career academic activities, K-15 developed a wider network of social relationships with all individuals and groups of academicians, professionals, technocrats, scientists, experts, intellectuals, artists, authors, literary figures, poets, bureaucrats, administrators, officials and others. In this social network, he constantly interacted with hundreds of individuals and groups who felt proud after meeting him. He met largest number of people during his official and academic career and afterwards. It was generally felt that one felt elevated and honoured after meeting and listening him. Even at present, when he is in 80s, he provides a live company. One loves to listen to him and finally loves him. His matchless oratory and literary-intellectual presentation remains unforgettable. Thus in his entire career, K-15 produced an educated and emancipated generation of Kashmiris. He nurtured their intellect, encouraged their academic-educational-intellectual activities, and made a radical change among them. His contribution to the cause of modern education in Kashmir stands comparable to the efforts of Sir Syed Ahmad Khan of Aligarh for IMs.

(vii) After education-service career and wider social network, he faced extremely upward and downward mobility. In terms of occupational-professional mobility, it was complete shift from a religious preacher-leader to professional educational expert. K-15 left all activities related to earlier occupation of the family. But, by adopting new occupation, i.e. government service, he refused all benefits of a feudal family. He could neither retain extra land in villages after 1953 land reforms nor could he inherit any Jagir. It was complete climb down economically in which all monetary and material benefits from feudal regime were discontinued. K-15 was conscious about this phenomenon and accepted it readily. He explained it in terms of a necessary measure in the process of dismantling the feudal system in the state.

(viii) On the other hand, K-15 had undergone highest degree of mobility from religious career to service career. In this long process, he felt psychologically elevated and socially progressive.

5. MARRIAGE AND FAMILY

(i) K-15's marriage was of exogamous type. He met her wife during the days of higher education in Delhi. In fact, they met, got introduced to each other's families, and got married. She proved an ideal choice. She was welcomed affectionately and with full customary and cultural celebrations. She was from a Muslim family of Lucknow with middle class background and had attained modern education. She felt at home in K-15 family and got well adjusted with all members, young and old and conservatives and radicals.

(ii) A point of importance was that though she was not a Kashmiri by birth, she always felt herself a Kashmiri, a rare phenomenon in social history of Kashmir. Even at the time of her death in the U.S., she wished to be buried in Kashmir. After her death, her family members had to spent about one million rupees for taking her dead body to Kashmir and bury her there. Throughout her life, she stood for Kashmir and Kashmiris. She used to keep her children attached to Kashmir and its culture. She was always concerned about the conditions prevailing among Kashmiri women and artisans. After retirement from government service, she used to work voluntarily for the cause of women in Kashmir.

(iii) K-15 established a new nuclear family household just after marriage. It was an exogamous and patri-local marriage. They lived with their unmarried children. But, after some time, all children left for the U.S. for higher education, got jobs there and settled there. This neo-local family unit had only two permanent members. Children used to visit them at regular intervals and kept in contact with their land of origin. While one of them emerged as a famous English poet, other became an expert in the field of English language. The third one became expert in the field of Indian sub-continental history. After the death of K-15's wife, he lives in the house lonely. But, the company of friends, admirers, students, followers and scholars don't leave him alone.

6. THE PERSONALITY TYPE

(i) As a direct result of process of socialisation and life experiences inside and outside Kashmir, particularly in the Western societies, he developed a 'personality type' for which K-15 was popular in Kashmir and outside. These characteristic traits of this personality were as follows:

- He was the most well read person in his generation. His study covered all subjects, particularly history, philosophy, science, sociology, education, religion, psychology, civics, Urdu and English literature. He was the usual buyer of every new book in the city. He used to study newspapers and magazines regularly. In brief, he must have gone through all important books in every subject.
- Since he was a feudal lord in origin, he could have involved himself in loot, plunder and exploitation. But, he represented a person who never thought in those terms. In fact, he was used to spend for others. He had established the record in not increasing his property but selling it for self and social purposes.
- He stood an unparalleled host. Everybody who met him became his honourable guest and got the treatment as per availability of consumer items in the kitchen.
- He believed in self-confidence and self work. He appreciated those who talk and act with confidence. That matched with his highly confident voice. At the same time, he believed and practised in self-work and self service within and outside family.
- He was considered matchless orator and unparalleled argument presenter. Even famous advocates could not match him. His speeches and lectures were heard with rapt attention and complete silence.
- He was fond of foods and drinks. He could spend any amount of money and time for getting choicest foods. He had adopted the western and eastern and Kashmiri standards in this regard.
- He stood super human helper to the needy, poor and suffering. He used to take personal initiatives to help the youth for different purposes. His sympathy and affection for lower classes, especially workers, washer-men, gardeners, domestic helpers and daily workers, was limitless and he used to keep them always happy.
- His approach in conversation with the youth was always oriented towards progress, change, development, mobility, achievement and humanity.
- He was one who loved by heart those young boys and girls who were considered zero starters.

7. SOCIAL LIKES AND DISLIKES

After lifelong, diverse and realistic experiences, K-15 developed strong likes and dislikes which included the following:

Social Likes	*Social Dislikes*
- Personal and social initiatives for change	- bureaucratic culture and rigid rules
- Always positive in approach	- political corruption and red tapism
- Always ready to help others in their needs	-poverty and poverty culture
- Modern attitudes and behaviour in life	- person of dual character
- Multi-cultural ideas and its ideal life	- social contradiction and conflict
- Indian Muslims' secular and progressive ethos	- religious fatalism and fanaticism
- Change and progress among lower classes	-illiteracy in all groups and communities
- Egalitarian social order	- educational drop-outs at primary stage
- A soft and truthful person	-communal mindset and communal disharmony
- Educated and emancipated persons	- economic exploitation of workers and artisans
- Gender equality and gender justice	-unequal agrarian structure
- Dress consciousness and dress code	-modernity with its sex image
- Democracy and its political practices	- oppression and suppression of people
- Celebration of festivals	- political ideology of feudalism
- Some aspects of irreligious life	- incompetent and corrupt teacher
- Capable researcher and scientist	-obsolete educational system and syllabi
- Intellectual company	- anti-social trends of crime and drug abuse
- School discipline of highest order	- irrational laws and rules
- Mass contact with scholars and students	- violent behaviour of youth
- Scientific educational planning	-violence against women.

8. CONCEPTS OF "I", "ME" AND "WE"

(i) K-15 showed strong sense of all three concepts. Keeping in view his affluent background, different kinds of association and adoption of different careers provided stimulus to psychological sentiments and social traits. This reflected in all three concepts. K-15 always thought of 'I' and he could never afford to forget it. He kept it alive always with different ideological shades, different dimensions, and at different levels. First, 'I' revealed in his sub-consciousness about his feudal status but refused to adopt its nomenclature and accept its worldly blessings. Second, after refusing the old system consciously, 'I' gave the inspiration for new competitive way of life and membership in a new world society. Third, 'I' gave consciousness of a man who struggled and achieved desired status, position, authority, power and honour. The concept of 'I' also represented his survival, submission and quality in his life and affairs of life. Finally, the concept of 'I' brought an evolutionary character of his life like 'I' as initiation, 'I' as determination, 'I' as action, 'I' as implication and 'I' as conclusion.

(ii) The concept of 'me' was also strong in K-15's life. Mostly, he equated it with the concept of 'my' which for him had an evolutionary form which may be explained in terms of 'me' as the past, 'me' as the present, and 'me' as the future. First, 'me' the past essentially referred to his hereditary status, his response to it, loosing of something and gaining of everything in struggle in this initial stage. Second, 'me' the present represented his achieved social status in competitive social environment with its essential implications. So, it was in actuality 'me' the professional, 'me' the family head, 'me' the community member, 'me' the social activist, and 'me' the cultural proponent. All these propositions were seen in respective social context and its effects.

(iii) The concept of 'we' too was very strong, specific and contextual. It was used in a wider social sense, a social collectivity with primodeal loyalty. In this context, 'we' was used as :

- The Kashmiris in comparison to Indians, Pakistanis and others.
- The intellectuals of high order.
- The academicians of higher social status.
- The aristocrats-bureaucrats with distinct social features.
- The administrators and officials with no commitment to values.
- The politicians with no political ideas and ideals.
- The community brothers having no moral ethics.
- The businessmen having no honesty and standard.

In this way, 'we' reflected positive and negative features. It also responded to different problems in a positive or negative way and gave rise to a respective situation. So, 'we' was attached to good or bad qualities of life, for example :

- We, the cultured and civilised people
- We, the non-violent people
- We, the honest and hard working people, and
- We the secular and progressive people.

At the same time, 'we' was attached to negative features such as

- We, the educationally backward people,
- We, the culturally not exposed people,
- We, the visionless people, and
- We, having no capability of self-criticism.

9. IDEAS OF EQUALITY AND INEQUALITY

(i) K-15 was a firm believer of equality in human society, especially in the field of education. Education in modern times, according to him, played the fundamental role in transforming human society and establishing an egalitarian social order. It was observed in the West that, only after achieving highest degree of literacy, those societies were in a position to attain highest degree of development. K-15 upheld that same experience revealed in the cases of Japan and China. At the same time, extreme level of illiteracy has contributed to backwardness and underdevelopment.

(ii) K-15 upheld the view that inequality in education led to societal inequality. Since education was considered as a material commodity, it led to more division, disharmony and disunity in society. People bought education according to their economic standard, so they became unequal individuals. The in-equal class education sharpened the existing system of social stratification, unequal pattern of change and development, and unjust social order. At the same time, inequality in caste education led to strengthening of ideal caste system, ideology of purity and pollution, *dharma* justification and inhuman treatment to SCs. In the case of gender, in-equal education hurt the basic cause of gender equality. It created more dissention and antagonism between sexes and violence against women inside and outside family. It finally contributed to subordination of women in all fields of life.

(iii) On the other hand, equal education to all classes, groups and castes remove basic obstacles in the way of change, development and emancipation. In addition to resolving all problems, it gave new direction to society. It certainly helped in constructing an equal social order.

10. THE IDEAL LEADER

(i) K-15 was highly impressed by the most prominent Muslim leader and scholar of India, Maulana Abul Kalam Azad (MAKA), the first Education Minister in Independent India. He was so impressed with ideas and ideals and political role of MAKA before and after partition of 1947 that K-15 gave him the status of 'greatest leader of modern India. He always referred to him as political ideologue and guide. He felt that MAKA's ideal features were unmatched but were not understood by a large section of IMs, especially in the catastrophic experience of partition of India.

(ii) K-15 considered MAKA at the highest degree of ideological clarity, truthfulness, boldness, Islamic personality, approach towards partition, position of Muslims in post-independence India, and rational approach to religion. In his ideological presentations, MAKA's knowledge, experience and thinking made Islamic concepts and theories reflected their relevance to worldly affairs at the national and international levels. In this regard, K-15 used to quote MAKA's famous statement as Congress President at Rampur session of Indian National Congress in 1939 that "he was a proud Indian and a proud Muslim simultaneously and there was no contradiction in this statement". He considered this statement as the future guide for Muslims in India after 1947.

(iii) K-15 felt that MAKA was always bold in his political views and positions, even about colonial and imperialist powers. He upheld his differences even with Gandhi and Nehru on many problems and issues. Despite heavy opposition, he stood by his particular ideas about partition of India in 1947 and emphasised all Muslims to stay and live in India as they used to be. He appealed to them not to leave this great land of world Islamic culture and civilisation. He reminded them that minarets of Jamia Masjid were telling them not to leave India. He used to cry: *is islam a iski miras ko kin key saharey chood rahey ho. Ye jamia masjid ke minar tumhey bula rahey hein.*

(iv) Finally, K-15 was highly impressed by the foresightedness about future of Muslims in the entire un-divided India. He proved correct word by word and emphasised Muslims to live like ideal Indians and Ideal Muslims.

11. GLOBAL SOCIAL ORDER

K-15 considered the establishment of GSO in institutional and organisational forms as most desirable objective. This order must primarily be education-based and education-oriented. It follows that there must be maximum input of desirable educational orientation, so that it leads to the fulfillment of educationally oriented output in newly established social order.

- It must reduce and eliminate educational disparity and educational differences and must make attempt to provide it free.
- It must eliminate differences between nations, communities and classes to the maximum extent.
- It must introduce cooperation and competition and not conflict within and between various societal groups and classes.
- Backward economic standard of any nation must not be allowed to involve its educational system through help and cooperation.
- Institutional and organisational efforts must be carried through this order to eliminate illiteracy from all societies, regions and nations.
- Ideal educational framework at the universal level must be formulated including educational planning, programmes, schemes and their implementation in this global order.
- Finally, education must figure at the top of agenda in any sphere of GSO.

12. RELIGIOUS LIFE

(i) K-15 was a sound believer and established scholar of Islam. His religious thinking was of high order because it was rational, scientific, scholarly, and always referred to basic religious sources and documents. He used to hold discourses, debates and exchanges on all religious issues at his home. He had also developed a comparative religious outlook. In his religious thought, he was highly influenced by MAKA's ideas and orientation and used to refer to his famous commentary of *Quran, Tarjamanul Quran.*

(ii) K-15 was a regular reader of western writings on Islam and Muslims. He studied all important books and other publications from the U.S. and Europe. He must not have missed even one such book. At the same time, he used to study the scholarly contributions of religious scholars and centers in India. Moreover, he was a keen observer of religious developments in the Muslim world. Thus Islamic religion became the source of wider and comparative religious understanding in which he had developed expertise during later part of his life. At that stage, he developed the image of top most expert in religious affairs with rational and scientific understanding.

(iii) K-15's family life was full of celebrations, not on particular days in a week/month/year but throughout the year, which were related to festivals and other celebrations. He had complete knowledge about basic realities of doctrinaire religion as well as folk religious practices in Kashmir. In reality, his religious orientation was completely academic and never tried to dabble in extra-academic exercises.

(iv) K-15 was a strong proponent of composite culture in Kashmir, especially KPs role in it. It was because of his association with KPs which was close, friendly and family based. They gave K-15 highest possible regards because of his highest excellence in education and acadèmics. He too showed respect to their successful careers in educational fields. He always proved helpful to them, especially during his official position.

13. THE KASHMIR PROBLEM

(i) K-15 was of the view that the Kashmir problem stood as a complex problem which could not be resolved in 1947. It was made more complex by the involvement of India and Pakistan in this dispute. The problem became further complex and expanded beyond limited proportions after 1948 when the GOI took it to UNSC and thus became an international political issue with superpower involvement. Among all partners involved in this problem, the Kashmiris stood as the most suffering lot.

(ii) K-15 put forward the point that non-resolution of Kashmir problem was mainly due to non-involvement of the intelligentsia of both countries in the process of this conflict resolution. The politicians of both countries dealt with it within their narrow nationalistic perspectives and domestic-foreign policies agendas. The politicians of all countries spoiled this issue, as a result of which it resisted any solution till date. Even a towering political figure and charismatic leader of India, Jawaharlal Nehru, could not resolve it.

(iii) K-15 was of the view that the Kashmir problem may be resolved by involving intelligentsia of all countries, India, Pakistan and Kashmir which may strive for balanced, durable and possible resolution of this 63 year chronic political problem. The intelligentsia which includes civil society representatives, ambassadors, diplomats, academicians, experts, media professionals, bureaucrats, officials, administrators, social notables, writers, etc. may be involved, who in all possibilities, will suggest a rational, just, balanced and realistic solution to this problem. Thus they must be allowed to play this crucial role as early as possible.

14. FUTURE KASHMIR SOCIETY

(i) K-15 explained future Kashmir society in terms of an order which stood education-oriented, education-directed which must be followed through scientific educational planning, programs and schemes and proper implementation. This society in its developed form reveal educational features mentioned below:

- Education must not be available as a saleable material commodity. It must not be commercialised like in the capitalist market. One must get necessary education at cheapest and affordable cost. The system must encourage and not discourage for attaining education.
- Educational inequalities between individuals, groups-communities, classes, at inter and intra level, must be eliminated. At the same time, educational equality must be established between individuals, groups, communities and classes and other social collectivities. Education as an ideal must strive for equality and not inequality.
- All generations must be educated in all subjects of modern times. All obsolete, dogmatic, fatalistic, and traditional subjects must be eliminated. Modernity must be utilised as cause as well as consequence of education. It must create an emancipated generation of human beings with human framework.
- Modern education must emancipate individuals from fanaticism, dogmatism, irrationality, and unfounded beliefs.
- Education must emerge as an instrument of change and development and not of status quo and backwardness.
- Education must create an environment of a healthy competition and not a disastrous conflict.
- Education must involve necessarily scientific progress and technological development in its most modern form.
- It must give rise to scientific culture and scientific temper.
- The educational ideals of education in that society must be peace, non-violence, stability and solidarity.

K-16 THE KASHMIRI YOUTH : RURAL SAYYID

1. SOCIAL CONTEXT

(i) The occupational-caste composition, inversely related to the KM community was explained in terms of *Sayyids, Khans,* occupational and service castes. (See author's book entitled *Castes in Kashmir).* These castes used to carry out specialised occupational activities and lived in separate localities of *Mohallas* like *Peer Mohalla, Dobi Mohalla, Chan Mohalla, Dasil Mohalla and Khan Mohalla.* All such castes were not homogeneous but hetrogeneous in terms of structure and function. In this stratified background, the *Sayyid* community too was stratified. The members of this community claimed their descent directly from the Prophet of Islam (PBUH)'s family. But, there were other *Sayyids* who can be characterised as "neo-*Sayyids*". They adopted different *Sayyid* names recently through the process of *sayyidisation,* according to which some families which were not using these names earlier, adopted *Sayyid* names now in order to claim higher social status. Now, a considerable number of *Sayyids* has emerged and they could not be challenged. In practice, it seemed difficult to differentiate between original and fake *Sayyids.*

(ii) In the context of dynamics of change, this community may be divided on the basis of their rural-urban belonging and social features. Thus we may differentiate between *Sayyids* who lived in rural and in urban areas. Their differences and associated social features are explained below:

Feature	*Rural Sayyid*	*Urban Sayyid*
- Education	High	Highest
- Employment	High	Higher
- Religiosity	Highest	Lower/Lowest
- Cultural Exposure	Low	Higher/Highest
- Social Mobility	High	Highest

They can further be divided on rural and urban basis on the lines of above-mentioned features. Thus we can have urban and rural *Sayyids,*each having two groups with following features:

URBAN SAYYIDS

Feature	*Group I*	*Group II*
- Education	Higher/Highest	Low/High
- Employment	Higher/Highest	Low/High
- Religiosity	Low/Lowest	High/Higher/Highest
- Cultural Exposure	Higher/Highest	Low/High
- Social Mobility	High/Highest	Low

RURAL SAYYIDS

Feature	*Group I*	*Group II*
- Education	High/Higher	Low/High
- Employment	High/Higher	Low/High
- Religiosity	Low	High
- Cultural Exposure	Low	Lower
- Social Mobility	Higher	High

(iii) In the preceding thematic framework, a basic occupational change was experienced among many rural and urban *Sayyids* by attaining higher education, adopting service career and professions and entering into business field. But, other *Sayyids* in rural-urban areas did not experience this type of change. Thus there emerged in-equal levels of change in the *Sayyid* community. With this, a concomitant change was observed in the institution of *Peer Muredi* which was primarily a social institution in which *Peer* and *Mureed* were interlocked spiritually with superior-inferior relationship and responsibilities and obligations on each other. The cultural background of this specific type of relationship was considered sacred and continued for life long period. In this relationship, while *Mureed* followed the *Peer* sincerely, followed all his orders and provided material and non-material help. The *peer* also took care about basic material needs of *mureeds.* Thus they fulfilled each others needs reciprocally.

(iv) But, this understanding and perception of *peer-mureedi* got disrupted making it non-functional. The accompanying change was felt in the manipulation and exploitation of this institution on the part of some *Sayyids*. The material aspect of this institution became its prime concern which led to its demoralisation and de-legitimisation and its traditional relations were discredited in urban and rural areas. In some cases, it gave rise to a group which only deceived simple and innocent people.

(v) In that changing situation, not only ideal relationship of *peer-mureedi* deteriorated, the ideal role of the *Sayyid* faced serious threat. While *Sayyids* left their traditional role completely, they opted for non-traditional occupations and there was very less scope for conventional activities. So, the ideal role of *Sayyid* was considered peripheral or irrelevant. But, the rural *Sayyids* responded to education and employment late comparatively, they remained socially conservative and culturally unexposed. K-16 belonged to this type of social context which helped in shaping his personality features.

2. IN-FAMILY SOCIALISATION

(i) K-16 was socialised in a *Sayyid* joint family in the city. But, against the general trend of migration from rural to urban areas, this family migrated from city to a village. This was done on the invitation of a *Mureed* of the

Peer who was a *mansabdaar* in that area and had a lot of property on his disposal. The *peer* was so sincere to the religious cause that he opted for silent village life in comparison to his busy city life. His devotion to religious cause also reflected in the fact that he used to go to *Hazratbal*, the place where sacred hair of the Prophet has been kept, from his residence bare footed. After migration to the village, entire family had to adjust in rural lifestyle. In this background, K-16 became the embodiment of rural as well as urban culture.

(ii) It seems interesting to note that K-16 family was committed to the social of religion, but it got modern education too, though late. At the same time, some family members were influenced by the reformist and radical trends of Islam, which were not in consonance with family's folk religious practices. These developments in K-16's family didn't stop family's *peer-mureedi* and was practised in an ideal form. The followers belonged to diverse social background such as from nearby and far off villages, urban and rural areas, all occupations/vocations/professions, all classes, castes and communities, men and women, young and old, rich and poor, literate and illiterate and so on. They attended the *peer* at regular intervals and sought his blessings in all matters. They used to pay high respect to children of the *peer* without any consideration of their religiosity. The *peer* used to advise them on worldly matters and performing some ritual practises. Everybody who used to come to his house usually, took some gifts which included eatables and daily consumer life items, which were sent to common kitchen to serve other guests and followers. In this environment, K-16 felt elevated and honoured and developed the image of *peer*'s loving son.

3. OUT-FAMILY ENVIRONMENT

(i) The out-family environment of K-16 was composed of relatives, neighbours, FFs and others. The relatives of K-16 were located in rural and urban areas because of its origin in the latter. He was in constant touch with urban relatives through regular visits and other formal contacts. This kept his urban belonging alive and his urban traits fresh. At the same time, he maintained good relations with rural relatives through intensive interaction, mutual visits and gifts. In fact, K-16 was the most mobile and most interactive person in the entire clan. It seemed that these relatives had accepted his impact and the reverse was hardly possible.

(ii) K-16 family had neighbours in the city but, after migration, that relationship collapsed. However, due to extreme social nature of K-16, he kept some social contact with them. The village neighbours were all non-*sayyids* and were followers or *mureeds*. They had patron-client relationship with some responsibilities and obligations. The *zaildaar* family considered it most esteemed and took care of all material and non-material needs of the *peer* and his family. K-16 family provided much needed legitimacy to the feudal order ruled by aliens. But, this relationship between two families didn't make K-16 family members as social parasites. They worked hard for education and subsequently got government service. Their positive and purposeful efforts led to their overall mobility. The neighbours were tied in such relationship which radiated its influence on them.

(iii) K-16's FFs were mostly persons of higher position, status, power, and authority. They included distinctive *mureeds, top officials, administrators,* bureaucrats, academicians, businessmen, professionals, police officials, politicians, etc. The second category of K-16 FFs were friends, colleagues and other acquaintances of children. Both these categories of FFs visited K-16's house regularly and he was impressed by their positions and got inspiration for his higher status position. He also started developing formal traits of those top positions for future from that stage.

4. EDUCATION AND CAREER

(i) K-16's early religious education and training was carried out at home as was a general practise in *Sayyid* families of that time. After that, his primary and middle education took place in a government school in nearby village. During that stage, he used to impress teachers due to his religious training at home. Subsequently, he joined the local town college for graduation which he completed successfully. Earlier, he was limited to the *Sayyid* company, but he got exposed to and developed non-*Sayyid* company now. After graduation, he joined a government job for some time and that stabilised his economic condition. Subsequently, he joined a post-graduate course and completed it with distinction. His academic interest and merit enabled him to pursue doctoral research in a central university which he got after some years of hard work and many difficulties and problems. His highest qualification and research training gave him an academic position in a university for which he had a lifelong dream.

(ii) After a long career of a student and scholar, he got a significant academic position in university. Long back, he had worked in a government department primarily for economic stability at that time. In fact, K-16 had thought for academic life in future which he got after a lot of struggle. But, soon after he resumed that job, he appeared in KAS entrance exam and qualified for KAS level official position. As everybody expected, he joined that job and enjoyed its status and power. Then came a radical decision of his life, i.e. he again preferred the academic job over administrative job. Though everybody around him was surprised, he showed his commitment to academics and pursued his career in this field. This change of mind on the part of K-16 can partly be explained by social-psychological factors. But, full explanation may be provided by the factor of "pre-determined destiny decided by God Almighty" as was held by famous sociologist, Dr. Ali Shariati.

5. ASSOCIATION AND OCCUPATIONAL MOBILITY

(i) It seems interesting to note that K-16 had developed different levels, types and degrees of association in his lifelong career. Once he met anybody, he used to establish relations that mostly continued and became a lifelong association. He had a variety of associations. First, he had the association of peer group youth who were mostly his class and batch mates. Second, other association was with academicians who included eminent professors, teachers, colleagues, researchers, scientists, experts and so on. Third, another association with police fraternity whose company he got for some period. It included top and petty officials and others concerned with police. Fourth, he had association of bureaucrats, officials, administrators and heads of various institutions and organisations. Fifth, he was in association with professionals, doctors, engineers, IT experts, mass media experts, lawyers and so on. Sixth, association with political people who included political leaders and activists of ruling and opposition parties. Seventh, association with big and small businessmen of Kashmir products.

(ii) K-16 developed the wider association and had multi-faceted character. It follows that his association was concerned with all walks of life; belonging to all classes, castes, communities and groups; all regions, cultures and languages; was serious and rational in this relationship; and developed these associations as permanent features in his life. He was well conscious about the culture of association which he maintained through verbal and non-verbal contact, continuous interaction, regular visits and electronic contact.

(iii) Taking into consideration lower socio-economic background, K-16's rise to the present prestigious position stood as a clear case of occupational mobility. His perception of academic career as lifelong busy profession, full of missionary work, dignified field of work, high-esteem profession and humanist oriented area made him convinced about his preference in life. He wanted top position in the field and excellence in performance that will make him accessible to national and international academic forums. Since he did a world tour recently, he was fully satisfied about global credentials and esteem for academic life.

6. MARRIAGE AND FAMILY

(i) K-16 was married in an endogamous type of marriage in which the girl belonged to the same caste. He was relatively late in the marriage market due to pursuing higher education and research. In fact, this type of marriage has emerged common among Kashmiri youth today. K-16 was married with a girl of a family which had comparatively higher socio-economic status. Though this marriage was not of hypogamous type, it proved a step forward in the process of social mobility in his life. Since the marriage partner of K-

16 was highly qualified and self earning, the marriage relationship proved durable and of egalitarian character.

(ii) K-16 lived in a joint family throughout and still loved to live in such social ethos. He was a strong proponent of this type of family. But, after marriage, he established a neo-local family unit in city where both partners were working. He, with his family, migrated to city where from his parents had migrated long back. In this way, his migration to city completed a cycle (of migration) which started from city and ended in city. Subsequently, K-16 constructed a house in a newly established colony in outskirts of the city. This act had three specific implications. First, he and his family made a settled and stable social life in the city. Second, he joined new class status, i.e. urban upper middle class, which stood radically different from his parental family. Third, he established small family household comprising three members only. This again stood radically different from his parental family which had joint family character.

7. SOCIAL LIKES AND DISLIKES

After going through tough conditions and harsh experiences in life inside and outside Kashmir, K-16 developed particular social likes and dislikes, some of which are mentioned below:

Social Likes	*Social Dislikes*
- Zero starter's personality	- crime and deviance in society
- Bold, upright and regular officer	- drug behaviour among the youth
- A person with sense of dress code	- violence against women at all places
- Social equality for all	- unjust social, economic and political system
- Gender equality and gender justice	- untrained and inefficient officer
- No class affiliation at all	- class differences in all manifestations
- No role of caste in society	- treatment with SCs in India
- No discrimination with any individual	- system of social stratification
- NGOs role in society	-exploitation of workers
- Social planning in all fields	- feudal system and its social impact
- Complete change and development	- sexual promiscuity
- Tough life orientation to problems	-having no national and cultural belonging
- Social policy for development	- violation of values and norms
- Role of Social legislation	- violent attitudes and behaviour
- Egalitarian social order	- mental health problems
- Cordial relations with all	- poverty and underdevelopment
- Hard work by students and scholars	- process of alienation
- Competitive life	- political suppression
- Social work among needy	- committing suicide
- Discipline in social life	- avoiding responsibility.

8. CONCEPTS OF "I", "ME" AND "WE"

(i) The consciousness of 'I' was at its highest degree in K-16's personality. It was always alive, dynamic and reminding in his mind. It was because of his experience of harsh conditions and acute problems in the past and struggle which he waged against these odd.

(ii) 'Me' represented a consciousness and identity about high level of 'I'. It represented accumulated lot of life experiences with positive as well as negative features and implications. So, this concept may be equated with:

- My struggle in life
- My efforts towards progress in life
- My encounters with real life situations
- My emotions and feelings about life
- My logic, patience and responsibility in life
- My attitudes, ideas and views about life
- My hard facts of life.

(iii) According to K-16, 'we' referred to direct phenomenon which stood as the product of collective life experiences with positive social image and implications. 'We' specifically referred to following features with associated social images and implications:

Life as 'We'	*Social image*	*Social implication*
- Academicians	dignified	social attachment
- Professionals	dignified	social attachment
- Experts	high status	social attachment
- Teachers	dignified	social attachment
- Social notables	dignified	social attachment
- Doctors	humanistic	social attachment
- Social workers	humanistic	social attachment

In all three concepts, I, Me and We, K-16 had a dominant element of pathology which created his 'I' as socially cornered, 'me' as socially regimented lot, and 'we' as the police collective social entity.

9. IDEAS OF EQUALITY AND INEQUALITY

(i) K-16 was a strong supporter of human equality on pure humanistic considerations. In this regard, he emphasised modern standard and religious-oriented equality whose chief characteristics are noted below:

(a) Modern standards of equality:

- Equality in economic position.
- Equal education to all children
- No division on the basis of caste
- Equal political and cultural rights
- Equality between nation at global level
- Support for political and civil rights of people
- Equality between opposite sexes
- No discrimination in selection of jobs
- Equality in competition and mobility

(b) Religious oriented Considerations:

- Human considerations in equality concepts, ideas and ideals.
- No differentiation or discrimination in any field of life.
- Rights of all people, especially elders, women, children and minorities must be safeguarded.
- No class, caste and race consideration in social life.
- No selfish interests in social life at the cost of others.
- Sharing economic prosperity with others.
- Social ethics and morality to be maintained in all situations.

(ii) K-16 felt that, in the above context, there was hardly any scope for class or caste inequality in society. He also felt that these inequalities must be systematically ignored, diluted and dropped.

(iii) K-16 was in favour of absolute equality between men and women. But, at the same time, some limitations like biological limitations must be considered while giving them broader social role. He felt that women throughout human history had been facing inequality and injustice. Now, in the modern times, that inequality and injustice must be eradicated in totality. This, according to K-16, can be done through social legislation and its effective implementation. For this macro-level effort, we need joint efforts of individuals and groups in an organised and systematic way. NGOs must be involved in this grand effort. K-16 also referred to the injustice perpetrated on women in domestic context. This intra-sex practise of injustice women must be done away with purposefully and meaningfully.

10. THE IDEAL CHARACTER

(i) K-16 had no particular individual as his ideal leader or character because, according to him, it was very difficult to develop and maintain continuously certain human standards of the highest-purest level in the present day situation. So, he thought about an ideal character which he tried to follow in his personal life. That was the ideal character of a teacher who follows certain social ideals, ideas, concepts, attitudes, behaviour and other life features. He was considered godly, noble and super-human in life situations. He follows god's profession and god's teachings and seriously worked for humanity to take it from darkness to light. These social ideal features and their degree of adoptability and level of quality, especially in the case of teacher, were identified as follows:

Social features-ideals	*Degree of adoptability-level of quality*		
	Highest	*normal*	*lowest*
- Sincerity and honesty	^	...	...
- Competence	^	...	...
- Specialisation	...	^	...
- Updated knowledge	^	...	...
- Intellectual caliber	...	^	...
- I.Q.	...	^	...
- Human approach	^	...	...
- Regulatory and punctuality	...	^	...
- Home preparation	^	...	...
- Scientific temper	^	...	...
- Commitment and dedication	^	...	...
- A person of a profession	...	^	...
- Not for money only	...	^	...
- Decent behaviour	...	^	...
- Oratory and public speaker	...	^	...
- Personal economic status	^	...	...
- Following values and norms	^	...	...
- Religious character	^	...	...
- Ethics and moral standards	...	^	...
- Upper caste/class b. ground	...	...	^
- Cultural standards	...	^	...
- Political ideology	...	...	s
- Anti-establishment	^	...	...

11. GLOBAL SOCIAL ORDER

(i) K-16 was of the view that emergence of GSO was needed in order to control the erosion of efficacy of basic social institutions in society. He felt that it can establish significance, utility and functionality of the institutions of family, school, religion and marriage.

(ii) First, the institution of family will be oriented to basic social training to children through internalisation of values and norms and will initiate the process of personality formation within family context. Second, school will be oriented to create social ethos and cultural environment that will lead to determination of relevant and desirable role and status for out-family situations. Third, the institution of religion will be oriented towards the totality of social life, particularly focusing on interaction between individuals, groups, communities and classes. It will also provide basis for cultural life and stable relationship with other cultures. The religion and culture together will affect all in-family and out-family activities, which will give rise to a stable social order.

(iii) Finally, the institution of marriage will be oriented towards its well established goals and create a situation of cultural transformation from ne generation to the next in the post-marital life situation. In this way, GSO will prove meaningful for the basic character of social order at the global level.

12. THE RELIGIOUS LIFE

(i) Basically, K-16 was a religious person, believing in all fundamentals and essential practices of Islam perfectly. He had correct notions of basic religions concepts, views and theories as he had studied *Quran* and *Hadith* in depth. In practise too, he followed all necessary religious practices and rules. In fact, K-16 was oriented towards this type of behaviour from the childhood stage. The religious traits in his behaviour were generally from earlier generations in the family.

(ii) K-16 believed with equal intensity in folk religious practices and upheld their ideology, which he always supported. He also justified the practices related to the *peer-mureedi.* He felt no contradiction between ideal-doctrinnaire Islam and folk religious practices in Kashmir. According to him, they go in coherence and reflected ideal and actual aspects of religion and represent internal and external facts of religious life. He was a regular visitor to all shrines on particular days but he never did saint-worshipping there, for which he had attracted wrath of *Mulla* there. He opposed some of the practices which violated the monotheism of Islam and duped rural-illiterate masses. K-16 maintained seriousness and sacredness of those places where he too prayed silently. He also celebrated particular days in a week/month/ year and prepared special dishes and drinks at home. He celebrated all *urs* in the valley.

(iii) However, K-16 had also developed contact with reformist and radical trends of Islam in Kashmir. It was mainly because of the impact of neighbours, FF, colleagues and others. Though he was impressed with these new religious ideological trends, he never joined them. He was extremely fond of folk religious practices.

(iv) K-16 had excellent relationship with KPs. As he had developed association with diverse social groups, he had developed close association with KP academicians, teachers, professionals, scientists, researchers, scholars, experts and so on. He used to visit their houses inside and outside Kashmir and used to get entertained by their traditional hospitality. He believed in the fact that KPs represented the most intellectual community in the country.

13. THE KASHMIR PROBLEM

(i) K-16 was interested in social aspects of the Kashmir problem related to the particular role played by political elites, families and ruling classes in its creation, evolution and resolution. He presented the view that actors of all these social collectivities in all countries, India, Pakistan and Kashmir, were responsible for prolonging this chronic problem in the sub-continent. The masses in these countries, especially masses in Kashmir, suffered extremely due to continuity of this problem. While ruling classes and elites in India and Pakistan made the focal point in foreign policies and core point in domestic political agenda, they hardly tried seriously and sincerely to resolve it realistically. These political actors of both countries, which included all political parties, organisations and groups, served their respective country's national interests. Thus these political exercises benefited ruling classes in both countries. On the other hand, people in Kashmir suffered continuously from 1947. But, the political elites and families too were benefited politically and economically irrespective of their ideological differences and also at the cost of masses.

14. FUTURE SOCIETY IN KASHMIR

K-16 had a particular ideological view of future society in Kashmir. That society must have to drop and, at the same time, to adopt certain social, cultural and political ideals in the broader social dynamics. These items included the following features:

Features to be dropped	*Features to be adopted*
- Cultural-religious singularity	- cultural-religious plurality
- Political dependence	- political independence
- Unscientific temper and behaviour	-scientific temper and behaviour
- No morality and no social ethics	- complete morality and ethics in social life
- Society without knowledge	- society with knowledge and scholarship
- Negative response to development	- positive response to change and development
- Violent lifestyle	- non-violent attitudes and behaviour
- Corruption and unemployment	- no corruption and employment-full society
- Gender discrimination	- gender justice
- Traditional notions of social change	-scientific social planning

14. SOCIAL PROBLEMS IN KASHMIR

(i) A*bsence of Social Ethics:* K-16 was very much concerned about deteriorating standard of public life, particularly in the field of academics. He always desired that minimum standards of social life must be maintained by all, particularly by professionals and academics. He lamented that academics in Kashmir were not fully committed to the profession of teaching and research. Only some of them were working regularly and seriously. Second, no serious and innovative scientific research were carried out. Third, some among them follow un-academic and amoral theoretical and political positions. K-16 felt that these practices on the part of academics were unscientific and unfair. They need to prefer sacred academic objectives in their activities and maintain standard practices in this regard.

(ii) *Non-seriousness among students:* K-16 was also concerned about non-serious behaviour of students, particularly in relation to study of syllabus books and attendance of classes. He felt that this problem stood alarming because of its implications on students future life. In schools, colleges and universities, they usually avoid attending classes and feel not inclined to study the prescribed books. The trend has emerged according to which they prefer to get 'notes' from some source and prepare for exams. In this way, they become 'uneducated graduates and post-graduates' with least knowledge about their subject.

In this context, this problem has emerged as a dangerous trend, according to K-16. It will certainly affect knowledge base and academic standard of society. Consequently, the society too will become poor intellectually. In view of these negative impact of this trend among students, it stood socially undesirable. So, this trend needed to be controlled and reversed necessarily.

K-17 THE KASHMIRI YOUTH – EX-MILITANT

1. POLITICAL CONTEXT

(i) The 1989 armed uprising of the Kashmiri youth against the Indian state signified one more violent effort in political movements for independence in modern times. The political uprising started after youth in Kashmir developed a perception according to which India will integrate Kashmir in its broader framework forcefully and will not allow KMs even to protest and assert their freedom demand democratically and peacefully. This happened in the aftermath of 1987 rigged elections in JK. When they were 'made' defeated, no alternative was left to the youth except to rise in revolt. They left for PAK, got arms training there, and came back to fight the Indian forces.

(ii) But, India crushed militancy with its military might of 7,00,000 armed forces. As a result of this forceful suppression, thousands of militants and civilians were killed, injured, disabled, tortured and disappeared and hundreds of women were raped, molested and abused. Other non-material and material loss was a great loss.

(iii) This armed uprising was started without ideological clarity, political consensus and intellectual participation. It is said that first group of militants was of semi-literate and lowly educated who lacked historical perspective, future vision and could not understand global-regional implications of politics. It was in this ideological and political vacuum that some petty elements exploited the uprising at the initial stage.

Others joined this struggle and made it a real political movement for *Azaadi.* It was at that stage K-17 joined the movement as its up-ground youth leader. He was a thinker, poet, scholar, idealist, ideologue and revolutionary. He was intellectual of the first order. He was not a dogmatic and fanatic religious follower but had global vision, international understanding and leadership qualities. More important, he was a proud son of Kashmir. People like K-17 gave the uprising a permanent and intellectual character.

(v) However, after some years of initiation of militancy in Kashmir, religious oriented political forces jumped in it. It was joined by their international colleagues called 'foreign' or 'guest' militants in Kashmir. This development radically changed the political situation vis a vis Kashmir's *Azaadi.* The Indian government carried out a successful campaign against this movement and dubbed it. Pakistan and Taliban sponsored and, so, it was characterised as "terrorist" movement. In that situation, the world opinion could not be convinced about indigenous political character. At the local front, the foreign-Afghan militants created deep reaction among local people because of former's undesirable acts and uncontrolled behaviour. In that political environment, the local intellectual dissident voices were silenced by intelligence agencies of India and Pakistan through their "unknown armed militants" (*namaloom bandook bardaar).* K-17 too fell to the alien bullets of alien armed men like many other great Kashmiri personalities.

2. IN-FAMILY SOCIALISATION

(i) K-17 was born in a far-off village family which had lower social and economic standard. As in case of others in the village, peasant families represented an average type in which they produced rice from agricultural lands for their self needs. In the second type, the peasants made a share-cropping with others. In the third type, earlier options were not available, so they opted for work as wage labourer. In the absence of all preceding choices, they worked in orchards or forests or other villages/towns as daily wage workers. In that agrarian situation, peasants life conditions were far from satisfaction. K-17's family was not an exception. But, even in those conditions, it maintained decency, culture and religiosity.

(ii) Despite this hard economic condition, K-17 family gave modern education to all children at primary and secondary level. The woman head of the family was an highly idealistic and an innovative person and used to give some ideal roles to her children. K-17 was socialised in this tough, harsh, difficult and poor life situation. But, he lived with it consciously and faced all its challenges throughout his life span.

3. OUT-FAMILY ENVIRONMENT

(i) The out family environment of K-17 was composed of relatives, neighbours, personal friends and others. First, the relatives of K-17 were living in same or lower economic, educational, social and cultural status. So, they had hardly any impact on his ideas and ideals. Second, his neighbours in the village belonged to the same status of poverty, dependence, backwardness. They too were not relevant for influencing the life of K-17. Rather there was opposite kind of impact observed.

(ii) Third, personal friends and acquaintances of K-17 proved highly influential and they decided the roadmap of his life and future of his personality. They composed a wider variety social personalities such as:

- Scholars	- researchers	- ideologues	- revolutionaries
- Religious preachers	- religious leaders	- eminent writers	- famous poets
- Administrators	- officers	- scientists	- academicians
- Teachers	- intellectuals	- professionals	- doctors
- Engineers	-politicians	- political workers	- businessmen

As all these categories of distinct people met and interacted with K-17, they found him :

- Highly universal in orientation	- highly revolutionary in ideas
- Highly emancipator in approach	- highly progressive in ideology
- Highly scholastic in presentation	- highly educated in information
- Highly scientific in thinking	- highly enlightened in views
- Highly modernised in lifestyle	- highly religious in attitudes and beliefs
- Highly intellectual in political ideas	- multi-faced personality

They accepted him for all these traits. In fact, they loved and showered affection on him throughout. In this way, he developed a broad network of well-wishers in rural as well as urban areas.

(iii) K-17 impressed all others mainly because of his personality features which included the following:

- Always knowledge gaining	- intellectual treatment of all issues
- Religious orientation in his whole life	- revolutionary perspective on all issues
- Anti-establishment in orientation in life	- literary presentation of ideas and views
- Rational-logical formulations always	- non-dogmatic and dynamic approach

In this process of constant interaction with those distinct personalities, he developed a new way of life. As his contacts extended, he became a popular person. Subsequently, he emerged as the student leader who was a great orator too. He used to deliver impressive speeches even during his student days.

(iv) His constant contact and daily interaction with political leaders and activists broadened his political contact and started playing the role of student cum youth leader. This image of K-17 spread from towns to the city where he got wider appreciation due to his academic, intellectual, revolutionary and literary credentials. He joined and established several student and youth political organisations which were mostly anti-establishment. But, at the same time, he didn't stay in one organisation for a long time and repeatedly shifted to other organisations. He was never satisfied with static position and static reality and wanted dynamic status and role.

(v) After the long journey in politics, he emerged as an established and legitimate leader in 1980s at the state level. Others who helped K-17 to reach at this stage included senior scholars, politicians, professionals, businessmen officers, professors, lawyers, doctors, academicians and so on.

4. EDUCATION AND INTELLECT

(i) K-17's primary and middle education was imparted in a nearby village in a government school. Despite unfavorable economic conditions at home, he carried out education and continued till higher stage where he topped in performance at all stages. The secondary level education was carried out in nearby town. For graduation, he shifted to main town where he met a lot of intellectual and politically-committed teachers. They appreciated his intellectual capabilities and encouraged him to follow the political career in future. After completing graduation, he joined the post-graduate course in the university and completed it. His performance became a standard and reference point. His literary styles were unique and promising. His revolutionary ideas, anti-establishment views, and radical political contents gave him wider acceptance at the state level.

(ii) K-17 left for Delhi for doctorate in a central university which he characterised as "so called Oxford of the East". Through his academic performance, he showed his excellence in research field and made his distinctive impression on the faculty. His writings were rated as 'master pieces' and were read repeatedly. But, at the same time, he had the limitation of not concentrating on a single work and work within a formal framework.

5. CAREER AND ORIENTATION

(i) It was clear from the beginning that K-17 will adopt career in politics. That he did consciously from his student days. So, he started his career as a student leader. The main issues of his politics those days were student problems, political instability-uncertainty and anti-establishment activities. While he was non-dogmatic, revolutionary, radical and non-compromising, his political views were directed against the Kashmir policy of GOI.

(ii) When his political activities extended, he became the youth leader in the town and city. He was popular for his personal qualities, especially oratory, revolutionary ideas and anti-establishment approach. The most important political objective of his life was to get independence for Kashmir. He was ready to sacrifice anything for achieving this objective. Though he was continuously monitored and disturbed by intelligence agencies of India and Pakistan, he never deviated from his ideal objective. K-17 was very clear that he was not pro or anti-India; or pro or anti Pakistan; but only pro-Kashmir.

(iii) After decades of political career, K-17 emerged as a mature political leader at the state level. He worked in political organisations and political parties on different positions. But, he maintained same political ideals and objectives, political values and norms, and political ideas and ideology. Taking into consideration his faculties and intellectual standards, he was offered by the ruling party the position of MLA. But, he refused categorically because it was against his political objectives. He behaved like a statesman and made a difference with his grace and dignity.

6. ASSOCIATION AND MOBILITY

(i) K-17's career of more than three decades determined his nature of association. This association was real, sincere and objective-oriented. The main groups involved in this broader network of association were as follows:

- political leaders	- political workers	- intellectuals
- scholars	- writers	- poets
- journalists	- professionals	- officers
- administrators	- bureaucrats	- businessmen
- traders and industrialists	- workers-labourers	- artists
- poor masses.		

He was highly conscious of the length and breadth of his lifelong association, so, maintained it consciously till his last moment.

(ii) Taking into consideration his background and lifelong struggle and its political status in the state, his mobility pattern was upward and significant. During his mature stage of political career, he was well respected by all political leaders in the state. Moreover, he was considered as 'star attraction' for public mobilisation.

7. MARRIAGE AND FAMILY

(i) K-17 was married in the village in his early age as was the custom prevalent there. According to this customary practice, males of early age used to be married in consideration of their initiating and establishing family role at an early stage. In the case of K-17, that marriage didn't prove productive. He used to remain away from home for weeks together for political activities in towns and city. After shifting to Delhi, he married another woman who was working there. In addition to lifelong company to him, this new relationship provided shelter and economic stability to him there.

(ii) This marriage was exogamous and matri-local type of civil marriage in which both partners belonged to same economic, social and educational status. Thus the male settled at female residence temporarily. After some time, they shifted to Kashmir. While the husband was devoted to politics of Kashmir, the wife got engaged in her profession. Both were active in their respective activities and their marital relationship was alive. But, this relationship collapsed after K-17 was killed in his ancestral home village. Subsequently, his wife remained alone with her daughter in nuclear family household and shifted to new house constructed in newly-established colony in periphery of the city.

8. SOCIAL LIKES AND DISLIKES

After going through his hard and tough life experiences, K-17 had developed following social likes and dislikes:

Social Likes	*Social Dislikes*
- Revolutionary ideas and ideology	- no ideas for innovative works
- Educated-emancipated personality	- person without political perspective in life
- Ideologically committed individual and group	- westernised life style
- Egalitarian political system	- gender inequality and segregation
- Agitation and protest of political nature	- politics of region and religion
- Literary meetings and activities	- cultural exclusiveness
- A big and happy family life	-an unproductive and ineffective political system
- Scientific and liberal approach in life	- an extreme Hindu revivalist organisation
- Moderate religious attitudes and behaviour	- political non-participation
- Equal status for all religions	- corrupt politics and politicians
- Youth agitating for their rights	- discrimination of any type
- Right to self-determination to all groups	- denial of basic human rights
- Political modernisation in relevant areas	- anti-minority politics by communal groups
- Charismatic leader and his authority	- an incompetent and untrained teacher
- Gender justice	- illiteracy and ignorance in villages
- Children with all facilities of modern life	- poverty and underdevelopment
- Marriage with austerity	- village isolation and dependence
-Internationalism in politics at higher stage	-social injustice with some particular communities
- Intellectual of the highest order	- drug behaviour of youth
- Life with all necessities available	- political instability and political uncertainty.

9. CONCEPTS OF "I", "ME" AND "WE"

(i) K-17 was conscious upholder of all three psychological identities, especially through the poetry of literary presentation of 'I', 'me' and 'we'. First, according to K-17, 'I' stood for ego called *khudi* by Dr. Iqbal. It does not convey arrogance or hot-headedness but humility and self-confidence; not a false notion but an actual reality; no sense of superiority-inferiority but egalitarianism and humanism. In this connection, a man and nation can reach to the highest level of material and spiritual development. That is why, Dr. Iqbal said

Khudi ko kar buland itna ki khuda tum se

Khud poochey bata nere raza kya hay

In this context, K-17 felt that 'I' stood for past, present and future; man's struggle in all stages of development and all situations.

(ii) K-17 held that 'me' essentially stood for 'my' contribution to society and humanity. Its contents were conveyed to all generations symbolically. These ideas were borrowed from Dr. Iqbal's famous poem *Insaan khuda ke hazoor me.* In this poem, man tells God bluntly that what he had done in the world. God replied and that reply prevailed over whole humanity, which conveyed the message of universal ideas, values and ideals. Finally, the poem concludes on the concepts of *Haq,* the status of man, and *Batil,* the status of his eternal enemy. In this context, 'me' referred to

- My culture	- my civilisation	- my creation
- My personality	- my views	- my ideology
- My vision	- my innovation	- my deeds and thinking

This concept of 'me' also referred to the struggle against *Shaitan* in all fields of life, especially politics, history, philosophy, economy, civics and others.

(iii) According to K-17, the concept of 'we' was an acceptance of the domination of society over individual. It could be equated with 'human whole', human aggregation at global level, their human relationship throughout history and finally made a comparison between 'we' and 'they'. Thus 'we' identified types and nature of their relations as follows:

- We the human .... And they the sub-humans
- We the eastern .... they the western
- We the Asians and Africans........... they the Europeans and Americans
- We the Muslims .... they the non-Muslims
- We the colonised............................. they the colonizers
- We the humiliated............................ they the humiliation imposer
- We the exploited.............................. they the exploiter
- We the subordinates .... they the super-ordinates
- We the *Haq parast* .... they the *batil parast.*

10. IDEAS OF EQUALITY AND INEQUALITY

(i) K-17 believed in absolute notion of equality in every human field but differently and contextually. It follows that while he upheld total equal status for men and women in life, some fields demand contextual and relative roles. So, equality has to be related with contextual needs and background demands. These notions of equality, upheld by K-17, were more poetic, philosophical, revolutionary and idealistic than, formal legal, realistic and actual. These were drawn mostly from revolutionary literature in Urdu language in the Indian sub-continent. These particular ideas and notions with their nature of applicability were identified as follows:

Life fields	*Caste equality*	*Class equality*	*Gender equality*
- Education	yes	yes	yes
- Economic status	yes	yes	yes
- Social status	yes	yes	yes
- Cultural status	yes, partial	yes	yes partial
- Religious status	yes	yes	yes
- Political status	yes	yes	yes
- Regional status	yes	yes	yes
- Science and technology	yes, partial	yes, partial	yes
- Scientific research	yes	yes, partial	yes, partial
- Professions	yes, partial	yes, partial	yes, partial
- Official positions	yes, partial	yes, partial	yes, partial
- Political leaders	yes	yes	yes, partial
- Health and medicines	yes	yes	yes

11. THE IDEAL CHARACTER

(i) *Agha Shoorish Kashmiri (ASK):* ASK was a prominent political and literary figure. He was born in India and died in Pakistan. He was a life-long editor of the famous Urdu weekly *CHATAN*. Throughout his life, he stood for anti-establishment ideas, ideology and policy. He participated in several anti-establishment movements in Pakistan for political justice and rule of democracy. *Pase Deeware Zindaan* stood as his testament for his anti-establishment ideology and approach in Pakistan. He consistently opposed all military dictators in Pakistan and was imprisoned several times. He was always revolutionary in ideas and actions, so never surrendered before totalitarian rulers in Pakistan. His name *Shoorish,* which means protests, itself reflected the essence of his lifelong objective.

(ii) K-17 was highly impressed by ASK because of four main reasons. First, he was a Kashmiri origin person. Second, he was a sincere revolutionary in ideas and actions and wanted radical changes in political order. Third, he always stood for anti-establishment ideology and participated in all anti-dictatorial political movements in Pakistan. Fourth, he always stood the ideal 'Kashmir cause' in Pakistan and criticised the military rulers in Pakistan not to follow this cause sincerely.

(iii) He was a contemporary of Faiz Ahmad Faiz in literary field and of his standard in literary status. He suffered throughout his life but never left the support to the suppressed-oppressed in his country and outside. He used to quote often the following lines of Faiz :

Qurban teri guliyon pa aay watan ki jahan

Chali he rasam ki koyi sar uthake ne chaley

His weekly newspaper *CHATAN* was like a regular diet for K-17 and he used to get political inspiration from this mouth-piece of ASK.

12. GLOBAL SOCIAL ORDER

(i) K-17 was internationalist in approach and wanted to follow social ideals in this orientation. So, according to him, the ideals of GSO must be followed within a distinct framework. It follows that this global order must suit super human values and must reflect in the literary dimension. It follows that different languages and literature of the world, in addition to the English language, must be allowed to play free and fair role in formulation, establishment, functioning and objectives of GSO. Its necessary features are noted below:

- equal treatment to developed and developing languages and literature of the world in addition to the global English language and literature in the formulation, evolution and functioning of the GSO;
- role of world languages in the input and output processes of literary developments in the maintenance of this global order;
- evolution and preparation of global literature from non-Western and non-English languages of the world;
- to put efforts to restrain from creating such a forum which will be of colonised type and serve the monopolistic interests at the global level; and
- to carry out consistent global efforts of translation of all important pieces of literature from developed to developing or under-developed languages and vice versa.

13. THE RELIGIOUS LIFE

(i) K-17 was a strong believer in Islamic fundamentals. He had developed rational understanding about Islamic concepts from authentic sources of *Quran and Hadith* directly. So, all basic concepts of Islam and their applicability in present day times was very clear in his mind. Since K-17 was a well-read person, he had developed comprehensive, historical and comparative understanding of Islam.

(ii) However, he had no consideration of folk religious practices. His view was that these practices were creation of local people who have made these (practices) as 'accessories' of Islam in Kashmir. There was no relevance and no role for these practices in ideal pure Islam. Moreover, these practices were exploited by ruling political leaders and *mullahs* for their political and economic interests respectively. As per his perception, villagers were prime victims of this exploitation. K-17 never visited shrines for worship but for political lectures. He never celebrated particular days in a week/month/year and never performed any rituals.

(iii) K-17 was a strong supporter of reformists and radical trends of Islam in Kashmir. He explained these trends as a reaction to corrupting pure form of Islam and the response to suppression of Muslims world over. He worked hard for expansion of these trends and used these for cause of Kashmir. So, he used these radical trends as ideology for political purposes.

14. POLITICAL IDEOLOGY

(i) K-17's political understanding was national as well as global in substance. He analysed issues and problems with proper perspective and objective critique of international level. So, he had broader and deeper global perspective of political ideology. He explained world ideologies in three major ideologies with their supporting systems. These ideologies were :

(a) *The Communist ideology:* K-17 explained this ideology in terms of totalitarian system and dictatorship of a few ideologues. It threw democracy and its system into the background, so it was not open but a closed system. It gave rise, from top to bottom to a corrupt and non-accountable system. It led to the massacre of thousands of people in the name of ideological revolution. It didn't provide any chance to grow any credible opposition from within. It denied basic human rights and civil liberties of all citizens. It could never establish ideal ideological or political system with its distinct economy, polity and society. It finally collapsed under its own weight and ideological contradictions.

(b) *Capitalism:* K-17 was also critical of capitalist political system because of reasons mentioned below:

- it could never establish egalitarian economic, social and political set-up and divided society into extremely different classes permanently;
- it could never benefit all members of society equally, thus increased and intensified gap between rich and poor, especially in Asia and Africa;
- in many cases, it led to domination and exploitation by those whose wealth was more than their needs over those who lack wealth even for their basic needs;
- it legitimised the system of economic exploitation through the interest-based financial dealings; and
- on the name of open competition, it benefited a few groups and betrayed larger groups of society.

(c) *Islamic Political System:* After making criticism of communism and capitalism, K-17 presented the concept of 'Islamic Political System'

(IPS), which stood non-existing and was to be established, whose prominent features were identified as follows:

- this system would establish democratic governance at all levels as suggested by *Quran and Hadith;*
- this system would have representative credentials in terms of representation to all groups, nationalities, ethnicities, religions and so on;
- all positive features of capitalism and communism would be incorporated into this system in order to make a balanced system;
- it would be ideologically directed system and would uphold and follow certain particular goals and objectives determined in advance;
- its social policy will be universal welfare-oriented;
- in domestic political matters, principal of consensus will be adopted and in external policy, the principal of justice and equity will be followed; and
- it would establish an egalitarian system in which every individual would have equal status and no discrimination would be made.

The above features stood as high ideal and not actual and needed to be applied in the proper political environment.

15. POLITICS OF THE KASHMIR PROBLEM

(i) K-17 felt that local politics always revolved around the Kashmir problem whose basics were not known to global audience. He saw this problem in totalistic perspective whose features were as follows:

(a) *Political:* The problem was created in 1947 and not resolved so far. It demanded resolution as per the UN granted RSD to the people in Kashmir.

(b) *Historical:* It was created by actions of India and Pakistan which made promises to Kashmiris to hold plebiscite at appropriate time. But, India backtracked due to its narrow nationalistic interest and occupied Kashmir permanently.

(c) *Social:* The intensive process of 'indianisation' of Kashmir was followed by GOI after 1947. But, the goal of national integration could not be achieved. The failure in integration led to non-violent as well as violent uprisings.

(d) *Economic:* After facing economic collapse after 1947, the economic dependence of JK on India was developed consciously and systematically. This situation also led to economic exploitation of Kashmir in the field of power generation, forests and mineral wealth.

(e) *Demographic:* After reducing population of Muslims in JK from 80% in 1941 to 62% in 2001, the GOI intended to change the majority character of the state in the near future.

(f) *Education:* In post-1947 era, while literacy rate in JK could not be increased impressively, the general educational backwardness could not be eradicated totally. There was also failure of achievement of the goal of universal enrolment at primary level.

(g) *Cultural:* The GOI attempted full cultural integration but faced opposition by the locals. Subsequently, various processes of cultural aggression were pursued.

(h) *Linguistic:* Though constitution of India ensured plural linguistic character, the proponents of Hindi language wanted to impose it forcefully. This was strongly resisted by the locals.

(i) *Psychology:* In this antagonistic situation, emergence of anti-Indian sentiment among Kashmiris could not be avoided.

(j) *Ideological:* There was no ideological similarity between India and Kashmir. Even then the former tried to impose the ideology on the latter, leading to ideological confrontation in Kashmir.

16. FUTURE KASHMIR SOCIETY

K-17 drew an idealistic plan for future society in Kashmir in the above-mentioned thematic framework in which he delineated its various features, which are mentioned below:

- Politically, it will be liberal, democratic, constitutional and representative
- Socially, it will be multi-ethnic, multi-national, multi-cultural and so on
- Economically, it will be liberal, interest-free and welfare-oriented
- Educationally, it will be 100% literate and 100% primary-level enrolment society
- Culturally, it will be multi-cultural showing patience and tolerance of all cultures and religions
- Linguistically, it will respect all mother languages and will identify and establish a link language

16 EXPERIENCE OF CONFLICT SITUATION

(i) As is clear now, K-17's first hand information about intellectual character of *Azaadi* movement, led him to emphasise the point that all groups, classes and communities must joined this point. In fact, the class factor became irrelevant in this type of political participation. Though this movement started with lowly educated local youth, it was subsequently joined by the intelligentsia, especially intellectuals. Those who joined or supported the movement included doctors, professionals, academicians, engineers, journalists, artists, thinkers, ideologues, writers, notables, religious preachers and leaders and other such personalities. Thus the movement developed high intellectual character.

17. SOCIAL PROBLEMS IN KASHMIR

(i) *Political uncertainty and Political instability:* K-17 felt that the problem of temporary accession of JK to India in 1947 created serious problems of political instability and uncertainty. While the latter was mainly due to non-resolution of Kashmir problem for ever, the former reflected in all post-1947 political regimes in the state. Consequently, neither political objectives of national integration could be fulfilled nor planned and systematic economic development could be pursued. So, the state remained backward in economic, educational and other fields. It had also disastrous effects for policy formulation, program implementation and planned development in the state. No private investment could be attracted in Kashmir. Even the GOI was hesitant to invest in this place on a long-term basis. That is why no worthwhile private sector with huge infrastructure could be developed.

The political uncertainty further introduced political corruption and bureaucratic bungling as they wanted to earn money in shortest possible time. In that situation, no respect was shown to democratic rights and civil liberties and no attempt was made for evolving genuine political participation in the national politics. Lastly, it contributed to the deterioration of ethics and moral standards in the state.

(ii) *Political Corruption:* The state of JK was deeply entrenched in the process of political corruption in which all major and minor political leaders from all political parties were directly or indirectly involved in corrupt practices for the benefit of their families and groups. This emerged as a common phenomenon in Kashmir after 1947 and particularly after 1953.

It is generally believed here that political corruption in Kashmir started at the highest level of politics in order to buy loyalty and support for Kashmir's accession to India. In the period after 1953, this corruption percolated to upper and middle level bureaucracy and administration which usually belonged to outside state cadre. They were given free hand to adopt any kind of tactics or method to make 'indianisation' of Kashmir a stable, strong and aggressive process. The continuous support to these practices by state and central governments in a way, legitimised the political corruption among the influential and dominant groups of society and, later on, expanded to civil society. This has now involved all political parties, organisations, groups, of all shades, views and ideologies. This political deterioration of political culture contributed partly to the emergence of political revolt against the governments in the Centre and State.

K-18 ELDER KASHMIRI INTELLECTUAL

1. SOCIAL CONTEXT

(i) Till early decades of 20th century, there prevailed an overall backwardness among KMs, especially in the fields of economy, education, and culture. This situation started undergoing change from 1931 when an organised and politically-directed movement for total emancipation of Kashmiris in modern times started. In this background, different sections of Kashmiri society responded positively towards modern education. The KPs were already literate. The other local literate group was of *Sayyids,* both men and women, who attained modern education, got government jobs and accepted other effects in life. Similarly, some lower class groups responded positively to education which was provided through the then-government-run schools. Like their predecessors, they got some jobs but petty and ordinary. When these individuals became in charge of their families and new generation, they pursued modern education necessarily. In that situation, a new trend of attainment of modern education got boost after 1947, particularly after 1952, when free education from primary till university was introduced in the state.

(ii) In the near future, this situation gave rise to a new generation of KMs. The associated development at that time was simultaneous growth of intellectual environment in Muslim families. That was not just possible before 1931 when there was no education, no economic standing and no cultural exposure. In that new environment, the intellectual activities reflected in social actions mentioned below:

- establishment of libraries in homes and borrowing books from public libraries;
- studying books, journals and magazines on various subjects and topics, and reading of daily and weekly newspapers;
- understanding and analysis of national-global issues and problems in an academic framework;
- holding discussions and debates on day-to-day issues and national-international problems;
- developing academic orientation and literary taste in life;
- liking arts, crafts and other related specialities;
- developing interest in regional, national, continental and global matters of common concern to all of us;
- inviting scholars, thinkers, writers, intellectuals and others for lectures and talks;
- understanding the religious thought, its basic and its application; and

- developing serious interest in the study of other religions and religious communities.

(iii) The academic-intellectual family environment with above-mentioned features was totally impossible before 1947. But, with broader changes, it emerged now in many families, as happened in K-18 family. In actuality, he belongs to that post-1947 generation of Kashmiris which started intellectual tradition in the community. He faced several difficulties and social opposition but upheld the new tradition.

(iv) Thus K-18 considered education as necessary step in the intellectual life. He used to borrow books from different libraries or buy for the purpose of study. He used to engage children, relatives, friends and others in discussions on every occasion. He also used to convey to his and others children to make reading a permanent habit and to involve in literary activities. This kind of academic, intellectual and literary activities was uncommon till recent past in Kashmir.

2. IN-FAMILY SOCIALISATION

(i) K-18's in-family socialisation took place in semi-literate environment in which his own family was literate, while others were illiterate. Same was the condition of his relatives and neighbours. In actuality, at that time, while 1930s generation was least educated-employed, 1940s and 1950s generations had initiated efforts to opt for literacy fully. So, more and more groups-classes started adopting literacy status and consequently accepted the impact on society, economy and culture.

(ii) K-18's family led to two sources of impact on socialisation. The first was from the side of his father who was a petty official. He was straight, hard, regimented, disciplined, authoritarian and realistic in life. These qualities of his father had some impact on the personality of K-18. Since he belonged to relatively economic background, it had sober effect on his life. So, he was serious in studies as well as in life in terms of following values and norms, discipline, laws and rules and elder's authority. In this way, K-18 had distinct perspective of life and maintained distinct lifestyle.

(iii) The second source of influence was outside family environment. Most of his relatives and neighbours were illiterate or getting literate at that time. They too affected his life. But, this impact proved partial and transitory and was within the parameters of tradition, religion, social structure, culture and education.

3. OUT-FAMILY ENVIRONMENT

(i) The out-family environment proved very effective in the life of K-18. His relatives were a mixture of literate and illiterate, lowly and highly educated, employed and non-employed. He visited and interacted with both categories of relatives but accepted the impact of the former. He also kept impressions about the latters' lives in mind and referred to these during his discussions as undesirable category. K-18 had a sense of 'past' and 'past of the community', especially in relation to poverty, ignorance and social-cultural backwardness. Some of his relatives were highly educated and politically active and connected. He often interacted with them and accepted many things from them except politics.

(ii) K-18's neighbours were mostly illiterate. While his family kept him away from their influence, his father too kept him at a distance from them. He was not allowed to interact freely with lowest sections of society. So, he developed a negative image of neighbours.

(iii) K-18's FFs were all sorts of people with distinct qualifications and qualities. They included well educated, highly cultured, professionals, officials, social notables writers, artists and others. He had adopted the cumulated impact of that friendship on his intellect, attitudes, views, ideas, behaviour and on the whole way of life. He often talked about these people and their desirable way of life. He remembered all their advices, lectures, talks and tried to apply in life through practical wisdom. So, he attempted to produce such a desirable family.

4. EDUCATION AND CAREER

(i) K-18's primary, middle and higher education took place in city's government schools where education was imparted free. These schools were all located in nearby localities. His high school had considerable strength of KP students because of a KP locality in the neighbourhood. His association with these students increased his intelligence, capability and merit that contributed to his bright future career. For college education, K-18 joined a city college of eminence in those days. There he was exposed to literary, social, cultural, minority and political groups which seriously affected his attitude and behaviour and determined his social life. Since he was a serious student, he got highest grades. He also participated in different activities in the college.

(ii) He did not opt for P.G. because his family needed his economic support. So, he tried for a job which he got in a semi-government office. He joined the organisation and served there till he retired. There he got several promotions and reached to one of the highest positions in the organisation. After retirement, he worked in other private offices and organisations.

5. THE INTELECTUAL LIFE

(i) K-18 was always of intellectual nature. He always remained alive in his life. This life reflected in the following activities:

- he made regular and systematic study of books, magazines, periodicals, journals and newspapers. While the books were related to history, literature, civics, sociology, anthropology, culture, language and international affairs. He used to study in mornings-evenings, on holidays and off-days. This study accumulated his knowledge in various fields and helped him in discussions and gave deeper understanding of life and its problems.

- K-18 established a good library having hundreds of books on variety of topics and themes. He used to bring books from different libraries and also buy books from market. He had the largest library in his entire clan.
- He used to involve family members, relatives and personal and ffs and others in serious discussions about current issues and problems. He used to read newspapers daily and get information about current issues.
- K-18 usually took part in all discussion on current national and international affairs. So, he had emerged a good debater. He had a lot of knowledge about religion, culture, social, linguistic, ideological, economic and other topics. In these discussions, he used to share his experiences of life to impress upon the audience. He also used to ask questions from his own and other's children on their subjects and GN.
- K-18 participated regularly in radio and television programs of literary, language, literature and general themes.

6. OCCUPATION, ASSOCIATION AND MOBILITY

(i) K-18's family in the past had no particular occupation. His fore-fathers must have been engaged in petty business activities. The observed fact was that his father belonged to lower economic background due to his petty official position. That was the adoption of new occupation in family which was accepted with all its positive implications.

(ii) The same occupational line was followed by K-18. In fact, his formal education prepared him for that role. His socialisation within and outside family oriented him towards this job. Finally, after graduation, he consciously opted for it consciously and adopted its lifestyle and day-to-day engagement pattern. The regular salary to the family at that time provided strong economic basis. So, new occupation proved to it helpful, beneficial and prospective.

(iii) K-18's career was followed by selective association of his colleagues and friends. They included senior-junior-equal status colleagues from all classes and communities and all regions and religions. He had developed life-long associations with them who visited his house most often. Special mention may be made about his association with KP colleagues. He referred to this association as materially rewarding, socially beneficial and culturally needed.

(iv) In the preceding context, significant degree of mobility was experienced in the family of K-18 from petty government official to a gazetted government official. This mobility was glaringly clear in the family life at home and so on. He was satisfied about this achievement and wanted this type of mobility too about his children, relatives and friends.

7. MARRIAGE AND FAMILY

(i) Marriage of K-18 was of exogamous type and the girl with whom he was married belonged to same economic, social, educational and cultural status. However, he claimed superior status for his family. Since the girl was educated, it became a mobility factor in his life. In totality, this marriage contributed to intellectual growth in the family environment.

(ii) K-18 lived with his parental joint family and shared its social life seriously. Even after marriage, he and his wife lived in the same family unit and became deeply involved in family life. This type of joint family life continued till the marriage of his sisters and subsequent death of his parents. At that stage, this family was reduced to a nuclear character in which K-18, his wife and their unmarried children lived. In this type of family, the sole authority rested with him and he developed authoritative and intellectual environment in it. His ideas and ideals regarding that environment became reality. His ideals of academic excellence, higher education, literary activities, modern lifestyle were practised with high degree of commitment.

(iii) However, the intellectual environment had a particular impact on the marriage of K-18's children. All of them were married in exogamous circles, particularly in elite families and professional groups. This was possible only because of the intellectual contact of K-18 within and outside Kashmir.

(iv) It seems important to note here that extreme modernity impact on the family did not prove beneficial in the long term. K-18's children, after getting higher education, higher jobs and affluent lifestyle, established their respective nuclear family units after marriage in a newly-constructed house by each alone in middle class colony in the periphery of city. From his joint family unit, there emerged three separate nuclear family unit in one house; first and second of his two sons and, third, of his own. This pattern of separate life in latter part of his life proved harmful for K-18 partly because he had to live a separate life at this age and partly because he had to work for earning at his advanced age.

8. SOCIAL LIKES AND DISLIKES

In the background of intellectual and literary background, K-18 developed following social likes and dislikes:

Social Likes	*Social Dislikes*
- Competent teacher and guide	- poverty and poverty culture
- Middle class neighbourhood	- illiteracy, ignorance and drop-ours
- Encouragement to talent and merit	- domestic violence against women
- Visiting near and distant relatives	- crime and drug behaviour
- Political statesmanship	- juvenile delinquency
- Higher grades in school examinations	- youth disarray and other problems
- Future vision of life and society	- unemployment problem
- Open worldview of the youth	- armed conflict situation
- Peaceful and non-violent environment	- limited cultural outlook
- Exogamous and simple marriage	- over-doze of modernity in one's life
- Cultural association with different people	- post-marital discard
- Higher economic standing	- political instability
- Gender equality and justice	- students who fails in examination
- Higher educational qualifications	- youth who abuse elders and others
- Students of prestigious institution	- corruption and nepotism
- Zero starter and hard worker	- inefficient and corrupt officer
- Inter-community interaction and dialogue	- inefficient and untrained teacher
- Collecting books in large numbers	- no reading of books and newspapers
- An intellectual and literary person	- class and caste inequality
- Holding cultural features in life	- social apathy and social pathology

9. CONCEPTS OF "I", "ME" AND "WE"

(i) K-18 had a strong sense of 'I'. Since he belonged to a lower social-economic background and, at the same time, had an intellectual bent of mind, it was natural and rational. He always showed high degree of consciousness of 'I' which determined and directed his life. In this broader context, K-18 always related the concept of 'I' with :

- tough economic conditions in the past
- life full of strain and struggle
- life full of activity and dynamism
- life with discipline, goals and objectives
- life with realistic estimates and assessment
- life with humble religious orientation

(ii) The concept of 'me' was inversely related to the concept of 'I'. In actuality, 'I' contributed to the growth of 'me'. Thus it represents higher level of 'I' as well as 'me'. We get a psychological framework which reveals individual's feelings, associations, reactions, speculation, creation, innovation, assumptions, achievements and, at the highest level, clear ideas and particular views.

(iii) K-18 was involved in 'we' by always thinking, talking, and discussing this concept and its various dimensions. This directed the social path of his life. He repeatedly referred to 'we' in terms of

- Kashmiri Muslims	- poets	- writers
- Kashmiri Hindus	- journalists	- doctors
- Professionals	- engineers	- artists
- Teachers	- academicians	- lawyers
- Officers	- colleagues	

K-18 always felt honoured and elevated in their company. He also felt associated and involved with their activities. This was a aesthetic and sacred relationship for him. His constant interaction with them was his lifelong desire.

10. IDEAS OF EQUALITY AND INEQUALITY

(i) K-18 had developed specific views about equality and inequality, particularly in the Indian context. Though these views were not systematic, coherent and logical, these represent his particular views. So, we present these here.

(a) **Equality:** He was a supporter of absolute class equality between all members of society. He was not in favour of different and dissimilar classes or groups. All such groups must be provided equal opportunities for competition and mobility. All social collectivities must be treated in an egalitarian way. At the same time, K-18 stood against caste, culture and religious based social differentiation. He held the view that Islam rejects all forms of inequality. He also opined that Hinduism must also reject in-equal caste system as was done by some reformist movements in Hindu society. In the case of gender, K-18 believed in 'contextual equality' because it suited them. All religions, especially Islam, have elevated and provided dignified life to women. He put forward the point that denying women an equal position in society can be equated to dehumanising them.

(b) **In-equality:** On the other hand, K-18 observed that despite the dominance of the ideology of equality, class inequality stood as the 'existential reality' and affected whole life. Though it was undesirable and deserve abolition, it existed in two particular ways. First, according to K-18, these groups, called *chute ghurik (*people of the rugs) and *soor wael* (vulgar people) which were illiterate, without proper jobs and proper economic activity, stood at the lowest of hierarchy. They maintain lower social esteem and position and were treated differently in marriages. Second, this class inequality was established and perpetuated through generation after generation through reservation system. Regarding caste inequality, K-18 had similar views. Despite religious opposition, this kind of inequality persists. This phenomenon proved negative vis a vis change and mobility.

(c) Gender: K-18 felt that since women faced some difficulties in social situations, it must be limited to certain appropriate fields only. This may be done in consideration of women's biological needs. These fields were identified medicine, nursing, education, teaching, scientific and technological research, IT, broadcasting, telecasting, academics, professions and other such fields.

11. THE IDEAL LEADER

(i) The ideal leader of K-18 was greatest Kashmiri political leader, SMA. As per his assessment, though SMA had become controversial in the present context, he will be remembered for centuries for his political contribution before 1947. It was precisely that contribution which K-18 considered and gave him the status of ideal leader.

(ii) K-18 was always reminded of the situation which prevailed in Kashmir during alien feudal rule. The extreme type of poverty was associated with system of forced labour, political suppression, forcible dis-arming, detached from cultural roots, and horrible tax system on peasants, artisans and workers. With that situation for centuries, there was no organised opposition and revolt on the part of local people. They suffered silently. In that background, there came a leader who raised consciousness for revolt against all that injustice, motivated people for common political action and organised the first politically directed movement of KMs in 1931 against feudal rule of *Maharaja*. After 1947, he and his party introduced revolutionary reforms in 1953 for overall change and development. K-18 didn't focus on his political role after 1953.

(iii) In the preceding context, K-18 believed that SMA emerged as the towering figure with positive political contribution in Kashmir. In actuality, he argued that SMA represented the demand of his time and responded to that situation positively. That is why his political movement was able to dismantle the centuries old feudal system in Kashmir.

12..THE RELIGIOUS LIFE

(i) K-18 was highly religious in his personal life. He was an ideal believer in fundamentals of Islam. In fact, he maintained a belief system which was enriched by his literary understanding and intellectual orientation. In practice, he behaved liked a committed Muslim, especially in his later part of life when he performed *hajj* with his wife. His religious preaching and practise had developed into a rational behaviour. He always maintained religiosity by performing all necessary practices in day-to-day life. He performed all sacred acts even during extreme winter season.

(ii) At the same time, he was involved in some folk religious practices. He used to attend shrines in Kashmir and outside at the time of annual *urs* and prayed there. Since a famous shrine in the valley was located in his old residential locality, he used to invite all near relatives on the occasion of annual *urs*. He also celebrated some particular days in a week/month/year.

(iii) He was a strong follower of *Sheikhul Alam Sheikh Noorud din Noorani,* the famous Kashmiri mystic and chief founder of *rishi* order in Kashmir. *Rishiat,* according to K-18, represented the ideology of other worldliness, no lust for material needs, effective control of self, and uniform spiritual and social order. His poetry stands most common in Kashmiri literature. It has been explained in terms of "*Quran* in Kashmiri language". The *Sheikh* upheld the ideals of other worldliness, refraining voluntarily from material comforts, egalitarian social order. He praised the common masses who followed religion sincerely but was critical of a group called *mullahs* who exploited the religion for monetary benefits and developed a hierarchy of their own in Kashmir.

(iv) K-18 was not attracted by reformist and radical trends of Islam in Kashmir. Most of the time, he was busy in his activities inside and outside his family. So, he never came in serious contact with the ideologues of these trends.

(v) K-18's lifelong association with KPs turned into permanent relationship he had developed reciprocally. They used to meet and interact at individual and family levels. They used to visit each others houses on different occasions and exchange gifts. Even after their migration to Jammu, he remembered many of them and kept the contact alive. He always held them in high esteem.

13. THE KASHMIR PROBLEM

(i) K-18 was not a political person nor had he any liking for politics. However, keeping in view the most dominant political problem in Kashmir, it could not be ignored by anybody, nor could he. He had some distinctive views about this problem which are mentioned below:

- K-18 felt that the Kashmiri leadership and masses had acceded temporarily to the union of India which was secular in theory and practise and was represented by MKG, JLN, and MAKA. They represented secular, democratic, liberal, progressive and composite cultural ideology and image of India. Kashmiri leadership had a lot of similarity with Indian Congress leadership. That is why INC and NC came near in opposition to ML. That is why also Kashmiri masses trusted the leadership of India.

- But, the problem started when India gave rise to communalist ideology and leadership represented by V. B. Patel, G. R. Godsey and S. P. Mukherjee. Subsequently, their ideology was represented by *Bhartya JanaSangh* and later on *Bhartya Janta Party* (BJP) which were openly communalist, anti-Muslim and anti-Kashmir. They opposed article 370 of the Indian constitution because it grants special status to JK. This ideology and its upholders wanted forcible integration of Kashmir in India. Though Kashmiris opposed it, GOI was successful in this policy with the help of politicians, bureaucrats, administrators, military and security forces. This gave a clear indication to Kashmiri masses that they committed mistake in 1947 by aligning with India.
- This situation created apprehensions among Kashmiri leaders and masses about India's sincerity and commitment to resolve the Kashmir problem after 1953. So, there were regular protests, demonstrations and uprisings against India started and continued till date. K-18 argued that till the political aspirations of Kashmiri people were not fulfilled, the problem will resist every solution.

14. EXPERIENCE OF CONFLICT SITUATION

(i) K-18 felt seriously concerned about health impact of two-decade long conflict. He observed that, in addition to mental health problems, there was rise of large number of cardiological, neurological, oncological, hyper-tension and other dreaded diseases among large sections of society. This fact has been established by many government and non-government agencies and organisations.

(ii) K-18 argued that gravity of the problem revealed that there was not sufficient health-care available in Kashmir. While sole psychiatric hospital caters thousands of mental health patients, three major hospitals were not able to cope with the rush of patients in the valley. This situation compelled a lot of patients to go outside JK for proper and specialised treatment. K-18 too had to go outside for specialised treatment. But, he raised a basic question in this regard, i.e. how many people can afford to go outside for proper treatment?

(iii) This grave situation, according to K-18, demand that special medical intervention must be carried out by official agencies of state government and NGOs. But, this had not been done so far.

15. FUTURE KASHMIR SOCIETY

(i) K-18 saw future society of Kashmir in the light of principles of social code/order developed in their poetry by two eminent mystic luminaries of Kashmir, *Sheikh Noorud din Noorani* and *Lale Ded (also known as Lale*

Arifa). These principles revolved around their ideology of *rishiyet* which was aimed t establish pure, ideal and un-corrupted social order in Kashmiri society on indigenous basis. Those principles may be identified as follows:

(a) renunciation of worldly-material comforts and to adopt other-worldly ideals;

(b) egalitarian social set-up keeping it away from all types of inequalities and differences; and

(c) in the preceding context, establishing and continuiting, with clarity of thought and action, the tolerance of all religions and cultures, representing different communities in Kashmiri society.

(ii) K-18 upheld the view that these humanistic principles of social life must be recognised formally and must be implemented sincerely. The application of these principles had following implications. First, social qualities of *rishiyet* will certainly lead to social order of *parhezgaar* with its multifarious consequences. It will also eliminate the basis of materialistic life of conflict, competition, antagonism and so on. It will create a society of *saleh* people. Second, it will create an egalitarian set-up based on equality in every field of life. With elimination of antagonism and inequality, social egalitarianism will certainly develop. In that situation, fulfillment of material pursuits will be minimum and spiritual objectives of life will be dominating. Third, in a situation in which equality and tolerance of various religions and cultures will be maintained, it will lead to religious-oriented human social order in which violence, conflict, inequality, and crime will be eliminated to the maximum limit. An ideal situation will be created would be as follows :

- We will uphold our religion and culture; they will uphold their religion and culture.
- We will follow our religion and culture; and they will follow their religion and culture.

(iii) Fourth, in the preceding scenario, the only possible social order possible will be tolerant, accommodative and responding to each other. This will ultimately lead to tolerance of various religions and cultures within the whole of Kashmiri society. In actuality, this will emerge as a cultural tradition and will be associated with the folk characters of Kashmir.

16. SOCIAL PROBLEMS IN KASHMIR

(i) *Ignoring the Elders:* This problem referred to consciously ignoring elders by their youngsters, particularly parents by their children, more by male than female children. This, according to K-18, happened in Kashmir in the background of the impact of modernity. After getting higher education, employment and prosperous status, the younger people after marriage generally developed modern lifestyle which was highly materialistic and individualistic oriented. While the former made them insensitive to religious based values, the latter averse to welfare of his family members, particularly his parents.

K-18 felt that this social dynamics led directly to ignoring personal care and social-economic needs of the aged in family. Some of them were left unattended or on the mercy of relatives. In this way, they suffer extremely in all fields. While some of them suffered economically, others suffered economically and socially. At that stage of later life, they need the family care most, which is denied to them.

It seems important to note that K-18 felt that this problem has not emerged in Kashmir in its form as has happened in Delhi and Mumbai. But, it has certainly started here. There are few studies which support this proposition and K-18 is personal witness to many such cases.

(ii) *Negative Impact of Affluence on Children:* K-18 felt that recent affluence in business, elite, professionals, politicians, bureaucrats and higher officials, families has spoiled their children in terms of their negative attitudes and behaviour. They may be characterised as 'deviant generation' and involved in juvenile delinquency. These families, as he observed, amassed huge wealth through corrupt and unfair means and spend on their children by buying things which spoil them further or spend themselves for the same negative purpose. This stood like criminal wastage of money.

It affected all in-family and out-family situations and entire social fabric. It affected children first by deviating them from the standards of serious life, making them unable to make careers, giving them life without struggle and finally involve other families' children in this degenerative effect. They developed dependable personalities like parasites. Their total parental support made them lethargic in social life. In consideration of negative effects of this social trend on entire society, this deviant behaviour needs to be controller.

K-19 PROFESSIONAL DOCTOR FROM SERVICE CASTE

1. SOCIAL CONTEXT

(i) The Kashmiri society was divided in various classes, castes, communities and groups. Each social collectivity had its own significance and specific role in particular context. The division on the basis of caste can be explained in terms of *Sayyids, Khans, Occupational and service castes.* All these caste configurations formed separate communities which lived in rural and urban areas and had traditional and specific structural and functional features and finally had faced some changes in the recent past.

(ii) The service castes formed the lowest strata in this system supported on ideational basis. They were engaged in different service occupations in rural and urban areas and lived in different *Mohalla*-type localities. These castes included the following:

- Sofi	- Gojri	- Hajam
- Kral	- Dhobi	- Misger
- Gilkar	- Roshanger	- Darzi
- Kundangar		

In their occupations, they maintained no segregation between men and women and no restriction on interaction between insiders and outsiders. In reality, they had developed occupation-suited structural and functional framework. Though they formed low esteem groups, they were highly conscious of their functional importance.

(iii) The status of these castes in the recent past was as follows. Economically, they were poor to very poor people. They were engaged in their occupations seriously which enabled them to maintain minimum standard of life. Educationally, these castes were near-total illiterate. Culturally, their life was contained and controlled by their own and other cultures. Religiously, they were highly emotional and extremely conservative and strong followers of folk religious practices. They all spoke local folk Kashmiri language. Socially, they proved traditional in values and norms and partial change resistant. Politically, they were active not as leaders but as followers.

(iv) However, a radical shift was experienced after 1947 mainly due to educational and economic progress and social-cultural mobility. This shift was encouraged by government's liberal policy towards backward classes of society. In that situation, all individuals and groups, irrespective of their class and caste affiliations, responded positively to available free education in government schools all over the state. They also opted for adoption of new occupations, especially government service, business, and horticulture. The service castes too responded in the same way. As a result, many young boys from these caste groups opted for modern education and government jobs. This reflected the pattern of change in these groups. So, two occupations emerged in these families, one with elder generation and second for younger generation with new generation. Some educated-employed persons from these groups still use their caste names in offices as follows:

- Dr. Dhobi	- Engineer Sofi
- Dr. Najar	- Engineer Dhobi
- Dr. Sofi	- Engineer Najar

(v) At the same time, some boys from these groups opted for medical and engineering fields. Some of them worked hard and got in these fields. Since these jobs were considered as 'status jobs', their families also got this elevated status. At this stage, two points of importance need explanation. First, service castes in urban and rural areas responded to that situation differently. While the former were fast, the latter were slow in showing their responses. Second, boys of these groups responded first than the girls. Thus we have a huge number of boys than girls in new occupations.

(vi) K-19 belonged to this social strata of society and his career developed within its social ethos. After getting general education, he worked for competitive examinations for medicine which he qualified in the first term. Subsequently, he became a professional Doctor.

2. IN-FAMILY SOCIALISATION

(i) K-19 belonged to service occupational family in which all members remained busy in occupational activities from morning till evening. There was no scope for educational and intellectual activities in this environment. This applied to all service occupational families. But, in a situation in which children of many families of relatives and neighbours got modern education and jobs, children of these families felt interested, inclined and ready for regular courses of general and professional education. This congenial neighbouring environment and governments' liberal policy proved added factors for their mobility.

(ii) This kind of in-family and out-family environment encouraged K-19 family to send their children for modern education. They felt impressed and attracted to get admissions in professional and technical courses. Through hard labour, they succeeded in getting admission in the courses. This was mainly because of hard work and perspective efforts, high encouragement of family and liberal policy of the government However, this didn't happen in the case of girls of these groups. That was mainly because of gender bias in education and employment. It was observed by K-19 that not many families responded to changes like his family. In that context, his family emerged as ideal and reference family. All these aspects of social life helped in the socialisation of K-19.

3. OUT-FAMILY ENVIRONMENT

(i) The out-family groups which had cumulative effect on personality formation, direction of life and determination of attitudes and behaviour of K-19 included relatives, neighbours, ffs and others. First, most of his relatives lived in the same locality in which he lived. Nearly all these families were engaged in service occupational activities. They hardly got enough time for visits to relatives' families. However, on different occasions and festivals, they used to visit each others' families, stayed there for days, exchanged gifts, and discussed about matrimonial matters. This type of relationship had not much effect related to education and career of their children. This only increased occupational homogeneity in cultural field and social solidarity in social field. But, the educational impact on K-19 family came from the contact with families, related or unrelated, which had established some educational credentials. Moreover, his family, later on, radiated influence to other families in the group.

(ii) Second, neighbours of K-19 family composed of other occupational communities wherein existed some exceptional cases of higher education and career making in some *Sayyid* families. This proved highly important for him and his family. Though they were not related in super-ordinate-subordinate type of relationship, the impact of ideal cases could not be ignored. In this way, the neighbouring environment proved influential to K-19.

(iii) Third, the FFs composed of men of their own and other occupational communities which belonged to different educational, social and economic status. They had least effect on his personality. Whenever they visited his family, men discussed family and occupational matters, women talked about domestic and matrimonial matters. They showed least interest in their children's education. But, this situation has changed radically in last few decades. This has materialised due to overall change and development and mass media impact.

(iv) Fourth, others composed of those who often helped K-19 in many ways and included clients, customers, businessmen, elite families, officers, political-religious leaders, *peers*, social notables, professionals and so on. In actuality, they took full advantage of their relationship from K-19's parents. In exchange of these services and duties, they helped K-19 in getting education, admissions and employment. In a way, this was a token of help and kindness on the part of these higher status people.

4. EDUCATION AND CAREER

(i) K-19's primary to secondary education was carried out in the city government school located in his locality. All family members, relatives, neighbour and other acquaintances encouraged him for pursuing formal education till higher stage due to his good merit and gentleness. Later on, they also encouraged him for attempting the competitive exam. in medical field. When K-19 was fully convinced, he attempted for a medical seat and got it in the first attempt. After getting inspiration from him, his younger brother attempted for engineering seat and he too got it in the first turn.

(ii) After completing MBBS, its house job and internship, he opted for M.S. and then for M. D. in a prestigious medical institution in JK. During these days, he got a regular job in a hospital where he started his career as doctor. While his hard work and level of intelligence was un-matching, his social traits were also unparalleled. So, he became most available, humane and popular doctor inside and outside hospital. After accumulating some service experience, he started private practise at home. Thus he stood most popular and most respected doctor in the locality.

5. OCCUPATION, ASSOCIATION AND MOBILITY

(i) The family of K-19 had a specific traditional occupation. Now this family had two occupations: one with parents and other with K-19. Since one parent passed away, that left the family with one occupation only. Taking into consideration past and present occupation, there seems a hell of difference and two occupations represented two extreme opposites. While the former had lost its significance, the latter has gained respectability and acceptability. This occupational change reflected a pattern of change among service occupational groups according to which when members (of these groups) got higher education and government service, they mostly dropped the traditional occupation and the new one completely. That exactly has happened with K-19 family too.

(ii) K-19 made a radical shift in occupation and adopted new occupation of high social esteem. This occupation got him higher perks and benefits, high social estimation and an ideal profession. In this context, he developed a popular folk character due to which he was associated with some kind of charisma and miracle among the villagers.

(iii) In the situation mentioned above, K-19 developed an association pattern having special relations with two varying groups. The first group was of relatives, neighbours and others related to his family. They were mostly traditional, half-educated, having no scientific perspective and no broader view of culture. On the other hand, second group was of members of peer group and his colleagues. While the former composed of class-batch mates, the latter referred to office and professional colleagues. They were usually highly educated, economically better, socially of upper status, culturally exposed, scientific in approach and rational life. These two associations had opposing effect on K-19 and his family. But, he was successful in establishing a balance between two extremes by adopting positives of both and rejecting negatives of both.

(iv) Taking into consideration nature and status of two extremely different occupations, K-19 and his family had experienced maximum degree of upward mobility which changed their entire lifestyle from a poor service occupational family to a professional middle class family.

6. MARRIAGE AND FAMILY

(i) Before his marriage K-19 was able to construct a new house in a newly-established colony in the periphery of city and had to shift to that house. That was because of two compelling reasons. First, the old house of large joint family had now shrinking place a large number of members. Second, the new status job of a doctor demanded a decent and spacious place of living. After some years of shifting, he was married in an endogamous and patri-local type of marriage. The girl belonged to the same endogamous occupational group. In reality, it was a marriage of equals, both belonged to same economic, social, educational and cultural background. Since the girl was an earning hand, it gave the marriage relationship the equality character. In totality, marriage proved a step forward in social life of K-19, especially his social and cultural progress.

(ii) K-19 lived with parents in joint family before and after his marriage. He and his wife faced no problem with parents and neither, parents had any problem. It was a normal social unit. He took full care of the health, social, economic and other needs of parents. But, after death of one parent and marriage of younger brother, the family got divided into two nuclear family units. K-19 also established his own family unit composed of his wife and unmarried children. It stood as a happy and prosperous family unit and fulfilled its social obligations. Its doors remained open for day and night for performing social obligation.

7. SOCIAL LIKES AND DISLIKES

After experiencing positive and negative aspects of life at different stages, K-19 developed following likes and dislikes:

Social Likes	*Social Dislikes*
- Simplicity, generosity and openness	- immoral and indecent acts of individuals
- Modern lifestyle in the family	- social and economic inequality
- Small families with social obligations	- discrimination against lower castes and classes
- Total care of women and elders	- illegal acts of youth
- Full and free medical care of all citizens	- corrupt official
- Due consideration of relatives and neighbours	- unjust and unfair political system
- Latest knowledge about chronic diseases	- shrewd and narrow-minded person

contd...

contd...

Social Likes	*Social Dislikes*
- A doctor with highest degree of patience	- a dishonest businessman
- A competent and committed doctor	- one who will not follow professional ethic
- Due care of individual health	- challenging the social ethics and morale
- Health care through govt. agencies	- corruption in any form
- Special health programs for the poor	- crimes against women and children
- Commitment to values and norms	- caste identity and its impact on society
- God fearing personality	- a *neta*-type political leader
- Free education for all children	- a system which perpetuates injustice
- Consciousness about immunisation	- the interest-based economy
- A religious preacher and leader	- a doctor with no social commitment
- Opposition to violence	- an illiterate and ignorant family
- Gender equality	- ideology of communal politics
- Basic needs of all to be fulfilled by state	- criminal behaviour in society

8. CONCEPTS OF "I", "ME" AND "WE"

(ii) K-19 had lower sense of 'I' and 'me' mainly because of his personality traits like :

- Informality	- truthfulness	- openness
- Submissiveness	- not offending others	- generosity
- Gentle behaviour	- politeness	- gentle behaviour
- Patient hearing	- rational response	

At the same time, he had developed higher sense of 'we' mainly of the social sensation related to :

- Social feelings	- social possibilities	- social sentiments
- Social ideology	- social objectives	- social initiatives
- Social images	- social symbols	- social views and opinions

(iii) K-19 explained 'I' in terms of "egoistic consciousness" about one's personality. Taking into consideration its implications in the context of interrelationship, it emerges as 'self-oriented' and 'socially undesirable'. So, according to him, it must be avoided and discouraged. If put in operation, it kills the talent and excellence of the person and make him sum total of arrogance and intolerance.

(iv) According to K-19, 'me' stood for tolerable in comparison to 'I'. It may be oriented towards one's personality or society. So, it can be used for positive or negative purpose and concerned individual has to determine its direction. Its positive and negative functions were identified as follows:

Concept	Positive function	Negative function
- Me	-utilised for all	-utilised for self
- Me	-established values in social life	-delegitimize values in social life
- Me	-used as a social trust and responsibility	-used as social deficit and irresponsibility
- Me	-was relevant to cultured lifestyle	-was irrelevant to a cultured lifestyle
- Me	-used for performance of social role	-important for self-role and gratification
- Me	-promoted selfless professionalism	- promoted selfish professionalism

Thus K-19's concept of 'me' dictated two sets of values. The first set composed of positive socio-psychological traits which must be used for societal good. The second set composed of negative psychological traits which must bc rejected for societal welfare.

(iv) K-19 saw the concept of 'we' as specific and purposeful and had clarity of meaning and implications. He used it for societal category distinguished by professional and other factors. In this regard, he gave the examples mentioned below:

- We, the professionals belonging to Kashmir
- We, the professionals belonging to Islam and Muslim community
- We, the professionals who are truthful, competent and qualified
- We, the professionals who committed and dedicated
- We, the professionals who have humanitarian approach
- We, the professionals who practise fully the social ethics
- We, the professionals who fulfill all moral responsibilities
- We, the professionals who follow distinguished careers

9. IDEAS OF EQUALITY AND INEQUALITY

(i) K-19 had developed some general ideas about equality and inequality in human society, which were purely idealistic and seemed least relevant for applicability. Since these ideas represented his perception, we present these ideas briefly.

(ii) He believed in absolute and complete equality in all fields of life like social, political, economic, culture, sex, language, region, religion, ethnicity, education, demography and so on. He viewed that if not completely equal, near-to-equal status must be established in society.

(iii) K-19 categorically rejected the basis of class, caste and gender for egalitarian set-up. It was because the bases of these concepts were inherently inequal. So, making in-equal into equal was not possible. He presented parallel basis of equality. These were (a) humanity: this concept provided solid basis for an egalitarian system in society. It follows that supreme ideals of equality lied in humanity in all situations., with all social collectivities and at all times; (b) justice: K-19 considered this full of potential for debasing all factors of in-equal system. At the same time, it will establish rules of equality because justice has to be made to every individual. Only those ideals will be adopted which will ensure equality; and (c) individual performance: the third criteria for establishing human equality in individual performance. It means that if one performed well, he will be rewarded and will ensure equality for family. If one performed bad, he will not be rewarded and will not ensure equality for others. This complex notion, according to K-19, gives priority to good or bad performance vis a vis equality. This performance is determined by religion and culture.

10. THE IDEAL CHARACTER/LEADER

(i) The ideal character of K-19 was a great physician of Kashmir, Professor A. A. Guroo, who was martyred in 1990s. It is believed that his greatness in academics and commitment to social-political fields was unmatched and unparalleled in the history of Kashmir. He was a proud son of Kashmir who devoted his life to his profession and to his society. Such a character takes birth after a long difficult time.

(ii) K-19 felt that Professor Guroo was a king in his profession. His excellence in teaching, research and treatment-practise was highly impressive, revealing and of world standard. He became a legendry figure during his lifetime because of his outstanding qualities.

(iii) Equally distinguished was his devotion and commitment to his motherland and its political independence. Despite his professional heights, he performed the role of a political ideologue and leader too. He had million dollar job/s abroad but he left all these positions for his political cause related to Kashmir. He was killed by none other than the enemy of Kashmir, be he Indian or Pakistani.

(iv) K-19 found a distinguishing personality in Professor Guroo. It was mainly because he had excellent and world-class academic and professional credentials and, at the same time, was committed to the political objective of Kashmir's independence. These qualities simultaneously exist unusually. His activities in both fields were so influential and impressive that he could not be forgotten for generations.

11. THE RELIGIOUS LIFE

(i) K-19 represented a perfect religious personality. He followed his religion completely, both in theory and practice. He had absolute faith in the fundamentals of Islam studied directly from original sources such as *Quran and Haidth.* In practise too, he was a strict follower of day-to-day religious practices. He performed the *hajj* in his younger age which is considered highly rewarding. In addition to professional and personal life, he always practised Islamic ideals such as *amanat, diyanat,* humanity, commitment to values-norms, generosity, affection, devotion and so on. All colleagues, relatives, neighbours and others felt impressed by his religious attitude and behaviour. All of them had unanimous opinion about him that he was most gentle and most religious person in his entire locality.

(ii) His religious personality had another sacred dimension. Many people in his locality believed that his medical practise was sacred as he had some spiritual powers. He was considered as a folk healer. He was also considered a doctor doing miracles during his practice. Those who came to him believed that they will be relieved from their health problem. This increased his popularity in the entire area.

(iii) He neither opposed nor supported folk religious practices. Since his family organised such practices and related functions, he participated in those religious activities without any devotion. He sometimes visited shrines for prayers but was never involved in polytheistic activities.

(iv) He neither intended nor had any time for developing contact with reformative and radical trends of Islam. They have approached him but he put a polite 'no' to them.

12. THE KASHMIR PROBLEM

(i) K-19 was completely a non-political person. But, in the situation in which Kashmiris were caught during last six decades, every Kashmiri had developed some particular views about Kashmir problem. So had K-19. According to his opinion, this problem was created after 1947 mainly because of opposing views about Kashmiri leadership and GOI. Though temporary accession with India took place, there was no real integration between the two. The political parties involved failed miserably to develop the sense of integration.

(ii) When central government attempted political integration of Kashmir through legislative, administrative and political measures, it was resisted by the local leadership. While the Indian intelligentsia and mass media was happy about one-sided integration, the Kashmiri intellectuals and masses characterised it forceful. The former felt pleased and the latter felt cheated.

(iii) The resolution of Kashmir problem, according to K-19, lied in rational understanding of Kashmiris' political aspirations. This might have lead to proper relationship between them and GOI and to realistic integration. It was in that spirit that article 370 was incorporated in the constitution of India, which ensured JK's special status in India.

13. EXPERIENCE OF CONFLICT SITUATION

(i) K-19 observed the conflict situation keenly throughout the period of two decades. He had firsthand information about all aspects and impacts of this situation. He treated thousands of patients who had suffered during that period. He upheld that people of lower classes suffered more comparatively. They suffered in terms of thousands of deaths, injury, disabled and disappeared. The people in general experienced dangerous medical and health implications.

(ii) In that situation, various diseases emerged such as neurological, hyper-tension, cancer-related and tension-based diseases. There was heavy increase in mental health diseases and problems. So, there were many cases of suicides and drug addiction in the valley.

(iii) Women and children suffered more in terms of health costs. They faced mental and physical health problems at all times, especially delivery of children. In many cases, there were fatalities and abortions.

(iv) Similarly, children faced various problems at the time of birth and after the birth, no regular immunisation, no medical treatment available, and no professionals and experts. That was mainly because of the collapse of health-care system in the state.

14. FUTURE KASHMIR SOCIETY

K-19 was highly conscious about health problems of common people in Kashmir. He desired a standard health for all citizens. He wanted this objective to be followed in the future society of Kashmir and his major concerns were as mentioned below:

- Government must essentially contribute to the establishment and maintenance of a wider healthy society in future;
- Regular health check-up of women, elders and children in hospitals and health centers in all areas;
- Regular and continued program of immunisation of all children in rural and urban areas and in all communities and groups;
- Community health objectives must be pursued in the policy, planning, programmes, schemes and their implementation;
- Short-term and long-term health goals to be determined and followed by government institutions, organisations and agencies;
- Pre-natal and post natal medical care of women in all villages, towns and cities in the state;
- All necessary facilities to be provided at the time of delivery of children;
- A large network of health care and emergency centers at each district, sub-district, tehsil, block, village and *mohalla* level;
- Availability of latest technology for diagnostic and observation purposes;

- Availability of all experts, professionals, surgeons, physicians, psychiatrists and others in all health-care centers;
- Special, technical, professional and super-specialty institutions in the city and its peripheries;
- Establishment of advanced level and world class institutes for research purpose; and
- Full care of mental health patients in their specialised hospitals.

15. SOCIAL PROBLEMS IN KASHMIR

(i) *Erosion of Professional Ethics:* K-19 thought that a common problem of medical professionals in Kashmir was to maintain their ethical standards in their field. He felt they got entire education and training from government-public funds, but then they exploited the same public after they had completed the course. While doctors exploited them through private practice, advice for making tests and observation and commission from pharmaceutical companies. Similarly, engineers get involved in corrupt practices in league with bureaucrats, politicians and officers.

(ii) According to K-19, doctors' private practise stood immoral and illegal because they exploited the same people who paid for their education and training and they get 50% more salary as non-practising allowance.

(iii) K-19 felt that maximum number of diagnostic and observation tests advised patients mostly in consideration of commission which they get from these labourtaries and centers. Though the tests seemed necessary for diagnosis and treatment, the financial consideration was also kept in mind. As an insider, K-19 knew that maximum number of doctors accepted commission from companies which stood as a clear case of corruption from moral and medical ethics. In fact, all these activities on the part of doctors directly contributed to the violation and erosion of ethics and morality. So, he advised them to stop this undesirable practice, but he himself was involved in it partly.

Children's Health Problems: K-19 observed in his surrounding locality that children of an early age group suffered from various health problems due to imbalanced diet, no regular immunisation and no medical care from their early childhood. While this situation could be explained in terms of ignorance and poverty, the least consciousness and lesser availability of health-care facilities were also responsible.

K-19 found that problem of unbalanced diet led to the rise of several body deficiencies, abnormalities and diseases. Similarly, no regular immunisation gave birth to a variety of dangerous diseases like cholera, TB, chicken pox, diaheria and so on. He quoted an expert doctor in the area who opined that 30% children of early age groups will face dangerous consequences of not getting regular immunisation dozes in next few decades. Finally, K-19 found that no medical-care for a long time created a dangerous situation, death of children of early age groups, and more cases of female mortality. In case government will not intervene effectively, the trend may involve more number of children in the area. The NGOs also need to initiate their efforts in that area. When both kinds of health organisations will work unitedly and effectively, then children of the area could be saved from dangerous health situation.

K-20 DOCTOR FROM MIDDLE CLASS

1. SOCIAL CONTEXT

(i) The class composition of the Kashmiri society in post-1947 era, especially from 1953 radical reforms, was determined by economic, political and educational changes at that time. It had qualitative and quantitative difference from pre-1947 composition when feudal rule was in operation and every Kashmiri was considered a subject of the ruler. So, post-1953 composition was different from pre-1947 type on the one hand and had different types in rural and urban areas on the other hand. While new agrarian hierarchy dominated the rural class composition, the lower-middle class composition dominated the urban hierarchy. In that situation, the following class composition could be observed:

- Upper class	- Upper upper class
- Upper middle class	
- Upper lower class	
- Middle class	- Middle upper class
- Middle middle class	
- Middle lower class	
- Lower class	- Upper lower class
- Middle lower class	
- Lower lower class	

(ii) The upper class was composed of elite, business, bureaucrat, professional and political families. They were politically committed to the state power because of their dependence on it. While economically, they were well off, socially and culturally they were mobile and exposed. Educationally, they were forward and religiously conservative.

(iii) The middle class was a new phenomenon and was in the stage of formation. It roughly composed of government employees, businessmen and other professional groups. A lot many people were getting into this class status at that time. Politically, it supported political regimes and their politics and got benefits in response. Educationally, economically and culturally, it was going ahead and enhanced its role and status.

(iv) At the bottom were rural and urban masses who provided legitimacy to the ruling regime. Though their conditions were not satisfactory, they were progressing steadily in economic, educational and social fields. In actuality, these conditions were far better than the conditions during feudal times. These masses became the backbone of all political movements in Kashmir.

(v) In the post-1947 period, politics played dominant role in Kashmir and determined all other developments. Many individuals and families played active role in day-to-day politics and, in return, got benefited by the state. While these individuals were staunch followers of SMA who was their supreme and charismatic leader they followed his dictates and were ready to sacrifice even their lives at his order. They formed a political group called *Shera* in direct opposition to MMMF's political group called *Bakra*. All of them were NC supporters, party activists and propagandists.

(vi) At the same time, many such families played active role in local political developments and helped political status quo to continue. These families, which belonged to all classes and communities, used to organise political meetings, rallies and other functions and forced the people to support ruling regime. In return, they got benefited in economic, educational and social fields. All these families belonged to middle and lower classes, specifically upper lower, middle upper, middle middle and middle lower classes. K-20 belonged to this group of families in the interior city which was heavily populated and congested. Despite this background, he believed in values and norms related to self effort and self achievement. With his personal intelligence, innovation, seriousness and commitment, he achieved a position of a doctor, which not many in that locality could achieve. The family proved a 'feasibility factor' only.

2. IN-FAMILY SOCIALISATION

(i) K-20 belonged to a family which had middle-lower class status in post-1947 developments. This family had experienced political, educational and economic impact at that time. In that environment, it had developed new political status and role which was noticeable in its actions. Thus the family had responded to education early and adopted service occupation too early. In that way, it distinguished itself from the neighbouring families.

(ii) The domination of politics in family in urban Kashmir was a registered fact. In fact, it could not be avoided in those political circumstances. It happened at two levels. First, at the individual level, family members became active ideologically and politically. They were lowly educated and employed, but their relations with the ruling party benefited them a lot. Second, at the group level, there emerged two varying groups, one supporting the establishment and other apathetic towards actual politics. The first group was composed of individuals with many features of political activism. The second group pursued the goals of higher education and higher jobs without political activities. The group members were interested in literary, academic and professional activities and developed relations with such groups. Thus two opposing groups in a family had different perspectives on life and society. K-20 was the product of latter group who preferred an academic and professional life.

(iii) In this way, K-20 was socialised in intellectual background. He accepted the impact of politics but to theoretical limit. He never participated in political activities and was not committed to any political party. In direct contrast to political activism, he became active in intellectual, professional and literary circles.

3. OUT-FAMILY ENVIRONMENT

(i) The out-family environment of K-20 was composed of relatives, neighbours, ffs and others. His relatives were more or less of same social, economic and educational status. Some of these families were later involved in marital relations. K-20 had a positive image of some families with which he established formal relations. These families used to meet on political functions, in addition to social, cultural and religious occasions, and discuss all matters.

(ii) K-20's neighbours belonged mostly to lower occupational groups and castes. They were lesser educated, of lower economic position, culturally not exposed, socially not mobile but politically active. These people were characterised as belonging to 'backward urban community' because its life conditions were below standard. But, the K-20 family was different because of its contact with government and ruling party. Despite ideological and political differences with neighbours, it didn't enter into rivalry, clash or conflict with them. At times, it helped them voluntarily in the spirit of *mohalla* solidarity. Socially, its image was soft but coloured.

(iii) K-20's FFs were individuals from politician and colleague families. While the former referred to political leaders and activists, the latter were intellectuals, bureaucrats, professionals, businessmen and so on. They also included prominent individuals from all fields of life, urban-rural areas, all intellectual-professional circles, from rich and poor background, from all classes-groups, and so on.

(iv) Others were mainly friends, acquaintances and colleagues of K-20 and his family. They composed of intellectuals, writers, researchers, scientists, academicians, teachers, religious preachers, businessmen, social notables, social workers, poets, journalists, artists, and so on. They represented the chief representatives of intelligentsia. Their visits to K-20 family gave it the intellectual image and affected his attitudes and behaviour constantly.

(v) Among all these groups related to out-family environment, K-20 was mostly influenced by last group, mainly because of its intellectual orientation and professional image. He showed respect to these professionals and adjusted their ideals in his life pattern. He also adopted their political ideas, but was always cautious and selective. He adopted those traits which rationality demanded. In actuality, he always held scientific approach and accepted new ideas as per scientific criteria.

4. EDUCATION AND CAREER

(i) The primary till matric education of K-20 took place in a city government school in his locality. He scored high in every class and retained distinction throughout. Subsequently, he got interested in medicine and attempted the medical text which he qualified in the first turn. In the college, he was exposed to further professional, intellectual and modern contacts of higher-elite classes. He used to spend sufficient time for these activities. From that stage, he was fond of discussion, debate, critical analysis, and objective assessment that became his lifelong features.

(ii) In addition to the job in a hospital, he carried out research courses of MS and MD in his field of specialisation. While his research guidance was done by a noted and eminent physician of JK, he produced a quality piece of research. After he got degrees awarded, and accumulated service record, he got several promotions till he reached to the position of Head of department.

(iii) Two points need to be mentioned here. First, after joining the government service, he didn't start private practise immediately but after a long gap. In that practice, he had lesser financial considerations than the medical interests of relatives, neighbours and friends. Even when he left for Saudi for a job, he could not stay there for more than two years.

5. OCCUPATION, ASSOCIATION AND MOBILITY

(i) K-20 family had a humble occupation in the recent past in which his father and grandfather were engaged. As a result, this family had attained the status of average economic standard in which minimum decent life was possible. But, in the post-1947 period, this family members adopted a new occupation of government service. This symbolised the occupational mobility in the family. Now, this family had not one occupation but many occupations simultaneously.

(ii) The association pattern of K-20 and his family developed on the basis of :

- Political affiliation, contact and interaction
- Professional affiliation, contact and interaction
- Educational affiliation, contact and interaction
- Social-cultural affiliation, contact and interaction.

(iii) K-20 developed a particular line and level of association which included the following nature and implications:

- Professionals for the professional association
- Doctors for the medical occupational association
- Engineers for the engineering occupational association
- Bureaucrats and administrators for the family association

- Journalists for the professional association
- Writers and thinkers for the intellectual association
- Academicians, scientists, researchers and technocrats for professional association
- Political ideologues and leaders for the political association
- Big businessmen for the economic association.

(iv) Taking into consideration traditional and present occupations, K-20 and his family experienced high degree of mobility. All family members approved and confirmed their mobility and in this environment adopted new political attitudes and behaviour.

6. MARRIAGE AND FAMILY

(i) After he got a job, K-20 married in an exogamous type. The girl belonged to family which was educationally, economically, socially and culturally higher in status. That was bureaucratic and aristocratic family. The professional excellence of K-20 was matched with high educational, economic, social and cultural status of girl's family. So, these two families were tied in equity-type relationship. In actuality, that marriage proved a step forward in the life of K-20.

(ii) K-20 lived in a joint family with his parents and their brother's children. It was a large and cohesive family unit but with divergent ideological tendencies. He stayed there till his younger brother was married. After that, he availed of official accommodation for some time and lived there with his wife and children, But, he didn't enjoy that because of feeling of alienation.

(iii) After coming back from Saudi Arabia, where he worked for two years, he constructed a new house in a newly-established colony in the periphery of city. After shifting there, he became a part of middle class colony life.

7. SOCIAL LIKES AND DISLIKES

After going through various experiences at different stages of life, K-20 developed following social likes and dislikes:

Social Likes	*Social Dislikes*
- Highly representative political system	- caste and class inequality
- Ideal social and economic equality in life	- gender discrimination and violence
- Ideas and ideals of social justice	- dictatorship and kingship system
- Community health and social medicine	- poverty and underdevelopment
- Fruit culture and balanced diet	- Harijan's status in Indian society

contd...

contd...

Social Likes	*Social Dislikes*
- Average economic standard of a family	- corruption, nepotism and favour
- Scientific social policy and social planning	-crime and drug behaviour of youth
- Nationalism as well as internationalism	- culture of elite families
- Basic human rights and civil liberties	- negative implications of affluence
- Liberal, ethical and committed journalist	- exploitative system and its impact
- Mass media pervasive impact	- degeneration in social and political life
- Scientific and technological progress	- ignoring elders, women and children
- Special treatment to relatives and neighbours	- illness, ignorance and distress
- Commitment to professional and social ideals	- economic depression
- Political issues in proper perspective	- arrogance and uncivilised behaviour
- A person with rational and scientific approach	- political repression and suppression
- Upholding human values and norms	- post-marital diseases in a family
- Respecting established role and status	- uncontrolled and deviant children
- Processes of modernisation	- violating medical ethics
- Reading of books and newspapers	- political exploitation and blackmailing

8. CONCEPTS OF "I", "ME" AND "WE"

(i) K-20 had balanced feeling of all three concepts which he had developed through his long experience and often reflected in his balanced personality. He always cared for 'I' and related it with personal qualities and experiences. He never felt himself outside the consciousness of 'I'. So, in the case of K-20, 'I' was usually used for :

- professional characteristics
- socially committed person
- serious, realistic and objective person
- morals and values-supporter
- political thinker and ideologue
- critical analyst of all developments
- scientific and intellectual person
- representative of social and political identity

(ii) The concept of 'me' was also used by K-20 without any break and never came out of it and referred to it repeatedly. During his arguments, debates and exchange of ideas, 'me' came out repeatedly through his particular emotions, ideas, views, ideology. So, 'me' was used for :

- My ideas and ideology
- My medical responsibilities and obligations
- My medical qualities and qualifications
- My academic and professional excellence
- My achieved role and status

- My social context and struggle for progress and change
- My relations with print media,
- My relations with political ideologues and leaders
- My relations with academicians, writers and researchers
- My association with relatives, neighbours and friends
- My association with colleagues.

(iii) Like the concepts of 'I' and 'me', K-20 upheld the concept of 'we' which, among other things, reflected his relationship of social collectivity and past of his fraternity. It touched political, economic, educational, cultural, social and medical fields and their associated communities of :

- Various classes and groups
- Various communities and sects
- Various majority and minority groups
- Various educated and uneducated groups
- Various urban, rural and hilly groups
- Various eastern and western ideologues
- Various modernists and conservatives
- Various medical professionals.

Finally, 'we' referred to social collectivity with special reference to professionals, doctors, political ideologues, social notables, social activists, human rights upholders and Kashmir ideologues.

9. IDEAS OF EQUALITY AND INEQUALITY

(i) In totality, K-20 supported the idea of absolute equality and he stood opposed to all forms and manifestations, even if religious or culture based. He upheld the view that inequality developed by interested individuals and groups for their respective interests. This led to deny basic rights of weaker individuals and groups and put them into extreme suffering.

(ii) According to K-20, the important aspect of that situation was that the existing political system was used to legitimize and continue the imposed in-equal order. However, this forceful system could not continue for long and was dislodged through counter political action. He argued that the logic must apply in the prevailing circumstances. That means the unjust and unequal system must be dislodged and a new system established through political actions.

(iii) K-20 felt that, in this process of transformation, the positive actions on the part of legislature, supported and defended by judiciary and implemented by executive, must be ensured, if necessary by initiating a political movement in this regard. He also felt that, in the present-day political society, this objective must emerge as consensus-based ideal to be supported by ideological justification, political support, economic strength, social-cultural set-up and literary-academic help.

10. THE IDEAL CHARACTER

(i) It was a difficult choice for K-20 to choose a particular ideal character. After a lot of thinking, he felt that it was Shamim Ahmad Shamim (SAS) who stood as one of the model personality of Kashmir by national and international standards. He rose from rural background and reached to highest level of eminence at global level. His personal traits and social capabilities were unparalleled. He will be remembered for three following distinguishing features:

(ii) First, he was an eminent statesman, politician and parliamentarian. His statesmanship reflected in mature political thinking and ideology; world-class political views and political performance; and provided the resolution framework for many important political problems. He was known for his political commitment to democratic political ideas and ideals and political opposition to dictatorial regimes. He was so innovative in political approach that he could not be fitted in conventional categories of politicians. His performance as parliamentarian in the *Lok Sabha* and state legislative assembly was historic, while his oratory was unmatched. His speeches in these forums were considered as 'treasures of knowledge and realities'.

(iii) Second, he was an eminent social activist and excellent journalist. He was an institution in himself in these fields. His newspaper, *AIENA,* weekly and later on daily, was standard mouthpiece of Kashmir. The highest level of excellence in journalism reflects in its writings which were usually critical, objective, realistic, comprehensive and scholarly in depth and orientation. The social criticism of the paper became an ideal and typical. It was a paper of its own class. It remained popular till his last writings in and out of JK. People used to wait for its publication and read it from A to Z repeatedly.

(iv) Third, SAS was the ideologue of and for Kashmir and Kashmiris. He was rooted in Kashmir's tradition and history. He worked throughout his life to portray the real situation in Kashmir before the world. He presented the Kashmir case in its originality, historicity and proper perspective. He presented Kashmiris as a group which was always suppressed and exploited and imposed a permanent suffering on them. He presented before the world courageously the aspirations of Kashmiris.

11. GLOBAL SOCIAL ORDER

(i) K-20 felt that establishment of GSO stood necessary in the context of emerging trends of social antagonism and social disintegration at the global level. It needs sincerity and commitment on the part of global powers to this cause. In the context of present day, global scenario of politics between dominant powers, GSO needed to be related to the following positions:

(a) the global powers of the world must not dominate or direct policy, program, management, organisation and objectives of the GSO;

(b) the dominant powers of the world must not take unilateral benefit of GSO in different regions of the world;

(c) GSO must not be developed like UNO, IMF, WB and ICJ in which the under-developed don't get political and economic justice;

(ii) In the preceding framework, K-20 suggested five specific objectives which must be followed vigorously by GSO. First, GSO must be oriented towards realistic and humanitarian goals and must treat all of its units equally. Second, GSO must reflect plurality and totality of all national units. All nationalities and sub-nationalities; all religious, regional and cultural communities; all races and languages; and all ethnic societies must be its component and organisational parts. Third, it must uphold all original identities and must ensure maximum degree of multi-cultural environment. Fourth, all ideas and ideals related to egalitarian set-up must be enshrined in its constitution. Fifth, the functioning of GSO must lead to peace and tolerance in the world full of conflict.

12. THE RELIGIOUS LIFE

(i) K-20 stood as a firm believer of all religious concepts and performed all related practices. But, he never posed his personal religiosity in social life nor presented himself as a religious ideologue.

(ii) He was not much interested in folk religious practices which were also performed in his family. He treated these as cultural activities and functions. He neither supported not objected to the performance of these practices.

(iii) K-20 was an admirer of reformist and radical trends of Islam in Kashmir. Regarding the former trend, he felt that this movement reformed many religious practices and changed orientation of people towards entire religious life. It isolated the religion from rituals, customs and occasional celebrations. More important was its contribution to separate *mullas* from actual religion.

(iv) At the same time, K-20 was critical of radical trend for imposing too much of politics on religion. It was used for limited community, sectarian and nationalistic political interests. This has in practise de-shaped and degenerated the original religion.

(v) K-20 had excellent relations with KPs even after their mass migration from Kashmir. Many of his close KP still maintained family ties and visited each others houses often. Some of his favorite teachers were KPs whom he paid full regards. But, at the same time, he criticised the KP political leadership for its narrow political approach which was suicidal to the community itself. Some of his KP friends shared these views.

13. POLITICAL IDEOLOGY

(i) K-20 upheld the view that individual in modern society gets exposed to political ideology necessarily. So, he must uphold particular political ideas. With this, he and other members participate in political socialisation and political culture. In fact, all of them participate directly or indirectly in political developments and share their positive and negative impacts. He argued that the individual could not remain aloof in this situation and thus play that role consciously. K-20 believed that political ideology of an individual must contain the following themes:

- ideological and political situation at global, regional and national levels;
- political economy at global and national levels;
- political developments in developed and developing countries;
- politics of domination and exploitation;
- politics of globalisation and its impact; and
- political development and change in Asian and African countries.

(ii) But, at the same time, K-20 believed active participation of every individual, especially of professionals, was not necessary. Practical politics was portfolio of politicians only. Thus while the actual politics was practised by politicians, professionals perform the job of political appraisal and 'watchdog'.

14. THE KASHMIR PROBLEM

(i) K-20 presented the Kashmir problem in a distinct perspective which must be applied for its comprehensive analysis. The perspectives presented were as follows:

(a) Global perspectives: It includes super power perspectives, especially of U.S., Western Europe, Russia and China

(b) Regional perspectives: it includes perspectives of South Asian, West Asian, and central Asian countries

(c) Involved countries perspectives: It includes perspectives of India (ruling and opposition parties, left-socialist and rightist parties and civil societies), Pakistan (ruling and opposition parties, rightist-leftist-liberal and civil societies), and Kashmiri (pro-India, pro-Pakistan, independence and civil societies) perspectives.

(ii) According to K-20, the application of these perspectives will lead to a broader, deeper, realistic and comprehensive understanding of this problem and will involve all actors involved directly or indirectly. This will certainly pave the way for durable resolution of this chronic problem.

15. FUTURE KASHMIR SOCIETY

(i) K-20 observed the future society of Kashmir was his favorite political gossip, i.e. how the Kashmiri society in future will be related to regional and international politics. In that context, he suggested that Kashmir must be made 'Switzerland of Asia' and not 'next Afghanistan in South Asia'. By these characterisation, he meant that Kashmir in future must be a place of

- peace, prosperity, reconciliation and cooperation;
- diplomacy, negations and stability;
- peace, and affluence in place of war and poverty; and
- cooperation and development in place of rivalry and domination.

(ii) Kashmir must emerge as the headquarter of local commonwealth of South Asian societies, economies and cultures. It must develop following prominent features in this regard:

- Heaven of tourism in South Asia
- South Asian super market of horticulture products
- Grand place for hydro-electric power generation
- Green wealth store of forests
- Mini-world of arts and crafts
- Cradle of Asian cultures and civilisations.

(iii) At the same time, Kashmir must not become next Afghanistan in any way, which necessarily meant the following

- No *talibanisation* of society and religion
- Maintain cultural plurality
- Patience and tolerance of varying religions and cultures
- Liberal, democratic and secular political order
- Developed, equitable and non-exploitative economic order
- Relevant ideological insights, vision-ful leadership and scientific-progressive worldview.

16. EXPERIENCE OF CONFLICT SITUATION

(i) K-20 was highly concerned about huge number of casualties in the armed conflict. During his duty, he used to see daily thousands of people in the hospital. According to him, most of them belonged 20s and 30s, many of them were women and children. They were mostly shot by security forces or caught in between cross-*fire.* Many of them were heads of their families and sole bread earners of the households. Those who were married left widows and orphans behind who had to face, grave problems.

(ii) K-20 felt that this tragedy was not limited to persons who died but extended to entire families and involved next generations. As per official and unofficial estimates, more than 1,00,000 people, mostly civilians, were killed in this conflict.

17. SOCIAL PROBLEMS IN KASHMIR

(i) *Political patronage of incompetent professionals:* K-20 showed concern about the problem of political patronage to professionals in different fields who were often incompetent, under-qualified and underscored. In reality, they seek the political support through surrender and submission to politicians and their authority. In this way, they developed a relation which can be characterised as super-ordinate and subordinate type of relations. This relationship has spoiled both-side actors and both occupations, particularly the professional and his field of specialisation.

(ii) K-20 felt that there were several intellectuals in his medical profession who were at top positions of hierarchy and were involved in this type of relationship. In this way, they lowered the standards of this profession and image and reputation also. He felt that they got involved in this relationship mainly due to their professional incompetence, no commitment to professional objectives and ethics, and extra-professional considerations. In that situation, they normally encouraged personalised system and its priorities; sub-standard knowledge and practices; and corrupt way of life.

K-21 FISHERWOMEN

1. SOCIAL CONTEXT

(i) The caste-occupational hierarchy in Kashmir was explained in terms of composing of 4 major castes of *Sayyid, Khan*, occupational and service castes. (See Dr. B. A. Dabla, *Castes in Kashmir*, Srinagar, 2011). There are numerous service caste groups which included the following:

- Haenj-Hanji	- Dhobi	- Zerger
- Najat	- Misger	- Gojri
- Sofi	- Kral	- Wani
- Darzi	- Kalaiger	- Roshanger
- Dander	- Ranger	- Sanur
- Sodager	- Artisans	- Thanthur
- Rafoger	- Kozger	- Ganie
- Wattal	- Sheikh	- La'el

All these caste groups were occupationally related to lower economic groups which were usually lowly educated and lowly mobile and culturally-religiously conservative.

(ii) However, there were some of these groups which have multiplicity of sub-groups and their respective economic-occupational functions. One such group was known as *Haenz or Hanji (*fishermen) occupational group. The sub-groups of this major group and their economic activities are mentioned below:

- *Gade Haenj (*fishermen) : this group deals with the occupation of fishing and both men and women are active partners;
- *Dal Haenj: this* group is located in and around the Dal Lake and is associated with all activities related to tourism. They play the roles of houseboat owners-managers, guides, travel agents and so on;
- V*eith Haenj: this group is located* on both sides of banks of *Jhelum* river in the city and towns of Kashmir;
- *Aram Haenj: this group deals with vege*table growing and selling occupation;
- *Material Haenj:* this group was active in providing solid material and commodities in the city;
- *Rasad Haenj:* this group used to perform the function of basic unit in 'public distribution system' of the government. In the changed situation, while most of units have been shifted to shops and houses, the group members have shifted to other occupations.

- *Shikara Haenj:* this group members used to ferry *shikaras,* i.e., small boats, in Dal Lake for tourists. With increase in tourist rush, they increased their economic standard considerably. But, with the downfall in tourism due to militancy, this group was compelled to change their occupation on the whole;
- *Mixed Haenj:* this group had no particular occupation. They used to perform different economic activities according to their speciality, contact and mostly season.

(iii) Among these sub-groups, the fishermen sub-group belonged to the lowest in the hierarchy of occupations and castes. They were extremely backward in economic, social, educational and cultural fields and their conditions of life were pathetic. K-21 was of that occupational background. An overview of life conditions of 'fishermen community' will provide information about in-family and out-family environment.

2. SOCIOLOGICAL PROFILE OF THE FISHERMEN COMMUNITY

(i) The fishermen community live in and around Dal lake in Srinagar, in and around Wulur lake in Bandipora and on both sides of Jhelum river throughout valley from its originto end. The community has a peculiar living pattern, i.e. living in houseboats floating on water. This stood quite different from the living pattern in concrete houses on solid earth. These houseboats are different from commercial houseboats for tourists and have distinct features. There is sufficient space for bed rooms, drawing rooms, sitting rooms, guest rooms and kitchen. There is no correct information available about their total population in the valley. It is estimated that their number must be in lakhs.

(ii) The sole occupation of this community was fishing from lakes and rivers of Kashmir and then selling in the market. When there was lesser production of fish due to shrinking and pollution in the Dal, Wulur and other waterways, they also used to purchase fish from governments' farms and sell in the market. Majority of these members continue to work in this occupation till elder age.

(iii) Economically, they can be characterised as poor of the poor in society. Their economic conditions were worse and pathetic. They work, earn and consume on daily basis. If they do not work regularly, they may not get meals regularly and necessarily. In that situation, they don't live, they only survive. Their selfish type of behaviour in economic activities can be explained in this context. They have no moveable-immoveable property and savings except small houseboats and household belongings.

(iv) Socially, fishermen stood as a distinctive group having its folk and tribal traits in their living pattern. They are strictly endogamous and have equal status families in marriage. Outsiders can never think in terms of taking or giving girls in marriage in this community. Generally, they perform marriage at earlier age and there is no dowry at all. They live in joint family structures/ clusters in a single houseboat and some establish nuclear family units after marriage. While their men wear common Kashmiri dresses, their women wear peculiar dresses and jewellary. They are informal in relations with others. They are considered 'loose' in their language. In this context, they usually attract derogatory remarks in markets by members of other service occupational groups.

(v) Culturally, they are committed to religious values, norms and its ethics. However, their conditions compel them to deviate from this commitment. They have common feelings of inferiority and sense of deprivation. This reflects in their entire way of life, particularly in female names which seem funny, derogatory and convey their lowest social status. These names were given to them by their *Peers* at the time of their birth and these were considered as sacred. Some of these odd names of fisherwomen were as follows:

- Khatiz	- Rahet	- Phazi	- Zooni
- Jel	- Gosher	- Shige	- Jigri
- Khazir	- Shamil	- Deder	- Kukil
- Sundir	- Sone	- Mugil	- Mukhte
- Phreche	- Azz	- Shame	- Male

(vi) Religiously, they feel conservative. Their commitment in actuality was to customary religious practices than to ideal religious practices of Islam. They necessarily visit shrines, *darghas* and *peers*. They are less particular about daily religious ethics because of their total ignorance.

(VI) Educationally, near-total community stood illiterate. All males and females belonging to all generations have not gone even for primary education. Children too are not sent to school as a rule but are trained in domestic role and occupational skills. Despite the fact that in Hazratbal area, where highest concentration of fishermen is located and, at the same time, Kashmir University is situated within a distance of one km., they have not sent a single boy or girl to the university during last few decades.

(vii) Though a lot of development work has taken place in their surrounding residential colonies and their life conditions, this community stands where they stood 70 years back. They have experienced least effect of governmental welfare programs. So, they suffer extremely in health, nutrition, education, employment, income, mobility, shelter, security and other fields. After observing this situation, one feels compelled to conclude that they have hardly been touched by processes of change and development and they hardly aspire for mobility. In actuality, they still live a tribal-type of life with primitive life conditions.

(viii) K-21 belonged to this social-occupational group and contributed an ideal role in her integrated community. She was socialised and trained in this in-family and out-family environment. In fact, she developed an isolated and alienated social personality. She and her family had not much contact and interaction with the outside world. They felt about themselves as "dissociated" and "discriminated" in the social arena.

3. OCCUPATION, CAREER AND ASSOCIATION

(i) K-21 was socialised in many roles mainly related to domestic life, marriage and occupation. She learned and personalised these roles at the younger stage. However, after marriage, she formally started domestic and occupational roles. This represents a 'cycle of roles' in the following pattern:

- Domestic role > post-marriage role > occupational role > domestic role

While 2 -3 generations of women were involved in this cycle of roles, the transfer of authority were functional and normal. K-21 too experienced this cycle and performed these roles in an ideal way.

(ii) Occupational and other roles in fishermen community were based on gender basis. There seems a clear cut division of labour between two sexes. For example, men always go to Dal Lake during the night for catching fish and women used to go to the market during the day for selling fish. Similarly, other works and responsibilities were pre-determined. K-21 adopted all these roles and related behaviour. Now, we are in a position to draw a list of occupational and other activities for men and women differently as follows:

Gender-wise Occupational and non-Occupational Activities

For females	*For males*
- Child bearing, rearing and caring	- child rearing in the day in houseboat
- Domestic jobs: washing	
- Cleaning the houseboat	- occupational activities during the night
• Sweeping	- catching fish
• Preparing meals and tea	- associated activities (day time)
- Occupational activities	- Elders care at home
- selling fish in the market in day time	
- Childrens' and Elders' care	
- Shopping in the market	

This division of labour reveals clearly heavy workload for women, establishing social contacts through women, women's role as the source of income and other matters. This role pattern seems similar to some tribal societies.

(iii) K-21 was found always busy in domestic, occupational and other activities day and night. This heavy schedule of activities of K-21 reveals in the following chart:

Chart of the female activities

Morning	*Day time*	*Evening*
- Washing - Cleaning - Serving breakfast - Market-preparation - Child care - Domestic jobs	- selling fish in the market with or without baby - shopping - daily purchases -	- serving dinner to family members - domestic jobs - children to Doctor (if ill) - cleaning

(iv) In the preceding occupational framework, K-21 has developed related association which was very limited in scope. While it can be explained in terms of no desire for expansion of relations on the part of this community, it can also be mentioned in terms of social ostracism imposed on them by the broader society. So, K-21 had limited association of families of same occupational group and used to spend all time with them.

(v) In this situation, how could K-21 aspire for change and development? She and other women in the community have developed the notion that they were born as fisherwomen and will die as fisherwomen. They have inherited this occupation from elder generation and will now pass on to next generation. So, there seems no scope for deviation or change in occupation. This was functionally correct because of no initiative for reforms in the community on the part of state or broader society.

4. MARRIAGE AND FAMILY

(i) K-21's marriage was done in the endogamous circle as is the rule with fishermen community which they follow strictly. They could never think of taking or giving girls to other social groups. Same is correct about rest of society. Though marriage with fishermen community is not illegal or illegitimate, it stands as complete taboo and in violation of this code is tolerated.

(ii) K-21 married with a boy who was her relative from her father's side living in different locality of houseboats. After marriage, she joined joint family of her husband which was of her equal status and was involved in same occupational activities. In addition to domestic roles, she also started the occupational role and contributed to family income.

(iii) In this way, she became the functional organ of the marital family. Subsequently, she developed and expanded her authority on the entire family covering her husband, children and elder males-females. Thus she became the dominant person in the whole family.

5. SOCIAL LIKES AND DISLIKES

After having lifelong experience in the families of parents and husband and out-family market interactions, K-21 developed certain particular social likes and dislikes as mentioned below:

Social Likes	*Social Dislikes*
- Eed festivities	- others comments in the market
- Marriage celebrations	- rough behaviour of people towards them
- Entertainment programs of folk music	- negative image and attitude of people
- Female domination in the family	- strict religious rules and behaviour
- *Peer-Mureedi* system	- dependence and discrimination
- Religious ideas, ideals and behaviour	- exploitation by other groups
- Attendance to shrine regularly	- social protest and opposition
- Early disposal of fish in the market	- no education and employment of their children
- Maximum profit margin in fish selling	- no proper shelter in the houseboats
- Means superior to ends	- political participation and disturbances
- Common civilised morality	- social distrust of fishermen community
- Social elevation from above	- other petty service groups and their role
- Participation in the process of change	- vulgarity of hoodlums in the market
- Living in isolation and alienation	- chronic and prolonging diseases
- A rich, generous and pious personality	- high rate of deaths among them
- Children with good health	- greedy eyes towards their girls
- Good post-marital life	- dowry in the marriages
- A morally high character person	- a dishonest fish businessman
- School in their locality	- social disorganisation and disorder
- A good alien customer	- gender differentiation.

6. CONCEPTS OF "I", "ME" AND "WE"

(i) K-21 had hardly any concept of 'I', especially in front of others. In fact, she and here community were lost in 'I'. They could neither find it nor feel it mainly because they considered themselves as the 'wretched group on earth'.

(ii) But, the concept of 'me' was used by K-21 in limited sense, i.e. she remained conscious about it some times and unconscious at other times. Thus she is 'me' in place of 'my' that was directly related to her background and family occupation. In this context, 'my' referred to my family, my relatives, my group/class and my caste. For her, 'me' referred to this limited social world.

(iii) K-21 held the concept of 'we' in a way in which it could partly be equated with 'me' and partly related to its independent identity. In the related society, according to K-21, we can find social features like positiveness, dynamism, activeness, and improvement in positive and negative senses. So, we have the concept of 'we' used for :

- A community with lowest standard of living;
- A community with highest mortality rate
- A community with highest degree of disease incidence
- A community having lowest social and cultural status
- A community having no chances of mobility and change
- A community which remained static always
- A community which didn't responded to the processes of development.

K-21 felt that this feeling of 'we' was so strong that there was very less feeling of the world at present and in future. They seemed to be satisfied with the present situation.

7. IDEAS OF EQUALITY AND INEQUALITY

(i) K-21 felt that she and her community represented an unequal lot in comparison to other communities living around them. She also felt that they remained at the lowest position in every hierarchy. She provided the rationale for this unequal status in her own way. She gave two main reasons related to historical context and social context. Historically, K-21 felt that they have inherited the unequal and degraded status from earlier generations and could never change it and pass it on to the next generation. There was also not any external effort to change their status. Socially, K-21 argued that the work her community was performing was actually god-ordained and god-sent. They could not change it, even if they wanted because it was their destiny. This reflected the religious justification for their status quo.

(ii) On the other hand, she argued that unequal status of fishermen community was because of their own weaknesses and deficiencies like poverty, illiteracy, ignorance, dependence, no proper shelter, disease-oriented health condition and prevailing culture. This system of inequality will continue and God will not help them. For the future of her children, she dared to start thinking differently.

8. THE IDEAL CHARACTER

(i) The ideal character of K-21 was *Peer Saheb* living in the nearby locality. She and her family had associated some religious qualities, merits, and miracles with him. They considered him most sacred and most ideal person who stood for them as unique. In actuality, these feelings became the basis of their beliefs about the *peer* and his super-natural powers. The resultant interaction led to among other things to *peer-mureedi* relationship. K-21 also contributed to strengthening of beliefs and related practices.

(ii) It may be noted *peer-mureedi* was functional in terms of religious education and training to the followers in whom they had complete trust. But, as time passed, this institutionalised relationship deteriorated and now it mostly stands for exploitation for material benefits of the *peer*. The illiterate-ignorant people like fishermen and women get exploited due to certain myths, dogmas, doubts, fears and other related practices imposed on them in the society. In this way, this institution was made to serve the *peer* at the cost of *mureeds*.

(iii) For K-21, *Peer Saheb* was spiritual and religious guru. She completely surrendered before him, followed his orders blindly, got satisfaction by his name, approached him for every problem, got his confirmation for every family decision and starting new works. Day by day, this relationship expanded and took others in this network. Thus he emerged as the sole arbiter of their community too.

9. THE RELIGIOUS LIFE

(i) K-21 was an illiterate person and had no basic knowledge about Islam from it direct sources of *Quran and haidth*. She was also not acquainted with folk religious practices in Kashmir. In actuality, she believed, adopted and performed a religion which was not clear to her. While she believed in myths, dogmas, miracles, and other such practices, her family had same ideas and views. In fact, all these beliefs and practices were inherited from the earlier generation through socialisation and other processes. They were not clear about fundamentals and basic concepts of Islam.

(ii) In this situation, K-21 and her family adopted a form of religion characterised by a series of rituals which cover the whole life, especially at the time of birth, death, marriage, disease, emergency and other occasions. These ritual performances were performed by a group of *peers* who were considered as the 'custodians of religion'. They had the notion that principles, ideals and values were not religious objectives but service to the religious custodians stood were real objectives. This exactly contributed to the exploitation of religion for material benefits and distortion of religion by changing the real perspective of religion.

(iii) Religion as sum total of customary practices, according to K-21, revolved around religious festivities, functions and ceremonies as customary practices. Thus these occasions were celebrated with funfair, high spirits and most delicious meals were prepared. These practices were partly devoid of religious meaning, contents, orientation, objectives and aspirations. These practices were considered by some as negating the essence of Islamic religion.

(iv) As K-21 and her family was less aware and had no knowledge about real religion. She also lacked the knowledge about folk religious practices. In fact, they were not made aware about the reality of religion by any individual, group, institute and organisation. There was not organised *tableeg* among them. So, K-21 and her family members were compelled to adopt the ritual-customary version of religion.

(v) K-21 had acquaintance with KPs with whom she had strong attachment. She remembered some of those families for humility, generosity and help. She used to take special fish to them on the occasion of *Heerath.* As she conveyed, she used to get heavy amount in addition to gifts on this occasion. She still remembered some families which took full care of her material needs.

10. EXPERIENCE OF CONFLICT SITUATION

(i) K-21 has a particular experience of conflict situation in Kashmir. During those years, she used to go to the City Center to sell fish in the market. In that busy market, she used to sit with a dozen of her colleagues in one corner to sell the fish. She used to go there regularly throughout the year even with her little baby in her lap during winter months of December-Feburary. She had selected that place for selling fish because of possibility of more customers there and probability of more profit and chances of quick sale of fish.

(ii) She used to go to that market even during peak militancy period where grenade-bomb blasts, cross-firing and killings by forces were common features of daily life. She came in contact with the officer and soldiers in the same locality. After meeting her and buying fish on daily basis, they showed their sympathy with her mainly because of her activity with a baby and in severe winter conditions. They took personal interest in her case and enquired about her family and its occupational activities and women's role.

(iii) This clearly reflected the human response of security forces which was expected from human beings. But, some days after bomb-blast and cross firing in that area. The same security personnel threw their fish on road and beat all fisherwomen present there. This was a pattern of reaction of security forces after such incident. They used to beat and injure innocent people and destroy their property.

11. THE KASHMIRI SOCIETY

(i) The active sentiments of K-21 about Kashmir and its identity were totally absent. She was hardly concerned about Kashmir problem and its resolution. She had no knowledge about origin, nature and dimensions of this political problem. She only knew about SMA as the great leader of Kashmir. Taking into consideration living conditions of her and other communities, she opined that no such fishermen community must exist in future.

K-22 SHIKARAWALLA

1. SOCIAL CONTEXT

(i) The service occupational groups have internal stratification based on income and occupation. In fact, in many situations, income emerged as sole criteria for its existence and functioning. In this context, we can trace status of sub-group of *Shikarawallas* in between many sub-groups up and down. This sub-group has its particular economic activities and social differences. The main service occupations, their related occupational activities and duration of work of the group of service occupations were as follows:

S. No.	Name of Occupation	Related economic activities	Duration of work
1.	Shikarawallas	- shikara-riding in Dal lake	7-8 months in a year
		- seasonal occupations	3-4 months in a year
		-other economic activities	1-2 months
2.	Foot-path Vendors	-fruit selling	whole year
		-vegetable selling	-whole year
		-other economic activities	-2-3 months
3.	Reddawallas	-fruit selling	-whole year
		-vegetable selling	-whole year
		-cloth selling	-whole year
		-all day-to-day use items	-whole year
		-other economic activities	-whole year
4.	Dhaba Tea Shops	-serving tea and cold drinks	-seasonal
5.	Sunday market-valley	-clothing selling	-on all Sundays
		-winter-summer items	-on all Sundays
		-day-to-day use items	-on all Sundays
		-all other consumer-domestic items	-on all Sundays
6.	Tourism related jobs	-different jobs in hotels	-seasonal period
		-Tourist guides and Travel agents	-seasonal period
		-handicraft items selling	-seasonal period
		-other tourist-related activities	- seasonal period
7.	Outside State jobs	-kashmiri handicrafts	-seasonal/whole year
8.	Other petty jobs	-all petty and seasonal activities	-seasonal period
9.	Manjgaroos	-selling local eatable items	-whole year

(ii) K-22 belonged to one such sub-group called *Shikarawallas*. He used to work for *shikara*-riding in Dal Lake for most part of the year. For rest of the year, he used to perform different seasonal jobs such as charcoal selling, chicken selling, eggs selling, and fruit selling. On the occasion of festivals, he used to sell different birds and other eatables.

2. OVERVIEW OF LIFE CONDITIONS OF SHIKARAWALLAS

(i) No accurate figures are available about total number of people in this occupational group. However, some estimates reveal their number in thousands. This sub-group was primarily an occupational group and stood one of the dominant sub-groups. Most of this community members lived in and around Dal Lake in their houseboats or in houses built on the banks. Most of them have encroached the dal land illegally. Some of them lived on the banks of Jhelum river. Thus most of them lived in urban areas and shared urban facilities.

(ii) Their occupation stood stable, well-paying, attractive and had regularity of activities. It had little inputs and more outputs. But, it was not in operation for whole year. This occupation has benefited the community economically till militancy started in 1989 in Kashmir. Subsequently, there were no tourists, so no *shikara*-riding. During last two decades, the community faced economic collapse because even their savings finished.

(iii) In old days, the economic condition of this community was stable and satisfactory. In a normal tourist season for the entire year, they used to earn sufficient amount for whole year and for savings. But, these conditions changed and all of them have shifted to seasonal and other economic activities for daily family expenditure.

(iv) Socially, they equated their occupational activities with other occupational activities and were performed in different areas. Their social image was not high and they considered as "undesirable" because of their uncultured attitudes and behaviour and language. They were always offensive and negative in their approach. They practised endogamous and patri-local type of marriage and considered them as natural and suitable. They were realistic in their approach to life and adjusted in all changed situations. They have developed patience for changing occupations often.

(v) Educationally, they stood illiterate and semi-literate. It was mainly because most of them either didn't join primary school and joined parental occupation from childhood. But, those who joined primary stage education certainly drop out later on to join their occupation. Thus they had hardly any functional utility for education.

(vi) Culturally, they felt conscious of their traditions, customs, values and norms. They showed total antipathy towards other petty occupational groups. They were hardly exposed to other cultural influences because of illiteracy and ignorance. Despite regular interaction with foreign and Indian tourists, they avoided their impact consciously. They were over-conscious about their lower status, which attracted other's criticism and disliking. Their lower status also reflected in their names which were advised by their *peers* at the time of birth. Some of these odd and degraded names were as follows:

- Naba	- Ama	- Nabir	- Mahmud
- Sole	- Nike	- Kabire	- Sabe
- Bule	- Bashe	- Gaffare	- Satare
- Qadire	- Bashire	- Nazire	- Hamide
- Aliye	- Amine	- Ramzane	- Rehme

Most of these names were funny, nicknames, offensive, derogatory and amusing. These were advised by the family *peer* who imposed these rough names on lower occupational groups and awarded good and sophisticated names to their own family children.

(vii) Religiously, they felt committed to all ideals of religion apparently, but not to pure, scriptural and doctrine version. In fact, they were committed to all folk religious practices which they considered as equivalent to religious fundamentals. Since they were completely illiterate and could not study basic sources of religion, they have developed lesser commitment to basic principles of Islam. Their *peers* introduced them only to folk practices which they believe as religion. In actuality, this service occupational community kept alive the institution of *peer-mureedi.*

(viii) Politically, they always served the ruling regimes. They participated in their sponsored rallies, protests and demonstrations for which they were paid. They also worked at the time of elections for the ruling party and managed its victory. This lumpen element was always used by SMA throughout his life. They considered him the great leader and called him *bab*, the most dear elder person.

(ix) In terms of change and development, this community was not benefited at all. They had not utilised the benefits of any development program and welfare scheme meant for them. Consequently, they suffered in all fields of life, especially health, education and mobility.

(x) But, militancy effected this community with serious implications. It was because of total dependence on tourism, total collapse of this sector and no productive economic activity. Their income was reduced even upto 90-95% and their savings were exhausted. In actuality, they could not withstand this downfall and were compelled to shift to seasonal occupational activities in which there were lesser monetary benefits. K-22 belonged to this occupational group and its changing environment.

3. IN-FAMILY AND OUT-FAMILY SOCIALISATION

(i) The entire in-family and out-family socialisation of K-22 was carried out in the occupational environment in which emphasis was on the adoption of occupational activities from childhood stage. In actuality, parents desired that their children adopt the concerned occupational role.

(ii) The occupational roles and required skills were developed by children not through formal training but through their informal participation before marriage. After their marriage, children were formally entrusted the occupational job and were expected to show their responsible role. This type of socialisation proved decisive and lifelong for K-22 as this group was competing with other rival occupational groups. Moreover, K-22's occupational group was socially considered as 'undesirable' by others, he had least positive social relationship with them. His own family life and its occupation had proved only socialising forces. In the environment of petty competition, he opted for his own occupational ethos.

4. OCCUPATION AND CAREER

(i) According to K-22, the occupation of *shikarawallas* was not operational for the whole year. But, it used to be functional for 7-8 months or more and rest of the period was spent in other seasonal activities. The tentative details about the economic activities of *shikarawallas* were as follows:

- January	Winter-related seasonal occupational activities
- February	- do –
- March	- do –
- April	*shikara-* riding in Dal Lake
- May	- do –
- June	- do –
- July	- do –
- August	- do –
- September	- do –
- October	- do –
- November	- do – and seasonal occupation
- December	-do - - do –

(ii) The main area of *shikara-riding* was the main Dal. The tourists used to go on all water routes at different occasions. Foreign and Indian tourists who stayed in houseboats used to have their respective *shikarawallas.* The locals too used *shikara*-riding for their family entertainment. The pre-marital and post-marital couples were also special clients of *shikarawallas.* K-22 observed that only men, elders, young, and children were involved in this occupation and women in general were not involved.

(iii) K-22 revealed that *shikarawallas* had old and new *shikaras* and one family had one or more *shikaras* which were well decorated and furnished so as give a grandeur look. In order to attract tourists' attention quickly, different name were written on the sign boards of *shikaras. Some* of those names include the following:

- King Point	- King Tourist	- Queen Tourist
- Suffering Moses	- Chinar	- Gulfam
- Zaffran	- Dal View	- Dal Scene
- Lotus	- Nightangale	- Paris Stop
- Kashmir Holiday	- Kashmir Holiday Shikara	- Kashmir Tourist
- Kashmir View	- Kashmir Darbar	- Kashmir King
- Kashmir Queen	- Kashmir Beauty	- Sheen Sheen
- London Avenue	- Bombay Stop	- Dulha
- Dulhan	- Maharaja	- Delhi Flight
- Chand Chandni	- Shah-e-Jehan	- Taj Mahal
- Calcutta Ferry		

(iv) In this ideal background, K-22 was involved in this occupation and developed a career in it. This started in his childhood when he developed necessary skills and was formally engaged in it after marriage. Subsequently, he performed the expert role and could play this role in all situations, especially when Dal becomes volatile due to speedy air waves. During the period ,tourists were not present in the valley, he used to perform other seasonal activities like charcoal selling, egg selling, vegetable selling, milk selling and so on. These activities continued till new arrival of tourists in April.

5. ASSOCIATION AND MOBILITY

(i) Since K-22's occupational activities were limited, his association pattern reflected this aspect of social life. So, his associational groups were composed of families of relatives and occupational colleagues. For him, rest of the association was partial, temporary, abnormal and selfish. Since they were looked down upon by other occupational groups, K-22 and his family's attitudes and behaviour was also antagonistic towards them. He always rated them below his status and standard. This led to their dissociation and segregation in the fields of contacts, interaction and so on.

(ii) At the same time, K-22 used to develop good rapport with foreigners and Indian tourists. They used to praise him always for which he was proud of. This gave him satisfaction in the occupation. But, he had not accepted any social or cultural impact.

(iii) In the preceding situation, K-22 was able to earn sufficient amount for yearly family expenditure and for future savings. He was satisfied with that situation. But, everything turned against him when complete economic collapse was due to militancy from 1989.

6. MARRIAGE AND FAMILY

(i) K-22 was married at an earlier age in a close endogamous group. The girl belonged to same economic, cultural, educational and social status. At that time, he was living with parents in joint family household. After marriage, K-22 and his wife lived in the same unit.

(ii) After his brothers and sisters were married and after death of parents, K-22 family attained the status of nuclear family in the cycle of change from nuclear family to joint family to nuclear family. This nuclear family household composed of he, his wife and their unmarried children. When children came to the stage of maturity, they worked in different fields for the family.

7. SOCIAL LIKES AND DISLIKES

After having long experience in his life, K-22 developed certain particular social likes and dislikes, some of which are mentioned below:

Social Likes	*Social Dislikes*
- Children with higher education	- arrogant and corrupt police officer
- Hospitality to foreign tourists	- poverty and dependency
- Multi-cultural environment	- corruption in all government offices
- A person with a government service	- a person having strict religious orientation
- Achievement through any way	- lower economic position and related status
- Ends justify the means	- extremely innocent and frank person
- Social commitment to values and norms	- illiterate individual and his family
- Work ethic and work culture	- corrupt and deceitful politician
- Opposing other occupational groups	- social inequality
- Social tension and conflict	- denial of gender justice
- A nuclear family household	- no change and no progress
- Neighborhood of the same status	- too much of hard work
- Celebration of festivals and other occasions	- negative feeling about *shikarawalas*
- Participation in all folk religious practices	- strong emphasis on rules and laws
- A charismatic political leader	- crime and criminal behaviour
- Marriage of endogamous and patri-local chr.	- drug addiction of boys and girls
- Certain degree of selfishness	- social deviation by children and youth
- No hard struggle in life	- begging as an occupation
- Affluence of all kinds	- all aspects of poverty culture
- Political participation	- political workers of other political parties.

8. CONCEPTS OF "I", "ME" AND "WE"

(i) K-22's concepts of 'I', 'me' and 'we' were vague in the sense that there was no clarity and specificity in their meanings. These were absolutely confused notions about 'I' and 'me'. 'I' was not associated with 'I' of the past and present. Similarly, 'me' was not associated with 'me' of the past and present. It was mainly because while 'I' and 'me' of the past was unbearable, shameful, unfavorable, unproductive, unthinkable, inhuman and horrible. So, they cannot live in that sub-human condition which tortured them every time and tried to hide 'I' and 'me'. The concept of 'me' in the past and present was also troublesome, torturous and problematic. It generally referred to 'my' and :

- my family which was in distress and disarray;
- my relatives who were in deplorable condition; and
- my group which was at the lowest level of hierarchy.

(ii) In this context, the concept of 'we' provided some solace. It could have been wider had they been educated and employed. 'We' of the past and present were favorites. While the former referred to their family not in stable condition and not in high esteem, the latter referred to the sense of our family and our community. This represented a higher stage of consciousness for stability, permanence and continuity of the community, especially in the prevailing unethical competition and conflict. They made difference between 'we' the upholders of particular identity in comparison to their identity. Thus 'we' led to a situation in which K-22 and his family make contrast in social status, economic position, political power and gender inequality.

9. IDEAS OF EQUALITY AND INEQUALITY

(i) K-22 felt that every individual must be rated in terms of humanity and in political, economic, social, cultural, educational, linguistic and other material terms. It follows that he favored a social system and social order based on principles of humanity irrespective of their different roles and status. But, at the same time, these differences seem crucial, socially and culturally rooted and difficult to uproot. In this crucial situation, inequality was prevalent in all fields and at every level and it was directly responsible for injustice, oppression, suppression, force, dependency and underdevelopment. It also gave rise to class, caste, and power hierarchies. In totality, K-22 saw inequality as a 'necessary evil' which they are living with, while it should have been uprooted. But, in this world, he lamented we were at the bottom and destined to be at bottom in future.

10. THE IDEAL LEADER

(i) SMA was sole ideal leader of K-22 who felt that neither such a leader was produced in the past nor will rise in future. He considered him the tallest leader in India, Pakistan and other countries of the world. He believed in super-human power and miraculous personality of *Sheikh Saheb* as he used to be called in Kashmir. K-22 considered him the supreme leader because of following reasons:

- his political leadership was unmatched;
- his popularity and following crossed the limits of age, region, religion and culture;
- he was proud, confident and popular leader who accepted all political challenges;
- he dedicated his life for the cause of Kashmir and Kashmiris;
- he was really the lion of Kashmir who ended the alien domination;
- he had the courage and leadership qualities who can face any leader in India and Pakistan;
- since he was called the *bab,* masses had emotional attachment to him;
- people in general followed his orders and dictates; they could have sacrificed themselves and their families, if ordered by the *bab;*
- he gave the freedom to the Kashmiris in 1947.

The individuals and groups, which believed in the above statements, were consciously and systematically used by SMA throughout his life for political purpose. They believe that he is still alive in the graveyard and comes out of it for visiting *dargah sheriff.*

(ii) K-22, like many others, was proud of lifelong follower of SMA. He put forth four reasons for that political support as follows:

(a) SMA was god-sent leader for the welfare of Kashmiris;

(b) he fought and got freedom for Kashmir in 1947;

(c) he always thought about interests of Kashmiri masses, especially down-trodden; and

(d) he constructed *dargah sharif* afresh.

11. THE RELIGIOUS LIFE

(i) K-22 believed in all religious fundamentals but with least clarity because of his total illiteracy and ignorance. In fact, he and his family members were not conveyed real and full knowledge about all these fundamentals in his folk perspective and were not also trained in basic religious practices. So, their religious life revolved around beliefs which laid emphasis on notions, myths, mysteries, miracles, rituals, spiritualism and so on. In the case of practices, he stressed for various ritual performances, celebrations of festivals and different *urs, Peer-Mureedi* relationship, shrine attendance and so on. All these practices stood of secondary and additional importance to actual religion in comparison to basic practices of *namaz, roza, zakaat, and hajj.*

(ii) In this theoretical and empirical situation, K-22 adopted a version of religious life which revolved around not ideal but folk belief and practices. He and his family were wholly devoted to this lifestyle. The adoption of this religious life had three broader and important implications which follow:

(a) mis-direction of the worldview of pure and real religion;

(b) distortion of basic principles and concepts of pure and real religion related to beliefs and practices; and

(c) exploitation of religion by particular clerical group for their monetary benefits.

12. KASHMIR PROBLEM AND FUTURE SOCIETY

(i) Since K-22 was lifelong follower of SMA, he had completely different views on the Kashmir problem. First, he believed that *Bab* had solved this problem once for all. He made Kashmir a part of India and we accepted it. Following this decision, we must follow it and live in India with satisfaction. But, all his children differed with him and upheld the political ideal of *Azaadi* from India. Second, K-22 upheld that we survive on the generous help from India (*Hindustanuk bate chi khewan).* So, we must not demand freedom from India. Third, Pakistan is not our friend and it will not favour us in the long run. It has shown its real face in 1947 at the time of tribal raid on Kashmir.

(ii) K-22 and his ideological friends adopted these ideas and themes from SMA's public speeches during his lifetime. They remembered all those speeches word by word and could not deviate from that despite opposite types of changes in Kashmir. But, K-22's children were different completely in their political perspective. They maintained that freedom of Kashmir, which India has grabbed by deceit, was their immediate political goal. Second, they upheld that freedom was their birth right which must be restored to them immediately. Third, they also joined the struggle for freedom which nobody can stop.

(iii) K-22 felt concerned with the role of his occupational group in the near future. As Dal is encroached more and more and getting polluted fast, it may restrict heavily the areas of *shikara*-riding. In that case, Kashmir will attract lesser number of tourists which will have direct negative impact on his occupation in future. They will be compelled to other occupational activities and thus his group will be affected adversely. That must be avoided necessarily and efforts in that direction must start immediately.

(iv) In this context, he could visualize an environmental and occupational disaster in the near future, which needed to be avoided in any way. As per his views, while government has to play central role, the NGOs have to play supportive role.

13. EXPERIENCE OF CONFLICT SITUATION

(i) K-22 conveyed his concern about future of Dal Lake as it was getting increasingly deteriorated by elements within and outside the Dal. With the increasing pollution, contamination, silting and other deteriorating factors, the Dal was dying its own death. While it will lead to ecological-environmental disaster, it will also ruin related occupations and its people.

(ii) K-22 felt that all this has happened in the recent past, especially during last two decades when people on sides of Dal grabbed its land illegally and constructed concrete residential houses in and around it. The *Hanjis* established floating vegetable gardens within Dal. This went on for decades without any effective check and control. Nobody could intervene in this process of debasing-defacing Dal ,because of political, militancy and sectarian considerations. On the other hand, the government was so busy in militancy that it could hardly formulate and implement any program for preservation of Dal. It was reported by K-22 that most of state and central governments funds got wasted because of large-scale corruption involved in the saving-Dal programs. Though national and international support in the form of technology, expertise and professionals was provided and used also but Dal deterioration could not be controlled.

(iii) K-22 felt that if this deterioration of Dal is not controlled effectively, it will certainly lead to the ecological, environmental and occupational disaster. Thousands of local people have to suffer the consequences of this disaster.

(iv) Last but the least, K-22 presented all these views about Dal deterioration. But the related fact was that he himself grabbed the Dal land and constructed his residential house. In that he stood equally responsible for the future disasters.

14. SOCIAL PROBLEMS IN KASHMIR

(i) *Social Differentiation among Occupational Groups:* Though this type of differentiation stood normal in many societies, K-22 showed serious negative concern about it. It was because it usually led to conflict, even on permanent basis. He also felt that in some cases, this differentiation stood natural and it has got its own dynamics of equilibrium and checks-counter and checks mechanism. But, when normal social principles were not followed, that led to social rivalry, social tension and social war.

According to K-22, this occupational group war was experienced in Kashmir too. While the caste factor provided basic factor providing basic elements of avoiding concerned equality, other factors gave it an extreme form of social cleavage which culminated into social conflict. Thus these groups look down upon each other, and compete in all fields that included physical hurting. They developed extremely negative images and felt safe in their own groups only.

K-22 held that social disliking and negative feeling against other occupational groups must end because both sides suffer in this type of relationship.

(ii) *Not Feeling about Hard Life Conditions in the Past:* K-22 felt extremely bad on the situation in which children were not aware about sub-human conditions of people in the past. They have developed the impression that people in Kashmir always got two meals in a day easily and comfortably. While K-22 himself and his generation had faced harshest life conditions in pre-1947 era, which the present-day children have not faced. They could not even imagine about those conditions.

While referring to those conditions, K-22 felt depressed and angry. He gave the entire credit to SMA who took out Kashmiris from that hell of extreme poverty.

K-22 wanted children to understand present as well as past situation in Kashmir and play a responsible role in broader society. The deviant, uncontrolled and criminal tendencies among them have ruined their life and they don't get on proper road to realistic social order.

K-23 RELIGIOUS IDEOLOGUE AND SAYYID–RURAL

1. SOCIAL CONTEXT

(i) The *Sayyid castes* are presumed at the top of hierarchy not only in ritual status but in worldly-material status also. In a broader sense, the *Sayyid* castes form a community with high degree of commonness, association, inter-relationship, endogamy, feeling of superiority and pride of foreign origin. In the modern period, their community was first to respond to processes of modernisation and development and, so, was ahead of other communities in education, employment, cultural exposure and social mobility.

(ii) Broadly speaking, this community does not stand for a homogenous unit of social, cultural and educational features and its response towards new trends of transformation. In this context, it can be broadly divided at two levels, rural and urban. While the rural *Sayyids* formed majority of this population, the urban *Sayyids* formed the minority. However, a large number of the former migrated to city after 1947 and, after getting modern education, dominated educational, intellectual, professional, technical and other fields. Second, *Sayyids* can be divided further in two categories which were (a) modernised *sayyids* in urban and rural areas and (b) conservative sayyids in rural and urban areas.

(iii) In the urban context, *Sayyids* proved more intelligent, open and responsive. Probably, this was second local community after KPs which adopted modern education, government employment, and were ahead in cultural, literary, intellectual and other fields. They also represented the first organised group among KMs which responded positively to the impact of trends of modernisation-westernisation. This response can also be explained in two types, fast and slow. The fast response came from educated and employed ones in urban areas who opted for modern cultural traits and lifestyle. Their women too stopped practising segregation and *purdah.* This behaviour later on became 'ideal type' for other women in Kashmir. The slow response came from those urban *Sayyids* who were not quick in adopting education and higher government jobs. They were also not exposed fully in the cultural field. Their women did not stop practising segregation and *purdah.* In direct contrast to earlier group, this group maintained traditions, values and norms. They also continued with certain ritual roles and *peer-mureedi.*

(iv) This response to modernity had two different aspects related to rural and urban areas. The urban *Sayyids*, including migrants, proved highly positive in case of modernisation-westernisation influence. Some eminent *Sayyid* families were at the forefront in this regard. It was observed that they experienced change in traditional role, occupation, in-family and out-family environment, religious attitudes and behaviour, lifestyle and new role of women. In direct contrast to this, the rural *Sayyids* were not exposed so much to modernity impact. In actuality, they maintained traditional role and status of men and women. Men worked for religious, ritual, customary, ceremonial and shrine purposes and some of them continued with *peer-mureedi.* Their men got education and consequently government employment, while their women remained confined to their houses.

(V) K-23 belonged to one such rural *Sayyid* family which maintained its traditional status. While men in the family got education and government employment, their women were prohibited to go for either They practised segregation and *purdah* seriously. They were not allowed even to go to their agricultural fields. Culturally, this family remained unchanged. Its elders discontinued with traditional spiritual and ritual roles and had to face monetary loss. In brief, while this family of K-23 maintained the image of *sayyid* family, its social and economic benefits were discontinued. Probably, his elders thought that was demand of the time. That is why, this family imparted education to its male children for active and dominant role in and out of family.

2. IN-FAMILY SOCIALISATION

(i) K-23 belonged to rural *Sayyid* family which was extremely religious in theory and practice. It practised religion in every field, especially related to women who were allowed to pursue education, employment and were not allowed to go to their agricultural fields. Education and employment was only for men. All members were sincere followers of Islam and upheld its norms and values in social life. It was the only male literate community in the village which lived with other castes/occupational communities in different *mohallas* like *peer mohalla, dab mohalla, dasil mohalla and so on.*

(ii) In addition to religiosity, gentleness and submissiveness, the family did not believe in the caste system or practice. Its members lived in an egalitarian set-up in which all other villagers were treated equally without any prejudice. The family didn't adopt traditional role of *peer* or *mulla* but preferred to get low government jobs. It also discontinued with *peer-mureedi* which could have given the family economic and social benefits. The members felt that this institution had deteriorated and become exploitative. The family even refused to accept a particular share in their paddy production which used to be given to *peer* at the harvest time. Other *peers* got this share. This family had developed a work culture in the home wherein men and women performed their pre-determined roles and jobs assigned to them. All in-family jobs were performed by women and their out-family jobs by men.

(iii) It was this family environment in which K-23 was socialised. He had developed all positive traits in his personality which practised throughout his life.

3. OUT-FAMILY ENVIRONMENT

(i) The out-family environment of K-23 was composed of relatives, neighbours, teachers, ffs and others. His relatives were all *Sayyid* families living in different villages and had not migrated to the city. They were relatively unchanged and not forward in education and employment. K-23 had least effect of these relatives but interacted with those only who were strict followers of religion. It was because their association provided religious knowledge, scholarship and literary works and news about national-international affairs. K-23 developed such habits in life. He was a regular listener of BBC, Urdu, VOA, Urdu, Radio Pakistan and AIR. He always remained well aware about current affairs at global level.

(ii) All his neighbours lived in the village who were illiterate, small peasants, labourers, artisans and unskilled workers. But, K-23 treated them well and proved their helper and well-wisher. He helped in all situations of crisis and emergency. He considered them equal partners in social life of the village and appreciated their role in religious, cultural, social, economic and others affairs. He never objected on their activities in public life. Thus K-23 family emerged most respected family in the village with more influence.

(iii) K-23 impressed teachers in the school. Since he was intelligent, innovative, religious and hard worker, they always took his care. For him, they as a group emerged as worth of highest dignity because they shaped ideas, ideals, attitudes and behaviour and busy-active social life. The teacher remained an ideal man in his life and he adopted the same role in his career. The prominent features of an ideal teacher were confident, revolutionary, hard worker, scientific, innovative, intellectual, reformer, and with a worldview.

(iv) The FFs of K-23 were his school-batch-classmates at different stages of life, and members, ideologues, workers and activists of his organisation. They also included intellectuals, poets, authors, writers, journalists, teachers, academicians, professionals, literary figures and others. He usually visited their homes and they too reciprocated. While his standard of hospitality was unmatched, he stood an exceptional host. He always involved guests in serious discussion on topics like poetry, literature, politics, religion, philosophy, history, science and other subjects. His presentations were always scholarly, academic and knowledgeful.

(v) Others included same kind of people who were actively involved in politics, religion, culture, literature, poetry and so on. K-23 was a well-read person, he used to convey correct and reliable knowledge. His arguments were logical, scientific and positive.

(vi) With all these intellectual connections, K-23 used to convey and learn a lot. In this process, he learnt about life and society and became a patient listener.

4. EDUCATION AND CAREER

(i) K-23's early religious education was carried out at home. He was taught religious scriptures and trained in Islamic practices. For modern education, he had to go to the nearby village where he got entire education in a government school. He passed every stage with distinction. He qualified graduation from a city college. Subsequently, he got a job in school as a teacher which he considered the ideal job and thus started his ideal career. Since he considered teacher a reformer, guide, missionary, leader and trend-setter, he attempted to follow all these desirable roles. In this way, he enhanced good image of his family and contributed to its income. During this period, R-23 carried out post-graduation in Urdu literature.

(ii) An important stage in K-23's missionary life came when he was offered a fulltime working job in a religious organisation in JK. He joined that organisation and stayed there throughout his life despite the fact that he had to face many financial difficulties. He worked on different organisational-managerial positions at tehsil, district, province and state levels. He was made chief and ideologue of that organisation. Taking into consideration his qualifications, qualities and capabilities, he was considered for several to administrative and organisational positions. But, the deteriorating health condition came in between and he had to work in the background.

5. OCCUPATION AND ASSOCIATION

(i) The *Sayyid* family's traditional occupation was ritualistic and sacred and revolved around roles associated with *peers* and *mullas*. All such occupations were hereditary and K-23 could have adopted those roles easily. But, he opted for the role of a teacher and considered it *namdaar.* He didn't like material comforts and lived a simple life within the framework of Islamic injunctions.

(ii) After he changed the occupational role, the association too had undergone change. The main association he developed was with personal-family friends, relatives, neighbours, colleagues and others. This particular association was characterised with features like intellectual credentials, political perceptions, social perspectives, religious orientation, cultural specificity and so on.

6. MARRIAGE AND FAMILY

(i) K-23 was married in an endogamous family circle and in patri-local type. Before marriage, he used to live in joint family of parents with unmarried brothers. After the marriage, his wife joined the joint family household and lived a combined life. She belonged to the same *Sayyid* caste and was of equal economic and social status but lower in education.

(ii) The post-marital life of K-23 was highly satisfactory. Both partners had stable feelings and interaction which led to a stable family. After death of parents and marriage of brothers, the family got divided into two nuclear units. In one unit, K-23, his wife and unmarried children lived and after their marriage, this unit developed into joint form. But, one deviation was observed in this process. Since K-23's children were educated and employed, their choice in marriage differed from their parents' choice. So, his senior daughter-in-law was from urban area and from exogamous group. In that social environment, while old cultural practices continued, some of these faced partial or full change.

7. SOCIAL LIKES AND DISLIKES

After going through conservative socialisation and other religious experiences in life, K-23 developed following specific social priorities:

Social Likes	*Social Dislikes*
- Islamic social way of life	- poverty at all levels
- Commitment to Islamic ideals and values	- crime and juvenile injustice
- Upholding principles in modern politics	- school without control, authority and effect
- Egalitarian Islamic social order	- western attitudes and behaviour pattern
- Regular literary and cultural activities	- irreligious way of life
- Poetry of high moral standard	- opposition to any religion and its community
- A highly qualified and talented teacher	- a person without values and ideals
- A polite, submissive and responsive person	- cultural domination and cultural aggression
- Never adopt rich standard of life	- colonialism and its disastrous impact
- No modernising-westernising lifestyle	- U. S., the sole super power
- Primary school in a far flung village	- role of communism vis a vis religion
- Health care for all in the villages	- politics of caste and communalism in India
- Full road connectivity to the city	- social and economic inequality in society
- Culturally exposed and plural person	- violence against women at all places
- Reading of books and newspapers	- extravagant marriage and heavy *maher*
- Awareness about international affairs	- class status and differences
- Opposition to communism and capitalism	- a *peer* who exploits the religion
- Urdu literature and its poetry	- ideal Indian caste inequality
- Zero starter and hard worker	- all sinful thoughts and actions
- The *Sufi* pattern of life	- political uncertainty and anarchy.

8. CONCEPTS OF "I", "ME" AND "WE"

(i) K-23 felt that, in abstract sense, 'I' and 'me' reflected arrogance in attitude and aggression in behaviour. But, he supported Dr. Mohammad Iqbal's concept of *khudi (*ego) in this regard. He explained 'I' and 'me' with the concept of *khudi* which in any way could not be equated with arrogance and aggression but with self consciousness, self assertion, and self identification. The self consciousness referred to :

In case of 'I'	*in case of 'me'*
- Awareness about self	- awareness about ordained self and role
- Awareness about self and creator	- awareness about others related associates
- Awareness about man with duties	- awareness about self and whole and their rela.
The self-assertion referred to	
- Awareness about God's message	- awareness about man as God's vicegerent
- Awareness about program of life	- awareness about man and his brotherhood
- Awareness about best of social order	- awareness about ideational role of man
The self-identification referred to	
- Awareness about man in environment	- awareness about my contribution to society
- Awareness about culture and civilisation	- awareness about man's historical role in civi.
- Awareness about parti. Region and origin	- awareness about totality of man,nature, God

(ii) K-23 felt that the concept of 'we' of higher ideational level which revealed 'wholeness' and 'totality'. It involved individuals and groups in a distinct role with distinct functions. Thus, 'we' was used for

- The Muslims who, like other humans, represent God on earth; and
- The Kashmiris as they suffer at the hands of India from 1947.

These and other features of we were explained as follows

WE the humans	*WE the Kashmiris*
- We the God's chosen for his mission	- we K. having distinct civilisational traits
- We the created for following His orders	- we K. as suffering lot throughout history
- We the upholders of universal values	- we K. who never surrendered before aliens
- We the deviant and corrupt lot	- we K. with strong religious and cul. Attachment
- We the elites and upper classes/rulers	- we K. who have strong nationalist sentiment
- We the poor and wretched on the earth	- We K. having non-violent behaviour.

9. IDEAS OF EQUALITY AND INEQUALITY

(i) In general, K-23 supported equality and opposed inequality between various groups. It followed that any position which is not equal stands for sin and that deserved dismantling. It also followed that any position of equality stood for which needed to be strengthened. In this background, he introduced ideas of Islam, i.e. 'self-action' and 'non-inherited status' which determine status, downward or upward. While the first emphasize personal actions and contribution that leads to higher status, the inherited status ask for stay and stagnation which determine the lower status.

(ii) So, according to K-23, positive actions may lead to dominance of good people over bad people, while negative actions may lead to dominance of bad over good people. This kind of equality between good people on the one hand and inequality between good and bad people provides a viable and realistic framework in comparison with the inequality created by caste, class and power. These ideas seem highly idealistic and non-operational.

10. THE IDEAL LEADER

(i) The ideal leader of K-23 was Mawlana Sauddin Taraballi (MST). He was a great person with great religious qualities. He was a mystic and had spiritual personality and was considered the founder of Islamic movement in Kashmir. He was not known much in public, neither he wanted to get publicity.

(ii) Apparently, MST stood as a religious scholar of the highest order. He got modern education in Panjab and later on joined as a teacher in a government school in Kashmir. While outside Kashmir, he came into contact with the Islamic movement in 1940s and felt impressed. After coming back, he started the movement in Kashmir in late 1940s. Though he faced tremendous difficulties, jailed several times, oppression and torture, opposition of traditionalists and secularists, but, he carried out his mission which led to the establishment of Jammat-e-Islami in Kashmir.

(iii) In a way, K-23 was a *Murd-e-Momin* and his personality had the following qualities:

- Helpfulness	- honesty	- supporting the needy
- Serving others	- generosity	- feeding children
- Feeling human always	- morality	- affiliation with joint family
- Upholding values and ideals	- solidarity with suffers	- patronising the poor
- Criticising unjust rulers	- hospitality	- correct understanding

(iv) According to K-23, MST represented many ideals in his character some of which are mentioned below:

- Ideal thinker	- ideal poet
- Ideal author-writer	- ideal civil servant
- Ideal teacher	- ideal organiser
- Ideal leader	- ideal manager
- Ideal missionary	- ideal revolutionary
- Ideal personal and family friend	- ideal proponent of freedom

11. GLOBAL SOCIAL ORDER AND FUTURE SOCIETY

(i) K-23 saw GSO in Islamic perspective. The prominent social institutions and their important functions were as follows:

FAMILY

(a) It must be established as positive and productive institution for socialisation and internalisation.

(b) It must give rise to the controlled generation of children.

(c) It must provide equal human status to women in all in-family situations.

(d) It must work for proper adoption of role and status for all individuals.

MARRIAGE

(a) It must be performed at an earlier mature stage.

(b) The exact amount of *meher* must be paid to the bride by the groom properly at *nikah.*

(c) It must not be involved in irreligious dowry practice.

(d) It must provide stable post-marital life.

KINSHIP

(a) It must be maintained in all situations.

(b) It must not lead to its undue consideration on social matters.

(c) It must not be utilised for illegal and corrupt practices.

(d) It must contribute to social relations and social solidarity.

(ii) Moreover, according to K-23, GSO referred to the ideal universal roles and functions in the preceding institutional framework. These are explained below:

WOMEN

(a) They must be awarded due status, role and regards.

(b) They must not be dominated, exploited, tortured, manipulated and divorced.

(c) They must be helped to develop desirable family household.

(d) They must be provided all benefits of gender equality and gender justice.

CHILDREN

(a) They must be properly socialised in the family environment.

(b) They must be trained in societal attitudes, behaviour, ideals and values.

(c) They must feel committed to ideas and ideals of social life.

(d) They must be provided all opportunities for their growth and development

ELDERS

(a) They must be treated well and taken full care by family members.

(b) They must be paid for health, diet and other expenditures.

(c) They must be provided social as well as psychological support.

(d) They must not be put in isolated homes or old-age homes.

12. THE RELIGIOUS LIFE

(i) K-23 had a distinct view about his religious life. He felt that he had his entire life stood for religion and it could not be compartmentalised. It stood as a cohesive unit and must be lived like a coherent unit with one ideology only. It follows that every act of an individual stood for *ibadah,* so all acts in life were sacred. Even sincere acts of manual and mental labour of an individual were characterised as sacred acts. The following material acts were also characterised as *ibadah:*

- talking with a person purposefully and politely;
- paying positive response to other ideas, views and opinions;
- reading a book and a newspaper;
- helping the needy and the poor;
- attending and taking care of children and elders;
- consideration and care of wife and children;
- kind in behaviour to neighbours, relatives and others;
- maintain simple lifestyle;
- opposing materialism and moral degeneration; and
- maintaining good manners, habits and behaviour.

(ii) K-23 argued that all these and other human acts may be considered religious in character. So, the entire life may be considered as religious in this context. He felt no need and no justification to portray religious life in separation from the social life.

13. THE KASHMIR PROBLEM

(i) K-23 felt that the Kashmir problem started after temporary accession of JK to India in 1947. Subsequently, India followed a comprehensive policy of 'indianisation' which was against the spirit of accession treaty and political aspirations of local people. Despite criticism from within and outside, this policy was followed through step-by-step legislative and administrative measures on the part of central government. These measures included abolition of the titles of *Wazir-e-Azam* and *Sadr-e-Riyasat*, extension of jurisdiction of SCT, ECI, CAAG. This also included the unanimous rejection of autonomy resolution by the Parliament passed by the state legislature.

(ii) In addition to its economic, social, cultural and other implications, this policy was followed vigorously which had deeper political impact in Kashmir.

(iii) All these developments had a cumulative effect which resulted in political protests and recurring political uprisings against India. This happened in 1953, 1962, 1973, 1989 and 2010. As is clear, these uprisings have proved against long-term interests of India. So, in order to establish peace in Kashmir, India and Pakistan must resolve this problem keeping in view political aspirations of people of Kashmir.

14. EXPERIENCE OF CONFLICT SITUATION

(i) K-23 had a particular type of experience of the conflict which not many people could reveal. It was the impact of conflict on religious practices. He felt that, in general, all these practices were disturbed and many religious places were desecrated.

(ii) As a result of continuous curfew and its strict implementation, complete disturbance of *namaz* was experienced. No regularity and punctuality in 5-time schedule could not be followed seriously. Moreover, this practise could not be performed in mosques due to curfew. Keeping fast during *Ramadan* became difficult because people could not get proper diet, eatables and other needed items. *Zakat* could not be paid properly and to proper persons or institutions. Even cheques could not be deposited in banks in this regard. *Hajj* aspirants too faced many problems related to their flights, transport, passports and training programs.

(iii) K-23 observed that not many people could attend shrine, graveyards and many religious places. People could not go to orphan and widows' houses for their help. People could not even visit hospitals nor homes for patient care. The visit to neighbours, relatives and others became a rare opportunity.

15. SOCIAL PROBLEMS IN KASHMIR

(i) *Irreligious Life of the Youth:* K-23 argued that deviation from traditional and religious oriented values and norms, adoption of materialistic-individualistic orientation, and practising westernised lifestyle created a situation of non-religiosity. This happened in the younger age groups which are prone to deviance and change. In actuality, this situation affected entire social life in general and youth life in particular.

The extensive and intensive impact of 'irreligiosity' was felt particularly in corruption, erosion of social ethics, crime and delinquency, favor, social crisis, bribery, dehumanisation, violation of values and norms, sexual promiscuity, violent attitudes and behaviour, red-tapism, and gender violence. All these undesirable social activities seriously affected the existing social standards and order. So, according to K-23, these trends need to be controlled and negated.

(ii) *Moral Degeneration:* K-23 argued that there prevailed a notion that religion stood limited to private life of the individual. It follows that religion was solely concerned with personal beliefs and activities and, at the same time, had no concern with political, economic, social, cultural and other affairs. This, according to him, stood illogical. Life as a unit could not be divided into private and public and this stood morally destructive because of its negative social impact.

K-23 further argued since this has been experienced in our society, it has given rise to a situation of moral degeneration. It has directly and indirectly involved all economic, social, political, educational, cultural, moral, psychological, ideological and other fields. Thus moral degeneration has necessarily led to human degeneration and to dehumanisation. K-23 argued that in order to restore moral and ethical basis of social order, this situation needs to be controlled effectively.

K-24 PROFESSSIONAL MUSICIAN

1. SOCIAL CONTEXT

(i) The KPs form the largest minority community having less than 2% of the total population in JK. A detailed introduction of this community has been given in chapter no. In direct contrast to other communities in Kashmir, KPs experienced high degree of migration which they considered a desirable trait for its educational, economic, social and cultural benefits. They in all areas and at all stages in history, carried out major or minor migration. In the early 20th century, KPs in rural areas of Kashmir experienced following types of migration:

Type one	*Type two*
- From rural areas of Kashmir	- From rural areas of Kashmir
• V	V
- Urban areas of Kashmir	- Urban areas of Kashmir
• V	V
- Urban areas of India	- Urban areas of India
• V	V
- Cities of foreign countries	- Cities of foreign countries
• V	V
- Urban areas of Kashmir	

(ii) In the way mentioned above, two distinctive types of migration emerged among the KPs. The first type may be characterised as 'linear' and permanent migration which reflected in this trend of population movement from rural to urban areas, from under-developed areas-countries to developed areas-countries, and from eastern regions to Western regions. The migrants in this type had no intension of returning back to original place/station and established residential households in the destination-arrival countries. In comparison to this type of migration, the second type was 'cyclical' and temporary in nature. It also reflected in the trend of population movement from rural to urban areas, from state-level cities to national-level cities, from cities to metropolitan cities, and from under-developed areas and countries to developed foreign countries and from those areas and countries to their native land. The migrants in this type of migration, though lesser in number, had clear intention of returning back to the native land and they didn't establish their households there.

(iii) These trend of out-migration among KPs had some pre-determined objectives which revolved around :

(a) attainment of higher and specialised education and training;

(b) getting higher position jobs in government offices and public-private organisations; and

(c) establishing household units at the places of arrival with higher standard of life and modern lifestyle.

It was observed that KP who settled outside Kashmir were successful in achieving these goals. Thus we see KP's present in all cities of the country and in the cities of U.S. and Western countries.

(iv) K-24 and his family belonged to the second type of migration which was meant to attain higher education and not to settle there. Thus he was involved in cyclical trend of migration as follows:

- From town to small city > small city to large city >
- Large city to metropolitan city > metropolitan city to global city >
- Global city to small city.

Thus K-24 was able to pursue higher education and professional career and came back to his native land with higher qualifications and technical-professional skills and capabilities.

2. IN-FAMILY SOCIALISATION

(i) K-24 belonged to the KP family which migrated from a small town to a small city. After this migration, the family changed its entire lifestyle which may be characterised more urban than the average urban family. It was because of acceptability and adoptability of mass urban culture. The family was located in a posh colony with mixed population of KPs, KMs, big business families, elite families, bureaucrats-administrators families, government officials and common Kashmiris. All members of K-24 family practised non-traditional occupations and had adopted modernised-westernised lifestyle. It stood as one of the reputed families in the colony.

(ii) There were three specific reasons for the top reputation of K-24 family. First, it was completely literate from earlier times. Its members were highly qualified and highly positioned in public and private sectors. Second, the family laid heavy emphasis in higher education in most modern, specialised, professional and technical fields. It was with the intention of getting professional and technical jobs of the higher status. Third, the family had no inhibition or reservation for following this kind of education outside JK and anywhere in the world. In fact, they were always ready to send their children for education anywhere in the country and abroad.

(iii) Two more points are worth mentioning here. First, many boys and girls of this family were getting education in these new fields in different institutions of India and foreign countries. Second, while this situation proved encouraging and inspiring, the educated-intellectual background provided support for new generation.

(iv) K-24 was socialised in this type of family environment. He got ideational orientation and practical support for adoption of distinctive professional course. Since the course he chose for higher studies was not taught in JK at that time, he proceeded outside state and country for this purpose. He was fully prepared for this purpose.

3. OUT-FAMILY ENVIRONMENT

(i) K-24's out-family environment was composed of the social collectivities of relatives, neighbours, ffs and others. His relatives were of the same economic, social, educational, cultural and professional status. They were also engaged in non-conventional occupations such as government service, public-private sector top employees, different professions and so on. They held regular interaction with K-24 family which led to constant contact with them and shared life experiences. Since most of them had migrated from the same town, they often used to get together on many occasions and celebration in the city. They took special care of the specialised and professional career of K-24.

(ii) The neighbours of K-24 were local big businessmen (dealing with Kashmiri handicrafts), elite families (of bureaucrats, administrators, politicians, and professionals), outsiders' families (working in central and state government offices) and common middle class Kashmiris. The relation of this family with all such groups were normal, but with Kashmiri groups, it was informal and cordial.

(iii) The ffs of K-24 family were mostly colleagues and friends of educational and post-educational stage who were now bureaucrats, officers, professionals, especially doctors and engineers, and technocrats. They also included outside friends and acquaintances. They visited the family occasionally which was reciprocated by K-24 family. This had effect of exposure to outside people and their society, culture and language. Consequently, K-24 adopted some non-Kashmiri attitudes-behaviour, different dresses and food-habits. He also developed a pan-Indian life perception which was generally uncommon in Kashmir.

(iv) Others included prominent citizens, religious leaders, politicians, social workers, and so on. They had limited interaction with limited objectives, most of financial, cultural and social nature. All this interaction had input effect for K-24.

4. EDUCATION AND CAREER

(i) All members of K-24 family were highly educated and highly positioned. They had strong desire for higher and specialised education for him. That is why he got entire primary education in a missionary and English medium school from 1st to 10th standard. He developed his potentialities in his school for his future life. He was educated in a city college where he got exposed to classmates, batch-mates, and others belonging to other cultures, regions and religions.

(ii) After a lot of thinking, K-24 was sent to a famous city of India to pursue a course in Musicology. This was a new world for him, in which he entered with confidence and competitive spirit. He qualified this course with distinction. His life was revolutionised when he adopted new ideas and ideology that shaped attitude to life.

(iii) After this course, he got an opportunity to visit Europe, particularly the U.K. There he got a chance to perform on the stage of BBC and other international organisations. It was the certificate of his practical experience at international level. When he applied for a job in India in a central government organisation, it was immediately offered to him. Subsequently, he joined it and started his professional career in Kashmir. He performed professional activities more outside office than in the office. In these efforts, he wanted to elevate the Kashmiri music to the world class quality.

(iv) After arriving here, he worked hard silently but sincerely and seriously. He believed in hard work ethic and its positive return. He used to say that spirit + performance + competition = Higher position and status. He was always busy in introducing new concepts, trends, understanding, perspectives and ideas to the Kashmiri music. For that purpose, he worked hard day and night, which revealed in his busy schedule of his daily occupational activities which follows:

Schedule of daily occupational activities of K-24

(a) Morning	- domestic and personal works
06.00 – 10.00 AM	- occupational activities- occupational practice
	- guidance-training to students
	- meeting with followers to discuss...
	- other related activities
(b) Day time	- office work
10.00 – 05.00	- occupational activities- meetings with official authorities
	- meetings with artists, authors, poets,
	- musicians, experts and others concerned
	- recording musical items, songs, programs and so on.
	- assessing the performance of staff and non-staff artists
	- discussion with different performers in music.
(c) Evening	- domestic, personal and official works
05.00 – 10.00PM	- occupational practice
	- helping others in learning music
	- attending guests and discuss about music
	- guidance and training to students
	- other related activities

(v) After putting a lot of efforts, he accumulated huge work in music production in Kashmir. Consequently, he became popular among Kashmiris inside as well as outside Kashmir. The Kashmiri diaspora too liked his productions and asked for the same. At the last stage of his career, he had contributed significantly and produced a large number of his followers.

(vi) During his career, K-24 visited the U.S., Europe, Russia, Central-South Asia and other countries and demonstrated his music there where he was highly appreciated.

5. PROFESSION, MOBILITY AND ASSOCIATION

(i) Taking into consideration K-24 family's occupation in the town, the present profession stood as complete departure. In fact, his contribution in this profession was acclaimed at regional, national and international level. People in general and professionals in particular considered him a 'national asset'. With this, he developed the image of a 'social notable'. This kind of mobility was more meaningful and useful than the material mobility.

(ii) After explaining professional contribution and its popularity, one can imagine about his nature of association. Most of his personal and FFs were intellectuals of the first order. While visiting his residence, they used to deliberate on social, cultural, literary and other issues. Another common topic of discussion was music of Kashmir. These friends included the following:

- Journalists	- Professionals	- Doctors and Engineers
- Professors	- Teachers	- Academicians
- Intellectuals	- Poets and Writers	- Artists
- Authors	- Media Experts	- Music lovers.

This association was profession-oriented, i.e. they were directly or indirectly related to the profession of music in or out of Kashmir. They included his followers, admirers, fans, students, favourites and general music lovers. They often visited his residence and office for the purpose of advice, guidance and discussing music-related issues and problems.

(iii) On the other hand, his association had no limits. One who heard his music or heard about him wanted to see and meet him. Those people included political leaders, religious leaders, cultural admirers, Kashmiri ideologues, NGOs, social activists and social notables.

(iv) The interesting aspect of K-24's association was that he never ignored his students despite migration from Kashmir. As the fact stands his students were males and females; rural, urban and hilly; Hindus, Muslims and Sikhs; poor and rich; locals and outsiders; and students, employees and others. He maintained constant contact and regular guidance to all of them. When KPs migrated out of Kashmir, he went to Delhi, but he did not snap ties with people in Kashmir. He guided and advised them in the normal way without giving any hurt to feeling. His example of secular attitude and behaviour was really unparalleled.

6. MARRIAGE AND FAMILY

(i) K-24 got married before he got the professional job in central government organisation. It was endogamous and neo-local type of marriage. The girl belonged to well-educated and respected family, while his family's status was higher than that. But, her family was quite ahead in education. It reflected in the situation in which the daughter was a lecturer in one college and father was Principal in other college. The girl was extremely beautiful and intelligent. In totality, K-24's marriage proved 'a step forward' in his life and they proved an ideal match. She used to say that "behind every man, there is a woman and behind him (as an eminent person), I stand."

(ii) K-24 lived with parents before marriage. But, after marriage, he established a neo-local family household in his official accommodation. It always remained a busy family, lot of guests visited them daily and the family proved hospitable. In that family unit, there lived K-24, his wife and unmarried children. After migration, they settled in Delhi and purchased a flat there. His family's commitment to Kashmir revealed in his efforts to train both sons in the classical Kashmiri music, *Sufiana* music.

7. SOCIAL LIKES AND DISLIKES

After having real life experiences, K-24 had developed specific social likes and dislikes, some of which are mentioned below :

Social Likes	*Social Dislikes*
- Openness of mind and heart	- inefficiency, incompetence and avoid work
- Zero starter and sincere worker	- poverty of mind
- To establish real secular credentials	- the communal ideas and ideology
- *Commitment to the growth of fine arts*	- *following rules and regulations strictly*
- All-round development of Kashmiri masses	- political participation in general
- Famous male and female singers of K.	- dehumanised police officials and soldiers
- Daily practise of music and singing	- discrimination of any type
- A nuclear family with lesser number	- social justice not for all members of society
- Socially ordered and disciplined person	- crime and drugs used by youth
- Ideas and ideals of *Kashmiriat*	- unemployed and unstable youth
- Tolerance of different religions	- a carefree and norm-less life
- Competition and mobility for all	- economic underdevelopment

contd...

contd...

Social Likes	*Social Dislikes*
- Efficient, civilised and regular officer	- illiteracy in all groups and communities
- Social workers	- anti-religious and anti-region orientation
- Functioning of NGOs in social sector	- mental and physical health problems
- Listening music from radio and television	- exploitation of religion
- Maintain norms of work culture	- no social harmony and solidarity
- A person having no bias towards others	- antagonism between various communities
- Equality of all must prevail	- corruption in everyday life
- No discrimination at all	- caste consideration in social life

8. CONCEPTS OF "I", "ME" AND "WE"

(i) K-24 had developed a specific meaning of the concepts of 'I' and 'me'. His polite, gentle, human and affectionate behaviour had given these concepts a character which was not arrogant, selfish and personalised, but attached these concepts to his values, norms, standards, principles and objectives. From this point of view, 'I' stood for human values, rational norms, scientific principles and humanistic approach. All these intensions and actions were not meant for individual but social ends. Thus 'I' could not be used for I but for one and all.

(ii) In this context, 'me' stood for '*my*' exclusively and single-handedly. It stood for as my efforts, my ideals, my attitudes, my behaviour, my ideology, my perception, my principles and so on.

(iii) For K-24, 'we' stood for a particular category of people with whom he was tied in long-term association. The ideal example of this category professional group of people and a category of people who called themselves as Kashmiris. The first group of professionals composed of following individuals and groups:

- IT, mass media and internet experts
- Teachers, students, scholars, scientists
- Doctors, engineers and town planners
- Professionals, researchers and academicians

(iv) On the other hand, 'we' specifically referred to the groups of Kashmiris to which K-24 belonged. He used it in the sense that 'we' were

- Upholders of religious plurality and cultural pluralism
- Ideologues of religious and cultural tolerance
- Followers of *Sheikh-ul-Alam* and *Lale Arifa*
- Founders of composite culture and society in Kashmir

- Proponents of distinctive historical tradition
- Supporters of liberty, freedom and scholarship

9. IDEAS OF EQUALITY AD INEQUALITY

(i) K-24 was of the opinion that there must be highest degree of equality between human beings. If there remained any inequality, it may be because of different levels of knowledge, performance, competition and achievement. All these must be determined in the social context. At the same time, K-24 upheld that inequality of all types and forms must be debased and destroyed practically. The caste and class inequality must necessarily be negated and destroyed because of their non-human foundations. Gender inequality must also be de-constructed because of dehumanised character.

(ii) K-24 upheld the view that absolute equality in terms of 100% was practically impossible in human society. So, the target must be maximum degree of social equality. The system of equality can be established in a professional framework, i.e. skills and capabilities of individuals. According to this view, every individual performs according to his/her skills, capabilities and specialisation. This will elevate the individual to a level where they will get their due which they deserve and need and not what they demand out of context. The professional competence becomes its factor in the achievement of economic position and social status.

10. GLOBAL SOCIAL ORDER

(i) K-24 was keenly interested in GSO mainly because it will serve humanity and will give rise to its ideal society. This will essentially lead to the emergence of global culture and civilisation which will suit all nationalities, ethnicities, regions and religions. It must be oriented towards the goals of humanitarianism at large and not to any world power and regional power, religious or cultural.

(ii) According to K-24, music may play a definite role in this regard. It may not help directly but indirectly in establishing GSO by :

- Enhancing its vitality
- Increasing its significance
- Establishing it relevance
- Strengthening its potentialities
- Ensuring its continuity

(iii) In this regard, the role of music may be explained in terms of

(a) demonstration of music shows of different cultures of the world;

(b) different music programs to be organised and presented in all countries, regions and continents; and

(c) publication of relevant literature and production of material related to music at the global level.

In simple words, K-24 meant that music must be used for global human brotherhood, its potentialities and sustainability. Music, according to him, has the capacity of that role.

11. THE RELIGIOUS LIFE

(i) K-24 was not a religious person. He was not also irreligious or anti-religious. In fact, he was religious, who didn't bother about religion and its role in society. He was also not concerned about its belief system and ritual practices. He hardly gave a serious thinking about its positive and negative aspects.

(ii) His primary concern was his profession and his life revolved around related activities. He remained so busy with his activities that he hardly got time to discuss and practise religion. However, he used to pray Hindu gods and goddesses for social formality.

(iii) In actuality, his religious belonging had not affected his professional and social activities. He was all out for non-religious treatment of others inside and outside his family. He was completely secular in approach. However, K-24 celebrated all Hindu festivals and other religious occasions in Kashmir. He made unusual visits to local temples.

(iv) The relations of K-24 with other religious communities were cordial and ideal. He hardly made any difference or discrimination on the basis of religion. While he showed tremendous concern about scientific temper, he hardly considered religious affiliation of his students and followers. He had established highest degree of secular credibility. Two more points may be added here. First, he remained more popular among KMs than among KPs. Second, despite migration from Kashmir, he never snapped his ties with KMs, he rather strengthened these ties.

12. EXPERIENCE OF CONFLICT SITUATION

(i) K-24 felt shocked when he had to migrate out of Kashmir. He resisted for some time but could not avoid it later on. After shifting to Delhi, he felt as a person thrown out of his culture, identity and ideology. He considered it as a total offensive against his ideal society.

(ii) After leaving Kashmir, K-24 never forgot it, its people and its music. First, Kashmir remained alive in his lifelike soul in body. He never came out of 'Kashmir dreams' and never felt alien to it. Second, he felt various Kashmiri communities as 'component parts of the body' whose separation was impossible. The migration in his case proved 'integrationist' than 'dis-integrationist' as it enhanced the consciousness of unity and similarity. Second, he always remembered and reminded the civilised, tolerant and non-violent way of life in Kashmir. He always felt proud of this Kashmiri heritage. Third, K-24 considered Kashmiri music as his real life, without which his life was meaningless. Thus his commitment to this music was complete. In all situations, it must be listened, promoted, developed, expanded and modernised. Finally, K-24 opined that Kashmiri music will play a positive role of integration, solidarity, harmony and cohesiveness of Kashmir and its people.

13. FUTURE KASHMIR SOCIETY

(i) In fact, K-24 was worried about the future of Kashmiri society. It was partly because of political and religious developments and partly because of the rise of particular social-cultural trends in Kashmir. As per his perception, these developments and trends will have direct bearing on secular ethos, tolerance of plurality of religions and cultures, non-violent way of life, ideology of *Kashmiriat* and inter-community relationship.

(ii) So, he suggested some efforts which may safeguard the traditional culture and other ideals related to *Kashmiriat.* All Kashmiris have to work for this grand objective, inside as well as outside Kashmir. They have to work in co-operation and collaboration. While the former has to become conscious, identify, maintain, safeguard, upheld and assert this distinguishing identity, the latter have to trust, support, assure and help the former in this great objective.

14. SOCIAL PROBLEMS IN KASHMIR

(i) *Music Career as Social Taboo:* K-24 remembered the time about 100 years old when music career and artists involved in this profession were not considered socially desirable and preferable. In fact, the social image of musician and singers was not 'good'. The music career was considered a social taboo. It reflected in general social image-impression of individuals and groups associated with music. They were considered belonging to degraded and not equal social groups and people generally avoided their company and that of their profession. Even in the marriage market, association with or performance of music was not considered a plus point but a minus point.

But, according to K-24, an extreme change has occurred in these attitudes mainly due to modern education, cultural interaction-exposure, overall modernisation-westernisation and related life-style. With these changes in social life in early 20th century in Kashmir, people in general got attracted, inclined and motivated to music. First, they got interested and started listening music. Second, they made music a respectable part of their life. Third, they started sending their children, boys and girls, for learning and training in music. While many of them wanted to follow it as a hobby, some of them followed it as career and became popular singers in Kashmiri.

K-24 felt pleased at this development. But, he still have fears about some individuals and groups who still oppose music in Kashmir. He opined that this opposition must be eliminated by the people's initiative and then by governmental action.

(ii) *Less Tolerance for Other Cultures:* According to K-24, it was observed that, despite the tolerant ethos intact, there has been some degree of deviation from that tolerance among the youth who have come up in last two decades of conflict. He felt that this development stood as cumulative result of three particular facts. First, negative policy of GOI towards Kashmir and its people. Second, practices of uni-dimensional culture by youth in Kashmir during last 21 years. Third, emergence of extremist groups which don't believe in tolerance of other cultures.

K-24 felt that this situation has hurt the basic feature of Kashmiri culture and it will have completely an undesirable implication in the long run. It will trouble every one who stood for *Kashmiriat* and *Sheikh-ul-Alam and Lale Ded*'s Kashmir. It will also give shock to all friends, admirers and ideologues of secular Kashmir.

So, he felt that there was a need to negate this trend completely and immediately. This can be done through social and cultural efforts on the part of whole society.

K-25 KASHMIRI PROFESSIONAL–JOURNALIST

1. SOCIAL CONTEXT

(i) Till the first half of 20th century, there existed lowest literacy rate in Kashmir. Not many people could read or write in the city, towns and villages. All classes, castes, groups and communities, except a few, were mostly illiterate. It was estimated that there prevailed below 5% literacy in JK in 1941. The only literate groups were KPs, some K. *Sayyids* and outsiders working in the state. In that situation, there was hardly any possibility of change and improvement in day-to-day life conditions. The forced labour and the burden of taxes had made the life a matter of survival. These harsh conditions of life made education a neglected field. However, the situation started undergoing change after 1947. Particularly after 1952-53 when some revolutionary reforms were introduced in rural areas of Kashmir. In actuality, the political, economic and educational reforms paved the way for broader processes of change and development. People in general in rural and urban areas and from all classes, groups and communities responded positively to these developments which created a congenial environment for attainment of education, economic change, occupational mobility and cultural exposure. In actuality, these changes in decades time stood for extreme opposite to the pre-1947 situation. It was in that newly-developed situation that certain occupations and professions emerged in Kashmir. As was expected, highly educated classes and groups responded to these professions in Kashmir first of all. They were mainly KPs whose education enabled them to dominate the scene.

(ii) In the following decades from 1060s, other classes and groups in Kashmir started entering these fields. Though they had to compete with earlier dominated groups, their large number enabled them to make their presence felt. This was done with encouragement of political leadership and liberal government policy. Thus middle class groups too entered in engineering-engineering fields; medical and para-medical specialties; print and electronic mass media; IT fields; teaching and research; and philosophy and religion.

(iii) The field of mass media in Kashmir was conventionally dominated by KPs, Panjabis, IMs and others. Local KMs were hardly represented in this field. But, after 1953 measures and changes engulfed this field. As a result, qualified, competent and confident local professionals were available from the mainstream society. This enabled the local mass media experts to compete in this field. Some of them were successful but most of them were not. That resulted in the continued monopoly of interest groups in this field. Moreover, social base of mass media in Kashmir was limited. There was no efficient infrastructure, no expert-trained manpower, no industrial set-up, no sufficient readership and no motivation for working in this difficult field.

(iv) Then came militancy in 1989. Among other implications of militancy experienced in Kashmir, there were some significant implications related to mass media. One of such implications was departure of non-local media professionals from Kashmir. This happened so fast that many national-international newspapers and newsmagazines had no representative in Kashmir. In that situation, the local mass media professionals, who had completed their courses and training in the field, joined the profession and started their careers. In this way, the field of mass media in Kashmir got Kashmiri complexion and local character.

(v) Now, non-local domination in Kashmir had gone and local professionals had to compete among themselves. In addition to working hard, they had to develop infrastructure, latest technology, IT involvement, and all facilities and contacts at national and international levels. All that happened with the locals' initiative in the private sector. At that time, two important developments took place in Kashmir. First, emergence of mass media fraternity composed of hundreds of journalists, columnists, photo-journalists, photographers, cartographers, IT professionals, technicians and other related staff. They worked for different national-international newspapers, news magazines, news agencies, television and radio channels, audio-video agencies and organisation; and official and unofficial agencies-organisations within and outside the country. Since Kashmir remained a live issue at national and international level in last two decades, these people were always busy in reporting to the whole world. It also gave rise to many prominent journalists, reporters, analysts and so on. Some of them attained the world-class status. They also figured among the list of eminent professionals in mass media.

(vi) Second, emergence of a large number of newspapers, news magazines and television channels in Kashmir. While the readership of daily-weekly newspapers has increased tremendously at large scale, the viewership has also increased on unprecedented scale. It was observed that number of daily and weekly newspapers has increased from some dozens in 1980s to more than 300 in first decade of this century, while the number of local television channels has gone into dozens.

(vii) It was in the above-mentioned social environment related to mass media which gave birth to the character of K-25 as a journalist in print media and adopted it as professional career. Subsequently, he and his family had to accept all major and minor implications of this career.

2. IN-FAMILY SOCIALISATION

(i) The family of K-25 was located in a far off village whose road-connectivity was also a problem. Like families in surrounding villages at that time, this family was backward in economic, educational and social fields. But, a trend of change was experienced after 1953 land reforms which led to some degree of development there. The K-25 family was religiously fatalistic, culturally conservative, and socially pro-status quo. However, the family had also paid a positive response to a religious movement and had accepted its ideas and ideals. In addition to adopting rational and reformed approach to religion, that movement emphasised the adoption of modern education, new economic activities, purposeful and egalitarian social order and new-scientific traits. It also stressed for dropping of folk religious practices, *peer-mureedi* and payment of fixed share of production to the *Peer*. These were considered as mini-revolutionary measures at that time.

(ii) K-25 belonged to this family where tradition stood intact but, at the same time, innovation was also introduced at the ideational level. This was made possible through modern education and new religious thinking. He was socialised in the family environment in which tradition and change existed side by side but was controlled by the serious ideational impact of a religious movement. Since resources of family were limited, it could not materialize all effects of education, employment and culture change. Later on, these effects were fully appreciated in the family when it developed a strong economic base. Accordingly, K-25 too adopted a revised pattern of social life.

3. OUT-FAMILY ENVIRONMENT

(i) The in-family socialisation had limited impact on K-25 than the out-family environment which was dominant and effective. This environment shaped his attitudes and behaviour in young age and determined his ideas and ideals. The first group in this environment was included relatives who lived in his or surrounding villages and had same economic, educational and cultural status. They too were undergoing various processes of change like educational attainment, occupational mobility, developing economic careers and opting for migration. K-25 got influenced from them and their efforts for elevating his position. In order to follow the same pattern of change, he adopted changes in personal and social life.

(ii) The neighbours of K-25 family composed of villagers living in the conditions of religious fatalism, educational-economic backwardness, and socially-culturally unexposed. But, they had not much impact on his personality growth. Instead, some individuals in his and other individuals proved more dominating because of their belonging to a religious movement which separated religion from dogma and emphasised on rational approach. It also stressed on dropping additional and folk religious practices and adopting pure and original religious principles. These new ideas affected K-25 in his attitudes, behaviour, ideology and perception of life.

(iii) The third out-family group of colleagues at different stages influenced

K-25 in his young age. Most of them belonged to better economic, educational, and social background and were from rural, urban and hilly areas. In actuality, they had reciprocal impact. In this process, K-25's rural traits started decreasing and urban traits increasing and finally he became more urban than his urban friends. More importantly, they helped him in his profession and in developing contacts and interaction with all important sections of society.

(iv) Others who influenced his perceptions and perspectives on life and society included the following categories, with whom he had constant professional interaction:

- Political leaders, ideologues and activists
- Religious leaders and preaches
- Intellectuals, scientists, academicians, researchers and teachers
- Professional, doctors, engineers and artists
- Bureaucrats and administrators.

4. EDUCATION AND CAREER

(i) K-25's primary education was carried out in the government school in nearby village. He had to take self-care of education because his family was illiterate. His secondary education took place in the nearby town. Since he was intelligent, he scored high grades and high merit that led to his distinction in many classes. K-25's college education took place in the town. There he was exposed to all sorts of impacts, especially to changing social behaviour. Here he faced the social reality according to which he got sufficient modern education, but was still committed to family traditions.

(ii) Finally, he shifted to the city for higher education. Since he was meritorious, he was able to get a seat for prestigious mass media course. After two years, he qualified it with distinction. He also got practical training. Subsequently, he qualified another P.G. course for enhancing the knowledge base and expertise and increase his academic credibility.

(iii) Just after completing mass media course, K-25 joined a local largest-circulated daily newspaper at that time. His work there was excellent and objective. He was highly appreciated for his stories on social, economic, political, cultural, environmental and other aspects of life. At that time, K-25 got introduced outside JK. So, he got opportunities to work for several national and international newspapers and news magazines.

(iv) Simultaneously, he tried for strengthening economic base. He got that chance when his close friend started books business in the city. He too jumped in through financial contribution. After some years, that business has prospered and K-25 and his friends reap the benefits.

(v) After getting accumulated a huge service record in the profession, K-25 offered his services to a reputed national daily, published from New Delhi. The management accepted his credentials and made him the chief correspondent of that national newspaper. After his contribution through this paper, he has emerged as an eminent analyst with high reputation. His status has enhanced to such a level that he was considered as a top professional. In this context, he developed close contact with largest number of people from all fields of life, especially politics, intelligentsia, academics, professionals, scientists and others.

(vi) K-25 was writing for several national and international newspapers and magazines on variety of topics from religion to politics and from economics to super-power rivalry. Now, he had started his weekly newspaper in which he comments freely on all local, regional, national and international problems and issues.

5. PROFESSION, ASSOCIATION AND MOBILITY

(i) K-25 reached to a high position in his profession. It represented a complete departure from traditional parental occupation, i.e. agriculture. He adopted different occupation consciously and as a deliberate choice. This conscious shift represented a change characterised by transformation from low status to high status occupation. In this profession, through hard work, he achieved overall mobility. He always remained conscious about this achievement and kept himself busy in various activities. The pattern of his daily work schedule reveals in following details:

Morning	*Day Time*	*Evening*
- Personal and domestic works - Occupational activities - Writing for newspapers - Collecting documents - Clippings and other documents - Studying material - Going through literature - Interactive sessions with different persons.	- Occupational activities.... - Treating guests	- Personal and domestic works - Occupational works....

In brief, the radical shift in occupational activities represented a radical departure which affected whole of his life.

(ii) This situation gave rise to new pattern of association in the case of K-25. In this process, old pattern of association was replaced by its new patterns. In this regard, the features of each pattern are mentioned below:

Old Type Association	New type Association
- Close and affectionate relationship	- Mmaterial and formal relationship
- Spiritual and moral relationship	- Ends versus means orientation
- Deeply felt feelings and attachment	- Highly individualistic traits
- Dedication and commitment	- No commitment and dedication
- Traditional and religious orientation	- Irreligious ethics in office
- Based on values and norms	- No personal feeling and no attachment
- Upholding traditional roles and status	- Asserting change in values and roles

(iii) Similarly, the pattern of relationship developed in the new profession determined pattern of new association which was closely related to professional activities. Thus K-25, like others in the profession, developed relations with politicians followed by association with them. Same type of association was established with religious leaders-preachers, businessmen, academicians and others.

6. MARRIAGE AND FAMILY

(i) K-25 was married when he stabilised his economic position. The girl belonged to city and Syed family. It was an exogamous, hypogamous and neo-local type of marriage in which the girl provided more economic stability with her working role in government office. In a way, this marriage proved a step forward in the life of K-25.

(ii) Before marriage, K-25 lived a bachelor's life first in rented and then official accommodation. After some time of marriage, he and his wife lived in the city family unit with his unmarried brothers and sisters. In this way, he had family in the city as well as in village. He with his family made regular visits to the village family, especially on different festivals and other occasions. He also took care of in-laws family. Thus he lived a peaceful life in the city family household.

7. SOCIAL LIKES AND DISLIKES

(i) After having long experience of life, K-25 developed specific social likes and dislikes, some of which are mentioned below:

Social Likes	Social Dislikes
- Objective social critique of every one	- A shrived and selfish politician
- A person having sound knowledge	- Poverty and under-development
- Political ideologue and dissidents	- Suppression and oppression of people
- Democratic system and it functions	- Illiteracy and ignorance in villages
- A happy family with children	- Dependence of villages on the city

contd...

contd...

Social Likes	*Social Dislikes*
- Zero starter and hard worker	- Extreme urban traits
- Social work and collective action	- A sponsored journalist
- Social change, planning and development	- Incompetent mass media person
- Processes of modernisation	- Corruption and nepotism
- Religious pluralism and tolerance	- A non-qualified academician
- Sufi music programs	- sexual promiscuity
- Limited kinship ties between families	- Social problems and complex issues
- Free education for all	- Social chaos and anarchy
- A hard but humane police officer	- Instable marriage and family unit
- Good post-marital life	-Change eroding values and norms
- A trained, competent and qualified teacher	- Indecent behaviour of individuals
- The moderate religious thinker	- Communal political parties and orgs.
- Secular outlook and personality	- Politics of region, religion and caste
- Independent and free-thinking journalist	- A sponsored newspaper
- Social and economic initiatives	- Non-governance in the state

8. CONCEPTS OF "I", "ME" AND "WE"

(i) K-25 had high sense of 'I' and 'me' in comparison to 'we'. That was mainly because of the nature and growth of his thought pattern in life. 'I' and 'me' were strong due to the fact that he had seen much difficult days in the past. Then he had to struggle and compete in life. So, his rise the result of sustained efforts with commitment and dedication, otherwise there was no place for him in this world. He believed that nobody cares about you unless you establish your relevance in society.

(ii) The concept of 'I' held by K-25 had two esteems, lower and higher. 'I' in the lower esteem referred to the part of life in terms of submission, politeness, gentleness, simplicity and truthfulness. These characteristic traits always guided towards general welfare of I and all. 'I' in this context conveyed the message of help, cooperation, and consideration of others. On the other hand, 'I' in the upper esteem referred to present the role and status which 'I' have achieved due to my efforts and which I deserve and enjoy also. It also implied that 'I' must give due benefit to my family, relatives and children. But, at the same time, this must not hurt others.

(iii) 'Me' also referred to both aspects. First, 'me' as many human qualities. At the advanced stage, broaden the conception of his efforts, his creations, his contributions and their implications. Thus 'me' was used as my experience in life, my struggle in life and my competition in life. 'me' is also used negatively for complexities and difficulties of life.

(iv) Finally, 'we' revealed consciousness about the feeling of commitment to primary social institutions in an objective way which signified support for some and opposition to other institutions. It also characterize and classify these social collectivities which were considered desirable or undesirable. In this context, 'we' referred to the following general and positive features:

- Close family unit	- Academic association
- Mass media fraternity	- All authors and writers
- All professionals and technocrats	- All engineers, doctors and associated experts
- Members of political parties/organisations	- Members of a religious group
- Members of castes and sub-castes	- Members of an ethnic community
- Members of an occupational group	- Members of a particular sect.

K-25 felt that there existed some negative features of the concept of 'we'. Thus it was used for :

- Opponents of the political parties/organisations
- Proponents of religious organisations
- Ideologues of civil and democratic rights
- Opponents of the ruling party
- Opponents of democratic and secular system

9. IDEAS OF EQUALITY AND INEQUALITY

(i) K-25 believed in the hard reality of existence of inequality at all levels and in all fields of life world over. This was characteristic feature of pre-modern societies and it has survived in all forms of societies. Thus the system of inequality based on class, caste, power and gender have hurt the entire society. Taking into consideration its past record, it has always proved disorganising and disordering and it could not be debased completely.

(ii) While K-25 supported absolute equality, he suggested that it could be made a reality through the establishment of its system. In it, equality of all individuals and other social collectivities must be ensured and its ideational foundations and value-oriented principles must be evolved properly. This system must provide social justice to every social entity in all fields. Social egalitarianism and social equilibrium must emerge as guiding principles. Its cultural ethos must ensure equal participation of diverse and different units. The ethnicity must reflect all its forms and dimensions.

10. GLOBAL SOCIAL ORDER

K-25 was a strong supporter of GSO. He argued that this order must follow certain specific social principles which must be meaningful, serve humanity than nationality, serve global rather than local interests and encourage internationalism than localism. In this regard, he argued that GSO must necessarily follow basic principles which included the following:

- Equality and fraternity
- Tolerance and patience
- Secularism, treating every religion at par
- Reciprocal relationship – two-way social relationship
- Liberty, in terms of availing basic human and civil rights
- Pragmatic worldview in the complex world
- Future vision for whole humanity
- Mutual understanding of cultures, religions and civilisations
- Peaceful co-existence of various nationalities
- Equal and just representation to all social entities in the world
- Scientific knowledge, technology and management
- Humanistic perspective of global problems and issues
- No discrimination on any basis
- No consideration of systems of class, caste, power and gender
- No scope for conflict between social collectivities
- Unification, similarity, accommodation, coherence, harmony and solidarity at global level

11. THE RELIGIOUS LIFE

(i) K-25 was a strong believer of religious formulations of *wahdat, risalt and qiyamat*. His strong belief also reflected in *Namaaz* and *Roza*. Since he had studied religion from original sources, his basic concepts of Islam were very clear in his mind. Equally strong was his adopted behaviour related to religious practices. But, at the same time he was not dogmatic or fatalist. He was pragmatic, scientific and realist in practical life. In his professional field, he was above the religious consideration. *He was fond of celebrating* festivals, especially *Eeds,* with his parents at their home in the village. So, on the occasion of every *Eed*, he with his family used to visit the village.

(ii) K-25 neither bothered nor responded to the folk religious practices in the village and later on. While he never attended shrines, he was also not involved in saint-worshipping. He never celebrated any particular day in a week/month/year.

(iii) K-25 was impressed by the reformist and radical Islamic trends in Kashmir. Though he was in contact with some ideologues of this movement, he neither agreed with their politics nor joined their movement. He always preferred to be away from them.

(iv) K-25's relations with KPs were close and cordial. He had some good KP friends in his professional fraternity, who were his colleagues at different stages of life. This friendship was based on bilateral understanding on common issues and problems.

12. THE KASHMIR PROBLEM

(i) K-25 always talked about complex nature of the Kashmir problem which was created by politicians when people of Kashmir were denied the right to decide their political future after 1947. Subsequent political developments made it complex and an international issue.

(ii) India ignored the implications of the Accession Treaty and followed intensive integration of JK which was even against article 370 of the constitution. The issue was taken to the U.N. by India. In the aftermath of cold war, India changed its position and policy on Kashmir which resisted the resolution of this problem.

(iii) Pakistan could not withstand its principled position of respecting people's aspirations and sent tribal raiders to Kashmir in1947 which reversed the entire situation. It linked the Kashmir issue with domestic and foreign policies and made it 'life line of Pakistan' and 'unfinished agenda of partition', which was strongly resented by India. This position resisted any solution of Kashmir as India strongly opposed that policy.

(iv) The Kashmir problem was discussed, debated and assessed repeatedly by involved countries of India and Pakistan and global powers in the UNGA and UNSC. But, this never helped in its resolution. The international intervention also didn't help. Thus the U.N. has failed miserably in the resolution of this problem.

(v) In the present regional and global political situation, the degree and dimension of complexity has increased further. That was because of the issues like emergence of *Taliban* in Afghanistan and rise of terrorism against America at global level. In this situation, the Kashmir issue got entangled in international politics.. This has contributed nothing except highest degree of complexity of this problem.

13. EXPERIENCE OF CONFLICT SITUATION

(i) K-25 reported for several newspapers about the Kashmir militancy during its entire period. He observed all developments personally and got most authentic information in this connection. He reported about killings, torture and interrogation of the local youth. In actuality, a large number of youth were arrested and tortured for days and weeks in most brutal way.

(ii) K-25 reported that hundreds of local youth were tortured severely and violently which led to some deaths. Thousands of them were injured, made disabled and declared disappeared. In fact, the entire young generation suffered at the hands of forces. It was also reported that some of the militant youth were virtually butchered.

(iii) K-25 observed that tortures had gone for years and nobody could stop them, even the political leaders of India. No national or international organisation could intervene in that situation. In this way, a whole generation was lost to the conflict.

14. FUTURE KASHMIR SOCIETY

(i) K-25 was a strong proponent of welfare-oriented state and society. So, the state's role vis a vis society must be oriented towards total emancipation of the latter. The state must also feel committed to achievement of highest standard of society. He specifically mentioned about some social efforts with clear objectives in this regard. The details of these efforts areas follows :

(a) The society must be scientifically and technologically developed and must serve the cause of change and development. In this connection, all scientific-technological innovations must be implemented at large. These must be made relevant to social life and its basic needs. Second, universal education must be considered 'compulsory' for all classes, groups and communities and in all fields. It must be considered human and sacred and not as 'market commodity'.

(b) The state must establish the system of social justice in which there will be no differentiation on the basis of class and caste. It must prove free and competitive society for all. No discrimination, positive or negative, must prevail there. The egalitarian status in relation to family-marriage-kinship ties must be practised. The institution of religion must perform the humanitarian and not sectarian role. It must be used for integration than for disintegration, harmony and not for disharmony, and for peace and not for under-development.

(c) In the field of culture, it must establish a plural and multifarious system which will contribute to tolerance and patience towards all religions and cultures.

15. SOCIAL PROBLEMS IN KASHMIR

(i) *Village Dependence:* K-25 felt that village as a unit was completely a dependent unit about 100 years back. In the recent situation, though the degree of dependence has decreased, the village continues to be dependent on town and city. Its contribution to the major economic sector, i.e., agriculture, has not given its due dividends. This economic dependence of village prevailed in the fields of economy, road-connectivity, health, education, polity, social-cultural affairs, change, development and so on. In actuality, every aspect of life in the village was compelled to become 'borrower' from town and city which became center of activities in the processes of development. In terms of implications of this type of dependence of village, the entire society in rural areas faced lop-sided development and denial of some basic human facilities. In that context, the situation negated the very basic role of development-oriented change.

K-25 argued that this trend of dependence needed to be arrested keeping in view long-term interests. In this regard, more importance must be attached to state policy, planning, programs and schemes to empower the villages to play positive and dynamic role in the processes basically related to development and modernisation. In order to the sufferings of villagers, K-25 suggested that the village must be integrated as a dynamic unit in processes of economic and social development.

(ii) *The Sponsored Journalist:* The sponsored journalist referred to a person who works in a newspaper for serving the cause and interests of a particular individual, group or agency. Thus that person stood for 'hired journalist' to serve particular interests in his published stories, presentations, analysis, reports and critiques. According to K-25, this was a rare phenomenon and stood as 'exception' than a 'rule'. In Kashmir, there were plenty of such cases due to chronic and complex political situation.

K-25 interpreted this phenomenon as deliberate distortion of news and news analysis. It directs the profession towards false perceptions and perspectives. It often presented non-reality as reality, major issues as non-issues, and major developments as minor developments and vice versa. In this process, the profession got deteriorated and degenerated.

K-25 upheld that, in Kashmir, various national security agencies were involved in such acts for long. It was essentially in this context that the local press in Kashmir was always under cloud. Its professional credibility was always questioned. Thus the sponsored journalist hurt the cause of profession for his selfish gains.

In the context of negative implications of this undesirable practise in mass media, it needed to be controlled and eliminated, But, it may prove a difficult task.

K-26 MILK-SELLER WOMAN

1. SOCIAL CONTEXT

(i) There exist a large proportion of occupational groups in the Kashmiri society. While these groups, known as service occupational castes also, deal with general service occupations which have comparatively lower social esteem. This group formed the lowest community in the caste hierarchy. On the other hand, the occupational castes deal with major societal occupation which are of higher social esteem. Though a lot of occupational mobility was experienced in last few decades in Kashmir, the co-relation between castes and occupations still exist. The occupational differences are explained below:

Occupational castes		*Service occupational castes*	
Name	*Activity*	*Name*	*Activity*
- Wani	Small business	- Hajam	Hair cutting
- Bhat	Large and small business	- Darzi	Tailoring
- Dar	Large and small business	- Dhobi	Washing clothes
- Kar	Large and small business	- Sofi	Bread making
- Magrey	Large and small business	- Gilkar	Measonary
- Tantry	Large and small business	- Chhann	Carpentry
- Shah	Large business	- Dandher	Vegetable growing/selling
- Shahdad	Large business	- Goor	Milk selling

(ii) K-26 belonged to one of the service occupational groups because of her occupational specialisation in which she played a significant role. This community was known as *Goor*, those who produce-sell milk and milk products. A brief sociological introduction of this community follows. Economically, they stood poor to very poor standard of life. But, their economic conditions changed in the recent past and came up to the status of average to middle income groups. It happened in the context of increasing purchasing power of the people and they started consuming more milk and milk products. This increased the income of *Goor* community. Some of its members get so much money that they invested it in business.

(iii) Educationally, K-26 community members were not motivated sufficiently at earlier stage. But, now they stood conscious about the role of education. So, they send most of their children to schools. But, the drop-out rate was also high among them. Only a few members were able to pursue higher education and higher government jobs.

(iv) Culturally, this community was not much exposed to modern influence and lifestyle. The elder generation live completely a traditional life and hardly any change has occurred in it. But, younger generation was not so conservative. Some families developed middle class lifestyle after getting modern education.

(v) Socially, the community faced two extremely opposite social images. First, they were seen as people who improved their economic condition and have undergone certain degree of mobility. So, they don't feel themselves belonging to lower esteem group. Second, there was opposite image according to which this community was considered economically forward but culturally backward. So, their social esteem was lower and they were considered even undesirable.

(vi) The *Goor* community maintained traditional forms of family, marriage and kinship ties. They gave highest importance to customary and conventional relations which they maintained through interaction, visits and gifts. While social solidarity among them was higher, they usually lived in joint or extended type of families which suited their occupation. They considered family as sacred and were committed to its safety, security and image. In response, the family provided much needed satisfaction and security. Marriage was also upheld in its conservative form. All customary practices were in vogue even in present day times. The marriage was mostly endogamous, monogamous and patri-local type.

(vii) Regarding change and development, the community was late and slow in its response towards these processes. Their practical life didn't reflect many development features, especially in the fields of health, nutrition,, basic life facilities, literacy and so on.

(viii) The most interesting feature of this community revealed in the structure of occupational activities which stood old and distinctive. Nearly all their families practise traditional occupation of producing and selling of milk and milk-products. Both sexes participate in these activities equally and shoulder to shoulder. There was not any clear division of labour between sexes but they performed different jobs as reveals in the following details:

Women jobs/activities	*men jobs/activities*
- Taking care of live-stock in the house - Domestic works - Taking care of children, elders and others - Selling milk and milk-products at home	- Taking care of livestock outside house - Selling-marketing activities - All out-family activities - Selling milk and milk-products inside and outside house and shops.

(ix) It seems important to note that no *purdah* and no segregation of sexes was in practise in occupational activities. In actuality, such social segregation was not possible in the institutional structure of this occupation. The occupational roles of men and women were tied in such a way that their separation was impossible. They interact with opposite sex of their customers without any reservation. In fact, they have no consciousness about separation of sex within and outside their families.

(x) In this context, the *Goor-Bai* (milk-seller woman) emerged as a unique character in which :

- women worked equally and with men shoulder to shoulder;
- there prevailed no gender bias in the occupation;
- no segregation of sexes was practised in the occupation;
- women in general enhanced their role and status in the family; and
- women in general took full part in decision-making bodies within families.

These were characteristic features which reflected in the ideal role of K-26.

2. IN-FAMILY SOCIALISATION

(i) K-26 was socialised in a milk-seller's family whose feature have been mentioned above. Her socialisation for a dynamic role in the occupation was perfect from the parent's family. It was a different role from the usual female role because it was not limited to personal and domestic jobs but extended to all related fields of occupation which involved daily interaction with outside male and female customers. She was prepared for this role and she knew how to deal with live stocks, prepare and sell milk products and how to treat variety of customers. She had developed expertise in these and other social affairs.

(ii) After marriage, she started this role immediately and she faced no serious problem. In fact, she became popular among child customers, on whom she used to shower her affection. She also took the responsibility of family life, children, elders and other individuals and groups related to the family. Thus everybody found her post-marital performance as satisfactory and considered her as the perfect occupational lady.

3. OUT-FAMILY ENVIRONMENT

(i) In the case of K-26, family proved more effective in comparison to relatives, neighbours, FFs and others. Her life was mainly shaped by family socialisation and she developed behaviour traits on expected lines. Outside the family framework, she was able to respond to the demands of customers and developed a busy role like that of a working woman in the office. That happened at her parental and later on marital family. In fact, her experience at parental home was repeated in the marital home.

(ii) Neighbors in both localities played least role in socialising her. They were mostly her customers and used to meet her at the time of collecting milk and milk products. They had no formal contact, no regular interaction and they could not develop reciprocal relationship with her.

(iii) The relatives and FFs were same people and they too had lesser social contact with K-26. In fact, they were of same social, educational and cultural status but the K-26 family was ahead in economic standard. So, she hardly considered them equal to her family. In fact, she became the ideal lady for their women and tried to follow her lifestyle.

4. OCCUPATION, MOBILITY AND ASSOCIATION

(i) K-26 had a permanent occupation related to production and sale of milk and milk-products. She adopted this role in totality which had many repercussions. She always remained busy from early morning till late evening in different occupational activities. Her busy schedule of these activities reveals in the following list of daily works:

Morning	*Day*	*Evening*
- Morning prayers	- attending relatives, guests and customer	- Personal work
- Personal works	- child-elder care	-Domestic works
- Domestic works	- family care	-Hospitality
- child care and elder care		- Visiting neighbours occasionally
- visiting relatives		
- Occupational activities		- Occupational activities
Milking cows	- ...	-...
Getting milk from outside		
Selling milk and milk products to customers		
Making curd and cheese		
Keeping records of finance dealings		

(ii) Many decades back, K-26 family's economic condition was not good. But, this condition changed in the recent decades. Broadly, a large-scale change was experienced in Kashmiri society which led to higher purchasing power. With this development, there was heavy increase in the consumption of milk and milk products. In turn, this contributed to heavy increase and economic affluence of *goor* families including that of K-26 family. They got money which was more than their needs. So, they saved extra money in banks, while some families invested it in the business of their children. K-26 family had acted in the latter way. In this way, this family experienced the occupational mobility in upward direction. With that came the affluence of K-26 family.

(iii) It was observed that this type of mobility was experienced in some fields only which were identified as lifestyle, construction of new houses, increasing income, food habits, dress patterns, dowry, fashions and so on. The fields which remained unaffected included ideas, attitudes, views, worldviews, and future vision. Thus while elders continued with old behaviour, youngsters underwent some significant changes. So, K-26 family experienced partial mobility.

(iv) Normally, change in occupational activity led to mobility and then to adoption of new association at individual and social level. But, that has not happened in the case of K-26 family. While some of its members maintain old associations strongly, lesser number of members have developed new association. It follows that economic change was not followed by psychological and social change.

5. MARRIAGE AND FAMILY

(i) K-26 was married earlier in life at the age of late teens. But, she was mature enough to undergo proper socialisation. Her marriage was performed according to the unwritten rules of endogamy, monogamy and patri-locality. Both families belonged to same social, economic, educational and cultural status. She faced no difficulty in getting adjusted in the post-marital environment. That is why she was able to develop new role in new family easily and comfortably.

(ii) Before marriage, K-26 was living in a big joint family. After marriage, she joined other such family unit. The framework of rights and responsibilities were same in both families. So, she was able to adjust in new family. She lived with husband's joint family with his brothers and their children.

(iii) She took full care of other members of her family and her husband who was an addict of a local drug which he used to consume at his shop with friends. This had dis-organisational and deviational effect on her children. But, due to personal qualities, K-26 took full care of her children and other family members.

6. SOCIAL LIKES AND DISLIKES

After getting practical experience of life in pre-marital and post-marital periods in the family context, K-26 developed some particular social likes and dislikes as follows:

Social Likes	*Social Dislikes*
- An active and dynamic woman	- Inequality between different sections
- Performing all domestic jobs herself	- Discrimination against anybody
- To shower affection on children	- Morally degraded persons
- A humble, polite and hard working bride	- Not serious about work and discipline
- Simple and dowry-less marriage	- Drug and crime behaviour

contd...

contd...

Social Likes	*Social Dislikes*
- Strengthening kinship relations	- Social deviation among children
- Dedicated and committed youth	- Not having basic facilities of life
- No cheating in occupational behaviour	- A person who plays fraud
- Folk religious beliefs and practices	- A person who doesn't bother about values
- Honesty and ethics in occupation	- Exogamous and polygamous marriages
- Stable post-marital life	- Illiteracy and ignorance
- Preference for other occupations	- Sub-standard food items
- Women's work as normal work	- A selfish person
- A family with large number of members	- A girl without value-orientation
- Following religious principles	- Portraying non-religious attitudes
- Accumulating money in the family	- Children with some career outside house
- Occupational fraternity	- Boys without any proper activity
- Affluence at home and outside	- Gender discrimination
- Education for all children	- Moral and ethical behaviour
- Busy activities in the house	- Wasting time uselessly
- A society with equal partners	- Extra-marital sex relationship

7. CONCEPTS OF "I", "ME" AND "WE"

(i) K-26 had folk and subdued notions of 'I' and 'me' but high sense of 'we'. Though she stood completely illiterate, she was able to convey her notions emotionally. Her actions and interactions also revealed these feelings. She took 'I' as a person who has suffered discrimination and exploitation in the past. That 'I' wanted to uphold 'herself' in terms of personality and identity but could not do it. This treatment was supported by culture and tradition and religion put agreement stamp on it. This 'I' was buried under the same three factors.

(ii) K-26 gave same treatment to the concept of 'me'. Though it meant a lot of qualifications – virtues, habits, attitudes, features and life situations, but all proved transitory and partial. 'Me' was lost in the process. So, she as 'me' was lost in life with benefit to nobody.

(iii) 'We', for K-26, was always a stimulating concept and 'I' and 'me' were integrated in it. So much integration has taken place that these two could hardly be identified and differentiated from 'we'. It was a superior concept and gave safety-security to K-26. In empirical terms, it referred to social collectivities which were directly or indirectly related to family. This, according to K-26, used for a group of :

- Occupational activists
- All family members
- Female customers fraternity
- Members of occupational families.
- Close and distant relatives
- All neighbours and FFs
- Lovers of child customers, and

8. IDEAS OF EQUALITY AND INEQUALITY

(i) K-26 had some distinctive ideas about equality and inequality among human beings. She started with observation that men and women, rich and poor, were born equal beings and had no particular feature. But, later on, they adopted systems of inequality which were not God-made but man-made. Man not only initiated these practices, but also established and legitimised them. In these processes and systems, inequality served the interests of few individuals, families and groups. They dominated, monopolised and exploited others, especially poor, women, elders, weak and children.

(ii) K-26 upheld that these systems of inequality must be fully opposed and debased. Subsequently, systems of equality must be established through religion-oriented principles.

9. THE IDEAL LEADER

(i) The ideal leader of K-26 was SMA whom she considered as the 'God-sent Leader'. His idea and image was more than of charismatic leader for her. He represented supreme leadership not only in Kashmir but also in the world. He stood as the only tallest leader in history. She was ready even to sacrifice her life on his orders. After the death of SMA, his role was made a folk character and she, like many others, believed him alive in the graveyard.

(ii) This kind of status for SMA during his life time was not available to many leaders in the world. He got this status because his followers attributed some achievements, correctly or incorrectly, to him and his leadership. Some of these achievements were identified as follows:

- He gave the freedom to Kashmiris
- He granted them regard, respect and dignity
- He gave them most needed distinctive identity
- He took them out of extreme poverty and complete illiteracy
- He served the Kashmiris through out his life
- He spent 22 years in prison for Kashmiri's political freedom
- He restored religion the dignity it deserved by constructing *Dargah Shreef*
- The *Kas*hmiris can never pay him back for his services
- He sacrificed everything for Kashmir and Kashmiris.

(iii) K-26 represented the women's generation which was wholly devoted to SMA and his political ideals. He organised them in a systematic way right from 1931. His wife helped him in this regard. Subsequently, they were necessary component in all political developments, particularly protests, demonstrations and uprisings. In this way, SMA utilised women's power for his politics. K-26 too was devoted to him without understanding his political ideals. She was a blind follower of SMA.

(iv) Thus SMA and his leadership got the credit of giving legitimacy to the political role of women in Kashmir. In fact, this new role stood unparalleled and unprecedented in the entire Indian sub-continent. In fact, Kashmir was the first place where equal political rights of men and women were approved through their inclusion in *Naya Kashmir Program.* He also started efforts for their free education and employment.

(v) K-26 felt that a leader like SMA never dies and can never be forgotten. So, her devotion to his leadership remains still alive.

10. THE RELIGIOUS LIFE

(i) K-26 was a highly religious person but in a folk way. She had no knowledge about basics of Islam and no awareness about fundamental practices of this religion. Since she and her family were illiterate, they never formed the audience of religious preachers. They continued with the oral or folk tradition of religion. In fact, this community was kept away from ideal religious form. Its members, especially women, never got or gave time to listen to folk religious preachers. They seemed neither interested nor involve/ motivated to develop proper understanding of Islam in their life. Illiteracy and ignorance further deteriorated their religious understanding.

(ii) In the preceding context, religion in K-26 family revolved around the performance of certain rituals, customs, practices and celebrations and so on. The major religious activities were identified as going to shrines regularly, following *peer-mureedi,* celebration of particular occasions and days/dates, festivals and *urs*. In this type of religious environment, the role of the *mulla and molvi* emerged important but exploitative.

(iii) However, in previous decades, some education has been attained by the children of this community which led to some degree of understanding of pure religion. Moreover, common folk religious preaching, radio-television programs, Islamic missionary activities, and different religious programs organised by various religious organisations on differed sacred occasions contributed to some degree of understanding of real and original religion. At the same time, this led to some conceptual clarity and practical relevance of basic Islamic ideas and ideals. For this situation, K-26 provided an explanation according to which *Mullas* wanted them to be illiterate in order to keep them away from original religion and continue their exploitative role.

(iv) Socially, K-26 family showed no interest in reformed or radical trends of Islam as all its members were illiterate. They could neither read their literature nor could understand them fully.

11. EXPERIENCE OF CONFLICT SITUATION

(i) K-26 faced a unique but important social problem during the conflict situation. It was related to milk feeding of baby kids in early age groups of 0-3 and 3-5 years of age. During these stages, particularly the first stage, the kids need milk-feeding necessarily in addition to breast feeding. This, according to doctors' views, was necessary for normal growth of baby kids.

(ii) According to K-26, this facility too was affected due to conflict. On many days of curfews, strikes and armed encounters, the parents or other family members were not able to collect milk for kids from K-26 house. Some parents used baby milk powder, but, it didn't suit some kids, others felt allergic to it.

(iii) The basic problem was not availability of milk for kids, but the attitude and behaviour of police and security forces who held lanes and by-lanes and didn't allow anybody to venture out of their houses, even for medical aid and emergencies like delivery of women. Those who dared to go out, were beaten mercilessly and injured critically. In that situation, kids could not get pure milk feeding due to which they suffered. K-26 could not tolerate that situation and condemned the attitude of the forces.

12. FUTURE KASHMIR SOCIETY

(i) K-26 had folk notions of future society in Kashmir. Some of these notions were fed by SMA during his lifetime. Most of these notions were highly idealistic and abstract but reflect the sentiments of K-26 and other such women. These notions included the following:

- Kashmir as an independent country with its own flag
- Kashmir society as a symbol of equality, brotherhood and harmony
- Kashmir society must have enough economic opportunities for all Kashmiris
- The poor in Kashmir must not suffer at the hands of rich
- No differentiation or discrimination between different groups and classes
- Political opponents must be treated politically and democratically
- Free education for all citizens from primary to university stage
- Marriage as a simple and dowry-less affair

- No segregation of sexes and no divorce to women
- Respect and support of parents in their old age
- No violence against women
- No crime against anybody
- Ideals of honesty and truthfulness upheld
- Providing employment opportunities to all unemployed
- Social progress of all disadvantage groups and communities
- Making broader awareness about kashmiri identity
- Exposing kashmiris to all modern sectors of economy
- Upholding secular ethos of the society.

13. SOCIAL PROBLEMS IN KASHMIR

(i) *Credit Borrowing:* A general practise in all societies, and in the Kashmiri society too, was borrowing from the market on credit and pay them after some time. K-26 had also this experience when some customers pleaded for credit-based supply. This usually applied to government employees who get regular salary after a month and to limited-fixed income groups. Keeping in view the past record of customers, K-26 allowed some of them to take milk on credit. While majority of them paid after the month regularly, some of them didn't do that. In the latter category, while some had genuine reasons for not paying, others were simply posing problems. In fact, their intentions were not clear. K-26 could differentiate between the real and fake customers.

K-26 considered this behaviour as 'unethical','immoral', 'illegal' and against civilised behaviour. She considered it undesirable and disastrous even for defaulters. In addition to getting undesirable social image and criticism, their next generation followed this practice.

K-26 talked about this problem in a specific way. She found that while many customers were honest, only some were not. She had the problem with them only and dealt with them harshly. In the context of this experience, she developed a principle that no milk should be sold on credit basis. If credit becomes necessary, it must be provided to those customers only whose record was clear.

(ii) *Adulteration:* It stood as a serious problem in which original and pure productions were mixed with fake and spurious products and sell on original high rates. This not only violated ethics, morality and ideals of occupational behaviour, it harmed the human body. So, it gave rise to many serious diseases and other health problems.

The *Goor* community in Kashmir was known for this practice. They usually mix water and other liquids with milk and sell it on original price. At other times, they consume powder milk, give it in liquid form, mix it with original milk and sell on the name and rate of original milk. This has created many health problems among customers whose treatment needed a lot of time and money.

But, K-26 was an exception. She used to buy and sell original milk openly and on standard rates. This variety suited elders as well as children. She was never found involved in this immoral, unethical, harmful and illegal practice.

K-27 THE KASHMIRI YOUTH: LOWER CLASS-CASTE

1. BIRTH-SOCIAL CONTEXT

(i) The service occupational groups/castes were characterised with diversity in their occupations. They were engaged in a variety of activities such as washing, tailoring, vegetable growing, bread-making, carpentry, masonry, milk-selling, hair-cutting, scanvangers' jobs, skilled-unskilled jobs and related activities. In theory, these activities had basic relevance to daily life but were considered of "low esteem", 'undesirable', 'impure' and 'menial'. These occupational groups/castes were not generally included in business fields.

(ii) However, a new development took place among these groups in recent decades related to change, mobility, occupation and migration. In fact, some among these groups responded positively to modern education. Subsequently, they got permanent government jobs that led to their occupational mobility. In this process, while they adopted new occupation of government service, they dropped the old one completely. They faced a situation in which elder generation continued with old occupation and new generation adopted the changed one. This situation led to an occupational crisis in which a vacuum was created because no local youth was available for these activities in urban areas. Even if available, they were lesser in number, not dynamic and commited, and were waiting for opportunity to shift to new occupation. K-27 belonged to that generation whose family also faced this changing occupational situation.

(iii) In that situation, the migrants from outside JK were attracted and they came in large numbers from Bihar, Rajasthan, U.P., M.P., and West Bengal. They were known as "*Bihari* labour" and were composed of skilled and unskilled manpower in lakhs. They have dominated some working sectors such as construction, tailoring, hair-cutting, bread-making, skilled-semiskilled jobs, agricultural-horticultural areas. It was observed that these migrants stayed in Kashmir for varying periods of some years to some decades. Some stayed for summer seasons, while others stayed permanently.

(iv) Despite facing various problems, the *Bihari* labour didn't face serious opposition, partly because there was scarcity of labour manpower here and partly because it was local people's own creation. The *Biharis* adjusted in the local condition and worked hard. As a result, they earned more than their needs and sent extra amount to their homes through bank, post office or other channels. This helped them considerably in improving economic conditions there, especially in Bihar. But, when negative brunt of this impact was felt seriously by the locals, there emerged a lot of sympathy with suffering local labours who were thrown out of jobs. This generated antagonism against non-local labour. However, this problem was solved because of anti-India political uprising in 2010 when about 85-90% of non-local labour had to leave Kashmir.

(v) It seems highly relevant to introduce the *Neyd* (hair-cutting) occupational community in Kashmir to which K-27 belonged. In terms of population, this community inhabited in *mohallas* in the city, towns and villages. They also lived in mixed colonies, especially in Srinagar. Their number was significant in comparison to other such groups and, as per unofficial estimates, their total number was about 4-5 lakhs. They worked in shops in city and on footpaths and roadsides in towns and villages. They also worked on different shrines.

(vi) Economically, their conditions were not well. They usually belonged to poor to very poor category because occupation paid them a meager amount. After recent changes, while urban groups got economically much benefitted, the rural groups still lived in poverty. Those who were totally illiterate faced acute problems. But, those who adopted change in occupations got their conditions improved and some among them jumped to middle class status.

(vii) Educationally, this community was not developed and still lacked basic, higher and professional education. While the city *Neyds* improved their position, those living in rural areas still lagged behind. Socially, the community stood traditional, conservative and pro status quo. The family provided stable, socialising and a controlling unit. It was joint family than that of nuclear family structure. Marriage in the community was endogamous, monogamous and of patri-local type. Traditional practices and customs were still followed strictly. Early marriage was a common feature. Kinship relations were still intact. So, there prevailed social coherence, cohesion and solidarity. Culturally, the community was not exposed to different impacts. It had not accepted modernising impact and maintained old lifestyle. In actuality, they lived a life of cultural isolation.

(viii) In the case of development and change, the community had shown less readiness and late response. Even in present day situation, they do not respond fully and positively to these processes. But, the response of such groups in urban areas was different which enabled them to get education and employment and responded to these processes differently.

(ix) K-27 belonged to one such family in the service occupational group/ caste which faced all such conditions in the urban context.

2. IN-FAMILY SOCIALISATION

(i) K-27 was socialised in an ordinary lower class family of service occupational group in the urban centre. As was generally condition in this group, i.e. illiteracy, ignorance, poverty and no motivation for change, his family was characterised with these features. In the urban political context, this family had developed certain specific traits which influenced strongly the personality of K-27.

(ii) The first trait was traditional ethos of the family under which this family emphasised traditional as well as new occupational structure, maintained religious oriented values and norms, and not allowed serious deviation from social ethics. The second trait of religious environment had mixed impact, i.e. effect of opposite religious trends. One was the established trend of folk religious practices and second was the reformative trend of Islam in opposition to the former. Since K-27 was educated, he had accommodated both trends and ideational impact in his personality.

(iii) The third family trait reflected in its political input as it was politically active in favour of ruling party. K-27 himself played a role of it as political activist and a strong follower of SMA. This directly led to the adoption of his political ideas, ideology and ideals related to the present and future of Kashmir. This impact in the family created 2-sided impact on K-27. On the one hand, he emerged to young ideologue of Kashmiri identity and, on the other hand, became the ideologue of anti-caste ideology. This bi-dimensional ideology was pursued by him through out his life.

3. OUT-FAMILY ENVIRONMENT

(i) The out-family environment of K-27 composed of relatives, neighbours, FFs and others. His near relatives belonged to same social, educational and cultural background, but were not equal in economic standing. So, they had lesser impact on his personality. In fact, they usually got benefited by K-27 because of his political and party contact.

(ii) The neighbourhood of K-27 had a tremendous impact on his young life. Since his entire locality was stronghold of SMA, the K-27 family felt politically mobilised for political participation. It also helped the family to establish a particular political image which established its contact with other such families. In addition to other effects, the neighbourhood also realised about political role of K-27 family.

(iii) On the other hand, K-27 lived in a locality where there was a shrine which attracted its followers from the entire valley. All particular days/dates in a week/month/year used to be celebrated there In this environment, there was huge crowd present always. All local residents participated in these functions and got socialised in the ideas and practices related to shrine celebrations and the *Mulla* role got legitimised. This situation affected the life of K-27 in many ways consciously or unconsciously.

(iii) Outside these influences, there was a serious impact of personal friends, who were his class-batch mates and office colleagues, on K-27's personality. While some of them belonged to upper socio-economic background, others were impressed by reformist-radical trends of Islam. Thus he got exposed to different socio-economic contexts and opposite political ideologies. As a result, he read some books on religion and politics and got doctrinal understanding of original Islam and politics.

(iv) Others, who influenced political thinking and ideology of K-27 were political ideologues, supporters, activists and workers of a popular political party. They socialised him politically and he worked for the party in spare time. As a result of these activities, he got political identity and particular political ideology.

(v) All above processes had a cumulative but diverse impact on personality growth of K-27. First, in politics, he supported one political party and one political leader – SMA. Second, in religion, he got devoted to follow religious practices in the shrine in the neighbourhood. On the other hand, he accepted some effect from the reformist religious trend and their literature. Third, he developed a revolutionary orientation and sentiment against the institution of caste and its upholders. He got a strong feeling after he got discriminated on many occasions after he was identified as of low caste origin.

4. EDUCATION AND CAREER

(i) From primary till secondary stage, K-27 got free education in a locality government school. By this, it was established that the response of his father was different from most of his occupational colleagues. That particular response was shown probably because of his increased economic position (due to city's central location of his shop) and his customers' advice to send children to school. K-27's family could afford to wait for his earning till he completed his graduation.

(ii) He qualified all exams easily as he was intelligent, clever, innovative and motivated to personal and collective actions. His college education took place in a city college where he qualified graduation in humanities. He was exposed to a new world of different classes, groups and communities and different ideas and ideologies. From that stage, he started thinking keeping his ideals about future in mind. There he participated in literary, cultural and political activities. He was a regular participant in all political protests and demonstrations.

(iii) After graduation, he was asked by his family to get a job for family support. So, he got and joined a clerical job in a government office. However, his officers were not happy with him because of his bluntness and expressing their limitations. They all worked against him which hurt his career in office by denying him the promotion several times. After decades of time, he was promoted to the position next to officer's position.

5. OCCUPATION, MOBILITY AND ASSOCIATION

(i) The traditional occupation of K-27 family was hair-cutting and was followed for generations. But, new occupational situation has emerged now which reflects in the operation of two occupations simultaneously, one with the elder generation and second with the younger generation. This had influenced his family life and gave it a new status and role. They felt psychologically elevated and all their children were enrolled in the school. A clear curve of mobility from low esteem occupation to high esteem occupation revealed in this family. This upward mobility was a great achievement which it had got after a lot struggle and opposition, which helped it financially, educationally and in other fields. It also ensured further mobility for future generation.

(ii) The association of K-27 family was determined by the pattern of occupational activities. While main association of elder generation was with relatives and occupational colleagues who were mostly religious, uneducated, and conservative. On the other hand, another parallel association was established by younger generation with their educational and career colleagues. They were highly educated and economically better off. Both associations continued in the family. It was felt by K-27 that the direction of change in association pattern was from traditional to new pattern and the latter will replace the former shortly.

6. MARRIAGE AND FAMILY

(i) K-27's marriage was carried out with a girl who belonged to same service occupational group. Though she belonged to same social and economic status, her family was behind in education and cultural exposure. In reality, it was an endogamous, monogamous and patri-local type of marriage. Since the girl was educated, it helped K-27 in the process of mobility.

(ii) Before marriage, K-27 lived with parents in a joint family. The bride joined that family and lived there for about a decade. But, after death of parents and marriage of brothers and sisters, this joint family got divided into nuclear family units. So, K-27 had to adopt a nuclear family household in which he, his wife and his unmarried children lived. In the recent years, K-27 constructed his new house in a newly established colony and shifted there.

7. SOCIAL LIKES AND DISLIKES

(i) After experiencing extremely different ideas, perceptions and roles in his radical orientation, K-27 developed certain specific social likes and dislikes which include the following:

Social Likes	*Social Dislikes*
- A person having revolutionary ideas	- Political exploitation and manipulation
- Political party representing people	- Rigging in elections by any political party
- Political participation, esp. elections	- Violence and crime against women
- A person without caste consciousness	- Crime and drug abuse
- A system which establishes social justice	- Social disorganisation and social deviance
- Gender equality in all fields	- A conscious and practising *Sayyid*
- Well-wisher of family and society	- The working *Mulla*
- A political ideologue of his society	- The unequal systems of class and caste
- The political workers and activists	- The capitalist system and its inequalities
- Progressive political forces	- The orientation less generation
- Change and development of all classes	- Urban problems and chaos
- Political modernisation of common masses	- Absence of work ethic and work culture
- Teacher with highest degree of charisma	- Kings, dictators
- Free education for all citizens	- The ex-colonial powers in the world
- No reservation on the basis of caste	- Hege-monistic role of the U.S.A.
- Religion without exploitation and distortion	- Opposition to genuine political leadership
- Cultural interaction and understanding	- The feudal times in Kashmir
- *Naya Kashmir Program* of NC	- Education as a material category
- *The ruling party* members	- Political instability and uncertainty
- *Attending* the *Urs* of *Sheikh-ul-Alam*	- Criticising the practise of shrine attendance
- Celebrating religious festivals	- Begger in the society
- Lower occupational solidarity	- Pro-hierarchy ideas and ideology

8. CONCEPTS OF "I", "ME" AND "WE"

(i) K-27 was conscious of all three concepts of 'I', 'me' and 'we'. The sense of 'I' was seen in dual time factor, i.e. past and present. Thus 'I' in the past referred to a person who :

- was enslaved and monopolised,
- was exploited and dominated,
- was forced to work but was not paid,
- revolted against unjust system but was crushed, and
- tried to establish equality but was defeated repeatedly.

On the other hand, 'I' in the present sense referred to a person who:

- Worked for justice, equality and freedom
- Opposed all caste and class considerations

- Established traditions of honesty and truthfulness
- Formulated ideas and ideals of social justice
- Implemented religious rules of life.

(ii) K-27 attached same features to the concept of 'me' in the past and present . Thus it is associated with the concept of 'my'. In the past sense, it referred to my poverty, my socialisation, my domination and shaping of my life. In the present sense, it referred to :

- My struggle to achieve affluent standard of life
- My effort to develop the system of justice
- My action to help the poor, needy and downtrodden
- My thinking on radical lines
- My following of the principles of humanity and brotherhood.

(iii) K-27 formulated the concept of 'we' in the past and present forms. The concept of 'we' in the past sense referred to 'we' the Kashmiris who were :

- Tolerant and non-violent people
- Absolutely hospitable people
- People with cultural and religious plurality
- People who lived in composite cultural set-up
- Pure human beings

At the same time, 'we' in the present sense referred to 'we' the Kashmiris who are :

- Violent and conflict-ridden
- Followers of individualism and materialism
- Non-tolerant people
- Ignoring neighbours, relatives and elders
- Socially deviant and delinquent

9. IDEAS OF EQUALITY AND INEQUALITY

(i) K-27 was strong supporter of equality in all fields. He was equally opponent of inequality in all forms. He rejected the basis of class, caste and gender inequality and upheld the grand concept of human equality. He explained its postulates as follows :

- It stood for an egalitarian social order to be established by a political leader and political authority
- It necessarily included universal principles, values and norms
- It must not provide any chance for any inequality and its justification

- Its political program and future vision were to be stated by the supreme political leader and safeguarded by his authority
- It was to be sustained and continued through ideological, political, economic, social and cultural measures

(ii) In a way, K-27 presented the concept of a system which stood authoritarian in nature and highly dominated by political leadership. He explained the necessary leadership which only can ensure equality among all citizens. It followed that, according to K-27, a system of equality on humanitarian basis could only be established and sustained by the political leader or political authority whose nature was totalitarian or dictatorial.

10. THE IDEAL LEADER

(i) The ideal leader of K-27 was SMA, the supreme character, whom he followed in life. He considered him God-sent and Prophet-favored political leader. He had strong political faith in this type of the personality of SMA, which provided the basis and permanence to his leadership.

(ii) K-27 followed SMA sincerely as a political leader through out his life. He never tolerated any opposition or criticism against him or his leadership. He used to say that he who is follower of SMA was my friend and he didn't follow him was not my friend. K-27 always tried to impose the supreme leadership of SMA on others and motivated them to join the ruling party.

(iii) K-27 always presented SMA as the greatest leader Kashmir had ever produced for reasons mentioned below:

(a) SMA was the ideologue of *Kashmiriat*. He formulated, upheld and propagated this ideology throughout his life inside as well as outside Kashmir.

(b) SMA was sole protector of Kashmiris' political interests. In reality, he represented, safeguarded and emancipated Kashmir and Kashmiris at all times and in all situations.

(c) *SMA was the only leader* who dismantled the alien *Dogra* rule in Kashmir. In fact, he initiated, organised and took to logical conclusion the movement for the abolition of feudal regime in Kashmir.

(d) SMA was the only leader who got freedom for JK in 1947 and then acceded to India temporarily under the constitutional safeguards of Article 370 of the Indian constitution.

(e) SMA had devoted his life to Kashmir, its people, its culture, its change, its development, its religion and its civilisation.

(f) SMA was the greatest supporter of workers, laborers and artisans and other such categories of people in Kashmir and tried hard to improve their standard of life.

(iv) Like other groups in the Kashmiri society, the youth in general, like that of K-27, gave total support to SMA in his political struggle. They were called *Sher-i-Kashmir Ke Diwaaney.* They could have sacrificed their lives on the orders of SMA. They could never tolerate his opponents. K-27 was a literate follower of SMA, who had read his autography.

11. GLOBAL SOCIAL ORDER

(i) K-27 had a particular notion of GSO which he felt, must be seen as a global agency or organisation to pursue certain specific humanitarian goals. It must be established for the global sufferers of inequality, injustice, domination, discrimination, colonisation and imperialism. These goals must reflect in all actions, principles and objectives of the global order. It must not hesitate to fight back socially and culturally the ex-colonial powers of Western Europe and sole super power of America. It must also reorient the social, economic and cultural objectives of GSO. It must not fall trapped in IMF, WB and other such institutions. So, the success of GSO, according to K-27, was in pursuance of its principal objectives.

12. THE RELIGIOUS LIFE

(i) K-27 had sound belief in all Islamic tenets. He emphasised on original contents because he had studied its authentic sources such as *Quran* and *Hadith.* Sociologically, there were two sources of his religious behaviour, scriptural and folk sources.

(ii) In terms of practices, he was like other Muslims in his society. He performed all necessary practices of Islam. While he could not pray 5 times a day, he was a strict follower of fast. It was also observed that K-27 talked much and practised less in his actual life.

(iii) K-27 had adopted diverse religious behaviour. The first religious behaviour as ideal and doctrine-based which revolved around beliefs and practices of *Quran* and *Hadith.* The second religious behaviour practical and folk-religious oriented, revolved around beliefs and practises of folk religion in Kashmir. The second type was dominant in the family life of K-27. In addition to all *Eed* and *Urs,* he used to celebrate all particular days/ date in a week/month/year. Since this ritual and customary aspect of religion was attractive and dominant, he participated in all such activities.

(iv) K-27 never got impressed with radical trend of Islam in Kashmir in theory and practice. He developed a view that this religious trend was more political than religious and was oriented to follow particular political objectives and interests. Since he was a staunch supporter of SMA, he opposed continuously this religious movement.

(v) K-27 was very cordial, friendly and brotherly with KPs who were his office colleagues. He never made political differences on the basis of religion. He accepted intellectual and *educational excellence* of KPs. He used to interact with them often and visited their homes on the occasion of *Heerat* and *Ram Navmi* festivals.

13. THE KASHMIR PROBLEM

(i) K-27 believed in Kashmiri nationalist ideology and was its proponent in life. The major formulations of this ideology were as follows:

- the JK state acceded temporarily to the Union of India under article 370 of its constitution;
- the trust between central government and SMA broke in 1953 which led to violation of the accession od treaty and arrest (of SMA), and initiation of the movement for freedom;
- the process of forced integration of Kashmir into India, under the policy of total indianisation, was pursued by central government through its formal and informal agencies in JK;
- all these developments in post-1953 period led to erosion of special status of JK through legislative actions of changing the nomenclature of *Sadre Riyasat* and *Wazire Azam;*
- *these* and other actions on the part of central government did not contribute to national integration but to alienation and isolation; and
- when the degree of alienation from national mainstream increased heavily, it led to political reactions like militancy in 1989 and mass uprising in 2010.

(ii) K-27 felt that resolution of the Kashmir problem lie in restoring the autonomy under article 370. This would give a separate identity to Kashmiris within a special relationship with India. So, the Kashmir crisis will be over by restoring this ideal autonomy, according to K-27.

14. FUTURE SOCIETY OF KASHMIR

(i) K-27 had a dream of future society of Kashmir, mainly borrowed from SMA's thinking, was in the shape of a 'buffer state'. This future state was explained in terms of following core features:

- it will be an autonomous state with its distinct identity and with all local-home powers like education, culture, development, domestic economic sectors and so on;
- the sovereignty of that state must be with India and Pakistan jointly in a special relationship which dealt with foreign affairs, communications, currency and so on;
- this state must have its own constitution, flag, President, Prime Minister and Legislature;
- the security of this state must have joint responsibility of India and Pakistan

- the armed forces of India and Pakistan will be stationed on two extreme boundaries of the buffer state, so that the chance or possibility of direct conflict between them is reduced considerably;
- Kashmir will emerge as the international hub for global peace efforts;
- it will create an environment of peace and development in the entire South Asia;
- the super power intervention in this region of the world will reduce considerably;
- about 50% of defence budget allocations in India and Pakistan will be saved immediately and can be shifted to development sectors;
- Kashmir will emerge as center of civilisation and knowledge in Central and South Asia;
- it will turn into global mall of economic activities, especially in sectors in which local resources were available in abundance; and
- in the tourism sector, Kashmir emerge as the real Switzerland of Asia.

15. EXPERIENCE OF CONFLICT SITUATION

(i) K-27 had two important experiences of the conflict in Kashmir. The first experience was related to the right of dissent. Since during 1990s there was all-over domination of 'gun', the opposition political entities were not allowed to speak, write or express their opinion. The pro-India political forces and mainstream political parties preferred to go into the background. Many of them had to confine themselves in their relatives houses. Those who could not do it, had to migrate to Jammu and other places in India.

(ii) The second experience was related to the security forces vis a vis national integration. The whole country believed that these forces were performing the jobs of national harmony and national integration. But, in actuality, their performance could only contribute to national embarrassment and disintegration. It was mainly because of their brutal, inhuman and uncivilised treatment of local population. They were found involved in molestation, rape, torture, harassment and other such practices in the case of women; and torture, killing, injury, harassment, disabling and other such practices in the case of young men. These forces, according to K-27, did not behave 'like the army of the same country' but as the 'army of the alien country'. This certainly resulted in the mass anti-India sentiment in Kashmir.

16. SOCIAL PROBLEMS IN KASHMIR

(i) *Caste Differentiation:* K-27 observed that the practise of caste differentiation was completely unjust. The purity and pollution aspect made it a dehumanising system. The most inhuman aspect of caste revealed in throwing out some castes outside the framework and characterised it as 'out caste' or 'untouchable caste'.

K-27 was of the firm opinion that Islam was completely for egalitarian social order and against the caste. But, at the same time, Muslims in India and Kashmir practised caste. In the latter case, they have been categorised as *Sayyids, Khans,* Occupational and Service Occupational castes. K-27 held that *Sayyids dominated* other castes like *Brahmins* in the Hindu society. So, he always opposed their superior status. In actuality, he challenged the entire system of caste.

K-27 felt that there were disastrous social implications of the caste. In addition to negative effects of caste structure and functions, this generated a lot of antagonism against upper caste/s among lower caste/s, which certainly tore apart the social system. In order to develop a just, equal and human system, the caste differences must be rooted out through social action and collective measures.

(ii) *Reservation Policy in Education and Employment:* In JK, there stands a practise of reservation in education and employment, which was granted on the basis of gender, backward areas and backward classes. This policy in the state was criticised by many professionals and experts and by K-27 too. The main points of criticism were. First, the policy of permanent reservation stood in principle against the policy of merit and open competition. Second, this reservation policy benefited only some families for generations together. In actuality, it gave rise to an interest group of families which want these benefits for their future generations. Third, it clearly hurt the distinguished and deserving candidates. Fourth, it gave benefit to undeserving candidates not only during education and employment but during promotions and service benefits also.

K-27 maintained that this policy of reservation must be abolished because certain particular individuals, families, groups, castes, and classes had monopolised these reservations. In order to stop this unjust policy and illogical practice, the state government must respond positively and formulate a realistic and needed policy of reservation.

K-28 KASHMIRI ENGINEER

1. SOCIAL CONTEXT

(i) The service occupational groups responded to processes of development in post-1947 comparatively late. In fact, the consciousness about their backwardness started from early 20th century, especially from 1931 freedom movement when these groups were organised for this cause. In the post-1947 period, especially after revolutionary reforms of 1952-53, responded significantly. As a result, these groups started attaining modern education and entering in new occupations. This also happened in the broader context of political developments, especially political socialisation of masses. Then there were particular factors for families that helped in the process of change and development. As a result, after some decades only, these lower groups pursued higher, professional and technical education and got adjusted in the new state apparatus in JK. Probably, this was the first or second generation of KMs belonging to lower groups which had undergone such a transformation.

(ii) K-28 belonged to one such families among those lower occupational groups that had experienced such radical change due to general and particular factors and had given their children a new occupation, new career, new mobility and new social life. The particular factors related to K-28 were as follows. First, he was adopted by a near-relative family which was economically better. Second, that family had come under the impact of educational mission of *Mirwaiz* family that started in Kashmir in late 1860s. In this regard, the family encouraged and appreciated all educational efforts of K-28.

2. IN-FAMILY SOCIALISATION

(i) K-28 spent early childhood in his parental family where from, after some years, he was shifted to a near relative family, which belonged to lower occupational group but had upper economic standing due to business activities. This economically prosperous family provided all necessary facilities to K-28 which changed future direction of his life. This family took note of his future aspirations and provided modern technical education to him which was not apparently possible in his family of birth. After he got the professional course at that time, it was a matter of celebration in the entire group. Since the economic standing of this family was better, K-28 faced no serious problem for educational expenditure. Moreover, the educational vision developed by the family also encouraged him to pursue this education. In this environment, he developed some specific social traits which included the following:

- hard work	- sincerity and truthfulness	- Social ethics
- academic commitment	- religious beliefs and practices	- no compromise on principles
- values and norms	- help to others	- education to all

(ii) K-28's personality had two aspects of in-family socialisation, one within adopted family and other within parental family. In totality, he accepted impact from both families but after assessing their moral and rational relevance, he accepted consciously more impact from the former than the latter family. In this background, he developed some social priority actions which included the following:

- Not speaking lie	- full regards to elders
- Helping the poor, needy and ill people	- proper educational guidance to children
- Social work among downtrodden	- support to all in the cause of education

3. OUT-FAMILY ENVIRONMENT

(i) The out-family environment of K-28 was limited earlier during his educational stage and broadened after he joined the professional course. In his early stage of life, he found his family in extreme poverty and abnormality. His near relatives faced the same plight in urban context. He could not be impressed by these relatives within and outside family. But, he observed two important developments at that time. The first was psychological in nature which compelled him to think why his family was caught in that situation? The second was social in nature and related to the reaction of his family situation by neighbours which was not sympathetic but socially undesirable.

(ii) Later on, when he got admitted in a professional college in the city, he got the association of many friends who were from middle and upper classes and none from lower class. In fact, there was very less number of students from that background similar to him. While he became conscious about their reality but accepted social-cultural impact from other classes.

(iii) Since most of the friends of K-28 were from prosperous economic background, they were also supporters and followers of the reformist trend of Islam. K-28 also got influenced by this religious trend and, as a result, adopted reformative/radical approach towards religion. This trend of Islam was in principle in consonance with the missionary ideas of *Mirwaiz* family in Kashmir, to which K-28's adopted family belonged. This religious impact prolonged throughout life in his attitudes and behaviour.

4. EDUCATION AND CAREER

(i) The primary education of K-28 was carried out in Islamic missionary school established in the city by *Mirwaiz* family in late 19th century. This was the school where most of the boys of locality got education. Since he was intelligent and innovative, he always stood at the top in class performance. He qualified matric exam. which proved the first milestone in his career. It was considered a difficult exam. In his community at that time. So, passing this exam. in the first attempt and with distinction was an occasion *to celebrate* in the community.

(ii) Later on, he was inclined to pursue the career of an engineering professional. He prepared, appeared and got admission for engineering course in a local professional college. This was considered an honour, by his family, which was celebrated for months. In that college, K-28 showed his intelligence level and intellectual power and participated in academic and social activities. Within a short period, he emerged as one of the forceful, dynamic and distinguishing character on the campus. He had not even thought about this type of education, but his intelligence and hard work enable him to reach to this college. When he completed the course, he had become a mature person with all academic qualifications and intellectual capabilities.

(iii) K-28's merit got him a job of an Engineer in JK government which was considered the 'real life achievement' at that time. Nobody in his occupational group could have imagined about this position. He joined this job and worked in different offices on different positions. He was promoted, awarded and appreciated several times for his work. He reached to one of the highest positions in his office career with dignity, dedication, competence and ethics. His career taught K-28 several lessons two of which were more important. First, life represents the accumulation of practical experience and proper understanding. Second, life must be having a worldview and perspective to guide in all situations.

5. OCCUPATION AND MOBILITY

(i) K-28 belonged to parental and adopted families which were engaged in low-esteemed occupations, which were generally hereditary. There was hardly any scope of change and deviation from this occupation. But, in his case, K-28 adopted extremely different occupation, i.e. government service, in place of traditional family occupation. This happened in other societies in decades and centuries and involved many generations. But, in his case, it happened in decades time and within one or two generation/s. How all this happened stood a basic question? It may be explained by sociological and psychological factors but the absolute explanation was presented by that argument that 'all in human life was determined by the will of Almighty Allah'.

(ii) In this type of occupational dynamics related to K-28 in particular, the relative occupational mobility followed. In his case, the mobility was basic, extreme, irreversible and of upward direction. While the previous occupation had one set of activities involved, the present occupation had new set of responsibilities.

6. ASSOCIATION

(i) As a general rule, occupations in all cases was followed by the respective association. K-28 had lesser association with relatives and neighbours. But, he had developed more closeness and association with colleagues at the educational stage and colleagues in the office career. Most of them belonged to social, economic, educational and cultural status which was usually higher, better, improved and changed in comparison to his own family. He valued this type of relationship and used to meet these friends often at his or their residences.

(ii) It seems important to note here that he made a conscious selection of association. He had strict, absolute and categorical criteria or choice in this regard. His positive and particular criteria for selecting or rejecting any association developed the following criteria:

- Strong and sincere religious orientation
- Morally upright character
- Economically sound position
- Socially affectionate environment
- Culturally humble and hospitable
- Ideologically committed

7. MARRIAGE AND FAMILY

(i) K-28 was married after he got the job. He was the most sought after groom in his relative marriage in service occupational group. Finally, he married a girl who belonged to same group and was economically ahead of and educationally behind his family. It was am endogamous, monogamous and matri-local marriage. K-28 had to stay with in-laws till he constructed his new house. Thus this marriage proved a step forward in his process of mobility.

(ii) It seems important to note that despite staying at matri-local residence till some time, no inferior status or lower image was associated with K-28, neither traditional patriarchal authority pattern was replaced by matri-local authority. In actuality, he was a dominating person and dominated the entire family under his personal authority. He imposed strict discipline in the family and was considered a 'hard task master'. He had an absolute control over the family, especially on wife, children and elder members.

(iii) Before marriage, K-28 was living with the families of birth and adoption. Just after marriage, he shifted to in-law's house temporarily. The girl remained in the same family in the post-marital family. After some time, he constructed a new house on the outskirts of the city and shifted there with his family. There he established a nuclear family household and provided ideal socialisation. As a result, all his children got highest education in their respective fields in Europe and the U.S. Now all of them are working in those countries and in the Middle East. This nuclear family was composed of the husband and wife only.

8. SOCIAL LIKES AND DISLIKES

After experiencing diverse, harsh and complex problems in life, K-28 developed particular likes and dislikes in social life. These include the following:

Social Likes	*Social Dislikes*
- An honest, truthful and intelligent person	- A corrupt, dubious and arrogant officer
- The scientific this in life	- Deviance and crime in society
- Educational advancement to highest level	- Children without control and socialisation
- Studying most modern sciences	- Drug addiction of the youth
- Religion as sole guide in human life	- Poverty and dependence
- Marriage of equal status partners	- Illiteracy and ignorance
- Domination of paternal authority in family	- Discrimination on class and caste basis
- A person with higher intellectual skills	- Sexual promiscuity and anarchy
- Excellent research centre	- Suppression of and violence against women
- Professional career	- Violation of values and norms
- No gender discrimination	- Completely irreligious attitude towards life
- A modern house with all facilities	- Marriage with dowry
- Maintaining social ethics and standards	- An arrogant bureaucrat
- No corruption in any way	- Political corruption in particular
- Disciplined life in family and outside	- Undue help to others
- Pure and ideal religious beliefs	- A school without competent teacher
- An educated person from lower class	- A person not truthful and sincere.
- Respect to elders	- Gender equation in the family
- A daughter in the family necessarily	- The corrupt police officer
- Following goals of development seriously	- Unplanned urban growth

9. CONCEPTS "I", "ME" AND "WE"

(i) Partly because of intellectual capabilities and partly because of complex past, K-28 was strongly conscious about all 3 concepts of 'I', 'me', and 'we'. The concept of 'I' was strong comparatively. Since he had considered life seriously and had to struggle with it, he always appreciated this concept. He used it in two inter-related parts. The first part was related to the past that means 'I' as an individual

- who was extremely poor,
- who was disassociated and not honoured,
- who was considered down trodden,
- who was dominated and humiliated, and
- who was never considered equal.

The second part of 'I' stood for a

- struggle against prejudice, injustice and discrimination;
- struggle against class and caste inequality;
- collective fight against exploitation and domination;
- collective fight for change and progress; and
- collective fight for humanitarian ideas and ideals.

(ii) The concept of 'me' was also strong and favored. It was consciously used in the sense of 'my' which had a long history of suppression, domination and alien control. In that context, K-28 explained 'me' equivalent to 'my' which was characterised by :

- my family background
- my occupational group background
- my class and caste background
- my historical background.

It also referred to

- my life under worst social conditions
- my life dedicated to help others to come out of these conditions
- my life of radical ideology and revolutionary perspective
- my life fully against the ideals of injustice and inequality.

(iii) K-28 upheld the concept of 'We' strongly. Since he was always dynamic, interactive and popular, he developed his image as an ideologue of many ideas and identities, which were determined by political and religious developments in Kashmir. In turn, the concept of 'we' in K-28's views referred to :

- The Muslims in Kashmir, in India and the world
- The Kashmiris in Kashmir, India, Pakistan and the world
- The members of backward developing countries in Asia
- The members of an international organisation working for poor of the world
- The trend setters in education, culture and social fields

10. IDEAS OF EQUALITY AND INEQUALITY

(i) K-28 was a strong upholder of equality between human beings at individual and collective levels. The basic formulation was that every religion, except Hinduism, has suggested egalitarian social order according to its principles. So, deductively-derived values and ideals can provide the basis for establishment of equal social orders in their respective societies. He gave the relevant examples of Islam, Christianity and Judaism in this regard. The religious ethos will provide the system of equality within their communities and between communities at the global level.

(ii) K-28 pleaded that original sources of every religion, especially Islam and Christianity, emphasize in categorical terms, the values, norms, ideas and ideals of equal social order irrespective of differences, in language, race, culture, social structure, ethnicity and nationality. So, all features of equality must be concentrated upon for implementation in different societies and cultures. Consequently, the resultant attitude and behaviour must be encouraged at all levels.

11. THE IDEAL LEADER

(i) The ideal leader of K-28 was Sir Syed Ahmed Khan (SSAK) of Aligarh who represented the ideology with rational thinking, scientific approach, historical context and future vision. After the debacle of 1857, he suggested a framework of thought and action which, according to K-28, only historical leaders and epoch-makers like SSAK could think. He suggested a particular approach to problems of Muslims in that situation which would ensure their present and future and, at the same time, safeguard Islam and Muslim interests in colonial India.

(ii) According to K-28, SSAK may be considered as an ideal leader of IMs for three reasons. First, he observed 1857 defeat of IMs in terms of its grave consequences. It totally collapsed the Muslim leadership and there was no chance of its renewal immediately. This defeat proved socially depressive, politically disorganising and religiously humiliating. In that chaotic situation, he stood up and suggested a way out of crisis. In his presentations, SSAK cricised of Muslim political attitude and behaviour towards the colonial power and suggested reconciliation with that power.

(iii) Second, according to K-28, SSAK adopted a tolerant and reconciliatory approach towards Christianity and British colonial empire. In fact, he stood for no conflict between two great religions and civilisations.

Third, SSAK suggested the path of modern education and cooperation with the colonial rulers for IMs revival and emancipation. This will ensure their future growth and development in India. Thus he was in favour of any political confrontation with the British as a long-term strategy and educational attainment through English language.

12. THE RELIGIOUS LIFE

(i) K-28 was a sound believer in Islamic fundamentals related to *eemaniyat.* He was ideologically very clear about its concepts, notions, theories and so on, which had been studied from its original sources. He had specialised knowledge on most of these topics/themes, especially the following:

- Islamic concepts and theories
- Islamic history in all regions of the world
- Islamic *Shariat* in all its fields
- Islamic philosophy and other modern philosophies
- Islam and modern ideologies, cultures and civilisations
- Islam and other religions of the world

(ii) He was a missionary type of person. He used to convey his Islamic knowledge to others through discussions, speeches and advices. He was always critical of others for their irreligious attitude and behaviour. Without any formalities, he used to convey his displeasure and appreciation for adopting religious attitude and behaviour.

(iii) In practise, K-28 was too religious. He never deviated from Islamic ideas and ideals and fulfilled all basic practical requirements of Islam. In fact, he was impressed by the reformist trend of Islam in Kashmir. So, he was a staunch believer and follower of that school of thought and action. He upheld the version of Islam which was pure and unadulterated. He never compromised with distorted or misinterpreted version of Islam. He considered the folk religious practices as 'extra' and 'additionalities' which were not necessary at all. He characterised these practices as *bidaat* and discouraged others to follow these.

13. EXPERIENCE OF CONFLICT SITUATION

(i) K-28 was strongly concerned about direct and indirect implications of conflict in Kashmir, particularly on intellectual growth of local youth. It was because he could visualize the disastrous impact of the current situation in future. He thought about these situations and questions they raised as mentioned below:

Conflict situations	*Questions raised*
- Students don't go to schools, colleges	- how can they study whole or part of content of colleges and universities and don't study of the syllabi? The subjects.
-People don't get and so don't read news Papers and magazines.	- how can they develop knowledge about current affairs?

contd...

contd...

Conflict situations	*Questions raised*
- People don't get new books, so are not able to read them.	- How can they get information about different fields of life in the world?
- people don't get time to discuss and debate	- How can they develop proper approach to Issues and problems in society. Various issues and problems?
- People don't listen and watch various programs from radio and television.	-How can they formulate opinions and views?
- Teachers don't prepare for their lessons.	- How the real knowledge can be transferred to the next generation?
- Researchers and scientists were not able to carry out research activities.	- How can they contribute to knowledge about Natural sciences?
- Academicians have lost interest of research	- How can an indigeneous understanding on their own societies. Of important developments?

14. SOCIAL PROBLEMS IN KASHMIR

(i) *Educational Backwardness:* K-28 was concerned about educational backwardness in Kashmir, especially among women and children and in rural and hilly areas. This phenomenon has extended backwardness to other sectors of life. Though some occupational groups and classes have improved their economic status, but it has not contributed to overall development.

The government seems not interested seriously in total literacy within a specific period. Its efforts may be characterised as lop-sided policy and half-hearted action. It had created enormous differences between rural and urban areas, between various classes and genders. There seems no clear perspective and objective followed by official organisations and agencies. Even if they stand functional, they have lost their direction.

In this situation, K-28 felt that government and civil society must share equal responsibility for educational progress in JK. The main job was to identify and follow the objectives of progress in education seriously and systematically. Some of the preferred areas and objectives to be adopted in this regard were as follows:

- Modernisation of education
- Education not to be treated as 'commodity' in the market
- Free education to all from primary to university level
- Specialised, professional and technical education for selected students
- Stopping of all reservations in the field of education
- No compromise on quality education

(ii) *Corruption in Government Offices:* K-28 was perturbed by major and minor practices of corruption in government offices in JK. The nature and scale of this illegal practise was so large that no office functioned without it. In actuality, it became a symbol of 'deviant work culture' in offices from top to bottom. His field of engineering, especially civil and mechanical, were considered notorious. The officers and officials, in league with politicians and bureaucrats, grab the entire amount of expenditure meant for public works. In some cases, it was found that the entire amount was grabbed without performing the job at all. K-28 knew a number of colleagues who had amassed wealth and property of billions of rupees through corrupt practices. It was essentially in that context that an international NGO, Transparency International, graded the JK state as "the second most corrupt state" in India after Bihar.

Since K-28 was a highly honest person, he didn't participate in this practise of corruption. He considered it *Gunnah which* he avoided and discouraged in his offices.

He was of the opinion that all major practices of corruption in JK were initiated and encouraged by politicians and bureaucrats for political objectives. This, in a way, legitimised the corruption practice. So, it seems difficult to rule out this practise in totality.

K-29 A COMMON POLITICAL ACTIVIST

1. SOCIAL CONTEXT

(i) The post-1947 period proved complex and difficult for Kashmiris, which composed of certain positives and negatives. While the former referred to positive educational and economic developments, the latter pointed towards negative political and cultural developments in JK. It followed in clear terms that the state made ideological progress and economic mobility but suffered due to political instability and uncertainty.

(ii) A wholistic view of this situation revealed in the underlying fact that all these developments revolved around certain degree of development. The process had considerable impact among certain groups of population and thus alleviated them only from lower to upper status. It was considered even better than in PAK. But, the associated fact was that political and cultural problems in post-1947 era negated the effect of development processes. Some of these developments and counter-developments are mentioned below:

- Forceful political integration of Kashmir into broader whole of India
- Political promises made at the time of accession not fulfilled
- Lacking the trust of Kashmiri leadership and its arrest in 1953
- Process of 'Indianisation' imposed on all fields of life
- Introduction of political corruption through rigging, toppling, imposing puppet leaders and regimes from New Delhi
- Denial of basic democratic, human and civil rights of Kashmiri masses
- Brutal suppression of people's movements and popular uprisings
- Introduction of pro-integration policy through cultural practices and educational curriculum

(iii) All these developments revolved around the sole objective of total political integration which was imposed through state apparatus, state policy and state approved actions. This directly resulted in non-integration acts on the part of people who consistently carried out passive and active resistance. The former referred to not believing in Indian nationhood, not participating in elections and political criticism of integrationist ideas, attitudes and perspectives. The latter reflected in open criticism of GOI's Kashmir policy, political protests and political uprisings and other political actions.

(iv) In this political environment, there emerged divergence of perception of the Kashmir problem between GOI and Kashmiri people. The economic and educational benefits were lost in political controversies and differences. K-29 belonged to that generation which first experienced the Kashmir problem after 1947 and then became a legacy for all post-47 generations. It was made the first victim of Indian politics and shifted this legacy to future generations till now.

2. IN-FAMILY SOCIALISATION

(i) K-29 belonged to an ordinary lower middle class family in the city in pre-1947 days. It was not satisfactory but were depressive. Neither proper socialisation took place in the family nor could it prosper.

(ii) Though K-29 family was in a position to send its children to school for education, he could not pursue till higher classes.. This was due to his personal limitation. His family wanted to engage him in some purposeful economic activity. Since K-29 was intelligent, shrewed, and jealous, he managed to study till pre-matric standard. While his class mates attained higher education and got good jobs in government offices in those days, he could not do so. But, his mental ability and alertness gave him social benefits which a normal person could not achieve. He had such personal power, future vision and soul-searching capacity that not many individuals could match him. In fact, he has performed miracles in his social life.

(iii) Thus despite his family background, K-29 socialised in different kinds of environment. Consequently, he developed different types of social, economic and political roles that of his parents, especially his father.

3. OUT-FAMILY ENVIRONMENT

(i) The out-family environment was male-dominated and determined the life conditions of K-29. This environment was constituted by relatives, neighbours and personal-party friends. Not much interest was shown by K-29 for near and distant relatives. He could have hardly accepted their impact. However, he had the interest in those relatives who were advanced in any field and kept constant contact with them through regular visits. This relationship played a minor impact on his personality formulation.

(ii) The relations of K-29 with neighbours followed the same pattern. Those who were influential and powerful were preferable for him and those who were poor and not influential were not relevant to him. He established close contacts with advancing families only in the neighbourhood. This helped him in going near to the families with top political contact and influence. He imitated and followed these families in political behaviour. Thus he used these relations to help his person and family. Though he was a devoted worker of the ruling party for decades and came near to political leaders, he was never given authority of power or position.

(iii) The friends of K-29 were political leaders, whom he followed, and political activists, with whom he worked. He himself was a political worker and used to work for the party. For all this, he got material benefits in many ways. In actuality, these political activities shaped his life attitude, behaviour, ideas, ideology, perceptions and perspectives. In this process of ideational change, he developed a future vision about standard of life for himself, his family and his grand children. In most of the cases, he was successful. This political background also enabled him to start small business in city in which he made change several times but continued the retail character.

(iv) All these developments had positive impact on K-29 which was much improved than the one which prevailed during alien rule before 1947. He had observed all major developments after 1947 and wanted to get more and more benefits. His intelligence and cleverness always compelled him to focus on personal and family interests in education, economic, cultural and other fields.

4. EDUCATION AND OCCUPATION

(i) K-29 family was in a position to send him to school for higher education but he made up to middle standard only. That was partly because of his need to contribute to the family economically and partly because of his personal disinterest in higher education. Due to his lower education, he could not get any good position either in the government or in the party. He was always considered as a political worker but was never honoured, the grudge which he had against his party.

(ii) He started a small retail business in several fields, one after the other. When one business field became less profitable, he shifted to other business field. He finally settled down in retail business in medicines. He owned a shop in the interior of the city and his business was always functional.

5. CAREER, MOBILITY AND ASSOCIATION

(i) K-29 had no formal career in a particular field on a particular position. His only career in continuity was in small-retail business which he shifted to many fields due to market trends. Taking into consideration his educational, economic and social conditions during pre-1947 era, his upward mobility was considerable and comparable. In this process of overall mobility, he developed good standard of life. His children, particularly his daughters, got higher education in different fields. He constructed a new house in outskirts of the city at a time when many rich people were only thinking about this. His family got exposed to modern social and cultural influences. Even his grandsons and granddaughters were all engaged in professional and technical courses in different educational institutions in the country. According to these social parameters, K-29 had undergone higher degree of overall mobility. But, he was not satisfied about it. K-29 had formal, impersonal and business like relationship with the occupational community and shop-keepers *biradari.* While he always showed skepticism about its members, they too had doubts about his personality. However, with political class, especially political elite families, he had developed one sided contacts with political activists and had no direct contact with-top political leaders.

(ii) There was a quality in the personality of K-29 which enabled him to develop higher level association in life and got benefited out of it. He never forgot the meeting with unknown person. Once he met somebody, he used to pursue relations intensively, leading to an association. K-29 had many such associations stored in his long life.

6. MARRIAGE AND FAMILY

(i) K-29 was married to a girl who belonged to the background of same economic, educational and social status. In actuality, it was an endogamous, monogamous and patri-local type of marriage. It proved a step onward in life of K-29. But, their post-marital life could not last long. After giving birth to 5 children, the wife passed away. K-29 didn't marry again and devoted his life to children and family. He used to say that he had performed the roles of father as well as a mother of a little children.

(ii) Normally, people in Kashmir gave more attention to male children during their upbringing. Butt, K-29 proved a different person. He gave more education to girl children than boy children and more attention to the former's career. As a result, his daughters got higher education at a time when KM women had not responded to modern education at large. They also got government jobs easily. K-29 attracted a lot of criticism for initiating girls education, but he never regretted.

(iii) After marriage, the K-29's wife had joined and settled in his parents joint family household. She lived there till her death. After some time, when K-29's parents passed away and his brothers and sisters were married, he was left alone with his unmarried children in nuclear type household. After the marriage of daughters, they left to their marital households. His sons also got married. They stayed for some time with their father, but could not live together for long. So, both married sons left his house. In this way, he was left alone in that grand old house.

7. SOCIAL LIKES AND DISLIKES

After going through ups and downs in his turbulent and disturbed life, K-29 developed very hard choices in social life. Some of these hard social choices were as follows:

Social Likes	*Social Dislikes*
- A gentle, sober and tolerant person	- Highly religious and rigid person
- Modern lifestyle in all possible ways	- A corrupt and arrogant bureaucrat
- Exogamous type of marriage	- A principled politician
- No dowry custom at all	- The quarrel with a doctor
- No gifts in social relationship	- No modern education to girls
- A highly qualified and most quoted person	- Women's inequality
- Detailed discussions and gossip	- second or third marriage in life

contd...

contd...

Social Likes	*Social Dislikes*
- Women's education in all fields	- A dishonest teacher and officer
- No consideration of traditional limits women	- No seriousness in life
- Women's working role necessary	- A young immoral person
- Less importance to social ethics	- Segregation of sexes in social life
- Commitment to family and relatives	- Caste or class consideration in social life
- Not forgetting the past	- Selfish person hurting others
- No conflict with a professional	- Education without a job
- A politician helping his own people	- Useless politicisation of masses
- Modern education must for all	- Social justice denied
- Qualifying exams. With higher marks	- Social equality ignored
- Zero starter and hard worker	- Lazy and having no initiative in life
- Clear objectives in life	- Following others aimlessly and uselessly
- Specific targets in life pre-determined	- Not a clever policy in life
- One who gains is called successful	- One who looses is called failure.

8. CONCEPTS OF "I", "ME" AND "WE"

(i) Since K-29 had real experience of ground reality, he proved serious and rational in his social life. These aspects of his personality were reflected in his notions and sentiments. So, 'I' and 'me' were of higher importance to him than 'we'. In other words, he preferred the personal concern to the social concern. So, 'I' was used by him as a :

- a poor man who fought against poverty and its impact;
- a semi-literate man whose children got higher education;
- a social observer who never followed values and norms seriously and sincerely;
- a committed political worker who could not get any position in the party; and
- a political activist whose sincerity was never trusted.

(ii) 'Me' was an important concept during his long life experiences in which he developed different kinds of relations with individuals, groups, associations, organisations, agencies and got his short-term and long-term goals fulfilled. He referred to the summation of these activities as 'my' actions. So, 'me' in this background referred essentially to :

- My family
- My girl children

- My relatives and neighbours
- My friends
- My contacts
- My colleagues
- My role in political party
- My response to new ideas and ideology
- My small retail business
- My newly-constructed house
- My work record

(iii) The concept of 'we' was not strong in K-29 case. In actuality, it was politically dominated and oriented towards its unfulfilled objectives. He represented the political identity and its co-relates. In the broader sense, 'we' was used for the people of Kashmir in collective form. So, 'we' specifically referred to :

- Kashmiris as the extreme sufferers of alien and feudal rule in the state
- Kashmiris as poor as they were not in a position to get two-meals diet to eat during that period
- Kashmiris who were trapped in usury system and unbearable taxes on artisans and workers
- Kashmiris who didn't allow their women to follow modern education in the past
- Kashmiris who have undergone a radical transformation in which all basic needs and facilities are available to every family
- Kashmiiris who got liberated from forced labour and its system
- Kashmiris who have gone for education in all fields and at all levels

9. IDEAS OF EQUALITY AND INEQUALITY

(i) K-29 had developed a distinct and relevant approach regarding equality. While he supported every or any form of equality, he opposed every dimension of inequality, especially related to class, caste and gender. Since majority of the examples of inequality fall in hereditary category, he suggested creation of the system of equality based on the introduction of new roles and positions. This may be done through the implementation of all objectives of education attained in the shortest possible time frame.

(ii) The education, as K-29 held, can provide strong and objective basis for evolution of egalitarian system. It will deal with existing problems in a scientific way and will impose responsibility to new educated generation. In this way, inequality and its theoretical basis will be negated, an egalitarian order will dominate the scene. But, for this situation to emerge, the level of literacy has to be achieved at the highest level.

10. THE RELIGIOUS LIFE

(i) Basically, K-29 was a non-religious person. Throughout his life, religion in theory or practise was hardly a consideration for him. But, in latter part of his life, he turned religious after performing *hajj*. He was a believer in all Islamic fundamentals but, like many other Muslims, he never bothered to know what religion meant for life?

(ii) Like common Muslims, K-29 was not following the basic practices of Islam in day-to-day life. He seemed not seriously interested in these practices. But, after performing *hajj*, he was a changed person. In fact, this type of behaviour stood as a common pattern of religious behaviour after performing *hajj*.

(iii) At the same time, K-29 followed some folk religious practices and participated in the celebration of particular days at the local shrines. He had developed good rapport with some *mullas* in the shrines.

(iv) K-29 felt not impressed by the new trends of reformative or radical Islam. He never bothered to take serious interest in their functioning and their ideology.

11. EXPERIENCE OF CONFLICT SITUATION

(i) K-29 was perturbed on seeing the negative implications of conflict on the social order. These implications have engulfed entire society in its influence by disturbing the normal functioning of basic social institutions, processes and dynamics of interaction.

(ii) In the case of basic social institutions, the family experienced this negative impact in terms of erosion of patriarchal authority, socialisation of children, and deviation from control. In the case of marriage, while traditional practices and customs could not be performed properiy, other problems like availability of equal-status match and late marriage could not be avoided. In the case of kinship ties, these were reduced to zero in effect. No purposeful interaction could take place.

(iii) The conflict also affected social processes like urbanisation, industrialisation, modernisation, secularisation, political socialisation, cultural impact and so on. The cumulative effect of this was felt in all societal groups.

(iv) Finally, interaction between various social collectivities also suffered due to conflict. The aspects of social harmony and solidarity got diminished. Very less interaction took place between distant relatives and between family friends. Reduced interaction was also observed between primary relatives such as parents and children, brothers and sisters, and so on. Very less interaction took place between families. Regular family get-togethers and other celebrations became rare. Interaction between doctors and patients, students and teachers, guides and scholars, businessmen and consumers, and so on were also reduced considerably.

12. SOCIAL PROBLEMS IN KASHMIR

(i) *Female Education:* K-29 felt that female education in Kashmir has always remained low. Even in the present situation, when there were equal opportunities of education, males were ahead of females. So, he felt that there still p*revailed* some ideological support for not giving full education to women.

K-29 felt proud of the fact that he was able to provide higher education to all his daughters. He remembered the criticism which he attracted at that time for sending his daughters in co-educational institutions. He believes that he was right at that time and time has proved it.

K-29 felt that ignoring women from attaining modern education was a social problem. This discriminatory treatment of women originates from some religious and ideological source. Since this problem has social origin, it must be treated at social level. The organised and systematic efforts towards women's education must not be limited to governmental efforts and allocations, but must be helped by NGOs, especially through civil society.

(ii) *Unproductive use of wealth:* K-29 had two sons-in-law, both working in the Middle East on higher professional positions for last many years. His daughters too joined their husbands in those countries and added further amount to their regular income. Over a period of decades, they have amassed wealth worth billions of rupees. What they do with this wealth worries K-29.

A maximum portion of this wealth, according to K-29, was spent on the construction of two palace-like houses in Kashmir and filled with all modern amenities and facilities. These can be compared with any palatial houses in the world. Many families could be accommodated in these houses.

K-29 felt perturbed about such a huge expenditure on houses which had to accommodate 4 to 5 members of family each. He characterised this type of expenditure as unproductive use of wealth which may be considered as wastage. He raised the question how much space could be used by 4-5 member family?

K-29 also felt the alternative way of invsting this money. It could be invested in upcoming costly IT industry or super speciality health sector in Kashmir. It would have benefited them as well as the people of their native place.

K-30 YOUNG ADVOCATE

1. SOCIAL CONTEXT

(i) The entire post-1947 era in JK was characterised with political uncertainty and instability. This political abnormality was caused mainly due to non-resolution of Kashmir problem. This had a direct effect on the process of integration of Kashmir to India. Since the integration was followed forcefully, it led to political alienation of Kashmiris. It also led to the creation of political elite families and puppet political regimes in the state on the part of central government. This also proved counter-productive. People did not participate in normal political processes but were forced to show their participation. This in turn eroded the political credibility and democratic credentials of GOI.

(ii) In addition to the political field, the conditions of political uncertainty and instability had completely negative impact on economic growth and development. Neither the economic infrastructure could be developed in the state nor could any heavy investment by Indian or foreign corporate sector could be attracted. The available resources in the state like water and forests could not be utilised properly for development. No policy, planning, programs and schemes could be seriously formulated. If some formulation work was carried out, there was no systematic implementation, mechanism and there was no allocation of funds. If funds were provided somehow, these could not be invested, leading to their transfer from Kashmir to Jammu region.

(iii) In these political and economic conditions, the youth in Kashmir could not be convinced about the ideology of Indian nationhood. On the name of national interest, the local political regimes carried out reign of terror against local youth, suppressed forcefully political aspirations of people and politically betrayed the Kashmiris. The political system was used for the petty individual, family and group interest and developed features of corruption, non-governance, incompetence and no commitment. The natural result was the rise of antipathy towards the Indian state. In actuality, the political regimes, irrespective of their differences, did great disservice to the cause of integration. When the local youth rose in revolt against this system, they were crushed, tortured, suppressed and even massacred. Thus their political sentiments were not allowed to be highlighted. What was left final subjugation of this youth was done by security forces after 1989 during anti-militancy operations.

(iii) The political implications of this situation were felt in two specific political developments of anti-Indian sentiments and rise of religious political forces. First, the experience of entire post-1947 period created a serious anti-establishment ideas and ideology with political attitudes and behaviour towards India and its state. More or less all intellectual and non-intellectual elements got involved in this process. Second, the mass anti-India sentiment got rationalised in Islamic perspective. The Kashmiri youth in large number got Islamic orientation of politics and developed particular political ideas and ideals about Kashmir. This impact was not limited to politics and youth, but was also experienced by the majority of population in all fields of life. They became more conscious about Islamic ideology and identity of Kashmir and followed radical trend of Islamic movements. But, this response on the part of Kashmiri youth was not uniform but different and diverse, though all of them were unanimous in their Islamic political stand.

(iv) K-30 belonged to a family whose youngsters were affected by this political impact. But, all three brothers in the family responded differently and adopted different versions of religious-political attitudes and behaviour which were as follows :

- First brother - extreme radical in attitude and passive in behaviour;
- Second brother - radical in attitude and active in reform groups; and
- Third brother - semi-radical in attitude and completely passive in action.

2. IN-FAMILY SOCIALISATION

(i) K-30 was born in a poor lower class family whose head was working in government office on a lower post. Despite his semi-educated status and lower economic position, he provided education to all male children. The family remained constrained economically till all children got education and jobs. When this happened, the family entered into middle class economic status. This reflected in the entire lifestyle, especially changes in tastes, food habits, dress patterns, entertainment and so on.

(ii) The family of K-30 was always alive with the problem of religion. The family environment, orientation and ethos was always religious in nature. All religious beliefs and practices were made practical realities in this family.

(iii) In this type of social, political and economic ethos, K-30 was socialised. Since parents had full control on its members, he could not deviate much from ideal role within and outside the family. In actuality, there was hardly any scope for deviation or violation of the traditional behaviour.

3. OUT-FAMILY ENVIRONMENT

(i) The out-family environment of K-30 composed of three main groups of relatives, neighbours and FFs. The relatives had lesser impact on him because they were educationally backward and economically poorer. Moreover, these relatives, engaged in service occupations and small retail business, were not psychologically elevated, emotionally not confident, and religiously not very active. They had only taught some and learnt some social traits.

(ii) The neighbours of K-30 represented a close community of same socio-economic status. They had regular interaction among themselves and had developed strong community sentiment. The degree of religiosity was high which had given rise to commonality, harmony and solidarity between members of this community. All these social aspects had serious impact on the relationship and association which K-30 developed outside his parental family. He was socialised in this environment to the maximum extent and participated in community activities which revolved around the local mosque, In turn, K-30 developed particular ideas, attitudes and engagements that gave rise to particular social role for him.

(iii) The FFs of K-30 had significant degree of impact on life and his family, especially in the fields of culture, religion, ideology and politics. Almost all of them belonged to same background.

4. EDUCATION AND CAREER

(i) K-30 had his entire education from primary till matric in the local government school. He got his education like other boys in the locality. Since, he had the qualities of seriousness, simplicity and religiosity, he proved a good and performing student. While he loved his teachers, they too showered affection on him.

(ii) After school, K-30 joined a city college for graduation, which was considered an achievement in those days. He qualified this degree with average grade. In the college, he got the company of serious and religious-minded students. He used to participate in academic, literary and social activities.

(iii) Then he opted for law graduation which he completed in the local university in time. During this course, he came across many people who played a crucial role in the field of judiciary. After completion of this course, he joined the local lower courts and started the career of an advocate. His perception of this profession was radically different. While all in the field of judiciary prefer to be realistic, practical, pragmatist and compromiseble, K-30 had different ideas and ideals for his career. In opposition to these ideas, he wanted to follow a tradition of truth, reality and no compromise on the principles of social justice, human rights and basic constitutional rights. He decided not to follow a single fake or false or fraud case in any court, nor will he be a party to those cases or judgements. In brief, he wanted to follow a career in legal profession which will be truthful. So, he has not failed, miraculously.

5. OCCUPATION, MOBILITY AND ASSOCIATION

(i) K-30 joined this new occupation consciously and willfully. He wanted to behave differently in this profession. He followed the ideal role of an advocate and wanted to make it a reality. The corrupt practices in the courts and among the lawyers-judges community had seriously disturbed him. After investing about a decade's time in different courts, he still believed in the highest principles of justice which will prevail in the ultimate end.

(ii) The work in this field was sacred for K-30 and he considered this work as *ibadah*. He felt responsibility of providing justice to everybody who comes to him for this purpose. In this great cause, he had no economic consideration. However, the fact stood that this new profession in family had benefited it economically and was able to maintain certain standard of life. By maintaining certain standard of principles and practices in the court, he had achieved economic mobility and professional credibility.

6. MARRIAGE AND FAMILY

(i) K-30 was married after he stabilised his position in newly-adopted occupation and ensured some regular income. The girl belonged to same social, economic and educational background and she proved an overall helper in the joint family. In reality, this was an exogamous, monogamous and parti-local type of marriage. The cumulative contribution of this marriage can be explained in terms of mobility towards higher status.

(ii) K-30 lived in a joint family before marriage and the girl joined this joint family and lived with his parents and married brothers with their unmarried children. The higher education of the girl proved beneficial in the family and she became popular because of her personal and social traits. Though K-30 and his brothers had political, ideological and religious differences, they maintained the joint life as per the wishes of their parents. However, after the death of father, this unity could not be maintained. All brothers constructed their respective houses. Thus K-30 was left with his nuclear family and lived a happy life.

7. SOCIAL LIKES AND DISLIKES

After undergoing various life experiences, K-30 developed some particular likes and dislikes, some of which are mentioned below:

Social Likes	*Social Dislikes*
- A man with all religious qualities	- A man having no religious qualities at all
- An experienced and religious personality	- Immoral and irreligious behaviour
- Maintaining religious values and norms	- Corrupt and arrogant politician
- Moral social ethics	- Deviation and c rime
- Necessary religious education for all	- Violation of values and norms
- Social justice for all	- Not following religious principles in life
- Honesty and commitment in legal profession	- Sexual promiscuity
- No dowry and gifts in marriage	- Uncontrolled female behaviour
- Close family ties with relatives	- Not taking care of parents and elders
- Friendship on the religious basis	- Westernised lifestyle

contd...

contd...

Social Likes	*Social Dislikes*
- A religious-oriented and competent teacher	- Not praying 5 times a day
- A humble and honest officer	- Opposing religious ideology
- Good image of the professional	- Criticising religious leaders
- A devoted and faithful husband	- Deserted mosques
- An individual following principled life	- Exploitation of workers and artisans
- The radical political and religious leader	- Political suppression and oppression
- Regular religious practices	- Prevailing corrupt practices
- A committed academician	- Corrupt legal system
- An honest businessman	- Social apathy
- No discrimination	- Moral degeneration

8. CONCEPTS OF "I", "ME" AND "WE"

(i) Despite high degree of religiosity in his personality, K-30 had high sense of 'I' and 'me'. It was because he had to struggle hard in life and belonged to humble economic background. So, he worked continuously for himself and his family. The religious ideas and ideals provided inspiration to his active world. So, he saw 'I' in the background of his belonging to the humble past and corresponding tough life. He almost won the struggle with the help of religious ideology. 'I' was used by him for an individual who was:

- a member of poor economic community;
- a member of suffering community called *mustazzaffin*;
- a member of community which never surrendered before despotic rulers;
- a member of community which struggled and revolted against tyrants; and
- a member of community which never tolerated injustice and inequality.

(ii) K-30's concept of 'me' was also strong in the emotional sense. So, 'me' was usually used in the sense of 'my' and specifically referred to

- My humble family
- My humble parents
- My humble relatives
- My humble neighbours
- My humble personal and family friends
- My life conditions in life in the past and present

(iii) The concept of 'we' was upheld by K-30 was dominated by religious orientation. So, it was usually used for Islamic believers or Muslims in totality. In this thematic context, it specifically referred to :

- We, the Muslims in Kashmir,
- We, the Muslims in India,
- We, the Muslims in the world,
- We, the Muslims who are backward in science and technology, and
- We, the Muslims who suffer most in the world.

9. IDEAS OF EQUALITY AND INEQUALITY

(i) K-30 was a strong proponent of human equality and strong opponent of human inequality in any form or any basis. He derived source of equality in Islamic ideology which clearly contributed to egalitarian social order and negated inequal social order. Isla, according to him, intended to establish absolute form of social justice among different human beings. This social justice emerges as the basic criteria against the existing criteria of caste, class, power and gender. He upheld the view that Islamic social justice will introduce maximum degree of social justice among all human beings in economic, social, cultural, educational, psychological, linguistic, ethnic, regional, religious and other fields.

(ii) K-30 was a strong believer in the system of equality and its manifested ideas and ideals. He gave less attention to the nature and contextual aspects of present-day inequality in the Muslim societies. So, his views reflected a bit of exaggerated ones. Moreover, this ideological and religious approach to the question of equality and inequality ignored basic existential or functional reality.

10. THE IDEAL CHARACTER

(i) The ideal character of K-30 was Usama Ben Laden who stood as the global anti-American character. He felt that this character must be seen in the light of strong criticism and strong appreciation which attracted the western powers and Muslim societies respectively. While the West characterised him as the greatest evil/devil on earth, the East considered him as the symbol of resistance to domination, oppression, colonialism, empirialism and exploitation of Western powers. K-30 argued that Ben Laden stood for a historical character as it does not emerge easily. It emerged after centuries.

(ii) K-30 held him in high esteem for 5 particular points which follow:

(a) Ben Laden represented a parallel lifestyle to that of his home-state, Saudi Arabia, lifestyle which has gone radically opposite to the luxuriant and corrupt kings and princes;

(b) Ben Laden represented a revolutionary character in the Arab society which fell against traditions of monarchy and feudal rule. He openly preferred the role of a revolutionary to a scandalous prince lost in the markets of London, Paris and New York;

(c) Ben Laden represented Islam in its original form. He rejected all conscious deviations and willful distortions in its form and content;

(d) Ben Laden stood for a courageous person of global status, who challenged supreme rulers of the world despite having no weapons to fight the world power; and

(e) Ben Laden represented the global level historical character which was aimed at to destroy the unjust world order governed by sole super power, the U.S., and replace it with just order dominated by developing and suffering societies in the world.

11. THE RELIGIOUS LIFE

(i) K-30 considered his active life as religious which could not be partitioned into parts or fields. This represents the unity of life. This conception of religious duty was so broad that it included all material and non-material measures in human life. In that theoretical context, integration of religious life was its distinctive feature. In this sense, religion, especially Islam, was complete way of life and its applicability cannot be restricted to some fields or parts.

(ii) His beliefs about religious conception of Islam was sound and authentic. He studied Islam from its primary sources, *Quran and Hadith*. So, he had clarity of concepts, principles and laws of religion of Islam. He usually clarified others' misconceptions and gave correct and authentic information.

(iii) K-30's knowledge about religion was correct, authentic and strong. He was also actively involved in performing day-to-day religious activities. In this regard. he did not consider anybody who could have misled him. In actuality, he stood one among few Muslims who practised Islam in its totality without any fear or apprehensions. He prayed daily 5 times without any break in all situations and at all places and asked other family members to follow. He also observed fast during the month of *Ramadan* and was particular about paying *Zakat* to the poor. He was serious and sincere in the performance of all other religious duties.

(iv) With regard to the folk religious practices in Kashmir, K-30 considered these as 'exterior' to real Islam. He felt these practices were actually not religious but cultural or customary.

(v) In totality, K-30 developed pan-Islamic perspective in his religious ideology which didn't recognise these cultural and social differences and features. He also showed his preference for the issues related to the Muslim world.

12. THE KASHMIR PROBLEM

(i) K-30 felt that Kashmir problem was related directly to the rise of extreme Hindu political forces in India. This problem started in 1947 when the Hindu extremist forces, under the political leadership of V.B. Patel, the first home minister of independent India. These political forces created a situation in and around 1947-48 in which accession of JK to India was made permanent without taking into confidence the people of the state. They also supported forceful integration of Kashmir into the broader whole of India. All political regimes at the center in post-1947 era were pressurised not to fulfill the promise of referendum and to abrogate article 370. They portrayed Kashmir as an integral part of India and made it a crucial issue in Indian politics, so that no political leader or party could fulfill the promise of giving Kashmiris a chance to decide about their political future.

(ii) Political leaders like S.P. Mukherjee, A.B. Bajpai and L.K. Advani followed that political legacy and hardened their attitude day by day. The political parties, especially *Bhartiya Jan Sangh (BJS),* and *BJP,* followed this policy vigorously and didn't change it at all. The religious-political organisations like RSS, VHP and other Hindu revivalist associations, organised the background public opinion to support that Kashmir policy. This politics made the K. problem more complex and an issue of life and death that didn't allow secular leadership to react. This communalisation of K issue made it so crucial for an average Indian that they could never think about India without Kashmir.

(iii) Regarding resolution of this problem, K-30 made 3 points. First, there must be complete separation between religion and K. problem. It must be considered a political problem. Second, the Indian Hindu masses must be informed about the actual historicity and nature of K. problem, so that they understand the political aspirations of people in JK. Third, they must be aware about negative consequences of the K. problem in the sub-continent and positive consciousness about resolution of this problem.

13. FUTURE KASHMIR SOCIETY

(i) K-30 thought of a Kashmiri society in future having features of extremely opposite nature. On the one hand, he wanted that family to develop features of modern societies which include the following:

- scientific and technological development,
- knowledge generation through latest means,
- scientific research,
- IT channels, organisations and agencies,
- higher economic standard,
- higher level of modern education, and

- urbanised and industrialised society.

(ii) On the other hand, K-30 wanted future Kashmir society to continue the conventional features which include the following:

- Maintenance of values, norms and principles
- Upholding and asserting the religious identity
- Conventional-customary lifestyle
- Religious attitudes and behaviour in life
- Education and research in traditional sciences
- Traditional practices of culture
- Overall development which will not hurt the moral ethos

(iii) Thus there emerged a scene of two extreme societies with two extreme cultures. How these two extreme types of societies will interact and accommodate each other was not clear. As this process will prove highly complex, one possible way would be adjustment and compromise between the two extremes.

14. EXPERIENCE OF CONFLICT SITUATION

(i) K-30 was concerned about the impact of conflict on children in the valley. He observed that armed conflict had affected children's entire life. It was found that their education was affected seriously in terms of significant drop-outs in primary classes and new enrolments, especially in rural areas. There was no regularity in attending schools, there were no regular teaching in the schools. All these effects deteriorated the quality of education which was related to militarisation.

(ii) The second field of concern of Kashmiri children was 'mental health' which has deteriorated to the dangerous level. There were thousands of cases of psychological and psychiatric problems due to constant tension, depression, stress, anxiety, and PTSD. This situation also was due to the acts of suicide, drug addiction, deviance, crime, juvenile delinquency. In this process, children got spoiled even before their youth. The tragic situation increased further when there was neither availability of sufficient experts nor required technology. Physically also, children have fallen prey to some dangerous diseases which were uncommon among them earlier.

(iii) K-30 felt that common children in Kashmir were robbed of their childhood beauties, engagements and entertainments. There were no life activities and no life interaction for them.

(iv) Thousands of children had no normal socialisation and control within their families. Traditions, principles, values and norms became irrelevant for them and they became deviant. Criminal and suicidal tendencies emerged among them. In that environment, children also developed antipathy towards work, education and knowledge.

15. SOCIAL PROBLEMS IN KASHMIR

(i) *Moral Degeneration:* According to K-30, it has been observed that generally some individuals having above-average influence and power deviate from established values and norms based on religious doctrines and principles.. They hardly care about religious and moral opposition. This type of conscious deviation led to broader behavioural changes. In this dynamics, they forgot their association with their family, group, community and other collectivities. They thought only in their individual interests.. In this approach, they felt compelled to become anti-human brutes. They dominate, exploit and dishonour every individual who suffer due to inequal, unjust and discriminatory system.

In addition to spoiling his personality and his family, they got involved in abusing and negating social conscience, ethics, morality and established standards of behaviour. All this led to deterioration of public life standards. This gave rise directly to the phenomenon of 'moral degeneration' which had socially negative implications for the social order at large.

This situation created a social crisis which encouraged all sorts of social evils and social undesirabilities. This destablised social ethos and polluted every sector and section of society. In order to maintain social stability and moral superiority, the social dynamics of this process must be treated and negated at its initial stage, so that it never matures.

(ii) *Unbearable Religious Behaviour:* K-30 felt that religious behaviour contributed to social solidarity, integration, cohesion and continuity. It performed necessary socialisation of individuals and groups and passed on the cultural heredity from one generation to other generation. It also maintained cultural order and regulated all cultural functions.

But, at the same time, he felt that religious behaviour, though necessary, was commonly considered 'undesirable' and was criticised on many points. The points included that religion stood irrational, unscientific, illogical, created division and confrontation, and took individual out of time and space. This criticism of religious behaviour was conveyed through the words *bekaar* and *faltoo.*

K-30 felt that this criticism was incorrect and unjustified. Religion has played more purposeful, meaningful and positive role and has disciplined the society. Moreover, those who had serious religious behaviour, were more intelligent, intellectual, educated, cultured, emancipated and belonged to all economic classes, upper, middle and lower.

Taking into consideration the contribution of religion to social life had positive as well as negative. In this context, K-30 felt that religious behaviour seemed highly desirable and preferable in the broader society.

Index